BUSINESS AND ITS ENVIRONMENT

McGRAW-HILL SERIES IN MANAGEMENT

Keith Davis, Consulting Editor

BUSINESS AND ITS ENVIRONMENT

KEITH DAVIS, Ph.D.
Arizona State University

ROBERT L. BLOMSTROM, Ph.D.
Michigan State University

McGRAW-HILL BOOK COMPANY

NEW YORK   ST. LOUIS   SAN FRANCISCO
TORONTO   LONDON   SYDNEY

BUSINESS AND ITS ENVIRONMENT

To Sue and Marge

PREFACE

The notion that just because we live in a business environment we understand it is a myth. There is much to learn, and this book seeks to aid that learning process. Likewise it is a myth to think that because our motives are good we know exactly how business ought to conduct itself. We can channel motives wisely only when we know more about business and its environment. Only then will we be able to develop the business policies needed to integrate business with its environment.

In this book we intend to look at the whole business culture as a dynamic social system. Students study business in functional pieces, and citizens observe it the same way, but finally it needs to be discussed and understood as a living whole. There are many value systems, such as law, economics, psychology, sociology, scientific management, public administration, and ethics, which are applied to business. Books about business and its environment usually are written from one of these points of view; however, our purpose is to *integrate all points of view* into a balanced analysis of the whole business culture. Further, we attempt to take a positive, constructive view of business, showing how knowledge can be used for progress, rather than a negative view.

We have designed this book for college students, business managers, and others interested in the business scene. In universities and colleges the book is suitable for first or second courses in Business Policy emphasizing the external environment of business and for courses in Business and Society, Social Responsibility of Business, and related areas. We have sought to present illustrations to make ideas more meaningful and practical. We have also tried to achieve a readable style, avoiding the technical language of specialized volumes written for one particular discipline. Another objective has been to include a discussion of international business in order to show how the concepts we are developing apply to business systems around the world.

We are grateful to many people who have helped with this book. Without them we could not have completed it. We especially thank Vice-president Joseph C. Schabacker and Dean Glenn D. Overman, who provided administrative encouragement when we were both at Arizona State University. Special thanks are extended to Dr. Harold Fearon, who contributed the section on relations with suppliers in Chapter 12. And we appreciate the clerical assistance of Mrs. Roberta Butler and Miss Sharon Sanders. Most of all we appreciate the patient encouragement of our wives and children.

We hope the effort has been worthwhile to you, the reader.

KEITH DAVIS   ROBERT BLOMSTROM

CONTENTS

CASES

APPENDIXES

1. THE AMERICAN BUSINESS SYSTEM: ITS ORIGINS AND DEVELOPMENT

CHAPTER 1   BUSINESS IN A
CHANGING SOCIETY

> It is now recognized that the direction of business
> is important to the public welfare, that businessmen
> perform a social function. . . .
>
> ROBERT D. CALKINS [1]

As twilight settled over a suburban Maryland community, the president
of a small wholesaling firm talked in quiet tones with his sales vice-
president; they were trying to decide what to do next with an alcoholic
salesman. On earlier occasions they had warned him and referred him to
a community agency, which he refused to see, but his problem had persisted until it was seriously affecting sales in his district. Was his work a
precipitate cause of his problem? Should more corrective action be tried?
What action?

Not many miles away in a high-ceilinged government office, three administrators with the National Aeronautics and Space Administration were
implementing a program change that required a private contractor to lay
off or transfer some three hundred men. They knew that the change was
unexpected and would materially affect the economy of a community near
the work site. What standards of action should be expected of the contractor in this situation? What standards would he actually apply? Would
he cause political repercussions for this sensitive government activity? Was
this situation a joint contractor-NASA responsibility?

Across the Atlantic in Africa the general manager of a British subsidiary tossed restlessly in his bed, wondering whether to reduce prices of
a retail product in an overpriced, semicartelized market. With his new
production facilities he was sure he had the lowest costs in the country

[1] Robert D. Calkins, "The Problems of Business Education," *The Journal of Business*, January, 1961, p. 4.

and could win any price war that developed. Competitive economics dictated a price cut, but from the *total view* would this decision be wise? How would the community and government react to a price war? How would his labor union react if he caused layoffs of its members in competitors' plants? What about effects on investors in native plants of this capital-poor country if he bankrupted a few native businesses in this price war?

The three incidents just discussed represent only a moment in time in a day involving thousands of similar decisions concerning business and its environment. Each new day brings thousands more new decisions, and so does the next—and the next. Business managers throughout the world are busily trying to make socioeconomic systems function effectively, and they continually face decisions involving the environment outside the firm.

This "world beyond the company gate" is the subject of this book. Going by the name "business and its environment" or "business and society," it is defined as the relationship of a business institution to values and institutions outside its own formal organization. This book is, in short, a study of institutional relationships from the reference point of business: How does business affect society, and how does society affect business?

The word "business" refers to the development and processing of economic values in a society. Business, in our broad use of the term, includes much more than private enterprise. It includes all economic and commercial activities, even when they constitute only part of the activities of an institution having other purposes, such as the actions of the business office of an opera company or the business activities of the Tennessee Valley Authority. The Metropolitan Opera Company, for example, negotiates with labor, invests capital, and makes layoffs in ways similar to private business. So also does the Tennessee Valley Authority.

In the final analysis, business actions are taken by men, not inanimate institutions; hence, our discussion will emphasize the businessman's role in business and its environment. Managers receive special emphasis because they are the group responsible for the general direction of business.

BUSINESS AS A SOCIAL INSTITUTION

The economic nature of business is well established in literature and the public mind. Likewise the technology of business is evident at every turn. What is often overlooked is the fact that business is also a social institution, having a broad influence on the way people live and work together. As stated in the quotation introducing this chapter, the direction of business is important to public welfare, and businessmen do perform a social function.

A Complex Society. Modern, complex society presents business with immensely complicated problems that it did not have formerly. One hundred years ago the three incidents mentioned at the beginning of this chapter would hardly be relevant to a business discussion. Societal relationships in those days were simpler than they are today, and even the meager complexities that did exist were usually overlooked. Decisions were clear-cut. If a man could not perform his work (the alcoholic incident), dismiss him; if a contract was canceled, lay off the men; and if you can do so, price your competitor out of the market. Each action was considered "in the public interest" because of its favorable effect on costs and prices according to the "invisible hand" described by Adam Smith.[2] If matters of community values were raised, a suitable answer was the "Bah! Humbug!" of Ebenezer Scrooge in Charles Dickens's A *Christmas Carol.*

One hundred years ago business was an uncomplicated relationship of capital, employees, and customers working together according to natural law, as represented by the triangle in Figure 1-1. Government and religion stood weakly on the fringes, having little significant influence. During this nascent period, revolutions in science, education, productivity, and culture were developing that would find their fruition in the twentieth century. It is estimated that human knowledge doubled between A.D. 1 and 1750, and again between 1750 and 1900. Then it accelerated to rocket pace, doubling again by 1950, and again in the ten years to 1960. It should double again by 1968, which means that the amount of gain in those eight years will be sixteen times what it was between A.D. 1 and 1750!

As knowledge expanded, so did institutions and interest groups, until today the chart of active participants in the business environment looks like the chart in Figure 1-1b. The president's suite in today's business is

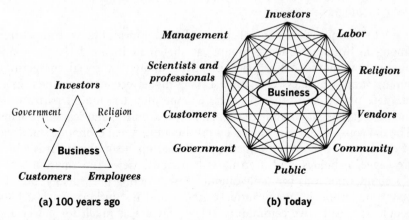

(a) 100 years ago   (b) Today

Figure 1-1   Business complexity 100 years ago and today.

[2] Adam Smith, An Inquiry into the Nature and Causes of the Wealth of Nations (1776), New York: Modern Library, Inc., 1937, p. 423.

less a place for autocratic decisions and more a place for reconciliation of the multitude of interests impinging on business. Although the number of competing interests demanding reconciliation has surely tripled, cultural guides to help an executive make the right decision have hardly expanded at all. In addition to the expanded *number* of interests pressing on business, the *kinds* of decisions needed and the cultural conditions for them have changed drastically, but without a corresponding change in cultural guides for business. The net result is that modern managers develop a *social vertigo* trying to balance all interest groups because they cannot relate to enough familiar points of reference. Like a pilot flying blind, they become disoriented and confused because the familiar horizon is gone. Likewise, the passengers on the airplane—who in this case represent the publics of business—rise in confused disharmony because they have lost the horizon too.

One company president comments as follows about the myriad pressures on a president: "If we used more accurate signs than we do, the sign on his door would not say 'President,' but would read, 'Department of Pushing and Tugging, Pulling and Hauling.'"[3] Without a doubt we expect a modern business to be:

A better place for investment
A better place to work
A better supporter of ethical ideals
A better company to buy from
A better company to sell to
A better taxpayer and supporter of government
A better neighbor in the community
A better contributor to social goals, public interest, and human progress

The unique development of modern business life is competition among institutional interest groups, as shown in Figure 1-1b. Economic competition in the marketplace has been diluted by social competition among various business claimants seeking higher economic payouts, more prestige, power, and other benefits. Competition has moved partly from the marketplace to committee rooms, business offices, and legislative halls. The old competition was judged by precise, impersonal economic standards of conduct, but the new competition is based upon social standards which are vague, nebulous, and overrun with personal views and emotions. The old competition was primarily among persons acting individually, but the new competition is among interest groups and institutions which act for people as a collective community. They may act as much for power and institutional survival as they do for people.

[3] John L. McCaffrey, "The Boss's Bosses," *The Management Review*, November, 1954, p. 712.

Even business investors in modern society are changing from individuals to institutions. Major investors today are mutual funds, insurance companies, pension funds, and other groups representing tens of millions of small savers. Employee pension funds in 1962 had over 35 billion dollars invested in corporate stocks and bonds, and their book value was growing at a rate of 14 percent yearly. In 1962 they were net purchasers of nearly 2 billion dollars' worth of common stock, while individuals—the historical capitalistic investors—were net sellers of 1.6 billion dollars' worth. All institutions together in 1962 made net purchases of over 4 billion dollars' worth of common stock; they have become a potent force changing the character of the stock market and business investment.[4]

The relationship of ownership to management has also changed. One hundred years ago the principal owners of business were also its managers. Ownership vested a person with the symbolic powers of leadership. He knew best how to manage his resources. Even when his leadership faltered, this turn of events was considered an exception to the rule, rather than a denial of the unity of owner and manager. If any conflict arose between owner and manager roles, it was internal, to be resolved within the person and never exposed to public consideration.

Today, as shown in Figure 1-1b, management is more of a differentiated role, semiprofessional in nature, with accession by competence rather than ownership. In many large enterprises the entire top-management group owns less than 5 percent of the company's assets—sometimes less than 1 percent. Management has become a distinct type of work with its own educational programs, literature, and criteria for achievement.

As management changed, so did labor. In early times employees acted primarily as individuals in their relationships with owner-managers. Increasingly, however, employment became governed by group contracts negotiated by labor unions. The union arose as a separate institution with its own institutional interests. Employees today find their employment conduct bound by management's rules, management-union contracts, and union rules, surrounded by a firm canopy of government intervention. In the crush of institutional claimants upon business, individual needs of employees are apt to be bypassed, as will be discussed in a later chapter.

Historically, labor unions have represented mostly manual skills, and as modern civilization became more complex, the burgeoning scientific-professional-intellectual groups tended to develop separate institutional interests. In the 1960s labor-union membership stabilized and actually declined as a proportion of the labor force (less than 25 percent), while membership in scientific and professional occupational groups expanded dramatically. As the 1960s began, unions represented less than 8 percent

---

[4] Daniel Seligman and T. A. Wise, "New Forces in the Stock Market," *Fortune*, February, 1964, pp. 92–95. Pension funds continued to make net purchases of about 2 billion dollars annually in 1963 and 1964; see *Business Week*, June 5, 1965, p. 110.

of white-collar labor and probably less than 1 percent of professional employees, but nearly all professional employees belonged to professional associations.[5] In the same manner that owners and managers differentiated their roles, it appears that manual laborers and intellectual workers are developing separate institutional claims on business, as shown in Figure 1-1b. This growth of professional influences has been one of the most striking business developments in recent years.

Religion has always influenced the actions of individuals both in business and elsewhere, but recently religious institutions have expanded their socioeconomic activities affecting business. Most church groups have developed social-action units which press for minimum wages, employment equality, real estate controls, advertising controls, wider distribution of material goods, and a host of other changes that fit their particular socioeconomic norms. Less metaphysical, but related in terms of their ethical interests, are many foundations which use their tax-exempt funds to advance specific socioeconomic ideas.

There is an ironic twist to the fact that the immense productivity of business has enabled modern society to support large numbers of idealistic social-action organizations which seek to change business conduct and restrain its influence on society. If, however, these organizations pursue their interests with balance and moderation born out of the knowledge that they are one of many groups to be represented, the net effect of their influence should be favorable to all concerned.

Modern business also gives vendors a more significant role than they once had. Increasing scientific complexity requires business buyers to work closely with their vendors to develop better schedules, methods, and product reliability. Major buyer-vendor relationships are long-run rather than consisting of a single commercial transaction. Sometimes deliveries are rescheduled or a part redesigned to fit a vendor's capabilities better. Vendors frequently have service representatives in buyers' plants, and buyers have their technical representatives in vendors' plants. When there is oligopsony with a powerful buyer purchasing a major part of a vendor's output, the buyer acts responsibly to help the vendor maintain competitive efficiency and stable schedules to avoid layoff and bankruptcy. Large mailorder houses and automobile manufacturers, for example, have actually served as management consultants to improve vendor business practice.

The increased role of government in modern business is well known and will be discussed in a subsequent chapter. The community, shown separately from government in Figure 1-1b, represents all *local* interests —including local government—in a business's employment community, and is discussed in a later chapter. It may appear strange that the public interest is separated from government and community in Figure 1-1b; how-

[5] Eldon J. Dvorak, "Will Engineers Unionize?" *Industrial Relations*, May, 1963, p. 60.

ever, neither government nor community—nor any other group—is sure to represent the public interest at all times. The "public interest" is an abstract, general term used to describe the greatest good for the greatest number. Where government is involved, powerful dictators, inept bureaucrats, or power-hungry politicians may work against the public interest rather than for it. We cannot say that Hitler represented the public interest merely because he represented government. Similarly, where a community is involved it may serve its own interests to the detriment of other communities; hence it cannot always act in the public interest. The public interest is actually an idealized norm which all people use to judge the acts of others. Most institutions claim to represent the public interest most of the time. The problem is that their views of public interest may differ.

A Pluralistic Society. The condition depicted in Figure 1-1*b* is a *pluralistic society,* in which diverse groups maintain autonomous participation and influence in the business environment. Business, in turn, participates in these other groups and influences them. Pluralism is a basic reality of modern business culture. Eells and Walton observe: "Pluralism always implies multiplicity, frequently diversity, and sometimes conflict. It is as much the generator as the result of freedom. . . . It is . . . as much opposed to the ambitious pretences of a James Stuart (the king can do no wrong), as it is to the Rousseauian version of democracy (the collectivity can do no wrong)." [6]

Since pluralism diffuses power, it suggests that progress is made through negotiation and compromise rather than by monolithic decision. In pluralism there are many power centers in society, none completely independent unto itself, but each with some autonomy.

Pluralism implies that business is a *joint venture* among responsible citizens and groups of citizens, such as investors, managers, workers, communities, scientists, and others. Together these groups offer diverse inputs and expect diverse outputs. Viewed as a whole, the outputs are more than economic because there are also social, psychological, political, and other expectations. This joint venture involving many groups is not necessarily a conflict or struggle for absolute power. Rather, it represents the efforts of people to reconcile their needs through a variety of organizational interests instead of one.

A key point in pluralism is that each person will usually have membership in several groups affecting business. In a drug firm, for example, one man is a member of management, a chemical-society member, an investor in the company, a consumer of its drugs, a citizen, a member of the local community, a church member, and so on. *Men* are not separated and assigned exclusively to one institution, but rather men divide *their needs* and assign different need fulfillments to different institutions. Ap-

[6] Richard Eells and Clarence C. Walton, *Conceptual Foundations of Business,* Homewood, Ill.: Richard D. Irwin, Inc., 1961, pp. 360, 363.

parently specialized institutions can provide improved payoffs to members
in relation to their membership investment in the same way that labor
specialization leads to greater productivity.

The net effect of institutional specialization is that institutions draw
their memberships from a more or less common population, instead of
each institution representing a class of separated people in conflict with
another class. Each man plays many roles in many institutions, rather
than belonging to only one institution representing his social class. Whatever conflict exists is not a class conflict, but an institutional effort to
resolve the different role needs of each citizen within the common population of a society. Workers, in addition to their employment needs, for
example, have consumer needs which cause internal struggles ". . . within
every man, between his interests as a member of some particular business
in pleasant conditions and security as a producer and his interests as a
member of society in plentiful goods at low prices for consumers." [7]

As civilization becomes more advanced and complex, there is a tendency to proliferate institutions in order to meet the expanding wants of
people; hence, the business environment is likely to become more complex rather than less so. Philosophically speaking, more institutions (assuming that they operate efficiently and in suitable balance with other
institutions) should give a man more fulfillment because they offer more
avenues for need satisfaction, and they should give a man more security
because the loss of membership in one will take away less of his total
membership investment.

Expanding institutions do, however, further divide a man's allegiance
because his membership role requires a measure of allegiance to each.
Writers in labor relations refer to a worker's "dual allegiance" to management and union;[8] however, in terms of the total business environment a
better term to apply to any person involved with business is *multiallegiant
man* because he allocates his allegiance among several institutions impinging on business. Multiallegiant man expects business operations to give
payoffs which are profitable in relation to his different membership investments.

Related to pluralism is the idea of *constitutionalism*. When each
person is a member of many organizations, there is a possibility that he
will be crushed by their collective power unless limits are put upon them.
Constitutionalism seeks to limit organizational power by means of written
documents, procedures, and social customs. It emphasizes due process of
law, justice, and protection from arbitrary exercise of power. Constitutionalism, for years a cornerstone in government, is now being applied to

[7] Lyndall F. Urwick, "The Purpose of a Business," *Dun's Review and Modern
Industry*, November, 1955, p. 52.

[8] Theodore V. Purcell, *Blue Collar Man: Patterns of Dual Allegiance in Industry*,
Cambridge, Mass.: Harvard University Press, 1960.

other powerful organizations affecting public interest: "The trend today is toward the extension of constitutionalist doctrine not only to *public* governments but to powers exercised by *private* organizations, and more particularly to such economic associations as labor unions and business corporations." [9]

BUSINESS RESPONSIBILITIES

In 1961, one of the world's largest shoe producers, Bata Shoe Company, of Czechoslovakia, sponsored a tour of the United States by twenty of their top managers representing plants in seventy-three nations. They spent four weeks studying management techniques and the structure of United States corporations. *Business Week* reported: "They felt that American managers, more than the rest of the world's businessmen, are actively groping for an explanation of business's place in a free society." [10]

Historically the mission of business, both public and private, has been to serve the economic needs of society. Business, especially in the United States, has been remarkably successful in this important function, so successful that it has become a dominant power in industrial civilization. Although its autonomy has been diluted by evolving pluralistic groups, its social power (or influence) actually may have grown in the last century. As it shared autonomy with others, its powers broadened beyond its own gates into the general community, until today business shares power for economic growth, social stability, community improvements, education, and a host of other public needs.

These expanded social powers are probably greater than the narrow property rights which business had a century ago and which gave control only over property. Business holds these social powers not by legal right, but by reason of responsible and competent performance. Out of these expanded relationships a doctrine of social responsibility is developing as a reciprocal of evident social power.

Social Responsibility. It has long been established in political science and scientific management that power should be balanced with responsibility. Since business social powers extend in numerous ways beyond the organization to community values and general welfare, social responsibility also exists. Stated simply, responsibility develops wherever power develops. It must also be emphasized that since other organizations, as shown in Figure 1-1b, are now more involved in business, their responsibilities to business are also greater than they were. If they act with intolerance or ignorance toward business, they avoid their own social responsibility.

[9] Eells and Walton, *op. cit.*, p. 404. See also Benjamin M. Selekman, *A Moral Philosophy for Management*, New York: McGraw-Hill Book Company, 1959, especially part 6.

[10] "Shoemakers Inspect U.S. Brass," *Business Week*, May 13, 1961, p. 136.

An institution by itself cannot take action. Men must give it life, so employees and other agents of business make social responsibility meaningful. Management assumes the key role because it is responsible for the general direction of business. Social responsibility, therefore, refers to a person's obligation to consider the effects of his decisions and actions on the whole social system. Businessmen apply social responsibility when they consider the needs and interests of others who may be affected by business actions. In so doing, they look beyond their firm's narrow economic and technical interests.

A number of persons have strongly criticized the idea of social responsibility for business. Levitt contends that the economic mission of business will become inefficient if diluted with the extraneous duties of social responsibility. Broad social responsibility could eventually lead to a new feudalism, with employees and customers dependent on business for almost all their socioeconomic needs.[11] Heilbroner contends that social responsibility is in part a ". . . transparent defense of privilege masquerading as philosophy, the search for sanction cloaked as a search for truth." [12] Yet the doctrine of social responsibility persists probably because it accurately describes reality. Businessmen have always championed responsibility for actions within the firm; therefore, when their influence extends beyond the business, we should expect them to honor responsibility as a reciprocal of their new powers. Rather than advertising, window dressing, or defending privilege, businessmen may be stating a profound relationship sometimes overlooked in other institutions.

Because of its importance, social responsibility will be discussed further in subsequent chapters.

Membership Investment and Payoff. As mentioned earlier, one person has a number of membership roles in the many institutions which constitute business and its environment. Each institution exists to serve certain member goals. Persons join and allocate their time and resources to an institution in expectation of a payoff greater than their membership costs. Simply stated, they expect outputs greater than inputs.

One person's total input represents his membership investment in an organization. His investment may consist of his time, tangible goods, his security, or other values useful to him. For example, a business owner may risk his prestige and reputation in a shaky venture. The venture's economic risk is minor to him compared with possible loss of prestige and self-esteem in the event of failure. Similarly a customer invests his time, economic resources, and judgment. If his purchase does not meet his expec-

[11] Theodore Levitt, "The Dangers of Social Responsibility," *Harvard Business Review*, September–October, 1958, pp. 41–50.

[12] Robert Heilbroner, "The View from the Top: Reflections on a Changing Business Ideology," in Earl F. Cheit (ed.), *The Business Establishment*, New York: John Wiley & Sons, Inc., 1964, p. 35.

tations, he may be more angered by his mistake in judgment than by his economic loss. Thus men will fight about a dollar or a word but will lose $1,000 with a smile because their total investment in each situation is different.

The return to a member for his investment is his payoff, and it may consist of any type of value—aesthetic, economic, social, or some other. Payoffs also vary in amount, certainty, and other ways. Since a business is involved with many claimants expecting different kinds of payoffs, society expects business to be socially profitable in a number of ways beyond economic gain. In business usage, the word "profit" usually refers to net economic gains to stockholders. Economic profit is one type of payoff; however, we use the term "socially profitable business" to refer to all types of payoff necessary to meet expectations of those interacting with business—including economic profit expectations. The socially profitable business gives a net gain to all those involved with it.

With regard to economic profit, a significant development has been Russian experimentation with the Liberman Plan in the 1960s. Russian economist Yevsei Liberman argued that industry should be judged at least partially by its return on capital, and a few factories have been freed from central planning to pursue this "novel" measure of efficiency. Apparently the Russian economy was deficient in this type of payoff and needed to give it more recognition in order to serve public needs better.

No one in society denies that business should be profitable, that is, provide a net gain in payoffs. Obviously its purpose is to provide outputs greater than inputs, and the greater the net gain, the better. The principal issue in an affluent industrial society, and the crux of the social-responsibility doctrine, is differing expectations of what kinds of net gains should be emphasized and what groups should receive them. Business managers, as the responsible agents of business, find themselves today answering to many types of "investors" with both economic and non-economic expectations. The idea of maximizing economic profit—so popularized by economists—appears workable only under idealistic, isolated economic conditions. As soon as all society is brought into the business environment, businessmen can talk of a satisfactory profit only because other values are involved. The responsibility of management, public or private, is to achieve enterprise needs while balancing payoffs to others in accordance with their investments in the enterprise.

Adaptation to Change. Society is undergoing its greatest transition in recorded history, including expanded education, growing urban centers, exploding technology, and new institutions. As it has done in the past, business is seeking to accommodate to these changes. To accommodate may be costly, in the same way that new technology has required expensive factory alterations, but failure to accommodate would be even more costly because business's ability to meet human expectations would decline.

Accommodation does not imply direct conformity to existing culture, for business is always transmitting values *to* society as well as receiving values *from* society. In fact, if business is to be a viable, vigorous institution in society, it must initiate its share of forces on its environment, rather than merely adjusting to outside forces as a bucket of quicksand does. Every business needs a drive and spirit all its own to make it a positive actor on the societal stage rather than a reactor or a reflector.[13] To expect business to be otherwise is to deny it the opportunities available to other institutions.

History shows that business is remarkably dynamic and responsive to change, as will be discussed in subsequent chapters on business history. Although business tends to be conservative in the values it holds, it is dynamic in applying those values. Generally it has responded faster than educational institutions, the church, or the judiciary. Some areas in which it has been especially progressive are technology, migration to frontiers, improved working conditions, and international development. As far back as the Jamestown colony of Virginia, business was a prime mover in developing the New World.

In connection with adaptation, one of the shallowest criticisms that can be made of business is that fifty or one hundred years ago it had some practices, long since changed, which by today's standards would be considered "bad." For example, it is said that business used to employ workers twelve hours a day, which is "proof" that businessmen were heartless villains. To evaluate this situation rationally, we must ask whether this historical practice was out of line with needs and practices of that time in history. Did business "villains" and shopkeepers work less than their employees or less than farmers or government workers? And was productivity so low that longer hours were necessary in order to maintain reasonable subsistence? Historical events need to be evaluated in terms of historical conditions and standards. For example, businessmen 100 years ago did not use atomic energy, which "proves" how technologically backward they were—or does it? Actually, criticisms of this type are merely evidence of business progress and adaptation.

The doctrine of social responsibility is partly one of adaptation to changing social and political conditions. There are several reasons for this adaptation. As mentioned earlier, businessmen are realists, and social responsibility is reality in a pluralistic society wherein business is interacting with many other groups capable of challenging its actions. Social responsibility is also the vehicle by which a businessman justifies to himself the usefulness of his mission and his expanded web of influence in complex society. Businessmen, like other members of the human race, are motivated

[13] See Peter F. Drucker, *Managing for Results*, New York: Harper & Row, Publishers, Incorporated, 1964.

by a sense of useful mission in their work, and they feel more secure in decision making when they have an idealistic basis for their actions.

The human psyche is basic, so self-justification of mission and power is probably more important to the *businessman* than justification to the public. To the business *institution*, however, justification to the public is required, or else public rabble elements will tear the institution to shreds and abort its mission. Exactly this is happening in some of the under-developed countries where general strikes, slowdowns, and sabotage are of such magnitude that a nation's gross national product is materially reduced and socioeconomic stability is diminished. Survival, therefore, is basic to a business. It must be able to renew its resources and be suffi-ciently profitable to give a payoff to all those interacting with it, or else its mission will abort. Adaptation is the essential means of survival, for the one "universal of the universe" is change in all aspects of time, season, and life. One writer observes:[14]

> Whether [business organizations] survive in the long run will prob-ably depend less on the international struggle with another (Communist) form of industrial organization than on how well they can adapt them-selves to meet the needs of the people who own, manage, buy from, sell to, or work for them—especially the latter.
>
> For that matter, the survival of Communist industrial organizations will probably depend, in the long run, on whether they can pass exactly the same test: satisfying the needs of the people who participate in them.

A powerful pressure for business adaptation is the public visibility of business, compared with other institutions. Since business is an ad-vertiser, a major employer, and a supplier of consumers, business acts are widely visible at all times and are therefore subject to judgment and com-ment by the general public. As a contrasting example, penal institutions have little public visibility. They are isolated spatially and socially, serve a limited membership, and restrict communication by means of minimum mobility. In sum, they have little contact with outside society, and they have changed very slowly over history.

Value Judgments. Techniques of production, science, and economics are philosophically neutral and impersonal. They can be used autocrati-cally or democratically, for progress or regression, or for goals judged "good" or "bad." The manner of use reflects the philosophy of business and of society. Values are the ultimate measure of civilized achievement. While science merely *discovers* what exists, values *determine* what should be done with what exists. They are paramount, ultimate, and determinate.

[14] Saul W. Gellerman, *Motivation and Productivity*, New York: American Man-agement Association, 1963, p. 80.

With few exceptions, managerial decisions involve value judgments. The hazy vagueness of values is compounded by uncertainty, since managerial decisions relate to the future, which by definition is uncertain. Whatever certainty managers have concerning values must be related to a specific environment, such as a particular country, culture, and time, because values differ around the world. Consider the highly publicized electrical conspiracy cases in the United States in the early 1960s.[15] In some other countries this kind of conduct is appropriate practice and is expected by buyer and public alike. But in this instance legal action and public wrath fell upon the offending corporations.

The dichotomy between rational scientific exactness and nebulous managerial judgment becomes especially evident when a scientist is promoted to a managerial position. Consider the situation of John Jones, a chemist promoted to laboratory manager. As a chemist, he typically knows when he is right, but as a manager he cannot be so sure. His decisions are restricted by such norms as profit, justice, and human relations, none provable by laws of physical science. When he is asked to decide whether a dangerous drug is ready for market tests, he needs to weigh new value systems before making his recommendation. Although he uses scientific facts in his decision, they are of lesser influence than when he acts as a chemist only.

It is evident that business is much involved in ethics, which concerns what is right or wrong, what is in the public interest or against it, what is fair or unfair, or what is a duty or a right. Ethics concerns man's relationship to man and his institutions in the broadest sense. Ethics refers to the norms that guide a person's actions, while morality refers to the quality of the actions themselves. To illustrate, businessmen make judgments on the basis of their ethics and then take actions of a specific moral quality.

Much current emphasis on social responsibility generates from humanism, which is a concern for people and their welfare. This philosophy is derived from Greek humanism and from Christianity. In the final analysis, is there anything more important than people? A professor of religion, for example, states ". . . that the making of goods is incidental and subordinate to the making of men." [16] The noble objectives of humanism have unfortunately been taken over in some cases by cults or have deteriorated into obsessions about certain groups, and the interests of others have been completely disregarded. These proponents adapt a *two-valued orientation*, meaning that they see a situation as all black or all white, overlooking the

---

[15] Clarence C. Walton and Frederick W. Cleveland, Jr., *Corporations on Trial: The Electric Cases*, Belmont, Calif.: Wadsworth Publishing Company, 1964.

[16] Raphael Demos, "Business and the Good Society," in Edward C. Bursk (ed.), *Business and Religion*, New York: Harper & Row, Publishers, Incorporated, 1959, p. 190.

multihued gray area between the extremes. Their obsession with one group or situation leads to social division and a reverse humanism in the manner of George Orwell's *Animal Farm*: "All men are equal, but some are more equal than others."

In January, 1965, for example, the Senate Agriculture Committee held hearings concerning farm labor, during which it was reported that oranges and lettuce were rotting in fields because farm labor was not available. Then a spokesman for a religious-action group testified: "As to the precious lettuce rotting in the fields, I can't squeeze out even a single tear of grief. I think people are more important than lettuce." [17] Did the speaker recognize more than a two-valued orientation in this complex economic problem? Did he show concern for people who grow lettuce and people who want to eat it, or was he concerned only for those who harvest it? Did he recognize the waste of human effort already invested that occurs when produce is unharvested? Did he recognize the connection of human wants with gross national product, productivity, and waste? Did he honor equally the employment desires of all people? Granted that people are more important than lettuce, does this fact make his view "right" and that of the produce growers "wrong"?

Even though the motives of an individual or group are indisputably exalted, this does not make them reasonable or accurate in their interpretations of business and its environment. Business relationships are intricate, complex networks in which a two-valued orientation rarely applies, and we shall try to take a broader viewpoint in this book—but we hasten to add that we do think people more important than lettuce! We also believe business cannot dispense utopia. Business can, however, help create conditions which contribute to human progress. That alone is a mission of great significance. Its successful performance will mean that we will have socially responsible managers exercising business statesmanship, no matter what we call them or think about them.

VIEWING THE WHOLE BUSINESS SYSTEM

Chris Argyris states that all organizations have three essential core activities. These are (1) achieving objectives, (2) maintaining the internal system, and (3) adapting to the external environment.[18] Typical books on management and organization tend to emphasize the first two core activities; however, our book is directed primarily toward the third: adapting to the external environment. We shall discuss the importance of this environment in management policy making and decision making.

Since business transmits values to society as well as receiving them

[17] UPI news release, *Arizona Republic*, Jan. 17, 1965, p. 4-A.
[18] Chris Argyris, *Integrating the Individual and the Organization*, New York: John Wiley & Sons, Inc., 1964, p. 120.

from society, it is involved with the values of our whole social system. Some of the disciplines which affect business are economics, marketing, sociology, finance, scientific management, human relations, ethics, religion, law, political science, and psychology. Our objective in this book is to integrate all these disciplines and value systems so that we can look at the business environment as a whole. The total system is generally something different from the sum of its parts. Consider an animal dissected and described in a laboratory. Even if the parts are sewn back together, they do not restore the living animal and show its living responses as a system. So is it with business in a whole society. We recognize that this book cannot truly picture a living business system, but at least its emphasis will be integrative rather than functional.

This is not a book on business ethics, but rather an analysis of business in its total environment. One factor in that environment is ethics, but there are many other influential factors. When it is necessary to discuss ethical norms, we plan to cover different points of view wherever practical so that each reader can make his own decisions. This book, therefore, does not offer a normative ethic of what business *ought* to do to be right with the world. Rather, it offers a discussion of how business and its environment interact mutually.

Business and its current environment can be understood best within a perspective of its long-run history. For that reason the next several chapters will cover the origin and development of business in the United States. We shall relate economic and social history to modern business ideas.

In Part 2 we shall discuss current issues in business, such as the managerial role, organization and the individual, technology and innovation, and the relationships between power and responsibility. In Part 3 we shall discuss some of the publics of business, such as customers, stockholders, government, labor, and the community. Each has certain institutional expectations of business. The international environment of business is treated separately in Part 4, in which we also survey the whole business society, with a glance toward the future.

SUMMARY

The discipline of business and its environment covers relationships of a business institution to values and institutions outside its own formal organization. The term "business" refers broadly to both private and public institutions which develop and process economic values in a society. Business is complexly related to other institutional groups, especially investors, management, labor, scientists and professionals, religion, customers, vendors, government, community, and the public. These groups and others comprise a pluralistic society in which diverse groups maintain autonomous participation and influence in the business environment. Management, as the agent responsible for general direction of business, attempts to reconcile all converging interests by providing a payoff that is profitable in relation to membership investment. Management is guided and restrained by constitutionalism, as are the other groups also. The socially profitable business provides net gains of all types, including economic profit, to those interacting with it.

The widening influence of business gives it social powers which lead to social responsibilities. Businessmen apply social responsibility when they consider the effects of their decisions and actions on the whole social system. Since change is ever present in a living society, business is continually adapting to new conditions and value systems. Managerial decisions are heavily influenced by value judgments based upon the ethics of society. An influential ethic is humanism, but the two-valued orientations (all black or all white) derived from it usually have not been realistic in a pluralistic society.

QUESTIONS

1. Is the relation of business to its environment important? Why?

2. What are the main institutional groups in the business environment today? In what ways do they relate to business?

3. What is the meaning of the following terms: social vertigo, pluralistic society, constitutionalism, social responsibility, membership investment, ethics, and humanism? What is the significance of each to business?

4. Discuss the separation of ownership and management and of manual labor and professional work.

5. What is the significance of different institutions representing different needs of a common population, compared with each institution representing a distinctly separate group of people?

6. Appraise this statement: "Although business autonomy has been diluted during the last century by evolving pluralistic groups, the social power and influence of business actually may have increased."

CHAPTER 2   BUSINESS IN ITS

HISTORICAL SETTING

> An adequate theory of business responsibility will
> recognize that the present business system is an out-
> growth of history and past cultural traditions. It will
> recognize that what we are today is, to a very large
> extent, a function of what we were yesterday.
>
> WILLIAM C. FREDERICK[1]

Questions of proper relationships which should exist between business and
the society in which it operates and what responsibilities business has to
that society have occupied increasing amounts of the time of business
executives, government officials, theologians, and scholars in recent times.
There does not seem to be any easy approach to this problem, but one
step toward progress is to examine the sources of values upon which any
business system is built.

Few, if any, would argue with the position that business is a product
of the value system of the particular society in which it exists. In turn,
any existing value system is the summation of individual beliefs of members of the society concerning the political, social, religious, and economic
institutions which make up the society. On the one hand, business often
appears to lead in shaping cultural change. Pressures for survival force
business to innovate. Driven by forces of competition, business produces
new products and develops new ways of doing things, which, in the long
run, result in a whole new way of life. For example, it has been suggested
that the Industrial Revolution in England was the greatest agent of social
change ever experienced in that country. Similarly, it has been predicted

---

[1] William C. Frederick, "The Growing Concern over Business Responsibility,"
California Management Review, Summer, 1960, p. 60.

that automation will bring a way of life totally different from anything we have known in the past.

On the other hand, various institutions of society shape business activity and establish rules within which it must operate. Business, like any other institution of society, exists for the sole purpose of fulfilling societal needs. When any institution ceases adequately or properly to serve the needs of society, it will be modified or destroyed by other institutions in that society. For example, antitrust legislation was a reaction against misuse of business power.

The next three chapters will be devoted to the evolution of business (particularly the American business system) and social philosophies of that evolution. From meager beginnings business has matured through a series of stages until today, in America, we have a highly complex free enterprise economic system called capitalism. *Capitalism* is an economic system which rests upon private ownership of property, the conduct of business for private profit, and freedom of individual initiative in business.

Over time the shape of capitalism changes. There are different kinds of capitalism, depending on the way basic elements are modified. Our modern capitalism is the result of a series of modifications which can be identified as separate stages[2] of development, distinguishable from one another, by examining the degree to which elements of capitalism are present or absent. Thus *precapitalism*, while recognizing private property, did not philosophically accept profit and in many cases imposed severe restrictions on individual business freedom. *Mercantile capitalism* was characterized by the use of private property primarily for merchant and commercial activities set within a framework of strict control by strong central government. Conversely, *industrial capitalism* emphasized freedom of individual initiative in business, little or no interference by the state, and the predominant use of private property in industrial production. *Finance capitalism* implies control of private property and means of production by financial interests and absentee ownership rather than by owner-managers. And finally, *national capitalism* denotes state regulation of business practice in the national interest and state determination of broad social policy.

In this chapter we shall discuss business as it evolved through the stage of precapitalism and into the stage of mercantile capitalism. Obviously, space does not permit a detailed examination of all the forces that worked to produce an evolving business system, and no such analysis will be attempted. Rather, we must be content only to call attention to certain socioeconomic, political, and religious philosophies and note how change

[2] Further details of ancient business heritage may be found in Miriam Beard, A *History of Business from Babylon to the Monopolists*, Ann Arbor, Mich.: The University of Michigan Press, 1962.

over time produced philosophies and values which became foundations for our American business system.

The next chapter will be devoted to the American business system as it evolved from English mercantilism, developed an American brand of capitalism, and prepared the way for industrialization. The final chapter in this part will discuss the phases of American industrial capitalism, finance capitalism, and, finally, national capitalism.

It has been said that answers to the future often lie in the past. This is only partly true. Certainly the future will be vastly different from anything civilization has even known. But examination of past cultural tradition provides us with some deep insights into understanding our present-day business systems.

BUSINESS EMERGES

No one can say at what point in history business activity first occurred. The Old Testament describes a relatively complex society based firmly upon private property, division of labor, and exchange. Transactions in local marketplaces as well as trade between distant places were clearly described, and the use of money was accepted as common practice. Archeologists have provided, and are continuing to find, evidence that fairly advanced business techniques were known and practiced long before the birth of Christ. Manufacturing and trade were widely practiced. Items such as wool, silver, slaves, and spices were brought to trading centers such as Ur, Uruk, and Uma by traveling merchants. Knives, hatchets, sickles, needles, and somewhat later (around 1000 B.C.) swords and other products of Mesopotamian craftsmen were transported long distances for trade. Ideas of division of labor, private property, medium of exchange, and market exchange were developed sufficiently to support a flourishing commercial system. Merchants of Mesopotamia were skilled in the use of contracts as early as 2500 to 3000 B.C. While headquarters for these activities were located in what we now call the Middle East, merchants ranged far and wide plying their wares as far away as the frontiers of western Europe. A large box containing dagger blades, needles, and sickles was unearthed in a Pomeranian moor, and a deposit in Brittany yielded 4,000 standardized hatchets (neatly bundled and bound with wire). The articles have all been identified as Mesopotamian in origin.

As might be expected, rules and codes of conduct were developed to govern relations between merchants and traders and also relations between merchants and governments. The oldest example of these codes is the Code of Hammurabi. Hammurabi, one of the great rulers of Babylon around 2000 B.C., promulgated a code consisting of over three hundred laws, many of which were directly concerned with commercial activity. For example, the following three laws deal with agencies:[3]

> If the merchant has given to the agent corn, wool, oil, or any sort of goods to traffic with, the agent shall write down the price and hand over to the merchant; the agent shall take a sealed memorandum of the price which he shall give to the merchant.
>
> If an agent has forgotten and has not taken a sealed memorandum of the money he has given to the merchant, money that is not sealed for he shall not put in his accounts.
>
> If while [a peddler] is traveling an enemy shall cause him to throw away anything he carries, the peddler shall swear the oath of God and he shall be quit. If a merchant gives barley, wool, oil, or any goods of trade to a peddler, the peddler shall write down the [amount of the] money and return it to the merchant; the peddler shall take a sealed receipt for the money which he gives to the merchant.

Other laws were in direct support of business and not only encouraged mercantile enterprise but also actually provided government protection in the form of business insurance (at no cost to the merchant). These laws put a direct burden of protecting traders on the shoulders of government. They also contained elements not too far different from some of our own concepts of social insurance. For example:[4]

> If the brigand has not been caught, the man who has been despoiled shall recount before God what he has lost, and the city and governor in whose land and district the brigandage took place shall render back to him whatever of his was lost.
>
> If it was a life, the city and governor shall pay one mina of silver to his people. . . .

Ancient Mediterranean Trading Cities. The pre-Christian environment around the Mediterranean was favorable for the development of business. As merchants developed skill and power, great commercial cities such as Carthage, Tyre, and Rhodes flourished along the rim of the Mediterranean. But why did they flourish? The strength or weakness of business as an institution depends in large part on its compatibility with other institutions and philosophies of the culture in which it exists. What environmental factors were favorable to the great trading cities?

From an economic standpoint the institutions of private property, exchange, money, and division and specialization of labor were firmly established in the great trading cities. A crude banking system existed, and there was wide use of credit and contracts. While agriculture was recog-

---

[3] The Code of Hammurabi (2000 B.C.). See Edward C. Bursk, Donald T. Clark, and Ralph W. Hidy, *The World of Business*, New York: Simon and Schuster, Inc., 1962, p. 9.

[4] *Ibid.*, p. 959.

nized as an important basic foundation upon which cities must rest, business was generally looked upon as being more productive. Agriculture provided the necessary items for life, but business provided items which raised standards of living and provided luxuries. In short, business generated wealth, and wealth was desirable.

Generally speaking no social-class system existed in these cities, with the exception of a distinction between slaves and freemen. What class distinction did exist was based upon wealth, so that the difference was between rich and poor. Furthermore, there was a high degree of mobility between the two classes. Business was regarded as one of the most honorable professions, and rich businessmen enjoyed the highest social status.

On the political side, a ruling class as such did not exist. Political leadership was expected from the most successful citizens. Success and wealth were nearly synonymous, and public offices were usually held by the rich, who, in most cases, were merchants. Poor men, it was thought, did not have time to administer even though they might be capable. However, every citizen, rich or poor, was allowed to vote on certain issues. Since those who governed were largely merchants, it was reasonable to expect that public policy would favor business.

Religion is always an important environmental factor. Pre-Christian religions were generally not opposed to commercial activities. Rather, in many ways religion contributed to business development. Temples often served as centers for local business transactions. Marketplaces were often established close to temples, and priestesses (not priests, in most cases) often became the chief moneylenders of the community and had no qualms about charging interest.

Environmental factors, then, were favorable to business. The society that existed in the early Mediterranean trading cities was one of the richest and most affluent of all ancient societies. No one can say how highly developed these societies might have become had they not been destroyed by the Punic Wars (246 to 146 B.C.).

Grecian Business Philosophy. While business continued to perform many useful functions in Greek society, it operated in an entirely different environment from that which existed in the great Mediterranean merchant cities. Grecian society was firmly founded on an economic base of agriculture with a basic economic philosophy that considered agriculture the most noble and productive of all human endeavors. There was a strong class system in which a ruling class and a military class were clearly defined, and there was little room for merchants. Businessmen were reduced to a very ignoble social position and were viewed as only a necessary evil.

However, inability to produce everything needed by society forced Greece to trade with other members of the Mediterranean community. In spite of philosophical prohibitions against business, Greek businessmen prospered. Commercial institutions developed a relatively high degree of sophistication. Local markets flourished, and Greek ports became centers for a thriving Mediterranean trade. Banking, too, was well established, both within religious temples and among private individuals. Competition appears to have been of some concern to those in the banking field, as evidenced by the following bank advertisement, which appeared in the middle of the third century B.C.:[5]

> TO CITIZENS and foreigners this bank gives equal dealing;
> Deposit and withdraw, when your account is correctly made up
> Let another make excuse: But Caicus even at night
> Pays foreign money to those who want it.

But the social philosophy of the time created an environment that was generally hostile to business activities. They were considered degrading, and those who engaged in them were relegated to the position of inferior citizens. The laws reflected these social philosophies. Merchants were not allowed to own property in Greek city-states, could not hold public office, and in times of war were pressed into military service in the lowest infantry ranks. (The cavalry was reserved for the military class.)

A brief review of the central ideas and social philosophies as expressed by the Greek philosophers gives an insight into the environment of Grecian business.

Plato (427–347 B.C.) on Trade.[6] Plato looked down on commercial activity as being base. Yet, in his ideal state, he recognized the necessity for division of labor and specialization. He began building an ideal state with the admission of mankind's needs and man's inability to be self-sufficient. According to Plato, the first necessity was food, the second was a dwelling, and the third was clothing and the like. Plato recognized that no two people have the same skills and that therefore there must be a place in the state for various kinds of artisans. But, reasoned Plato, almost no city is capable of supplying all man's needs, and therefore there must be a merchant class to bring goods from other cities.

Plato also recognized a need for a division of distribution. In addition to the merchant class, which brought merchandise to the city in large quantities, he saw the need for someone to buy and sell in the local marketplace. So he distinguished between the wholesaler and the retailer.

While Plato readily admitted the necessity (even the desirability) of commerce in his ideal state, he did not seem willing to admit it into the world of reality. In his *Laws,* he recommended such strict regulation of all commercial activity as to virtually stifle trade.[7] He made a basic assumption

---

[5] Charles J. Bullock, "Bank Advertisements: Ancient and Modern," *Barrons,* July 30, 1928, p. 3.

[6] Plato, *The Republic,* trans. by B. Jowett, Oxford: Clarendon Press, 1881, pp. 47–53.

[7] Plato, *The Laws of Plato,* trans. by E. A. Taylor, London: J. M. Dent & Sons, Ltd., Publishers, 1934, pp. 309–313.

that exchange activities and "roguery" were synonymous and proceeded from there. He attempted to legislate the pricing function of the laws of supply and demand by controlling price and to legislate a code which would control virtually all business activity. In order to enforce this code, he recommended that there be Commissioners of the Markets and Curators, who were to have wide punitive powers. Fortunately, his suggestions were never adopted.

Aristotle (384–322 B.C.): *The Idealist.* Aristotle followed Plato by only a few years and had studied under him. While his writings, in his own time, were generally considered secondary to those of his teacher, his philosophies had more influence on later social and economic philosophies than those of any other man. He discussed economic questions such as exchange, division of labor, money, interest, and usury, and his ideas had a great influence on later economic philosophies, particularly medieval church doctrine.

Like Plato, he recognized business (exchange) as performing a useful function in household management. To Aristotle, household management encompassed far more than one individual household. It could easily be expanded to include management of whole city-states. Exchange benefited society, according to Plato, only if two articles of equal value were exchanged, but he had difficulty defining what value consisted of. While laboring with his "theory of just price," he neglected to include values such as time and place utilities added by merchants.

Aristotle shared Plato's dislike for commercial activities, particularly those engaged in by businessmen for profit. The following quotation summarizes his philosophies on business:[8]

> Of the two sorts of money-making one, as I have just said, is part of household management, the other is retail trade: the former necessary and honourable, the latter a kind of exchange which is justly censured; for it is unnatural, and a mode by which men gain from one another. The most hated sort, and with the greatest reason, is usury, which makes a gain out of money itself, and not from the natural use of it.

Xenophon (440–355 B.C.): *The Realist.* Business was not entirely without its champions. Xenophon viewed business activities from a different point of reference than either Plato or Aristotle. While they saw business from an idealistic point of view, Xenophon took a much more practical and realistic approach. He looked at business as an agency for increasing state treasuries and urged that commerce be encouraged, rather than stifled. He viewed commerce as contributing to the total social well-being of Athens.

Foreigners and merchants were looked upon as an asset by Xenophon.

[8] Aristotle, *Politics*, found in Philip C. Newman, Arthur D. Gayer, and Milton H. Spencer (eds.), *Source Readings in Economic Thought*, New York: W. W. Norton & Company, Inc., 1954, p. 11.

He argued that they paid taxes imposed upon aliens but were not eligible for public pensions. They provided a great variety of merchandise for consumption and helped to dispose of surpluses. And in addition, if they could be induced to settle in Athens, they would pay taxes and circulate money.

But, argued Xenophon, in order to receive these benefits, the state must do everything possible to encourage merchants to settle in Athens. He suggested that foreigners be allowed to own land and build buildings, that they be exempt from conscription into the army, that they be honored with seats of distinction on public occasions, and even that merchant ships be built with public funds and offered for hire.

Roman Business Philosophy. The Roman scene was not greatly different from the Greek. The highly compartmentalized society of Rome after the Punic Wars allowed only a very low place for businessmen. But in spite of its agricultural foundations, a society dedicated to militarism found it difficult to provide the necessities of life for the populace, let alone any luxury items. Roman agriculture simply could not produce enough food. But, as in all societies, there was a large class willing to supply those items wanted by others—at a price. Without businessmen, the Roman Empire could not have survived. Merchants provided food for the masses, luxuries for the elite, and money for military conquests by rulers.

Roman ruling classes shared Greek disdain for businessmen, and Roman social philosophy differed little from Greek philosophy. However, the Roman Empire did leave two important legacies for succeeding centuries. First was a body of law which served as a basis for later systems of law, and second was the concept of natural law. According to Roll:[9]

> During the height of its [the Roman Empire's] power when, for a time, the patricians, the new landowners, and the commercial classes lived in comparative peace, there was evolved a body of laws which has had the most profound influence on later legal institutions. In the first place, the intercourse with other people which Rome had had from very early times brought into contact different legal systems and created an interest in the problems of their relationship. The *ius gentium* was the body of all those laws which were the same in different nations and were created by the necessities of the same historical development. This concept led later to the idea of the natural law which had a considerable influence on the evolution of economic thought. Of more direct economic importance were the doctrines which Roman jurists evolved for the regulation of economic relations. They upheld the rights of private property almost without limit and guaranteed freedom of contract to an extent which seems to go beyond what was appropriate to the conditions of the day.

There should be added a third legacy, if the Roman Catholic Church can properly be termed a legacy. Certainly it was to be a major influence

[9] Eric Roll, A History of Economic Thought, 3d ed., Englewood Cliffs, N.J.: Prentice-Hall, Inc., 1956, pp. 37–38.

in shaping the social, economic, and political institutions in Europe for the next several centuries. From the business sector came a well-developed commercial and financial mechanism.

THE MIDDLE AGES

The time span covered by the Middle Ages is generally agreed to be roughly from the fall of the Roman Empire in the fifth century to the middle of the fifteenth century, and has been characterized by many historians as a period of stagnation. Compared with the rapid changes which occurred in later centuries, the slow cultural evolution which took place during those 1,000 years appeared not to move at all. But move it did, from its foundations in the Roman Empire to its disappearance into the age of commercial capitalism.

The essence of medieval society lay in sharp class divisions, political disunity, and dominance by the Catholic Church, all of which sat firmly astride a solid agricultural base. While the first two factors were important in shaping the social structure and economic activities of the Middle Ages, the third was by far the most important. But so closely related and entwined are these characteristics that none can really be considered in isolation. All were deterrents to business development.

Class Division. Well-defined class divisions were inherited from the Roman Empire, and the medieval system of manorial landholding emulated the Roman *latifundia system.* During the early phases of the Roman Empire, agriculture was based on slavery, but as the agricultural system matured, shortages of slaves and high costs of maintaining them caused large estate holders to change their operating methods. Slavery was replaced by a system of serfdom, which prevailed throughout the Middle Ages. Serfs were bound to the landlord, worked his estate (or manor), and served him in a military capacity. Landlords, in return for these services, provided the serf with a small plot of land which he worked to produce his own livelihood. Those who belonged to neither the landlord nor the serf class were "freemen," who, as the term implies, were free to move about if they chose and to pursue whatever activity appealed to them. From this class came the merchants. Superimposed upon these three classes was the clergy.

Division into the above four classes and the permanency of class structure was the very foundation of medieval society. Inequality of men on earth was recognized and accepted without question, and acceptance of this philosophy provided a social stability that has not been equaled since. Division between lord, clergy, serf, and freemen was sharp. Rights and obligations of each were clearly defined, and every man knew exactly what his position was in relation to that of everyone else. Born into a particular class, a man expected to stay there, and was assured that his children (if any) would inherit neither a higher nor a lower social position. Since he knew the rights, privileges, and obligations of his station, he knew exactly how to behave, what was expected of him, and what he could expect life to provide in the future. He also knew what to expect from everyone else. His world was in equilibrium.

While there is much to be said for social equilibrium, one thing is certain—institutions do not change rapidly. Medieval society, which stressed institutional stability and continued to do things in the same way year after year, provided a poor environment for business development.

Political Disunity. The early medieval political system was also a logical transition from the Roman system. The Empire did not collapse overnight, nor was Roman civilization swept away overnight by waves of wild barbarians, as has been suggested by some historians. Heaton points out that at the time the Roman Empire collapsed, civilization was already well on its way to decay and that the barbarians were really not wild.[10] As the Empire declined, more administrative duties fell into the land-lords' hands, thus forming the basis of the manorial system. Left without the central authority of Rome, large portions of land were seized by those who became kings. They in turn subdivided their holdings into estates and transferred them to past supporters, who administered the estates within a very broad political framework; many became political entities unto themselves. As towns developed and became independent of land-lords, they soon became self-governing. Left without a central governing body, each manor and town passed its own laws and controlled its own activities as it saw fit. The result was a political patchwork which in itself was an important deterrent to the development of commerce. A traveling merchant moving across the countryside was often subjected to tolls by every landlord whose land he crossed. Towns also extracted heavy tolls, in many cases, and imposed laws which favored local trade and penalized the foreign trader.

Universality of the Church. Probably the most important institution of medieval society was the Roman Catholic Church. More than any other one force the church shaped social philosophy of the times, and more than any other single factor it worked as a deterrent to business development. Not only was the church universal in the sense that it was "the one" church, but it also attempted to take responsibility for all men's actions, both spiritual and temporal. All human activity was governed by canon law, and explanations of all worldly activity were in terms of ethical and moral considerations.

The power and influence exercised over men's lives by the church, particularly during the early centuries of the medieval period, were a

[10] Herbert Heaton, *Economic History of Europe*, New York: Harper & Row, Publishers, Incorporated, 1948, p. 60.

natural transition from the decay of Roman power. There were several reasons for this strength.[11]

First, by the end of the eighth century, the church was the greatest landowner in Christendom. Since riches and property which belonged to the church were set apart for serving God, liberal giving to the church was considered a pious act. The common belief prevailed that sins could be bought off and divine forgiveness earned by transferring property to the church by gift or bequest. The clergy ruled as landlords over these vast properties and drew large incomes from them. Much income was received in produce, and although some of it was consumed in everyday operation of the estate, much went into streams of commerce. As landlords, the clergy faced the same problems as nonecclesiastical landlords, and they solved these problems in exactly the same way.

Second, the autonomous nature of feudal political units did not provide any ties of national unity. Canon law provided uniform codes governing social behavior without regard for political boundaries, and the church became a great administrative body possessing widespread judicial powers in secular as well as spiritual matters.

Third, the church found strength by offering a spiritual doctrine which gave meaning to men's lives. Born in a period of uncertainty and crisis, Christianity offered to thousands a framework within which they could judge their relationships with others and justify their daily activities. To them the Kingdom of Heaven was a reality, a reward for successfully surmounting the trials of earthly existence.

The combination of secular and spiritual power and the harmony which existed between these powers allowed the church to claim the ordering of all man's worldly conduct as well as preparing the way for his spiritual salvation. Indeed, the church found itself deeply involved in practically all aspects of social, political, economic, and religious activities of the day. One historian comments that the church acted as ". . . a governor, a landed proprietor, a rent collector, an imposer of taxes, a material producer, an employer of labor on an enormous scale, a merchant-man, a tradesman, a banker and mortgage broker, a custodian of morals, a maker of sumptuary laws, a schoolmaster, a compeller of conscience—all in one." [12]

Church Philosophy versus Business. The role of the church was salvation—guiding the actions of men so that they would attain the Kingdom of Heaven in the hereafter—and the teachings of churchmen were di-

[11] For a detailed discussion of reasons for the strength of the church, see H. Pirenne, *Economic and Social History of Medieval Europe*, trans. by I. E. Clegg, New York: Harcourt, Brace & World, Inc., 1956, pp. 13ff.

[12] James Westfall Thompson, *Economic and Social History of the Middle Ages: 300–1300*, New York: Century Company, 1928, p. 648.

rected toward shaping men's lives in that direction. They were concerned with relations of one man to another and attacked business as it affected these relations. Ecclesiastical hostility toward trade was not an attack on trade and commerce per se. Rather, hostility was based on the belief that commercial activity turned men from the search for God. All commercial activity, it was believed, had self-interest and the pursuit of gain as its foundations. Covetousness led men into sin. Tertullian reasoned in the third century that greed was the root of all evil and argued that to remove covetousness was to remove the reason for gain and, therefore, the need for trade.[13]

Though church doctrine was based on the teachings of the Gospels, early canonists also relied heavily upon the philosophies of Plato and Aristotle. They accepted the natural economy of household management and rejected as unnatural the art of moneymaking. Trade, it was admitted, was indispensable in supplementing the deficiencies of one country with the surpluses of another. But heavy restrictions were imposed against such practices as selling an article for profit; and taking usury, in the eyes of the canonists, as in the eyes of Aristotle, was the basest human activity.

During the early centuries of the Middle Ages, church dogma was generally appropriate to the economic system as it existed. But in the latter part of the Middle Ages, these views became incompatible with an expanded economic system based on private property. Increased emphasis on trade (and manufacturing, to a lesser degree), caused by the development of trade routes, growth of towns, and expanding markets, rendered church dogma not only unrealistic but also unworkable. As the manorial system decayed, more emphasis was placed on business activity, which depended heavily on money, profit accumulation, and use of credit. Clearly canonist philosophy, which strongly condemned making a profit from sales and taking interest on loaned funds, was at odds with a social philosophy which increasingly stressed material well-being. Businessmen could not successfully engage in economic activity and at the same time conform to church dogma. What businessman would labor in the markets without expecting to be rewarded for his labor through profits? Similarly, what man would risk losing his wealth by loaning it to another without some compensation for that risk? Economic environment forced a change in social philosophy which incorporated in its value system acceptance of commercial activity and the economic institutions necessary for commercial growth (profits and interest).

As the economic environment changed, the church itself had increasing difficulty adhering to its own teachings. In its multiplicity of roles, the church became caught in the same environmental pressures and motives as the merchant. Priests borrowed money to build churches, other

[13] Roll, *op. cit.*, p. 45.

priests loaned money to needy parishioners at interest, and still others profited from commercial activities in their roles as landlords. Tawney comments on the extent of church violation of its own teachings:[14]

> From the middle of the thirteenth century a continuous wail arises against the iniquity of the Church, and its burden mav be summed up in one word, "avarice." At Rome, everything is for sale. What is reverenced is the gospel, not according to St. Mark, but according to the marks of silver.
>
> The Papacy might denounce usurers, but, as the center of the most highly organized administrative system of the age, receiving remittances from all over Europe, and receiving them in monev at a time when the revenue of other Governments still included personal services and pavments in kind, it could not dispense with them.

As business activity increased, the church found it necessary to modify and reformulate its tenets in order to reconcile them with existing economic conditions. St. Thomas Aquinas (1225–1274) led the way. He looked at the concepts of both profit and interest and made some sweeping revisions in theory. St. Thomas Aquinas considered trade a necessary evil which was inevitable in the imperfect world of men. Gain, he felt, did not necessarily involve anything dishonorable since it might be directed toward some necessary or even honorable ends. Profit was to be considered a wage for the labor of the trader, much as wages were a reward for the services of the skilled artisan. Thus, the use to which profits were put rather than the profits themselves became the subject for consideration. It became right for a man to seek such wealth as was necessary to support his family in its proper station. Also, trade was good when its object was to benefit the country or to provide for the needy.

Views on usury (interest) also changed. With the development of commerce, opportunities for monetary transactions increased. From the secular point of view, lending of money at interest enabled men to take advantage of those opportunities, and justification was found in Roman law. While St. Thomas Aquinas followed Aristotle closely in condemning usury as unjust gain, he did distinguish between loans for consumption and loans for use. Loans of items which were to be consumed, or money to purchase items for consumption, should not bear interest. But an item which was loaned for use and then returned (such as a house) could command a price for the use, even though it was returned intact. It sounds more like rent.

Another major relaxation of church prohibitions against interest came with the concept of a penalty for failure to repay a loan within the agreed-upon time. The lender was allowed to exact a penalty in addition to the return of the principal sum, an idea not a great deal different from today's

[14] R. H. Tawney, *Religion and the Rise of Capitalism* (1947), New York: Mentor Books, New American Library of World Literature, Inc., 1962, pp. 32–33.

practice of imposing interest on an open account after it has become due. Other justifications for taking of interest followed. Loss of a chance for gain because money was loaned and therefore not available to the owner for other opportunities became justification for taking interest, and this idea was soon followed by the admission that interest should be looked upon as a payment to the lender for risks which he undertook. By the sixteenth century, virtually the only remaining canonical prohibitions against taking interest were those against taking interest on loans where no risk was involved or on genuine consumptive loans to the needy.

The Protestant Revolution. Religious fetters of social theory which hampered business during the Middle Ages were virtually abandoned by the sixteenth century. Religious theory and economic theory were generally recognized as two separate divisions of social theory, each playing its own separate and special part, while at the same time contributing in its own way to general social philosophy. Tawney summarizes this thought as follows: "Society, like the human body, is an organism composed of different members. Each member has its own function: prayer, or defense, or merchandise, or tilling the soil." [15]

The Protestant revolution of the sixteenth century further swept away church condemnation of commercial activity.[16] The new theological point of view recognized a temporal calling as well as a spiritual calling. Although early canonists condemned business activities as base and distinct from godly pursuits, teachings of Protestant reformers, particularly John Calvin, encouraged business. Calvinism, like Catholicism, preached that the key to Heaven lay in man's actions while on earth. Unlike Catholicism, it preached that some measure of spiritual worth was to be found in the successful pursuit of a temporal calling. Thus, Calvinism emphasized traits such as diligence, industry, thrift, and conservatism; equated spiritual worth with temporal success; and provided a religious climate which encouraged business activities based on the profit motive. Worldly success, to a large degree, was measured in terms of accumulations of wealth. But there was no place in Calvinist theory for indulgence. Wealth was to be used for church support, contributions to charity, and other worthy philanthropic pursuits, not for lavish indulgence or "conspicuous consumption."

Herein lie the elements of the "individual ethic" that we, today, are prone to point to in our heritage—the belief that the individual, by diligence, thrift, wise investment, and prudent management of funds, can rise to a position of wealth.

Many historians believe that one of the major underlying factors in

[15] *Ibid.*, p. 27.

[16] For a discussion of the Protestant revolution, see Max Weber, *The Protestant Ethic and the Spirit of Capitalism* (1905), trans. by Talcott Parsons, New York: Charles Scribner's Sons, 1958.

the rise of capitalism was the change in social philosophy exemplified in the teachings of John Calvin. Heilbroner comments: "Calvinism fostered a new conception of economic life. In place of the old ideal of social and economic stability, of knowing and keeping one's 'place,' it brought respectability to an ideal of struggle, of material improvement, of economic growth." [17]

MERCANTILISM

Mercantilism, or mercantile capitalism, is the name given to the political and economic system that replaced feudalism. As the name implies, emphasis was placed on merchant activities because they were the source of social well-being, and industry remained small and handicraft in nature.

While the mercantile period is generally considered to have begun in the fifteenth century, where the Middle Ages left off, there was no sharp dividing line between the two periods. Rather, the transition from one to the other was gradual and occurred over several centuries, and it is incorrect to assume that no elements of mercantilism were present in the earlier period. But, in order for mercantile capitalism to emerge, it was necessary to have an environment which was quite different from that which existed during the Middle Ages. A different set of laws, customs, and political institutions was necessary, and during the latter part of the Middle Ages many forces were at work to sweep away the feudalistic social system. Among these forces were (1) the growth of central governments, who, anxious to destroy the power of the church and appropriate authority of feudal lords, emphasized a greater concern with wealth; (2) the Protestant revolution, which supplied a central doctrine favorable to economic activity and accumulation of wealth; (3) a revolution in farming methods which resulted in increased emphasis on production for the market, rural overpopulation, and severe social dislocations; and (4) maritime discoveries which hastened expansion of foreign commerce.

The force of these changes ushered in the era of mercantile capitalism. Based upon a wholly different set of underlying philosophies, mercantile policies were devoted to building strong nations through economic superiority. This was a system based upon mutual dependence between state and commercial interests. National good and merchant profit were two sides of the same coin.

A discussion of mercantilism should start with an examination of the relationships between political and economic ideas and institutions. Among the more important aspects of mercantile philosophy were (1) the identification of money with wealth, (2) unification and strong govern-

[17] Robert L. Heilbroner, *The Making of Economic Society*, Englewood Cliffs, N.J.: Prentice-Hall, Inc., 1962, p. 55.

ment, (3) protectionism and state intervention, and (4) power. But so closely entwined and interdependent were these elements, that it is virtually impossible to discuss one without touching upon aspects of others.

Importance of Money. Accumulation of treasure in the form of hoards of precious metal and money was nothing new to the mercantile period. For centuries a market economy had been developing which was dependent upon money. Persons who had the largest hoards of money or precious metal were considered to be the wealthiest, and wealth (in the form of treasure) gave the holder power—power to command goods and services.

Mercantile philosophy expanded the concept of wealth to the nation, but there was one important difference—at least in the early development of mercantile doctrine. National well-being was considered to be dependent upon the stock of money which lay more or less dormant in the national treasury. Little concern was given to how this money could or should be used, and since wealth was equated with a store of treasure, policies were designed to prevent flow of money out of the country and to encourage it to flow into the country.

Awareness of the connection between trade and treasure existed well before the end of the Middle Ages. For example, wool merchants in England were required, in 1339, to bring in a stipulated amount of metal for each sack of wool exported, and the British Navigation Act of 1381 contained a prohibition against exporting gold and silver. However, methods of acquiring a satisfactory supply of treasure were modified and refined during the mercantile period. Prohibitions against movements of gold and silver gave way to a balance-of-trade concept similar to that in effect today. The theory was simple: A country that exported more than she imported was bound to have a net inflow of money. Later theory included a "value added" concept. Not only were exports supposed to exceed imports, but emphasis was placed on (1) importing those items of raw material (relatively low in price) which were needed for home industry or consumption and (2) exporting finished goods (of relatively high value).

Importance of Central Government. Medieval atomization of political power, vested in the hands of feudal lords and autonomous towns, was strongly at odds with growing commercial interests. The ability of towns and feudal lords to levy taxes, impose tariffs, coin money, and regulate trade, all of which were different from political boundary to political boundary, created nearly insurmountable economic barriers and severely hampered commercial intercourse.

National economic power depended upon unification of political power—a centralized political unit strong enough to impose and enforce a uniform set of commercial laws, uniform tariffs, and a uniform monetary system. To these ends merchant capitalists joined forces with rising central monarchies by financing their struggles against feudal lords and

authoritarian powers of the church. With successful establishment of national monarchies came a variety of benefits for merchants. First, domestic
markets were widened. Second, national unification brought safer movement of merchants and goods. Third, royal courts dispensed justice according to uniform laws of the land. Property and rights of individuals
were protected. Fourth, monarchies improved internal communications
systems by building roads and bridges. Fifth, central governments stabilized currency (at least to a degree). Sixth, important commercial concessions and monopolies were often granted to merchants for political
support.

Protection and State Intervention. Mercantilists demanded a strong
central government to protect and encourage ever-widening trade interests.
However, in the early phases of the mercantile period, the crown did
little more than replace rigidities of the feudal system with rigidities of
nationalism. Rather than establishing a political atmosphere in which
individual entrepreneurs could move ahead, authoritarian governments—
particularly under Elizabeth and the Stuarts—placed more barriers in the
way of commercial expansion than they eliminated. Seeking to build up
revenues and at the same time hoping to build a loyal following, the
crown turned to the system of economic monopolies. Grants of monopoly
privilege covering virtually every economic endeavor were sold, and then
a royalty was imposed on each item sold. Hacker states:[18]

> There were monopolies imposed upon the soap, salt, glass, starch,
> vinegar, wine, alum, cloth-finishing, gold and silver thread manufacture,
> and the pin industries; upon the selling of playing cards and dice; upon
> the importation of tobacco; upon the issuance of licenses for the keeping
> of taverns, the engrossing of wills, and the printing of linens. . . . There
> was a grant for the weighing of hay and straw in London and Westminster.
> Another patent was given for the gauging of red herrings. There was
> one for the marking of iron, another for the marking and gauging of
> butter casks, still another for the gathering of rags.

From the standpoint of producing revenue for the crown, monopolies
were quite successful. It is estimated that in 1639 Charles I ". . . was
getting £30,000 from wine licenses, £13,050 from tobacco licenses, £30,825
from soap licenses, and £750 from playing card and dice licenses." [19]

Thus, the crown did encourage commercial and industrial enterprise
during this period, but the system favored a few at the expense of masses

---

[18] Louis M. Hacker, *The Triumph of American Capitalism*, New York: Simon
and Schuster, Inc., 1940, p. 74. Examples of the monopolies of the playing-card
makers and the felt makers in England are discussed in George Unwin, *Industrial
Organization in the Sixteenth and Seventeenth Centuries* (1904), London: Cass and
Company, 1957, pp. 142–147.

[19] *Ibid.*

who were disenfranchised from economic opportunity. Discontent grew and was finally manifested in the Long Parliament, which was called in 1640, and the Puritan revolution, which occurred between 1642 and 1647, led by Oliver Cromwell. The whole philosophy of the mercantile system was challenged, and emphasis shifted from state intervention to state protection and from monopoly to free trade.

Mercantile policy after the Puritan revolution was addressed to several propositions, all directed toward one central aim: to make the nation as nearly independent of other countries as possible. In order to accomplish this task the following basic concepts were stressed: First, England was to produce all its own foodstuffs and manufactured articles. Second, England was to control its own carrying trade (merchant shipping). And third, the colonial system was to be developed in a manner which produced raw materials for home industries and absorbed any surplus of manufactured goods.

Concept of Power. Although the concept of state power remained much the same after the Puritan revolution, the use of this power changed. Political and military power were closely related to economic power and were mutually dependent. Under the new concept, government concerned itself with solutions to social problems and protection for economic activities. Military power was necessary to obtain and hold foreign markets and to protect shipping. Successful development of a colonial system depended heavily upon military power. State power, in turn, depended upon economic activity to provide the money necessary to protect commerce, enforce laws, and fight wars. Colbert summarized these relationships neatly when, in a letter to his cousin in 1666, he said: "Trade is the source of [public] finance and [public] finance is the vital nerve of war." [20]

SUMMARY

No one knows when business activity actually began, but from its humble beginnings, somewhere in antiquity, business development can be traced with a reasonable degree of certainty. Phases in business maturity can be established, and environmental factors that either encouraged or discouraged growth and maturity may be identified.

Business's place in society has always been (and continues to be) a function of its compatibility with other social institutions and the general social philosophy which surrounds it. Putting it another way, the place which society accords to business depends upon how well it serves in reaching social objectives. As perceptions of social needs change, so also

[20] Quoted in Eli Heckscher, *Mercantilism* (1931), trans. by Mendel Shapiro, New York: The Macmillan Company, 1935, vol. II, p. 17.

must business change. Sometimes leading the way in social change and sometimes following, business has progressed over the centuries to its present maturity.

The present chapter has been concerned with business as it developed from crude beginnings in antiquity to a reasonably sophisticated system during the period of mercantile capitalism. Environmental factors of social, economic, political, and religious philosophies have been examined. Social attitudes toward business have varied over the ages from encouragement during the early years before the birth of Christ, to general hostility during the periods of Greek and Roman power and during the Middle Ages, and back again to encouragement during the mercantile period.

The next chapter will discuss the origins and development of American business during the colonial period.

QUESTIONS

1. What names are given to the five phases through which business has passed? How may each be characterized?

2. Appraise the following statement: "An adequate theory of business . . . will recognize that . . . what we are today is, to a very large extent, a function of what we were yesterday."

3. Contrast philosophies which surrounded business in the Mediterranean trading cities with those surrounding it in Greek and Roman culture.

4. In what way did medieval church philosophy affect business?

5. Why was the Protestant revolution important to business development?

6. Discuss the more important aspects of mercantile philosophy.

CHAPTER 3 THE FOUNDATIONS OF
MODERN BUSINESS

> In America, the wisdom and not the man is attended to; and America is peculiarly a poor man's country. . . . They find themselves at liberty to follow what mode they like; they feel that they can venture to try experiments, and that the advantages of their discoveries are their own.
>
> THOMAS POWNALL[1]

Born into a capitalistic climate and reared in the cradle of British mercantile policy, America was destined, from the very beginning, to develop as a capitalist nation. Max Weber commented that it was sufficient ". . . to call attention to the fact that without doubt, in the country of Benjamin Franklin's birth (Massachusetts), the spirit of capitalism . . . was present before the capitalistic order." [2] But, as is often the case in relationships between parents and children, the child rebels against parameters of behavior set by the parent. He must develop according to his own personality and talents, and he must formulate his own philosophies and value systems. Rarely can he be forced into a preconceived mold.

So it was with English and American business relations between 1607 and 1776. At the beginning, colonial business activity fitted well into the British economic scheme, but as colonial business expanded, it ran head on into restrictive British mercantile policy with all its suffocating effects. Like a child hampered from growing to manhood by domineering parents,

---

[1] Thomas Pownall, A *Memorial, Most Humbly Addressed to the Sovereigns of Europe, on the Present State of Affairs between the Old and New World* (1780), quoted in Albert Bushnell Hart (ed.), *American History Told by Contemporaries*, New York: The Macmillan Company, 1929, vol. III, p. 76.

[2] Max Weber, *The Protestant Ethic and the Spirit of Capitalism* (1905), trans. by Talcott Parsons, New York: Charles Scribner's Sons, 1958, p. 55.

39

American business had to revolt against a system that suppressed, at every turn, its attempts to develop its own social, business, and political institutions. Once free to experiment, America experienced the growing pains of adolescence, that difficult time when ideas, values, and philosophies are tried and tested. This chapter will cover the period between the founding of the first colony and the Civil War, and it will be our purpose to examine the origins of American ideas and philosophies and the environment in which they developed.

It would be incorrect to say that the Revolutionary War was the result of social domination by the British. It would be equally incorrect to describe it as a war against religious intolerance, "taxation without representation," or suppression of manufacturing, even though each, in its own way, was a contributing factor. The American Revolution was really a reaction to a strange collection of contradictions in English policy brought about by conflicting power groups. Miriam Beard described the Revolution as ". . . indirectly a product of the mental unrest and the industrial and commercial pressure of pre-Machine Europe." [3]

COLONIAL FOUNDATIONS OF AMERICAN BUSINESS

An examination of the American business system must start with its colonial foundations, which in the eyes of the mother country were never intended to be the underpinnings of a business system at all, especially not a business system as we know it today. However, the whole British concept of colonization sprang from the philosophy of mercantile capitalism, and the Colonies were designed to support the mother country. From the viewpoint of British mercantile philosophy, the Colonies were supposed to perform only two functions. First, they were to furnish products that were in short supply in England, and second, as markets, they were expected to absorb manufactured goods from English mills.

Arguments for supporting colonial policy continually stressed the need for raw materials and markets. Lippincott commented:[4]

The substance of the various arguments was that the Indians in time would become large consumers of British goods; to this would be added the demands of the colonists; the growth of trade would promote the development of the merchant marine, increase the number and skill of the sailors, and provide a substantial basis of a larger and stronger navy; the colonists would afford a source of supply for many raw materials of manufacture, and a place where the idle population of England could find occu-

[3] Miriam Beard, A History of Business from Babylon to the Monopolists, Ann Arbor, Mich.: The University of Michigan Press, 1962, vol. II, p. 46.
[4] Isaac Lippincott, Economic Development of the United States, New York: Appleton-Century-Crofts, Inc., 1925, p. 49.

pation. . . . Meanwhile, the Royal Treasury would be augmented by duties on tonnage and taxes on commerce.

In these very arguments lay the seeds of contradiction that shaped American ideas, beliefs, and philosophies.

Capitalist Origins of American Business. American business was bound to be capitalistic. Our institutions were born and matured in an environment that was capitalistic from the start. With few exceptions, the Colonies were founded squarely on the opportunity for private gain. Georgia was founded directly by the crown as an experiment in growing mulberries, as well as a political effort to contain the Spanish in Florida, and New York and Nova Scotia came directly under control of the crown through war. But the British crown in most cases played only a passive role. Reinsch observed: "The mere glory of possessing colonies had little attraction for the liberals. They had no desire to tax themselves for the pleasure of governing others." [5] All the other colonies were formed by groups of individuals stirred to action by the profit motive. Charter companies and individual proprietors were the chief agencies of settlement. Here the crown did play an important part by transferring large tracts of land to private ownership, much of which found its way into the hands of individual farmers.

While England still wrestled with the vestiges of feudalism, settlers moving to America found an environment free from feudal organization and institutions. Vast amounts of land, available for little effort or money, allowed the American farmer to start out as a capitalist farmer, owning his land and tools and producing for a market as well as for himself and his family.

American craftsmen, too, started as capitalists. During the early colonial period, English industrial production remained under monopolistic authority of craft guilds which controlled production, set wages, and dictated the status of apprentices, journeymen, and masters. While the craft system of production followed immigrants to America, the guild system did not. Any craftsman possessing sufficient skill and capital could set up shop in America free from guild restrictions and free to employ capital and take risks in any way he saw fit (within mercantile restrictions of the time). He also enjoyed freedom of competition. At least he enjoyed freedom of competition on a local scale. Mercantile policy (which will be discussed later) put severe restrictions on his ability to compete in foreign trade, but in local markets craftsmen competed freely among themselves as well as with foreign goods. Industrial procedures in America were never subject to the restrictions of national guild monopolies.

[5] Paul Reinsch, *Colonial Government*, New York: The Macmillan Company, 1902, p. 6.

American merchants were also capitalists from the beginning. With the exception of those who acted as agents for the large trading companies, the merchant was an entrepreneur in every sense of the word. Free from monopolistic restraints of English merchant guilds, he traded in whatever commodities offered a profit, took title to merchandise as well as handling consignments, in many cases owned means of transportation, and, as he expanded, employed people for wages.

Thus, whatever type of business endeavor the colonist might choose in the new country, all the elements of capitalism were present. Assuming that he had enough capital or sufficient credit, he was free to own property with no restrictions and to employ his property according to individual initiative and toward any opportunity that appealed to him. However, it is incorrect to say that the colonist enjoyed complete freedom of choice of business endeavor. Until the close of the Revolution, he was always subject to restrictions upon activity imposed by the mercantile system. But within the system he was free to make entrepreneurial judgments, and often he moved outside the system as a matter of either convenience or necessity. The influence of British mercantile policy and its application to American business, political, and social ideas will be discussed in the next section.

Mercantilism versus Business and Political Freedom. Most colonists came to America from countries whose business systems were based on philosophies of mercantilism—a system not wholly unlike totalitarian systems of today. Mercantilism was both a political and a business system which worked somewhat on the theory that what was good for the state was good for the individual. Writers such as Schmoller[6] and Heckscher[7] identify mercantilism with state making. They viewed mercantile policy merely as a means to the end of strong national states and believed that state regulation of business was essential to both business growth and national strength. On the other hand, it has been pointed out that merchants favored a strong state only to the extent that they could manipulate it to their own ends.[8] But Eells and Walton raise the interesting question: ". . . if the government subordinated business to its national purposes, the real question of who controlled the governors remained wrapped in enigma." [9] It seems clear that the system was based on a mutual dependence between state and commercial interests. National good and merchant profit were two sides of the same coin.

[6] Gustav Schmoller, *The Mercantile System and Its Historical Significance* (1895), Gloucester, Mass.: Peter Smith, Publisher, 1931.

[7] Eli Heckscher, *Mercantilism* (1931), 2 vols., trans. by Mendel Shapiro, New York: The Macmillan Company, 1935.

[8] Eric Roll, *A History of Economic Thought*, 3d ed., Englewood Cliffs, N.J.: Prentice-Hall, Inc., 1956, pp. 37–38.

[9] Richard Eells and Clarence C. Walton, *Conceptual Foundations of Business*, Homewood, Ill.: Richard D. Irwin, Inc., 1961, p. 32.

For two reasons, however, the American Colonies did not fit well into the British mercantile scheme. First, colonization, to some extent, was a protest movement. Many American settlers had fled their home countries to escape governmental tyranny in business, social, political, and religious realms, and their belief in mercantile philosophy was already weakened by the time they arrived in America. Limitations, restrictions, and penalties imposed on colonial development by a government 3,000 miles away did little to strengthen the colonists' belief in strong central government. Laissez-faire philosophies and emphasis on natural rights of the individual, as these ideas were reflected in the American Constitution and the Bill of Rights, were logical outgrowths of experience under British mercantile policy.

Second, British mercantilism did not work well in America because England refused to accept the Colonies as a separate economic unit, viewing them instead as an extension of British agriculture and extractive industries. According to the mercantile scheme, the Colonies were viewed as a support element whose principal functions were (1) to supply commodities that could not be produced at home and (2) to absorb finished goods from English manufacturers as well as services of merchants and financiers. Herein lay the contradiction that led to the breakdown of mercantilism in America. Colonies were expected to import more from England than they exported, thereby creating a balance of trade in favor of England. Moreover, balances were to be paid in gold and silver. But, since the colonies bought more than they sold, there was no way for them legally to obtain money necessary to pay these balances and still stay within the mercantile system. Andrews summarized the situation in the following manner:[10]

> One problem that neither the [English] government nor the [English] mercantilists were ever able to solve was how to meet the need of hard money in the colonies or to provide an adequate medium of exchange for the doing of business. . . . Because the mercantilists wanted the balance of trade always to be in England's favor and the drift of money always in one direction, and that toward England, they saw in the colonies not a separate commercial group with interests of its own, but a channel through which an additional supply of Spanish and other foreign gold and silver might eventually reach England.

Mercantile policy, as applied to the American Colonies, consisted in defining colonial business activities according to whether they supported England's economy or competed with it. Activities that supported England's economy were encouraged by bounties, remission of import duties at English ports, and various other favorable legislation. On the other

[10] Charles M. Andrews, *The Colonial Period of American History*, New Haven, Conn.: Yale University Press, 1938, vol. IV, pp. 350–352.

hand, those activities which competed with England's economy were discouraged by unfavorable legislation or were forbidden outright.

In order to understand the extent of limitations imposed on American business freedom by British mercantilism, it is necessary to compare the products wanted by England with colonial ability to produce them. Equally important is a consideration of British mercantile policy and the manner in which it was enforced.

Business Autonomy. According to the British Navigation Act of 1660 and subsequent acts of trade, all items moving either into or out of the Colonies were confined to British and colonial ships, and to ensure control, shipmasters were required to declare at English ports all foreign cargoes destined for America. Depending upon durability, exports from the Colonies were controlled by "enumerated lists," [11] bounties, prohibitions against entry into England, and discriminatory duties. During early American business development, these acts were generally beneficial to the Colonies, and when parliamentary regulations cramped business opportunity, the colonists were generally prone to ignore or circumvent them. It was not until late in the colonial period that serious conflict developed as a result of England's attempt rigorously to enforce restrictive legislation, and pressures developed differently in the Northern Colonies from the way they did in the South. For this reason the two sections will be discussed separately.

Commerce of the Northern Colonies. Although the Northern and Middle Colonies produced little that England wanted, in the beginning they fitted rather well into the British scheme. England wanted furs and forest products, which were available in vast quantities throughout the North. Chittenden referred to Northern America as the "richest and most extensive field for collecting fine furs upon the face of the earth." [12] Northern forests provided a virtually unlimited supply of lumber which was particularly suited to shipbuilding. Also the whaling waters of the North produced a supply of whalebone that was much in demand in England for the manufacture of ladies' garments.

But in the production of other commodities the North was less fortunate. Northern soil and climate lent themselves particularly well to production of agricultural products such as beef cattle, work animals, and cereal grains, all of which were barred from English ports. Even though England wanted iron and copper, limited deposits were largely smelted

[11] Enumerated articles were articles which could be sold only to England. They were usually given preferential tariff treatment to encourage production. Among the more important enumerated articles were sugar, tobacco, ginger, indigo, rice, molasses, copper ore, crude iron, furs, whale fins, hemp, potash, pearlash, lumber, and a variety of naval stores.

[12] Hiram M. Chittenden, *The American Fur Trade of the Far West,* Stallo Vinton (ed.), New York: Barnes & Noble, Inc., 1935, p. 86.

in America for home consumption rather than export. And the rich fishing banks provided fish, which were also barred from English ports.

All in all, New England and the Middle Colonies had little to offer in direct trade with England. Lack of English markets forced Northern colonists to search for other outlets which could absorb increasing volumes of colonial products and thereby furnish money with which to pay for English imports. Many products found their way into European markets, where they could be sold for cash or bills of exchange. This was particularly true of fish. However, most lucrative of all were the markets of the British West Indies. British planters needed beef to feed the white population and fish for the black slaves. They needed cereal grains for food and lumber for building. Since the British West Indies were part of the British colonial system, trade between the two areas was encouraged.

Need to dispose of Northern surpluses stimulated the growth of a large merchant class. Risks of transporting quantities of goods were great, but profits for the successful were also great. Rapid expansion of merchant activities also stimulated shipbuilding in the North. As early as 1700 shipbuilding had become one of the major industries of the North. For example, records show that 1,118 vessels were built in Massachusetts alone between 1696 and 1713.[13] Some ships were sold to England, but most were absorbed by colonial merchants themselves.

Colonial merchants dealt in many commodities, but probably the single most important item of trade was rum. Its nearly universal appeal made it an item which could be converted into remittances to England with relative ease. It was an important item in trade with the American Indians. It was carried by coasting vessels to other colonies and exchanged for products which could be sold to England. But most important, it became the cornerstone of the famous (some call it infamous) triangular trade with the West Indies and Africa.

Based solidly on rum, the triangular trade operated as follows: American ships, loaded with cattle, grain, fish, and lumber, were taken to the West Indies, where the cargoes were sold for cash or traded for sugar and molasses. These items were then taken back to New England, where they were converted into rum. Rum, in turn, was taken to Africa, where it was traded for gold dust, ivory, and slaves. The first two items were used as direct remittances to England, while slaves found a ready market in the West Indies, where they were sold for cash or traded for more molasses. Figure 3-1 shows the three-cornered relationship between the West Indian Islands and the American Colonies.

Thus, the Northern Colonies were able to generate sufficient money to pay the ever-increasing balances of trade created by importing greater

[13] Louis M. Hacker, *The Triumph of American Capitalism*, New York: Simon and Schuster, Inc., 1940, p. 134.

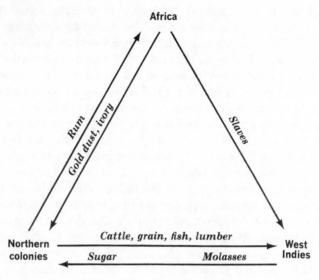

Figure 3-1 Triangular trade.

and greater quantities of English manufactured goods. Concerning the volume of imports into the Colonies, Edmund Burke commented in an address to the House of Commons in 1775: "The trade with America alone is now within less than £500,000 of being equal to what this great commercial nation, England, carried on at the beginning of this century with the whole world." [14] Therefore, the problem that faced Northern colonial businessmen was that of expanding their commercial activities fast enough to meet the rapidly expanding balance of trade. As the colonial period wore on, American merchants were forced to move more and more outside the British mercantile system, ignoring many of the navigation acts, with their attendant restrictions on trade. High costs of operating British West Indian plantations, coupled with high export tariffs from West Indian ports, encouraged American businessmen to turn increasingly to foreign islands for supplies of sugar and molasses. Twenty to forty percent could be saved by trading with French and Dutch islands rather than with English plantation owners. Thus, a substantial part of American trade with the West Indies was illicit. It has been estimated that only about one-eighth of the annual consumption of sugar and molasses by all the Colonies came from British planters. The balance was smuggled past British customs from foreign islands.[15]

[14] Edmund Burke, *On Concilliation with America* (1795), quoted in Charles A. Beard and Mary R. Beard, *The Beards' New Basic History of the United States* (1944), Garden City, N.Y.: Doubleday & Company, Inc., 1960, p. 57.

[15] Arthur M. Schlesinger, *The Colonial Merchants and the American Revolution*, New York: Barnes & Noble, Inc., 1939, p. 43.

Attempts by the British to maintain a monopoly of the sugar trade for English West Indian planters by enforcement of navigation acts contributed heavily to the political and economic revolt of Northern businessmen in 1776. Had England been able rigorously to enforce the navigation acts as they applied to the West Indian trade, the entire economy and prosperity of the Northern Colonies would have been destroyed.

Agriculture in the Southern Colonies. The economy of the Southern Colonies was in sharp contrast with that of the Northern Colonies. Climate and soil, along with consistent encouragement by England, gave the South a distinct advantage in agriculture. Almost from the time of the first settlement, the South had made tobacco its staple export item, but here the colonists confined themselves to producing the plant and left marketing almost entirely to British merchants. Protected and encouraged by English law, the South had a substantial advantage in producing tobacco. Acting as agents for the planters in marketing, and transporting tobacco to England in English ships, British merchants could make substantial profits by financing Southern planters. During the eighteenth century considerable attention was also given to growing rice and indigo, both of which were enumerated articles and enjoyed the protection and encouragement of English law. The Southern Colonies were also liberally blessed with forests, from which lumber and naval stores were produced in substantial quantities.

Probably the most striking difference between the Northern and the Southern Colonies was that while the economy of the North developed primarily as a commercial economy, with the preponderance of native capital invested in merchant activities, the South developed as an agricultural economy, with native capital invested almost exclusively in plantation-type agriculture. From these large landed estates grew social, political, and economic systems based upon sharp class differences and a pseudoaristocracy which claimed rights to leadership by virtue of race and birth.

Native Southerners did not ordinarily become merchants because merchant activities were generally looked upon as inferior to agriculture. There were several reasons. First, remnants of feudalistic beliefs and associations of power with large landholdings remained. Second, emphasis was placed on large landholding and agriculture from the very beginning of the Southern Colonies. Third, protection and encouragement of agriculture by British mercantile policy gave it a favored position. And fourth, high financial returns possible in tobacco and related activities made agriculture, initially, an attractive outlet for English capital. Commerce, typically, was left to English merchants.

Commercial relations were maintained between planters and English merchants in two ways, both equally uneconomical for the planter. First, he could deal directly with a British merchant at home on a commission basis. The merchant transported tobacco, rice, or other products to England and disposed of them in the home markets. In return he furnished and delivered to the planter's dock the variety of goods needed for the following season. Or the planter could deal with a resident agent, or *factor*, maintained in the Colonies by the British merchants. Factors kept a supply of consumer and industrial goods on hand which were advanced on credit against the following year's crop. Both systems provided generous credit and encouraged wasteful methods and overbuying by planters.

Southern plantation owners, even though they enjoyed a favored position in the British mercantile system, experienced much the same basic difficulties as the North, that is, the problem of finding enough hard money or salable commodities to meet an ever-increasing balance of payments. A number of factors contributed to the planter's dilemma. First, the plantation system was a high-cost one. In addition to the ordinary costs of farming, slavery was an extremely expensive and uneconomical form of labor. Second, not only was transportation in English ships expensive, but also payments for shipping stayed in England. Third, charges for insurance on cargoes of tobacco were high. Fourth, although generous credit was always available, interest rates were quite high. Fifth, tobacco prices were controlled in the English markets. To make the position of the planter worse, the nature of tobacco itself is such that it rapidly exhausts the land upon which it grows. These factors, plus the extravagant nature of the planter class, combined to place them in a continual and ever-increasing debt position. Tobacco crops were usually mortgaged before they were grown.

The planter, then, found it necessary to move continually westward, and availability of Western land was his salvation. Fresh, cheap lands allowed him to maintain and even increase production, but more important, he could speculate in land. Indeed, land speculation became the backbone of Southern planter economy. Hacker has observed: "The ability of planters to make a profit (not on the cultivation of their staples but in their role as speculative landlords) furnished the incentive for the flow of short-term capital from England into the southern colonies. . . ."[16] In addition, the Western wilderness provided a rich harvest of furs which furnished a cash crop and means of meeting trade balances.

When England began to deprive Southern planters of means of paying their debts, as she did by changing her colonial land policy in 1763, the entire Southern economy was threatened with wholesale bankruptcy. Under pressures from British capital interests, the entire area west of the crest of the Appalachians was closed to colonial land speculators by the Proclamation Line of 1763. Jurisdiction of Western lands was taken from colonial governors and placed in the hands of special agents of the crown who were sympathetic to British land speculators. Fur trading was also

[16] Hacker, *op. cit.*, p. 131.

monopolized by British interests through the device of licensing fur traders. The net result was virtual exclusion of colonial capital from the West and complete frustration of Southern ability to remain solvent.

Thus, when Southern business interests, already fighting for their very existence, clashed headlong with British business interests apparently bent on destroying them, the Southern Colonies enthusiastically joined the North in a rebellion of survival.

American Manufacturing. Manufacturing did not develop in colonial America to any appreciable extent. Blame for lack of expansion has often been laid at the feet of the British mercantile system itself. And to some extent this is true. There were prohibitions against manufacturing many items for export, such as iron plate and woolen commodities. On the other hand, England did little to interfere with manufacture of articles for consumption within the Colonies. Nails, candles, soap, blankets, clothing, and a variety of similar products were widely produced in homes for family use, and local craftsmen often produced articles such as bricks, leather, iron utensils, and wagons.

Reasons for lack of expansion in manufacturing, even in the Northern Colonies, must be sought outside the British mercantile system. First, abundance of land encouraged immigrants to become farmers. By 1800 there were approximately five million people in America, but they were scattered from the Canadian border to Florida and from the Atlantic Coast westward to the Mississippi River. Less than 10 percent lived in towns of 1,000 or more population. The rest were farmers, who, in the colonial tradition, remained as self-supporting as possible.

The second reason, a direct result of the first, was the shortage of labor and resultant high labor costs. No laboring class developed in America until well into the nineteenth century. Sources of labor were generally limited to slaves or indentured servants, both of which were uneconomical. Skilled artisans, too, were difficult to employ. Generally they were better off financially if they became independent businessmen than if they offered their services for hire.

Third, price competition from abroad operated against expansion of colonial manufacturing. Maturity of the English factory system brought products of higher quality than could be produced in America, and mass-production methods of English factories resulted in lower unit costs. Even when the costs of transportation were included, English goods enjoyed a substantial price advantage over most American products.

Fourth, and highly important, was lack of capital. Other business opportunities offered local capital much higher returns on investment. Merchant activities, and opportunities such as shipbuilding which were related to trade, promised higher and faster returns. British capital, too, looked unfavorably upon investing in colonial manufacturing. There was no desire on the part of English capitalists to invest in anything which competed with British manufacture, but more important, they, like the colonists, could gain larger profits through trade.

Social Autonomy. Tendencies toward social autonomy were present in the Colonies from the very beginning. The colonists did not bring with them the social order of Europe, a social order based upon a rigid hierarchy of kings, lords, clergy, and peasants and a society based upon a scarcity of land and with strict class lines which were rarely crossed. Rather, American social philosophies were largely the result of modifying old ideas and beliefs.

Nearly all early American settlers were either farmers or settlers with no fixed "stations" in life. Even as classes based on economic prominence began to appear, no barriers to movement between the classes developed. On the contrary, intermarriage between economic classes strengthened community social ties, and intermarriage between the Colonies built strong continental relationships. In addition, social interaction developed a permanent set of customs, ideas, manners, and views which were different from those of the Old World. As family ties with Europe faded and as the American economic environment developed in its own unique way, colonists began to think of themselves as Americans rather than as part of a distant European social system. They thought of themselves as part of a separate and distinct social system with beliefs, problems, opportunities, and duties quite apart from and different from the European systems from which they had come. And as the Colonies matured, intellectual leaders molded scattered ideas and philosophies into a systematic social philosophy which raised and answered questions about the origin of government, relations of the Colonies and the mother country, various business opportunities, and relations which would promote the welfare of American people; in a more abstract vein, they inquired into the ends of human life. Intellectual leaders wrote books, pamphlets, and magazine and newspaper articles on nearly every aspect of these questions, and they wrote for a large audience. A high rate of literacy and growth of the colonial postal system aided in the dissemination and consumption of such literature. Continued discussion of common problems set in a familiar context gradually led to the formulation of social philosophy which was uniquely American, a philosophy which centered around equality, freedom, and justice.

Political Autonomy. Political autonomy was also developing side by side with social and economic autonomy throughout the colonial period. From the standpoint of both political philosophy and experience, continued concern with, and participation in, politics and government prepared the colonists well for the break with England.

From early times, colonists enjoyed considerable self-government, while at the same time submitting to overall political control from the crown. From the very beginning, colonists demonstrated their drive toward self-government, as illustrated by the Mayflower Compact, a document drawn up by the Pilgrims binding themselves together for the purpose of making laws for governing the colony. Similarly, the founders of Massachusetts established an assembly composed of representatives from each town. All the charters of joint-venture companies contained clauses for the establishment of self-government. Even the colonies established by royal land grants to individuals (proprietors), such as Maryland and Pennsylvania, contained provisions in the charter compelling the proprietor to seek the counsel of free men in making laws.

As additional colonies were founded, each formed its own popular assembly, with representatives from each town who were elected by qualified voters. In general, colonial assemblies had wide powers. They could make laws concerning the colony, impose taxes to support colonial government, appropriate money to pay colonial officeholders, and generally legislate on matters of property and freedom, subject only to veto of the Royal Governor. Colonial governments were, in general, free to legislate in all matters that were not contrary to English law or the provisions of their colonial charter.

However, the Royal Governor had extensive powers. He was charged with enforcement of both English and colonial law. He appointed high-ranking civil officers, and he was judge of the highest court and acted as military commander in chief. For the most part these men tried to deal amicably with the colonists, but conflicts between British and colonial interests often put them in difficult positions. They were expected to enforce the laws of England, and if English law conflicted with colonial interests or actions of colonial legislatures, they were bound to favor the English position.

On the other hand, colonists were free to govern themselves within the framework of British law, and even when conflicts arose, they were free to petition the Governor and argue their case. Indeed, colonists were gaining experience in virtually every aspect of government, from drafting legislation to administration of laws, and by the time of the Revolution, they were quite adept at handling the public affairs of America.

THE MIDDLE PERIOD: EXPERIMENT IN FREEDOM

In the period following the Revolutionary War, American business continued much as usual. The main accomplishment of the war was to free America from the fetters of the British mercantile system and allow her to develop her own brand of mercantilism. Businessmen did not rush to establish manufacturing enterprises for exactly the same reasons given earlier. Rather, they remained, for the most part, occupied with merchant activities and land speculation for the simple reasons that (1) more profit could be made in transporting and selling commodities than in manufacturing them and (2) these were familiar activities.

The end of the British control literally opened the whole world to American merchants. Trade with France which began during the war flourished. Holland began to buy substantial quanties of raw materials which had previously been on the enumerated lists, and Spain also became an important market. Furthermore, non-British West Indies trade expanded, and rich commercial relations were formed with China, India, Russia, and the Near East. To make commercial enterprise even more attractive, England and France declared war in 1793. Americans were quick to move into the void and capture much of the trade previously held by these countries.

Speculation in Western land was also a familiar activity for American businessmen and attracted large amounts of capital. Aided by a liberal land policy, speculators obtained large tracts of land which they disposed of in small parcels at substantial profits. All lands belonging to the crown became the property of the new nation, and after the war, property of those who had remained loyal to England was confiscated. Anxious to obtain revenue and to encourage settlement of the country, the government set about transferring public land to private ownership. From the standpoint of revenue, it seemed most logical to dispose of it in large tracts at low prices. For example, a 5-million-acre tract north of the Ohio River was sold by the government in 1787 for 66 cents per acre. Even though land was to be sold at auction for a low minimum price per acre, few settlers had sufficient capital to purchase the minimum number of acres. Laws concerning the disposal of public lands favored the speculator and provided opportunities for profits by transferring the task of settlement to the speculator.

National Concern with Manufacturing. Although businessmen failed to be concerned with developing manufacturing, political leaders recognized its importance to national growth. Washington urged the support and promotion of all "manufactories" which would make the United States independent of other countries, particularly for military supplies. Hamilton, too, was a staunch supporter of manufacturing. He had learned well in the school of mercantilism. Clearly recognizing the relationship between manufacturing and national strength, he strongly advocated the adoption of mercantile policies to encourage growth of manufacture in America. Hamilton's recommendations, which appeared in his *Report on Manufactures*, published in 1791, were strikingly reminiscent of British mercantile policy against which he had rebelled only a few years earlier. Not only were his recommendations in keeping with accepted mercantile policy, but many also have the familiar ring of views held by many businessmen today. Below are recommendations from Hamilton's *Report on Manufactures*:[17]

1. Protecting duties—or duties on those foreign articles which are the rivals of the domestic ones intended to be encouraged. . . .
2. Prohibitions of rival articles, or duties equivalent to prohibitions. . . .
3. Prohibitions of the exportation of the materials of manufactures. . . .
4. Pecuniary bounties.
5. Premiums.
6. The exemption of the materials of manufactures from duty. . . .
7. Drawbacks of the duties which are imposed on the materials of manufactures. . . .
8. The encouragement of new inventions and discoveries at home, and of the introduction into the United States of such as may have been made in other countries; particularly, those which relate to machinery. . . .
9. Judicious regulations for the inspection of manufactured commodities. . . .
10. The facilitating of pecuniary remittances from place to place. . . .
11. The facilitating of the transportation of commodities. . . .

Not only was business in general apathetic toward large-scale manufacturing, but also political leaders of the agrarian interests strongly opposed Hamilton's policies. Led by such men as Thomas Jefferson, George Logan, and Thomas Cooper, who considered agriculture to be the most beneficial and productive of all human enterprise, the agrarians opposed manufacture at every turn. They considered manufacturers to be purveyors of vice and viewed industrial cities as threats to morals, health, and liberties of man. They fought protective tariffs, bounties to manufacturers, chartering of banks, immigration of industrial workers, and every public policy that in any way might benefit infant industry. And to a very large extent they were successful. Very little Hamiltonian policy was implemented in its recommended form before 1800.

In spite of the many obstacles facing industrial development, some substantial starts were made. Groups of capitalists pooled their funds and petitioned state governments for business charters. Between 1781 and 1785 eleven such charters were issued; twenty-two were issued between 1786 and 1790; and 114 were granted by the states between 1791 and 1795.[18] Many of these companies were formed to build turnpikes, canals, and bridges, to improve rivers, to speculate in land, and to establish com-

[17] Alexander Hamilton, *Report on Manufactures* (1791), extracts reproduced in William MacDonald (ed.), *Selected Documents Illustrative of the History of the United States, 1776–1861*, New York: The Macmillan Company, 1898, pp. 111–112.

[18] Hacker, *op. cit.*, p. 179.

mercial banks, but also many of them were formed to manufacture iron, woolens, sailcloth, and glass. One French traveler of the times reported that in 1790, "a fine ship, called the Massachusetts . . . had its sails and cordage wholly from the manufacture of Boston; this single establishment gives already two thousand yards of sail-cloth a week." [19] He also reported fourteen breweries in Philadelphia; referred to the "infant woolen manufactory at Hartford," which produced about 5,000 yards in 1789; noted that "Pennsylvania, New Jersey, and Delaware, make annually three hundred and fifty tons of steel, and six hundred tons of nails and nail rods"; and observed that in the same three states there were ". . . sixty-three paper mills which manufacture annually to the amount of 250,000 dollars." He further commented on the manufacture of glass, noting that one glassworks employed 500 persons; on the printing of calicoes, cotton, and linen; on the increase in sugar refineries; and on twenty-one powder mills in Pennsylvania, which produced 625 tons of gunpowder a year.

But for the most part manufacturing in America remained small. Little or none of the large accumulations of capital found its way into manufacturing. Coxe, Assistant Secretary of the Treasury in 1793, commented in one report: "A large proportion of the most successful manufacturers in the United States are persons, who were journeymen, and in a few instances were foremen in the work-shops and manufactories of Europe, who, having been skillful, sober and frugal, and having thus saved a little money, have set up for themselves." [20]

Manufacturing was done largely by hand, and only crude processes were used at the turn of the century. The factory system upon which modern industrialism rests had not yet reached America. Indeed much of American manufacturing in the period from the end of the Revolution to the Civil War remained mercantile in nature; that is, merchants—not manufacturers—were the big enterprisers. Often called the *cottage system* or the *putting-out system*, merchants did not own the tools of production but, rather, acted as financiers and purchasers. They furnished raw materials to small, independent producers who worked in their homes, and later they purchased the finished goods for movement into the channels of trade. Coxe described the extent of this practice: "Household manufactures are carried on within the families of almost all the farmers and planters, and a great proportion of the inhabitants of the villages and towns. This practice is increasing under the animating influences of private interest. . . ." [21]

[19] Jean Pierre Brissot de Warville, *Manufactures and Trade of the United States 1790*, found in Albert Bushnell Hart (ed.), *American History Told by Contemporaries*, New York: The Macmillan Company, 1929, vol. III, p. 52.

[20] Tench Coxe, *Industries of the United States 1793*, found in Hart, *op. cit.*, p. 66.

[21] *Ibid.*, p. 63.

Most manufacturing continued to be characterized by numerous small producers well into the nineteenth century. For example, the boot and shoe industry and the meat-packing industry, two of America's leading industries today, continued largely under the household system until the introduction of machinery shortly before the Civil War. The notable exception was always the cotton textile industry.

False Start toward Industrialism. In spite of the predominance of small manufacturing, America conducted one concentrated experiment in industrial growth early in the nineteenth century. After 1806 the outlook for profit from manufacturing looked bright indeed. Political policies toward England and France which foreshadowed the War of 1812 placed American manufacturers in a favorable position. The Embargo Act of 1807 and the Non-Intercourse Act of 1809 resulted in the disappearance of fine manufactured goods from the American market, and American manufacturers were called upon to fill the gap. The startling realization of the extent to which America depended on foreign manufactured goods led to the adoption of many recommendations made by Hamilton nearly twenty years earlier. Premiums and bounties were offered for the manufacture of fine goods, and technical improvements were encouraged by revising and strengthening patent laws. Capital for expansion came from accumulated saving and from merchants whose overseas commercial activities were substantially limited by the hostilities with England. Some cities even invested in factories. Millions of dollars were invested in capital equipment.

But this was a short-lived prosperity for many American manufacturers. When the war was over, they were once again subject to the grinding competition from abroad. They were not prepared by way of either experience or financial solvency to compete with the volume of foreign-made goods that was dumped on the American market. British manufacturers, involuntarily holding large backlogs of finished goods, flooded the limited American market with all types of goods at ruinously low prices. Business and financial difficulties occasioned by the panic of 1819 added to the number of bankruptcies, so that only the most efficient survived.

Mercantilism Prevails. If the ill-fated experiment in large-scale manufacturing did nothing more, it proved that America was not yet ready to be a full-blown industrial nation. Agrarian as it was, with its isolated markets, undeveloped sources of raw materials, lack of a labor force, and lack of technical knowledge, the right combination of ingredients was missing.

Attention was turned instead to opening new Western lands and further developing America's commercial position. High profits in shipping and land speculation caused attention again to be centered in transportation. Land served by adequate transportation brought higher prices, and there was also profit to be made from freight and passenger revenues.

Hard-surfaced roads first attracted attention. Canals and river improvement rapidly followed as objects of interest. Financed partly by private capital but largely by states and development companies whose securities were taken up by public investments, canals began to crisscross New York, Pennsylvania, Ohio, New Jersey, and Indiana. Even Southern states developed elaborate plans for canal development. It has been estimated that by 1838 American states had contracted indebtedness in the amount of 200 million dollars, most of which was for public-works projects such as canals, roads, and in some cases railroads.[22] Most of these issues of stock had been subscribed by foreign investors—largely English.

But of all the transportation facilities, railroads played the most dominant role. Waterways were limited by the physical features of geography. Rails could be laid virtually anywhere, thus providing service to much wider regions than could ever hope to be served by canals. Slower to develop than canals, railroads rapidly overtook and surpassed them. While the panic of 1837 literally pronounced the death sentence on canal building, it did little more than slow railroad building for a time.

PREPARING FOR INDUSTRIALIZATION

The middle period between the Revolutionary and Civil Wars was one of experimentation, adjustment, growth, and development. But above all, it was a period of transition which not only shifted business emphasis from mercantilism to industrialism but also heralded sweeping social changes which were to alter the whole environment of business after the Civil War and raise serious questions concerning relationships between business and society. Socioeconomic relationships resulting from the new environment will be discussed in the following chapter. The balance of this chapter will be devoted to discussing changes which were necessary to set the stage for the booming industrial development that occurred after the Civil War.

Population Growth. By 1860 there were more than thirty-one million persons in the United States, scattered from coast to coast. Table 1 shows increases in population between 1810 and 1860 by selected geographical areas. Both increases and dispersion of population were important to business. First, with numerical expansion of markets came increased demands for manufactured articles. Second, the ever-increasing number of mouths to be fed stimulated the farm machinery industry. Third, while population was increasing rapidly through natural causes, immigration played a very important role in two ways. Those who went West needed farm machinery and a variety of other necessities. Those who did not have money to move West and take up farming remained in the cities and helped satisfy the ever-growing demand for labor in industrial mills. Table 2 shows the number of immigrants reaching America between 1820 and

[22] Hacker, *op. cit.*, p. 230.

TABLE 1   Population of certain divisions
at given periods, 1810 to 1860 *

DIVISION	1810	1830	1860
East North Central	272,324	1,470,018	6,926,884
West North Central	19,783	140,455	2,169,832
West South Central	77,618	246,127	1,747,667
Mountain			174,923
Pacific			444,053

* Lippincott defines the geographical divisions as follows: The East North Central division consists of Ohio, Indiana, Illinois, Michigan, and Wisconsin; the West North Central division consists of Minnesota, Iowa, Missouri, Nebraska, Kansas, and the Dakotas; the West South Central division consists of Arkansas, Louisiana, Oklahoma, and Texas; the Pacific division consists of California, Oregon, and Washington; and the Mountain division consists of the western part of Texas, Kansas, and Nebraska.

SOURCE: Isaac Lippincott, *Economic Development of the United States*, New York: Appleton-Century-Crofts, Inc., 1925, p. 143.

1860. Fourth, geographical dispersion of markets and the need to consolidate and service these markets encouraged the development of transportation.

Transportation. Adequate transportation was vital to business develop-

TABLE 2   Immigration into the United States,
1820 to 1860

DECADE	PERSONS
1821–1830	151,824
1831–1840	599,125
1841–1850	1,713,251
1851–1860	2,598,214

SOURCE: Isaac Lippincott, *Economic Development of the United States*, New York: Appleton-Century-Crofts, Inc., 1925, p. 137.

ment. Industrial development was dependent upon facilities to distribute manufactured articles and to transport raw materials to manufacturing sites. But railroads could be built only by attracting large quantities of capital. Public subscription of railroad stock (much of it by foreign investors) provided part of the necessary capital. Liberal grants of public land put the railroads in the land speculation business, which provided more capital. And in addition, outright subsidies in the form of cash payments for each mile of track laid helped finance many of the railroads. By the time the Civil War broke out, a fairly respectable railroad net had been established to serve the country. During the decade of the 1840s, only 6,000 miles of track was laid. (Most of the mileage was around Boston.) But in the following decade nearly 21,000 miles of track was constructed—most of it in the West. By 1860 the American railroad net connected such Western Cities as Milwaukee, St. Louis, Chicago, Memphis, and New Orleans. Chicago boasted in 1860 that it had fifteen lines and 100 trains. The completion of the first transcontinental railroad in 1869 opened the far-flung markets of the West to Eastern manufacturers.

Communications. Closely related to needs for transportation were needs for communication. Population growth and westward expansion rapidly magnified communication problems, and in these problems American businessmen saw opportunities for profit. In addition to railroads and canals, the magnetic telegraph and postal service provided other much-needed communication. The telegraph reduced the time necessary for people to communicate with one another from days or weeks to hours or minutes. Once the practicality of the method was demonstrated, businessmen were quick to develop it. By 1850, there were telegraph lines connecting the East with such Western points as Chicago and Detroit. By 1861, Western Union had completed its lines to the Pacific. Thus, by the time of the Civil War, far-flung American markets were relatively well tied together by transportation and communication nets.

Invention. The importance attached to innovation and the concern with finding new and better ways of doing things are reflected in a comparison of the number of patents issued at various times. Only 276 patents were issued between 1790 and 1800, compared with over sixty-four hundred issued in the ten years from 1840 to 1850, and in the following decade, 1850 to 1860, the number increased to 25,200. But this number gives only a rough idea of the extent of innovation which occurred. Many ideas were not patentable, even though they were valuable, and this applies to innovations in forms of business organization and in management as well as to mechanical invention. Sometimes innovation consisted in discovery of new resources or of new ways to utilize raw materials.

Inventions by the hundreds were being applied to virtually every form of economic endeavor. A few of the great inventions of the prewar period were the sewing machine, the rotary press, the magnetic telegraph, the reaping machine, the Bessemer process of making steel, and machinery for processing and canning food. The result of these inventions was to broaden the scope of industry and to increase production. Invention in many cases created new industries, thus creating new skills and new jobs for thousands of workers. Increased production also increased demand for many raw materials. The extent to which invention paved the way toward industrial expansion is illustrated by the following statement in the 1860 Census of Manufacturing concerning the sewing machine:[23]

[23] *Preliminary Report, Eighth Census of the United States, Manufactures,* Washington, D.C.: Government Printing Office, 1860, p. 64.

It has opened avenues of profitable and healthful industry for thousands of industrious families to whom the labors of the needle had become wholly unremunerative and injurious in their effects. Like all automatic powers, it has enhanced the comforts of every class by cheapening the process of numerous articles of prime necessity, without permanently subtracting from the average means of support of any portion of the community. It has added a positive increment to the permanent wealth of the country by creating larger and more varied applications of capital and skill in the several branches to which it is auxiliary. The manufacture of machines has itself become one of considerable magnitude.

Resource Development. The development of resources in the period before the Civil War was remarkable. Western and Southern agricultural lands were opened and brought into production. By 1860 the Western grain and livestock industries were competing vigorously with similar industries of the East. The Southern states concentrated on cotton and were so successful that it became the largest single export of the country. Some of the great iron deposits of the West, particularly around the Great Lakes, were opened, and both bituminous coal and anthracite coal were being produced in quantity. The gold supplies of California had been tapped, and the minerals of the Rocky Mountains were under development. Copper also had received its share of attention.

Such discovery and development provided tremendous supplies of raw materials for factories and created a demand for several kinds of manufactured goods, such as farm machinery and mining equipment. And a firm foundation was laid for the remarkable growth that occurred after the Civil War.

Corporate Form of Business. Business organizations in the middle period were typically individual proprietorships or partnerships, and the amount of capital invested in any one enterprise was small compared with amounts invested in firms of later periods. Widespread use of the corporate form was slow to develop. States, in most cases, looked upon corporations as potential monopolies and doggedly held on to their ability to modify business charters at will. In spite of the decision of the Federal Supreme Court in the Dartmouth case,[24] which declared corporation charters to be contracts and not subject to unilateral changes by State Legislatures, states continued to find ways of changing charters. New York, for example, did not fully concede to incorporation under general laws until 1840.

Earlier in the century, the corporate form of business had been used largely for the development of railroads, banks, and canals. However, inventions and expansion of markets stimulated the growth of business enterprise. Large amounts of capital were necessary, and these could best be raised by distributing the risk and the potential profit among individuals

[24] *Dartmouth College v. Woodward,* 4 Wheaton 518 (1819).

of limited financial means as well as those with substantial capital resources. Partly because of recognition of economies of scale, partly as a
result of a changing business environment, and partly because of changes
in public attitude, the corporate form of business was quite popular by mid-
century. By 1850 security exchanges had been established in New York,
Boston, and Philadelphia.

Political Foundations. The political foundations of industrialism were
also being laid during the middle period. When the Founding Fathers
set about writing the Constitution, they were mindful of producing a
document which would be the foundation of a strong nation and, at the
same time, would provide protection against injustices which were inherent
under the types of governments they were familiar with. They had just
fought a war to escape the economic tyranny of England. Armed with
their own experiences and supported by the laissez-faire concepts of such
men as Adam Smith,[25] it was only natural for them to conceive of the
government's relation to economic activity as being supportive rather
than regulatory. The question was: Which kind of economic activity
should be supported—agriculture or manufacturing?

In spite of the rapid movement into industrial activities during the
1840s and 1850s, the political environment posed severe restrictions on
full development. Depressions of 1819–1821, 1837–1843, and 1857–1858
had demonstrated to business the need for protective tariffs, a sound banking system, a cheap and nonmilitant supply of labor, and sympathetic
courts. But the Southern agrarian aristocracy remained in firm control of
the executive, legislative, and judicial branches of the Federal government,
and they strongly opposed those things needed by business. They opposed
protective tariffs; were against Federal support of railroads, turnpikes, or
canals; favored state banking and cheap money; fought chartering of a
Pacific railroad; opposed homesteading; and would not support a favorable
immigration plan.

The election of 1860 provided the wedge. Quick to take advantage of
the split in the Democratic ranks, the Republican party offered sanctuary
to the abolitionists and included economic planks in the platform which
offered to industrialists reforms needed for expansion. Republican success
in this election pushed the Southern leaders into an untenable position,
one which seemingly could be resolved only by secession.

New Breed of Capitalist. For the most part, the industrial capitalists
of the post–Civil War period were a different group from the merchant
capitalist class of earlier periods. Few merchants transferred their capital
into industrial development. It is true that there were exceptions. Almy
and Brown, who financed Samuel Slater's cotton textile mill, were mer-

[25] Adam Smith, *An Inquiry into the Nature and Causes of the Wealth of Nations*
(1776), New York: Modern Library, Inc., 1937, book IV, chap. 9.

chants, and there were others. But generally these men looked for other investments. As the shipping trade became overextended, many old merchant families of New England moved into public-works promotion, insurance, and banking. They invested in turnpikes and canals, financed railroad construction, became large-scale speculators in Western lands, and formed mortgage companies.

If, then, merchants did not become industrialists, where did the class of industrialists known as the Captains of Industry originate? They came, largely, from the independent farmers, skilled craftsmen, and small storekeepers. Eli Whitney and Cyrus McCormick came from such backgrounds. Andrew Carnegie came from a family of country weavers, John D. Rockefeller's father was a peddler, and John Gates spent his early years on a farm.

To build the industrial complex which was put together after the Civil War, talents different from those of the large Eastern merchants were necessary. Development of these talents produced a breed of men with different outlooks, interests, and visions. By the close of the Civil War, these men, who were capable, shrewd, brave, visionary, and ruthless, stood ready to take advantage of the vast opportunities which existed on every side.

SUMMARY

America began as an integral part of the British mercantile system with all the beliefs, values, and philosophies of the mother country. But her inability to perform adequately her role within the mercantile system of England and still survive as a separate economic entity led to inevitable conflict, which culminated in the Revolutionary War.

Born into a capitalistic climate and left largely to survive as best she could, America early began to develop as an autonomous unit with interests, beliefs, values, and philosophies quite different from, and often in open conflict with, those of the mother country. By the time of the Revolution, America had developed a high degree of autonomy in business, social system, and politics. Experience gained under British mercantilism prepared Americans well for their experiment in freedom.

While American mercantile philosophies as they existed at the close of the eighteenth century were adequate to support a free nation, they were not adequate philosophies upon which to build a great nation. The period between the Revolutionary and Civil Wars was a period of experiment in philosophies, a period of trial and error, and, above all, a period of transition. During this period those factors necessary to support a transition to industrialism developed. By the time the Civil War ended, all the needed ingredients for industrialization were present in our society.

QUESTIONS

1. Why did the American Colonies, as a whole, not fit well into the British mercantile system?

2. Explain the following statement: The main cause of British-American conflict was England's refusal to recognize America as a separate economic unit.

3. Contrast the economies of the Northern and Southern Colonies. In what ways were the business problems of the two areas different? The same?

4. What reasons can you give to explain why there was no development of large-scale manufacturing in America during the colonial period?

5. How do you explain the fact that by the time of the Revolutionary War, America had developed a considerable degree of both social and political autonomy?

6. What is meant by referring to the middle period as a period of social and economic adjustment and experimentation?

7. A number of factors developed during the middle period which set the stage for American industrial expansion. Discuss these factors and their relationships to one another.

8. What evidence can you give of an emerging American philosophy of individualism? Human rights? Due process of law?

CHAPTER 4 AMERICAN INDUSTRIALIZATION:
A WAY OF LIFE

> The chief business of the American people is business.
>
> CALVIN COOLIDGE[1]

The Civil War has, from a variety of viewpoints, been considered a turning point in American history. Particularly is this true from the standpoint of business development. It may be incorrect to attribute the sweeping changes that occurred in America to so brief a point in time, but certainly the ten years preceding and the ten years following the war produced significant economic and political changes.

Social change does not occur quickly. When an event of crisis apparently ushers in dramatic revisions of social structure and philosophy, change often appears to occur nearly overnight. However, analysis of events preceding the crisis usually reveals that a number of factors have cleared the way and set the stage. What appears to be a sudden change is really the culmination of several smaller, less noticeable changes.

American business growth and the social change which accompanied it from 1865 to the present will be discussed in this chapter. Various phases through which business has passed in its development over time were identified previously. It should be noted here that in the centuries preceding the Civil War, business had progressed only through the stage of mercantile capitalism. However, in the relatively short time since the Civil War, business has progressed rapidly through industrial capitalism, finance capitalism, and into the present phase of national capitalism. What is really significant about this comparison is the tremendous increase in the

---

[1] Calvin Coolidge (speech before the Society of American Newspapers Editors, Jan. 17, 1925). Text of the speech appeared in *The New York Times*, Jan. 18, 1925.

rate of change during the last one hundred or so years. Starting just prior to the Civil War, change has occurred in a geometric progression. Today the fantastically rapid rate of change is creating major social problems such as the paradox of high unemployment levels concurrent with high employment levels, rapid educational and skill obsolescence in a highly educated society, and poverty within the most affluent society in history.

AMERICAN CAPITALISM, INDUSTRIAL STYLE

In many ways the Civil War and circumstances surrounding it acted as a catalyst in the nineteenth-century transition from mercantilism to industrialism. Many factors essential to the transition were present to one degree or another in the United States society before the Civil War. It is inevitable that the industrial system would have evolved regardless of the war. However, the real question is: Would it have evolved as fast?

The Impetus of Civil War. In a number of ways the pressures of war stimulated combinations of social, economic, and political factors to produce an environment necessary for industrial capitalism. First, the Civil War demanded integration of industry. Military needs favored consolidation of small enterprises and growth of large-scale use of mechanized processes. Armies demanded an adequate and dependable supply of standardized products, such as boots and shoes, blankets, uniforms, processed foods, firearms and ammunition, iron, salt, and paper. Integration of production processes within single firms was also spurred by wartime sales taxes on manufactured goods which were imposed at each phase of production. Additionally, poor and undependable railroad service brought pressures for pooling rail facilities and centralizing management.

Second, mechanization and integration were expensive and depended upon the adequacy of the national capital fund.[2] Expansion in the capital fund came from the war itself. In order to finance the war, the government found it necessary to expand the basic national credit resources. Some 3 billion dollars was added through bond issues and issues of greenbacks. High profits from government contracts made industrial capital accumulations possible.

Third, public fiscal policy favored industrial consolidation and expansion. Excise taxes were imposed on production to finance the war, but these could easily be passed on to consumers. Republican support of a high protective tariff insulated American business from foreign price competition, thus maintaining profits and encouraging industrial capital accumulation.

Fourth, because of both wartime monetary difficulties and projected future monetary needs, a national banking system was established by the National Banking Act of 1863. The new system eliminated wildcat bank-

[2] Louis M. Hacker, *The Triumph of American Capitalism*, New York: Simon and Schuster, Inc., 1940, pp. 252–256.

ing and unsound currency, absorbed a substantial part of the government bond issue, and stood ready to convert greenbacks into 6 percent government gold bonds on demand. In short, it provided the financial stability necessary to support war and postwar business expansion.

Fifth, disposal of the public domain aided industrial development in two ways. Settlement of the West provided a national market for manufactured goods. Western farming provided surplus cereal and meat products, which went into world markets, thereby providing foreign balances with which to pay for machinery and other capital goods.

Sixth, chartering of Pacific railroads assured Eastern businessmen a consolidated national market. Western settlement and agricultural production were of little value if farm products could not be moved to the East and manufactured goods could not be moved West. Pacific railroads which were built after the war solved this problem. Financed by the government, an intercontinental railroad net was built which linked the West firmly to the East.

Seventh, immigration acts provided the labor supply necessary for industrial expansion. Thousands entered America under liberal immigration laws. Many migrated to Western farms, but many more, skilled craftsmen and unskilled industrial workers, remained in the cities, where they provided labor for the factories and swelled the ranks of industrial laborers.[3]

Eighth, many inventions from the first half of the nineteenth century were developed, improved, and utilized during the war years. Industrial processes were refined and improved, and forms of business organization were tested. Business emerged from the war with a strong technical foundation.

Thus, many factors were at work during the Civil War that prepared the way for American industrial and social change. None was especially significant by itself, but their combination produced a dynamic industrial system. The maturity of many industries, along with the size of capital accumulations made possible by the war, led one observer to comment: "The power accumulating in the moneyed classes from the concentration of capital in large masses is attracting the attention of close observers of the money market. It is one of the signs of the time and will probably exert no small influence over the future growth of our industrial and commercial enterprise." [4]

Important, also, to emerging industrialization were evolving social

[3] Carter Goodrich and Sol Davidson, "The Wage-earner in the Westward Movement," *Political Science Quarterly*, June, 1935, pp. 161–185; March, 1936, pp. 61–116.

[4] *Commercial and Financial Chronicle* (1866), quoted in E. D. Fite, *Social and Industrial Conditions in the North during the Civil War*, New York: The Macmillan Company, 1910, p. 165.

philosophies. As has been mentioned in an earlier chapter, survival of any economic system depends upon value systems which surround and support it. Certainly industrial capitalism and finance capitalism depended upon reaffirmation and refinement of value systems that stressed private property, *laissez faire*, the Protestant Ethic, individualism, freedom, and pragmatism. Business methods and new forms of business organization, along with philosophies supporting social change, will be discussed in the next few sections.

Captains of Industry. Led by a group of capable and visionary men, American business moved forward rapidly after the Civil War. Known as Captains of Industry (or often less affectionately as Robber Barons), these men built business complexes whose size and power had marked social significance.

Having come largely from simple backgrounds and having been well indoctrinated in the economic philosophies of Calvinism, these men moved with a singleness of purpose toward economic supremacy. They have often been described as shrewd, energetic, resourceful, frugal (at least during their early careers), unprincipled, and unscrupulous. To accumulate wealth and power seemed to become their purpose in life. Some were industrial builders, some were developers, some were exploiters of natural resources, some were consolidators, and some were speculators. All seemed well adapted to the new era of unbridled monopolistic competition. Many historians have described how they took advantage of opportunities to bribe public officials, corrupt employees of rival companies, ruin competitors, bilk the public, and appropriate government funds to their own use.

Activities of the Captains of Industry had a profound effect on social philosophy toward business both then and now. Modern antagonism toward business can often be traced to their reputations. There is little question that they did much to revive and reinforce the Aristotelian and medieval church philosophy that business was base and founded on avarice and greed. But we must not become two-value-oriented as we appraise these men. They were "doers." Even though some social groups appeared to have suffered some inequities at their hands, they must be given credit for the unprecedented economic growth experienced in the United States after 1850.

The story of American business cannot be told without recounting the business careers of men such as Leland Stanford, Collis P. Huntington, James J. Hill, Cornelius Vanderbilt, John D. Rockefeller, Andrew Carnegie, Jay Gould, J. P. Morgan, and many more.[5] Obviously space will not permit an examination of each man and the enterprise he directed. Rather, we must be content to review only one business venture. We have selected Leland Stanford and his associates and the building of the Central Pacific

[5] For biographies of many Captains of Industry, see Gustavus Myers, *History of the Great American Fortunes*, New York: Modern Library, Inc., 1936.

Railroad because both the character of the men themselves and their business activities are typical of the times.

When Leland Stanford, Collis P. Huntington, Mark Hopkins, and Charles Crocker formed the Pacific Associates, they had no specific intentions of building railroads. Rather, this was a speculative venture pure and simple, formed to take advantage of any opportunities that might arise.

Entry of the Associates into the railroad field was more by accident than design. A chance meeting with a young engineer named Theodore Judah, who was intrigued with the idea of a transcontinental rail system, was the opportunity the Associates had been waiting for. They promptly formed the Central Pacific Railroad Company and issued stock in the amount of $8,500,000, regardless of the fact that they had less than $200,000 in actual cash.

Armed with stock certificates and a sizable portion of the existing cash, Judah went to Washington to secure the contract for his associates. His activities in Washington are not clear, but when the contract was issued the Central Pacific Railroad Company was named as official builder of the western portion of the transcontinental rail line. In return for building the railroad, the company was to receive 4,500,000 acres of land along the right-of-way, $16,000 for every mile of track laid on level ground, and $48,000 for every mile of mountain construction.

The Associates now had a problem. Before they could collect any money from the government they had to build trackage, and they were embarrassingly short of money. Most of the original $200,000 had been used in securing the contract. Fortunately, Stanford had recently been elected Governor of California, and he did not hesitate to use his office to further his own affairs. At his "suggestion" the city of Sacramento contributed $400,000, and Placer County generously provided another $500,000. Having obtained enough capital to build the initial section and receive payment for track completed, each succeeding section financed itself.

Financing construction of a railroad and making a personal profit are two different things, and the Associates were interested in personal gain. Nothing could be gained immediately from the sale of stock. In fact, when Central Pacific stock was offered to public subscription in 1863, only fifteen shares were sold. But from a long-range point of view the Associates perceived the potential value of these securities and, as directors of the railroad, blandly issued to themselves some 33 million dollars in Central Pacific stock and 49 million dollars in bonds. But for profits in the short run, two relatively simple devices lay close at hand. First, thousands of acres of land belonging to the railroad were transferred to the partners as individuals. Much of this was choice suburban land which became extremely valuable as cities grew. To help in this department, Huntington convinced the government that the original land grant was insufficient and obtained an additional grant of 4,500,000 acres, much of which the partners appropriated to their own use. Second, and more immediate, was the device of a construction company. The Credit and Finance Company —a construction company—was formed by the Associates to build the railroad. It was a simple matter for the Associates, who were directors of the railroad, to sign an exclusive construction contract with their own construction company. The difference between the actual cost and the charges to the government made its way into the partners' pockets. The actual cost of the railroad, according to the Pacific Railroad Commission,[6] was $27,217,000, but the government was charged in the neighborhood of 80 million dollars, a tidy sum to be divided among the Associates.

It has been observed that the railroad retarded rather than stimulated economic development.[7] Certainly the actions of Stanford and his group justify such an observation. While the government perceived the role of the railroads to be one of ensuring competition and providing service to the West, the Stanford group viewed them as a mechanism for generating maximum personal rewards. High freight rates were the key to personal gain, but high freight rates were possible only under monopoly conditions.

Nearly as fast as charters for other Western railroads were issued in Washington, the new railroads were absorbed by Stanford's group. Before their own line was complete, the Associates secretly purchased the California charter of the Southern Pacific. As a result of outright bribery of public officials and illegal laying of track ahead of the Texas Pacific, this line was soon forced to sell to the Associates. Control of the Atlantic & Pacific was obtained by blocking progress at a critical mountain pass and then buying the charter. Thus the entire railroad network of the West came under control of the four partners.

Having gained monopoly control of rail transportation in the West, the partners imposed the highest freight rates in the country. So enormous were the charges that in some cases it was cheaper to ship goods to Europe and then transship around South America to California ports.[8]

Practices such as those described above were not peculiar to Western railroad builders. Much the same story can be told about Eastern railroads. Issuing worthless or watered stock, bribing public officials, appropriating lands granted to the railroad, and defrauding both local governments and the Federal government (not to mention one another) seemed to be the order of the day. Results, too, were always the same. Having secured a monopoly position and personal financial control, railroad owners invariably used the railroad for economic domination of those it served. Farmers

    [6] Pacific Railroad Commission (1887), quoted in Robert L. Heilbroner, *The Quest for Wealth*, New York: Simon and Schuster, Inc., 1956, p. 177.

    [7] Stuart Daggett, *Chapters on the History of the Southern Pacific*, New York: The Ronald Press Company, 1922, p. 270.

    [8] Heilbroner, *op. cit.*, p. 196.

were often charged more for shipping wheat than they could get for it in the market, and businessmen were at the mercy of arbitrary freight rates.

Nor was this breed of man peculiar to the railroad industry. They were active in virtually every facet of economic development, and accounts of their activities make fascinating reading. But, while men like Gould and Fisk left little behind except a wide trail of worthless stocks and empty pocketbooks, many others were putting together the industrial giants which shaped the industrial structure of America.

The period prior to the Civil War was the golden age of the small entrepreneur. The typical concern was owned by a single proprietor who was also the manager or by two or three partners. Few corporations existed. However, inventions and utilization of laborsaving machinery during the war had demonstrated the profitability of large-scale firms. Part of the size increase was the result of internal expansion, part came from one company's absorbing smaller companies, and part resulted from small companies' voluntarily joining together.

Business Consolidation. As business size began to increase during the war, old forms of business organization became inadequate and unsuited to business needs. Consolidation depended, in large measure, on increased use of the corporate form. But heavy capital outlays required for a profitable mechanized firm made it necessary for several people to combine their assets. The amount of capital needed was usually beyond the means of a single individual, and risks were usually too great for a single individual to bear.

With the increased economic activity that followed the war came a stiffening of competition. Rate wars, for example, between railroads drove fares and freight rates below costs in many cases, and in the sugar industry, about forty refineries were driven out of business from price cutting.[9] Size and power seemed to be the answer to survival. A few single proprietorships grew and prospered, but most business giants of the times resulted from combinations of individual resources. When John D. Rockefeller combined his resources with several others to launch the Standard Oil Company, he gave as the reason: "to stabilize the local oil industry."

Finance Capitalism. However, as capital resources of the country became more highly concentrated in the hands of a few, a new kind of competition appeared. In a way, it could be referred to as a new kind of competitive game. Elements of competition remained the same, but the players changed. Rather than many small firms competing freely among themselves, the monopolists began to compete with one another, and this competitive struggle led to further consolidation of business. Finance capitalism was emerging.

Financiers, who often had no knowledge of operating an industry, now

[9] Harold Underwood Faulkner, *American Economic History*, New York: Harper & Row, Publishers, Incorporated, 1949, p. 432.

gained control. Most early industrial combinations were put together by men who were themselves industrialists. They were principal owners of large firms and were actively engaged in the operation of the firm. Typically majority ownership and management of the firm were not separated. But as competition became more severe and larger combinations were needed, control shifted to financial interests. Ownership and management became two different groups.

The more sophisticated forms of combinations were pools, trusts, and holding companies. A pool is an organization of several companies. Members attempt to divide and apportion all available business in some predetermined manner, thereby controlling competition and stabilizing prices. Allotments of business were often apportioned on the basis of territory, market, sales, or output. Although pools were declared illegal by the Interstate Commerce Act of 1887, secret agreements continued.

After the passage of the Interstate Commerce Act pools were largely discarded in favor of trusts. A trust, unlike a pool, is no loose agreement between companies. Rather it is an actual consolidation of interests for the purpose of putting several firms under centralized control. Stockholders of various companies, under a trust agreement, deposit their stock certificates (along with the rights and privileges attached to the stock) with a trustee. In return, stockholders receive trust certificates. The purpose was always to create a monopoly. Standard Oil experimented with the trust idea as early as 1879. A "whiskey trust," a "sugar trust," and a "cotton-oil trust" all appeared in 1884, but the trust form of organization did not become generally popular until after 1887.

Antitrust legislation, that is, the Sherman Act, led to the adoption of the holding company. A holding company is an organization created to control other companies by owning a controlling interest in their stock. Adoption of the holding company concept encouraged the pyramiding of businesses, one upon the other, until the final result was complete domination of an industry.

Misuse of Monopoly Power. Pools, trusts, and holding companies may be formed without creating a monopoly, although it is apparent that those formed during the latter quarter of the nineteenth century were formed for this purpose. Likewise, monopolies may be formed which are not contrary to public interest and which in some cases are considered to be in the best public interest. We have, in our society today, many monopolies sanctioned by law and considered to perform certain economic tasks in the best way. For example, the United States postal system and a whole series of public utilities are monopolies pure and simple, but they are looked upon as being socially desirable.

The question, then, concerning business concentration from 1865 to 1890, and the public reaction which arose, did not revolve around the desirability of large-scale business per se. Society enjoyed a greater quantity and variety of goods and services than at any previous time. Rather the question concerned the use of monopoly power. Attacks on business occurred not because of size or form of organization but because business abused the power inherent therein.

From an economic viewpoint, arguments both for and against large-scale monopoly appeared. Some of the more popular arguments favoring monopolies are the following:[10]

1. Large resources make possible the use of best located plants and most efficient machinery.
2. Large-scale production allows more utilization of by-products.
3. Large-scale production allows use of division of labor and specialization between plants.
4. Administrative expenses can be saved by eliminating duplication of high-salaried jobs.
5. Inefficient methods are more easily detected by comparing like plants.
6. Greater strength exists in dealing with labor.
7. Marketing expenses are decreased by eliminating duplicate advertising, sales effort and cross shipping.
8. Control of market price of both raw material and finished price helps stabilize price and production and is thereby a healthy economic force.

However, closer examination shows that the alleged monopoly advantages are really economies of scale and are applicable to any large-scale industry regardless of whether or not a monopoly exists. Even admitting the above arguments as potential advantages, opponents claimed that the advantages accrued only to the monopolists themselves. In actual practice, claimed the opponents:

1. Savings were not passed on to consumers but were retained by monopolists.
2. Evidence indicated that the public had been injured by unreasonably high prices.
3. Price to suppliers of raw materials was forcefully depressed.
4. Monopoly resulted in careless and inefficient service to consumers.

In actual practice consumers, suppliers, and competitors were all at the mercy of the monopolists. History abounds with evidence of misused monopoly power. Through economic dominance, monopolists crushed competitors by controlling prices, dictated to suppliers by the same means, and subjected consumers to high prices, poor quality, and undependable service. In 1905 *The Literary Digest* published a cartoon depicting a man (obviously John D. Rockefeller) contemplating a huge rose (labeled Standard Oil Company) growing out of a pile of small skulls. The cap-

[10] *Ibid.*, pp. 444–445.

tion proclaimed: "The American Beauty Rose can be produced in all its splendor only by sacrificing the early buds that grow up around it." [11]

With economic power came political power as well. Through bribery of public officials, business leaders controlled public policy and were always able to manipulate it in their favor if the occasion arose, as it did frequently. Disposal of public domain, awarding of municipal contracts, legalizing monopoly practices, control of labor through court protection, and protection from criminal acts all attest to political power wielded by business.

Social power was also a by-product of economic power. Rich businessmen and their families rose to social prominence rapidly after the Civil War. In the social whirl of the period, the austerity of the Protestant Ethic, under which these men rose to riches, gave way to the philosophy of conspicuous consumption. Social leadership was equated with extravagance, each family trying to outdo the other. Fortunes were spent on palatial houses, lavish parties, and other extravagant displays of wealth. Americans did not begrudge the businessman his wealth, but when he began to flaunt it in the face of the less fortunate and squander it in the midst of need, a negative social reaction took place. The "idle rich" came under severe social censure.

SOCIAL IMPACT OF INDUSTRIALIZATION

Hand in hand with economic change went social change. Many social institutions and social philosophies of today had their foundations in the latter half of the nineteenth century. The American way of life changed. New social groups gained prominence. And business, as a social institution, took on new dimensions of power.

Invention and Changes in Living Conditions. The wave of invention that swept America during the nineteenth century brought with it unimagined changes in patterns of living. It was truly an age of innovation that carried American society to new high standards of living. New products appeared, old products were improved and refined, new services were offered and others modified, and all this was accompanied by a general lowering of prices. Articles which before the Civil War had been luxuries now became staples in many cases. Ready-made clothing and shoes, processed foods, iron and steel implements, and machinery, to mention only a few items, were generally within the economic reach of the masses. Transportation and communications were broadened and cheapened, and innovations such as electricity and natural gas were widely available. Writing in 1889 one reporter noted over forty-five "inventions, discoveries, and ap-

[11] *The Literary Digest* (1905), found in Arthur C. Bining, *The Rise of American Economic Life*, New York: Charles Scribner's Sons, 1949, p. 389.

plications" which were in wide use.[12] His list ranged from butter to hydraulic cranes and many practical uses of electricity.

Labor Emerges as a Power Group. Working for wages was not specifically a development of post–Civil War years, but relations between employers and employees changed shape and intensity after the war. Prior to the war, relations (speaking in very general terms) between employer and employee were largely paternalistic. Smallness of firms encouraged personal acquaintance and a sense of responsibility on the part of the employer.

With the growth in size of firms, separation of ownership and management, and increased immigration and movement to cities, relations changed. Many immigrants who came to America during the 1840s and 1850s remained in the cities. Thousands more were brought to work on railroads, only to drift into cities as soon as the major job of laying rails was finished. As the factory system grew, so did the demand for workers. As greater numbers of persons filled cities and became wholly dependent upon wages for their livelihood, a labor movement which had been largely ineffective began to gain strength.

Emergence of the labor movement changed the shape of society and complicated the job of businessmen. As the labor movement grew, it added another dimension to the society which business served, and it added another power group with which business had to reckon. Space does not permit further exploration of the idea of labor as a power group here. It will be expanded in a later chapter.

Emergence of Professional Managers. The separation of ownership and management which occurred during the last half of the nineteenth century made it necessary to depend on hired managers who held little, if any, ownership in the company they managed. Increased use of the corporate form of business spread ownership among large numbers of persons, so that no longer were owners and managers the same persons.

Even though a majority stockholder retained ultimate control of, and responsibility for, a company, he often found it necessary to depend on hired subordinate managers. As business firms grew in size through both vertical and horizontal integration, it became virtually impossible for one man directly to oversee all activities of the firm. Owner-managers were forced to rely heavily on subordinate managers to help run the firm.

Dependence on hired managers increased as financiers, rather than industrialists, gained control of business. Uninterested in day-to-day operation of business and geographically separated from the firms they owned, absentee owners were forced to depend on hired managers.

Gradually, then, management became recognized as an activity sep-

[12] David A. Wells, *Recent Economic Changes* (1889), quoted in Hacker, *op. cit.*, p. 403.

arate and distinct from ownership, a vital element in economic growth. Some economists modified the list of factors of production by adding management to land, labor, and capital. The word "management" was gradually substituted for "capital" in the common vocabulary. Capital no longer received praise for economic advances; rather, management was congratulated. And labor no longer vilified capital but directed its attacks against management.

Business Philosophies and Value Systems. Business systems are a product of beliefs, mores, and customs of the society in which they exist. Indeed, their very existence depends upon social philosophies which condone and support various kinds of business action. Philosophies are important from two points of view. First, businessmen (whether they realize it or not) must have some basic set of philosophies to guide their actions. Beliefs and value systems concerning what is right or wrong are basic to all business activity and serve as a justification for doing or not doing things in a particular way. Second, the society served by business also develops philosophies and value systems against which actions of businessmen are judged. Societal value systems and philosophies evolve from concepts of social well-being or common good, and business actions are always judged by how well they contribute to social well-being.

As long as value systems and philosophies of businessmen are compatible with those of society and resulting business practices contribute positively to social goals, society will accept, support, and encourage contemporary business practices. On the other hand, if value systems and philosophies of businessmen give rise to business practices which society believes are contrary to the common good, society will initiate and enforce curbs against those practices.

Practices of the Captains of Industry during the period between the Civil War and 1900 become quite understandable when viewed against the background of business and social philosophies of the times. Businessmen found justification for their actions in philosophies which were widely accepted by the public they served. Several major philosophies of the times will be reviewed in this section. Undoubtedly, similarities between popular philosophies of this period and views held by many businessmen today will be recognized.

Individualism and the Protestant Ethic. Individualism has always been considered an integral part of the American heritage.[13] As a philosophy it stresses man's relations to his environment. Based upon the belief that the individual can control and master his environment, the philosophy taught that man was limited in his accomplishments only by his own capabilities and initiative. Inherent in this philosophy were concepts of

---

[13] For a discussion of individualism as a social philosophy, see John William Ward, "The Ideal of Individualism and the Reality of Organization," in Earl F. Cheit (ed.), *The Business Establishment*, New York: John Wiley & Sons, Inc., 1964.

equality of opportunity and individual freedom, man's freedom to pursue his own interests as he saw fit, without interference from outside forces.

Closely related to individualism was belief in the Protestant Ethic. Every man, according to the Protestant Ethic, has a spiritual and temporal calling. While the first responsibility was to worship God and live by His laws, man's worthiness to enter the Kingdom of Heaven was judged by how well he fulfilled his temporal calling. Diligence, hard work, frugality, initiative, and judgment were considered godly traits, and a man's ability to amass material wealth was a major criterion for judging his success on earth.

Thus, businessmen, operating after the Civil War, found two philosophies by which they could justify their activities. And the common man accepted business activities for exactly the same reasons. While few men actually achieved great wealth, it was important to everyone to know that opportunities for wealth were open to any individual *if only he chose* to take advantage of them. The Protestant Ethic provided the spiritual justification.

Laissez Faire and the Classical Tradition. America had, in the eighteenth century, fought a war with England over government and business relations. Difficulties resulting from government interference with American business under British mercantilism were still fresh in the minds of businessmen. It was no wonder that the men who framed the Constitution were careful to define the role of the new government in terms of *laissez faire* (the term as used here is defined to mean "let business alone").

Adam Smith, whose widely read book appeared in 1776,[14] was a staunch advocate of *laissez faire* and provided theoretical support for this philosophy. Government, it is true, played a part in Smith's economic system, but its role was supportive. It should provide defense and justice, construct and maintain public works, and provide other essential activities that would not be carried on by private business because they could not be made to yield a profit. But Smith felt that government should not in any way become involved in workings of the market system. The greatest public good could be achieved, in the Smithian system, by businessmen bidding freely among themselves and by supply and demand freely adjusting to each other. The key to the whole system was freedom of competition, which assured the greatest good for the greatest numbers: the system always produced full employment, lowest operating costs, lowest prices, and economic growth.

American political and economic philosophies of the nineteenth century warmly embraced Smithian theory as an ideal model. While the model did little to describe the business system as it actually existed, it did provide a philosophical model against which to judge government-

[14] Adam Smith, *An Inquiry into the Nature and Causes of the Wealth of Nations* (1776), New York: Modern Library, Inc., 1937.

business relations and socioeconomic activities of business. Many remnants of classical economics, as founded by Adam Smith, are reflected in today's social philosophies, even though the Smithian model no longer describes (if it ever did) our contemporary business system.

Social Darwinism. Approximately one hundred years ago, Charles Darwin published a most provocative book entitled *The Origin of Species*, which indirectly provided the basis for one of the most popular nineteenth-century philosophies of business behavior. In its original biological context, Darwinian theory proposed that all forms of life evolved, over time, from a few basic types and that through a process of natural selection, only the strongest and most fit survived.

When Herbert Spencer applied the theory to society and explained social development in terms of social evolution, he gave America a new business philosophy.[15] Applying Darwinian theory to society as a whole, Spencer reasoned that if environment were not tampered with, the most able men would rise to leadership through a process of "natural selection." Nature somehow endowed only a few persons with exactly the right combination of characteristics to master their environment fully. Noninterference with the natural selection process, according to social Darwinism, would produce the greatest good for the greatest numbers by placing the most fit in positions of leadership.

Here was a philosophy ready-made for the Captains of Industry. As the nineteenth century wore to a close and society became more intolerant of business practices, business leaders championed social Darwinism as a rational justification for their position, their riches, their actions, and their power.

Philosophies of Machiavelli. Threads of Machiavellian philosophy also appeared in nineteenth-century business philosophy and continue to appear today. Niccolò Machiavelli (1469–1527) in his famous book, *The Prince*,[16] discussed the problems a prince faced in ruling his people. In his discussion, he not only identified with great clarity many problems in political administration but also suggested what he considered appropriate solutions to the problems.

Relationships between means and ends are illustrative of Machiavellian philosophy. According to Machiavelli means should be subordinate to ends (power of the Prince); that is, a Prince should take whatever measures are necessary to keep his subjects "united and obedient." Adapting this to business philosophy, it became popular to think of the businessman as feeling justified in resorting to any means to reach the end of profit. Strong arguments can be made to demonstrate that the Robber Barons were guided by this philosophy.

[15] Richard Hofstadter, *Social Darwinism in American Thought*, rev. ed., Boston: Beacon Press, 1955.

[16] Niccolò Machiavelli, *The Prince* (1513), Oxford: Clarendon Press, 1909.

The phrase "Do unto others before they do unto you" is also Machiavellian in origin. He referred to those who fared better by "overreaching men by their cunning" than to those who trusted to honest dealing, and he concluded that the Prince should be prepared to deal with individuals at their own level and beat them at their own game. In short, one should be prepared to use unlawful means if necessary.

While most businessmen today do not operate according to either of these philosophies, it is important to recognize that many people perceive business as being based on the above principles.

Pragmatism. William James[17] and John Dewey[18] added another facet to social philosophy. These philosophers viewed social progress as a process of change which could and should be controlled by man. Unlike social Darwinism, pragmatic thought viewed man's environment as a variable which could be controlled and manipulated. Experimentation with new ways of doing things would produce the greatest good for the greatest number, and the test of experimentation was: Does the new way work better than the old?

From the businessman's point of view, pragmatic thought was a mixed blessing. It encouraged industrial development and experimentation with the business system at large, and as long as results were socially profitable, businessmen received support from the rest of the social system. On the other hand, when results from business activity were viewed as socially unprofitable, the whole business system became suspect and subject to change.

Nineteenth-century Philosophy and Today's Business. Philosophies concerning today's business system and the place of business in society are a curious mixture of nineteenth- and twentieth-century philosophies. This creates a dilemma for the modern businessman. Modern business has, in large measure, discarded the philosophies of the Robber Barons of the previous century and has become genuinely concerned with its proper role. It is trying to define and assume its responsibilities in today's complex society. In order to do this, business must overcome the reputation created by misuse of monopoly power during the previous century. But this is not an easy task. People tend to forget slowly and continue to view the businessman as though he formulates policy in exactly the same way and for the same reasons as his nineteenth-century predecessor. To receive the social confidence it needs, American business must clearly demonstrate, by both words and actions, that its policies are entirely compatible with overall social objectives.

[17] William James, *Essays in Pragmatism*, New York: Hafner Publishing Company, Inc., 1948.

[18] John Dewey, *Human Nature and Conduct* (1922), New York: Holt, Rinehart and Winston, Inc., 1935; and John Dewey, *The Public and Its Problems*, New York: Holt, Rinehart and Winston, Inc., 1927.

Business as a Leading Power Group. Consolidation of business after the Civil War brought with it concentration of power.[19] Unlike business and social relationships of the early nineteenth century, in which entrepreneurial decisions had only local and limited ramifications, decisions of business giants affected wide segments of society. Business, then, became the leading power group during the latter part of the nineteenth century. So great was its power that it was virtually unchallenged during much of the period. America for all practical purposes had a monolithic society. One can only speculate as to the results had business not misused its power. Had business realized that the very possession of power over society makes it responsible to that society for proper exercise of that power, many current problems business faces in its relationships with government, labor, the public, and others might well have been different and less complex.

THE AGE OF REFORM

The point has been emphasized several times in the preceding chapters that society will support social institutions only as long as they contribute to the well-being of that society. As long as business activity contributed positively to social and economic growth, social philosophy supported and encouraged business, but when business began to oppress and even defy society, as it did in the latter part of the nineteenth century, society manifested its dissatisfactions by imposing legal curbs on business activity.

Social Dissatisfactions. Public dissatisfaction with the business system stemmed directly from business's disregard for social and economic rights of the "little man." When businessmen began to strangle competition through huge corporations, pools, and trusts; when prices were artificially maintained; when products and services were not improved; when public property was freely appropriated to private use; and when labor was forcibly suppressed, a rising tide of protest appeared, in spite of the predominant laissez-faire philosophy.

The period between 1880 and World War I has been called the Age of Reform. Perhaps more properly it should be called the Age of Revolt. Beginning in the 1870s and gathering strength through the 1880s, a social revolt against unrestrained monopoly business practices took place. The first legal attacks on big business came with the Granger movement, although some illegal retaliation from an organization known as the Molly Maguires[20] occurred earlier than, as well as concurrently with, the Granger movement. The Molly Maguires were a secret group (composed

[19] For a discussion of nineteenth-century business power, see Heilbroner, *op. cit.*
[20] Wayne G. Broehl, Jr., *The Molly Maguires*, Cambridge, Mass.: Harvard University Press, 1964.

largely of coal miners) who were organized to carry out a campaign of physical violence against mine owners and mine bosses. Beatings, sabotage, and murder, as well as the strike, were their weapons. After conviction and execution of their leaders in 1877, for criminal acts, the organization disbanded.

The Granger Movement and Antimonopoly Legislation. The Granger movement, on the other hand, was a legal attack on big railroads. Working through State Legislatures, farm groups attempted to enact laws that would prohibit greater charges for short hauls than for long ones, forbid consolidation of parallel rail lines, and establish maximum rates and fares. Several state laws were passed to regulate railroads as a result of the agrarian movement and were upheld by the United States Supreme Court until 1886, when it reversed itself, saying that states had no right to interfere with interstate commerce.

Clearly, to those opposing railroad practices, a Federal law was needed, and in 1887 the Interstate Commerce Act was passed. Successful evasion of the law and court decisions favorable to the railroads in the years immediately following its passage made it ineffective. It was, however, a start toward regulation of business, and after the turn of the century it was strengthened by remedial legislation. The Elkins Act of 1903 made rebates illegal. The Expediting Act of 1903 gave preference in circuit courts to ICC and Sherman Act cases. The Hepburn Act of 1906 gave the Interstate Commerce Commission wider jurisdiction, increased the number of members on the Commission, gave it express authority to determine rates, and made it a regulatory body, placing the burden of court action on the carrier. The Mann-Elkins Act of 1910 further enlarged and strengthened the Commission's powers. Other minor amendments gave further strength to the act. By 1915, the political and economic power of railroads was firmly checked.

Muckrakers and Trustbusters. By 1890 public revolt against monopoly practice was widespread, and the clamor for antitrust legislation was loud and sharp. President Harrison also urged monopoly legislation, and the first piece of general antitrust legislation—the Sherman Act—appeared in 1890. Much like the Interstate Commerce Act, early results of the Sherman Act were disappointing. The act was written in such broad terms that it was virtually useless until clarified by court action. Only eighteen suits were initiated by the government in the ten years following passage of the Sherman Act, and of these most were unsuccessful. Administrations under Harrison, Cleveland, and McKinley exhibited little interest or talent in enforcing the act.

Interest in business regulation and antitrust activity was revived after the turn of the century. A group of writers led by Ida Tarbell, Lincoln Steffens, and Upton Sinclair, who became known as the "muckrakers," dissected American business for public view in various magazines of the times. This literary movement emphasized the worst facets of government and business. Supported by public opinion they revived the crusade against business. President Roosevelt and Governor Robert La Follette, of Wisconsin, led the political battle against the business giants, La Follette at the state level and Roosevelt at the national level. Under Roosevelt nineteen civil suits and twenty-five criminal suits were successfully prosecuted. The most significant piece of legislation to appear during the period was the Pure Food and Drug Act of 1906 and its revision in 1907.

Antitrust policies were even more vigorously pursued under Taft. However, the two most significant cases prosecuted during the Taft administration—the Standard Oil Company case and the American Tobacco Company case—even though decided in favor of the government, were only hollow victories. In both cases, the giants were divided into several parts. Each part was to be organized as a separate autonomous company, and each part was forbidden to hold stock in, or cooperate with, any other part. These measures were taken to ensure competition, but little was really accomplished. Through voluntary cooperation the separate parts seemed to work together as well as they had before dissolution.

The antitrust movement reached its peak with the passage of the Clayton Act and the Federal Trade Commission Act in 1914. Since that time, however, there seems to have been a reversal in the roles of the public and government concerning the enforcement of antitrust laws. While government activity in antitrust enforcement has steadily increased since 1915, it has been observed that public concern has lessened. Hofstadter[21] suggests that the reason for this reversal in government and public roles may be that the whole antitrust issue has become so complex that it is beyond the full comprehension of the average man, with the result that only an organization of specialists in case law and economic theory can cope with the problem.

STATE CAPITALISM EMERGES

By 1930 a marked change in relationships among American social institutions was evident. Social dissatisfaction with the business system had been evidenced by the growing body of antitrust legislation. Until 1930 the function of government had been primarily to support the business system in its role of economic leadership and to mediate between business and society. After 1930, however, the role of government changed from passive judgment of business behavior to actual economic leadership. Putting it another way, government's role changed from judging how well business performed its social responsibilities to defining what those responsibilities were. In a sense, after 1930 government appropriated many

[21] Richard Hofstadter, "What Happened to the Antitrust Movement?" in Cheit, op. cit., p. 151.

functions that previously had been reserved for business. According to Cochran and Miller:[22]

> Under the New Deal the federal government became a great employer of men, the greatest user of the nation's savings, the greatest underwriter of debt. The government assumed much of the risk-taking activity of private enterprise. It assumed leadership in finance and construction. Above all, it supplanted private business as the chief planner of the nation's economic life.

The Great Depression. The stock-market crash of 1929 and the subsequent national economic collapse put American free enterprise squarely on trial for its existence. Widespread unemployment, decline of purchasing power, collapse of markets, and declining standards of living all threatened American social stability. These problems were placed squarely in the lap of American business. Business, however, was unable to respond. When it became evident that the business system, by itself, could not generate enough momentum to stimulate economic recovery, Americans began to look to other social institutions for corrective action. Government quickly took the initiative. The story of recovery legislation under the Roosevelt administration of the early thirties is well known and need not be discussed here. What is important is the change in social philosophies which occurred during the thirties and the resultant change in business environment.

Individualism versus the Social Ethic. The individual ethic, so popular in the last century and early twentieth century, was being replaced by the social ethic during the thirties. The term "social ethic," as used here, does not imply belief in socialism as a political system. Rather, it is used to describe an ever-increasing belief that man no longer can control his environment or be master of his destiny. Implicit in the social ethic is the belief that individuals have become so interdependent and so subordinate to various power groups in our society that they are dependent upon these groups for physical, social, and economic security.

The New Business Environment. Within the framework of the social ethic, and beginning in the thirties, government set about defining in legal terms many social responsibilities of business. Wage-and-hour laws, safety codes, and social security obligations imposed by government are illustrations of the new environment. Concurrently, a redefinition of power relations among certain social institutions took place. The Wagner Act established labor as a major power group in society, and labor, too, imposed social restrictions on business behavior. Improvements in working conditions and emphasis on real wages were stressed. Indeed, by 1940 business found that it was no longer *the* major power group in society,

[22] Thomas C. Cochran and William Miller, *The Age of Enterprise*, New York: The Macmillan Company, 1942, pp. 355–356.

but only *one* power group, whose decisions were shaped and challenged by other groups equally powerful—notably labor and government. Business found itself in a different environment from the one it had had a scant fifteen years earlier.

World War II also added new dimensions to the business environment. National problems associated with the war effort were far too complex to be solved by any one social group. Joint effort between government, labor, and business was called for. Nor has the need for cooperation between the three groups diminished. If anything, the need has become greater. The magnitude of national problems resulting from our increasingly complex industrial society will call for stronger bonds of partnership, greater understanding, and mutual respect among the power groups. Meanwhile business must face the problems of defining what its responsibilities are in society (no small problem in itself) and finding socially profitable ways of exercising those responsibilities. It is reasonable to predict that business policies of tomorrow will be shaped to a substantial degree by how well today's businessmen recognize what society expects of the business system, both today and in the future.

The balance of this book will be devoted to examining the contemporary environment of business and analyzing relationships between business and the many groups with which it must relate. It is hoped that the preceding analysis of American business in its historical environment has provided some insights into current social decisions faced by businessmen.

SUMMARY

Many social changes were at work before the Civil War, preparing the way for post–Civil War industrial growth. Guided by a new breed of capitalist, the Robber Barons, and supported and encouraged by social philosophies of the times, industrialism produced social gains unimagined a few decades earlier. As long as business activity continued to produce social gains such as new products, improvements in old products, improvements in services, and lower prices, society supported business activities. But when a few men began to use the business system to emphasize private gain at the expense of social gain through the misuse of monopoly power, society responded by discarding laissez-faire philosophies and strengthening state governments and the Federal government.

Early government interference with the business system in the form of antitrust legislation was largely a protest movement against the power position of business leaders. But in spite of legislation against it, business continued to be the most powerful single group in American society until the Great Depression of the 1930s.

The inability of business to stimulate recovery from the Depression caused a redefinition of the roles of business and government. Government assumed, in the early thirties, many functions previously reserved for business. Encouraged by success and supported by the social ethic, government began to define by law some social responsibilities of business. Labor, too, was legally recognized as a social group by the Wagner Act and began to impose social restrictions on business.

Finally, World War II and the attendant national problems established an entirely new and different environment for business, an environment calling for mutual attention to problems by the three major power groups. No longer can social problems be solved by one group alone; they require the attention and cooperation of all major power groups in society.

QUESTIONS

1. In what ways did the pressures of the Civil War stimulate the growth of industrial capitalism?

2. Prepare a short biographical sketch of one or more of the following men. Include such information as family origin, how he started in business, business and/or political activity, and amount of his fortune at death.

John Jacob Astor	Russell Sage
Marshall Field	John J. Blair
Cornelius Vanderbilt	Leland Stanford and Associates
Daniel Drew	J. P. Morgan
James Fisk, Jr.	John D. Rockefeller
Jay Gould	Andrew Carnegie
Stephen B. Elkins	James J. Hill
Andrew Mellon	James B. Duke
The Guggenheim family	The du Pont family

3. How can you explain the business-consolidation movement that developed during the latter quarter of the nineteenth century? Describe various types of consolidation that were popular during this period.

4. Differentiate between industrial capitalism and finance capitalism.

5. From a social point of view, evaluate the arguments for and against monopolies.

6. Compare the popular social philosophies of the nineteenth century. What relationship can you see between these philosophies and business?

7. Explain this statement: The antitrust movement of the late 1800s and early 1900s was largely a social-protest movement.

8. Contrast the individual ethic with the social ethic.

9. How does the environment of business today differ from that of thirty years ago? Fifty years ago?

2. CURRENT ISSUES IN BUSINESS

CHAPTER 5   THE MANAGERIAL ROLE

> So, for those who would benefit their fellow man
> —as a deep-seated matter of ethics and as a matter of
> effectiveness—I know of no way better calculated to
> provide a good result than the conduct of a productive,
> profitable business.
>
> ROGER M. BLOUGH[1]

> More and more people are coming to understand
> that when business hurts, so does the whole econ-
> omy. . . .
>
> CHARLES G. MORTIMER[2]

The main linking pins between business and its environment are business managers, so it is appropriate to learn how they view their roles. The two introductory quotations by board chairmen of two large corporations give rather typical comments. Higher managers do believe in the importance of their activities, and they believe that their work is significantly related to the progress of society. Although their *motives* are often criticized, they appear certain that their *behavior* is an essential and important function in society.

In this chapter we shall develop the idea of "role," and in order to tie this chapter in with earlier historical material, we shall summarize the evolution of the managerial role to its present state. Then we shall discuss

---

[1] Roger M. Blough, chairman of the board, United States Steel Corporation, "Management: An Open Society" (speech at the University of Texas, Feb. 19, 1963), New York: United States Steel Corporation, 1963, p. 13. (Mimeographed.)

[2] Charles G. Mortimer, chairman, General Foods Corporation, "Developing a Climate Conducive to a Growing Economy" (speech at the University of Chicago, Mar. 27, 1963), New York: General Foods Corporation, 1963, p. 7.

the types of role behavior required of managers and the value systems they develop in their role.

ROLE BEHAVIOR

Meaning of Role. Role is a fundamental idea in understanding social organization. William Shakespeare described role, in his famous passage from *As You Like It*, as follows:

All the world's a stage,
And all the men and women merely players:
They have their exits and their entrances;
And one man in his time plays many parts.

Man does indeed perform many roles, and managing is one of them.

Role is social behavior oriented to the patterned expectations of others. A manager perceives himself in a certain job and set of relationships with others, and he tries to act on the basis of what he thinks is expected of him. In other words, society's expectations influence his behavior. Just as a computer is programmed by people, so is a manager programmed by society for a role.

Since many claims press from all sides upon a manager, each action he takes is really a balancing or commingling of all these claims. When claims of two parties are different, a role conflict exists which the manager must resolve before taking action. For example, the people of his community want a pleasant city, but his business produces fumes and dust. The fumes and dust could be prevented, but that action would displease customers by raising prices 50 cents and would require several hundred thousand dollars of capital that might otherwise be used for stockholder benefit. Much of his working day each manager is required to resolve conflicts of this type, although usually not of this magnitude. His decisions are a shade of gray, rather than all black or all white.

Assuming that a claim is perceived, a manager's next step is to screen it on the basis of its legitimacy or propriety. Let us take an example. If a local action group comes to him in the United States insisting that woman's place is in the home and that no women should be employed, he will pay little heed because this demand seems to him out of line with current realistic thinking and, therefore, has weak legitimacy. After screening, many legitimate claims usually remain, so he must further resolve them on the basis of the values he holds. He seeks role action which brings net outputs greater than inputs according to his perceived values. The inputs and outputs may be social, psychological, economic, or any other type of value.

The managerial role requires different conduct with different people, rather than uniform conduct. One pattern of conduct is required with a subordinate, another with a fellow manager, and another with the local mayor; yet all three are managerial-role actions. Since these role variations are expected, managers need to develop role sensitivity for appraising each situation and do role thinking to select the most appropriate action.

Similarity in Managerial-role Perceptions. The most significant fact about the general role called "management" is that managerial perceptions of it appear fairly uniform throughout the world, at least in industrially developed nations. Kerr and others, on the basis of international studies lasting a decade, developed evidence that industrialization tends to cause a uniform work culture, including the managerial role. Generally speaking, as industrialization advances, there is a move toward more democratization of employee and managerial roles.[3]

A study of role perceptions of higher managers in Israel and Australia, nations with distinctly different industrial heritages, reported substantial agreement between the two countries.[4] Cross-cultural comparisons showed that role perceptions and work values were similar on most items surveyed. The study concluded that similar institutional pressures act on managers in both countries to promote similarities in attitudes and perceptions.

One comprehensive study covered written responses of 2,800 managers in eleven countries. Research showed general uniformity in role perceptions regardless of country; however, responses of managers from certain clusters of countries were distinguishable as being slightly different. Separate clusters existed for northern European, southern European, and Anglo-American countries. In all groups there was agreement on the importance and desirability of performing the functions of "directing" and "cooperating." For "reprimanding" there was agreement, except that Spain stood out with extra-strong support for this activity. For "persuading" there was more dispersion, and Germany stood out in its lack of support for this role activity. These variations show that cultural traditions do affect role perceptions, partly offsetting technological pressures for uniformity.[5]

In Chapter 1 we explained that the term "business" included business operations in all types of economic and political organizations—private, governmental, nonprofit, and others. In further support of this view, re-

[3] Clark Kerr, John T. Dunlop, Frederick H. Harbison, and Charles A. Myers, *Industrialism and Industrial Man: The Problems of Labor and Management in Industrial Growth*, Cambridge, Mass.: Harvard University Press, 1960. See also A. Inkeles, "Industrial Man: The Relation of Status to Experience, Perception, and Value," *American Journal of Sociology*, vol. 66, pp. 1–31, 1960.

[4] The Israeli-Melbourne correlation was .79, significant to the .01 level, and the Israeli-Sydney correlation was .54, significant to the .05 level. Y. Rim and Bilha F. Mannheim, "Factors Related to Attitudes of Management and Union Representatives," *Personnel Psychology*, Summer, 1964, pp. 149–165.

[5] Mason Haire, Edwin E. Ghiselli, and Lyman W. Porter, "Cultural Patterns in the Role of the Manager," *Industrial Relations*, February, 1963, pp. 95–117.

search discloses that managers in various types of enterprises have essentially the same understanding of their managerial role. Israel furnishes an excellent example because it has a mixed economy of enterprises owned and operated by private groups, by government, and by labor unions (the Histadrut). A casual observer would think that managers in these three enterprises would view their jobs differently because of their different objectives and modes of operation. In the Histadrut, for example, leadership is determined through hotly contested political elections, and positions are allocated according to votes obtained. The leaders of private industry, however, are chosen by higher authority, as in the United States.

In spite of these differences in ownership control, management in all three enterprises is essentially the same. One study reported: "Managerial functions, attitudes and limitations are uniform to an astonishing degree among the larger private, Histadrut, and government-owned enterprises." [6] Another study of Israeli managers reached the same conclusion, reporting that the managers' role definitions were similar regardless of the ownership control of their enterprise.[7]

In conclusion, cultural differences among countries and variations in ownership control do lead to variations in managerial-role perceptions; however, higher managers substantially agree on the managerial role regardless of country or ownership control. The managerial job itself, wherever it exists, is substantially the same. This uniformity in function tends to promote similarities in perceptions by managers. For successful performance, for example, managers need to understand the nuances of authority and the relationship of cost to productivity regardless of their cultural heritage.

Historical Development. Certainly managerial-role perceptions have changed historically. Centuries ago nearly all management was performed by a dynastic rulership operating through rights of monarchy, military power, church rank, or land ownership. However, as industry expanded during the eighteenth and nineteenth centuries, political philosophy, economics, and biology combined to support a managerial role of economic individualism and autocratic leadership based on natural survival of the fittest. The Declaration of Independence of the United States was made in 1776, the same year that Adam Smith published his *Wealth of Nations*. Smith related political liberty to an economic liberty and showed that self-interest pursued without governmental intervention would promote the welfare of all. Smith's philosophy added an ethical purpose—welfare

---

[6] Milton Derber, "Plant Labor Relations in Israel," *Industrial and Labor Relations Review*, October, 1963, p. 59.

[7] Rim and Mannheim, *op. cit.*, p. 156. There were some differences, such as that 46 percent of private-business managers believe that an enterprise making larger profits is usually more efficient than other enterprises, but only 22.5 percent of government-business managers agreed.

of all—to the manager's political view that he as an individual should be free to pursue his economic interests.

Economic individualism was reinforced by the views of Herbert Spencer. He interpreted Charles Darwin's theory of evolution to show that the most capable persons rose to the top by best adapting to the natural conditions of life. This social Darwinism further justified power over others and supported managers in their belief that they were chosen leaders who could best serve public welfare by pursuing their own personal goals. Observe, however, that even in this era of rampant self-interest, managers still viewed their role as ultimately providing public service through the route of industrial growth. Like other citizens, they were socialized to fit a certain culture and were, consequently, trying to do their job as they saw it. As a matter of fact, they did contribute greatly to expansion of the frontier, more national wealth, and industrial development.

The next managerial role, paternalism, grew naturally from the manager's perception of himself as a leader who rose to the top through superior capabilities. As a superior leader with a broader perspective than an ordinary citizen, he believed that he had better knowledge of what was best for industrial society. Since responsibility goes with authority (an ancient management precept derived from the realities of work), the manager felt responsible for introducing these better conditions to his workers. In the public interest he felt he should oversee their welfare. If he could protect them, they could produce more, just as a cultivated orchard produces better than an unkept one. And if he could improve their health and morals, they could do more, just as he, with his superior ability, had been able to do more than they. Accordingly he built company towns and stores, developed profit sharing, supported recreation halls and libraries, held picnics, and encouraged education of workers' children (but usually not of the worker himself, as is done today). In spite of the unselfish aims that some managers had in applying paternalism, it made the worker and his family psychologically dependent on management. As soon as a worker felt able to seek similar benefits on his own, he was ready to throw off the yoke of paternalism as a gesture supporting his personal dignity and freedom. Paternalism was weakened further by the fact that some managers were notoriously poor judges of what workers wanted.

There are a number of similarities between the experiences of business paternalism and current developments in public welfare. Views have been offered that excessive welfare places the citizen and his family in a psychologically dependent role. Citizens may respond with hostility in spite of the economic and social progress being made, just as they rose against business paternalism in spite of the economic and social progress made during its period. More accurately, perhaps, business paternalism was cast out because of progress made during its term; that is, business paternalism served as a useful stage on the continuum of progress, but that same progress eventually called for an improved form of relationship. Will a similar philosophy apply to current public paternalism? Will progress under it soon call for it to be cast out in favor of an improved form of relationship as world society matures? As education makes a more sophisticated citizen, as medical advances make him more healthy, and as technology and business give him more wealth, will the citizen move, as the business employee did, to a new level where he expects less paternalistic conditions?

Definition of the Modern Managerial Role. The modern managerial role has developed a well-defined set of characteristics which may be called its *role definition*. Since society is dynamic, the definition will change as it has in the past, but it is expected that changes will develop gradually through evolution and adaptation rather than drastic revolution. We call the modern role *career management* because management is a differentiated occupation which one enters on a career basis.

First, career management is a *system regulator* because it functions at key junction points in the intricate social system that forms an organization. In fact, an organization may be defined as a cluster of roles having a common objective. As part of the system, management is both independent and dependent, initiating action on others and having action initiated on it. Some earlier views of management made it exclusively an independent force initiating on others, but this view lacked realism in terms of actual operating conditions. Management is one of many interacting forces within a firm, and as presented in Chapter 1, management also interacts with groups in the larger social system outside the firm. Management is, therefore, a dynamic system relationship rather than the static authority structure pictured on an organization chart.

Second, in its dynamic system, management operates as an *innovator* or change agent. Change is a natural condition of organizations, and managers, as the responsible directors of organizations, are continually involved with it. They initiate changes on their own behalf, apply changes required by others, and adjust to new environmental conditions.

Although management needs to motivate others to be creative, the management role itself emphasizes innovation more than creativity. Creativity deals with the generation of ideas, but innovation deals with making them work. Compared with research scientists, who emphasize creativity, managers are more concerned with innovating to bring ideas to fruition. Since creative ideas are of no usefulness until implemented, the innovative role of management becomes more important as more and better ideas are generated in modern society. Ideas without implementers simply increase the burden of conscience on society because people know that there are better ways and are frustrated by their deficient implementation. Modern society, having generated ideas beyond our capacity to absorb them, is turning more and more to management in order to implement them. One analyst states: "All in all, ideation is relatively abundant. It is its implementation that is more scarce." [8]

Third, the limits of management's innovative role are largely defined by its role as *productivity catalyst*; that is, the kind of innovation that management is supposed to stimulate is one that is more productive. Nearly all societies place this role expectation on management. Most managers recognize it and are able to state it explicitly with comments such as the following: "To make the best in quality at the lowest possible cost" and "More and better things for more people." If managers can improve their operations enough to increase gross national product only 1 percent in a year, the increase will be about 6 billion dollars in the United States. While managers do not usually think in terms of gross national product, they recognize that more productivity of goods and services is a public service, and they regularly remind the public of this service in their speeches and policy statements.

A fourth role, related to productivity, is that of *trustee*. Society commits to management its human and capital resources with the expectation that management will employ them wisely in producing goods and services. As with legal trustees, management is expected not to dissipate the resources under its care and to enhance them if at all possible. Legitimacy of management, therefore, rests more on successful performance of its function than on legal rights. Management holds its power because of the effective job it does as trustee within the system. Legal rights support the system, but in the long run they will undoubtedly be amended to the extent that management fails to meet citizen expectations regarding use of resources entrusted to management. The trusteeship role is discussed further in the chapter on ownership.

Fifth, management performs the role of *boundary mediator*. Just as a fluid system in physical science has boundary conditions, so also does a dynamic organization have them. These are its points and forms of contact with its environment, and management mediates or resolves these boundary contacts in order to keep its organization effective. Its role is to meet organizational objectives while supporting social objectives also. Managers direct an open social system, not a closed one. They should expect external pressures of all types and be prepared to mediate them. Through resolving these pressures they integrate their organization with society. Their role is largely one of mediation because they have no direct authority to order society to take—or not take—any course of action.

The sixth part of management's role definition is that of *leader*. Society expects management in all its actions to use leadership, which is defined as behavior which induces energetic, emotionally committed,

[8] Theodore Levitt, "Creativity Is Not Enough," *Harvard Business Review*, May–June, 1963, p. 73.

cooperative followers. As has been said many times, management is not expected to perform society's operative tasks but to motivate others to do so. If better men can be attracted and motivated, then better results should be reached, other things being equal. Some of history's great business leaders recognized this role, such as Andrew Carnegie, whose epitaph reads:

> Here lies a man
> Who knew how to enlist
> In his service
> Better men than himself.

Although part of the leadership role is an acquired technique, much of it is a matter of comprehensive climate and spirit which a leader develops through sensing the needs and goals of people and relating them to organizational objectives. Men follow because they see reasons, both emotional and rational, for following. Leadership finds those reasons and makes them more appealing. It encourages average people to give above-average performance.[9]

In summary, the role definition of management calls for many behavioral expectations. Six important managerial roles are those of system regulator, innovator, productivity catalyst, trustee, boundary mediator, and leader. In one way or another, all six requirements relate to introducing and responding to change in a dynamic environment. Unless a person promoted to management can handle change effectively, he is unlikely to be a successful manager. This ability to handle change is so widely needed in our dynamic modern world that one analyst concludes that "the critical problem confronting business today is the lagging supply of managers capable of grappling with the problems of change." [10] From the role point of view, we can say that management is administering change through people. Because of society's immense needs and fast growth, this role of administering change becomes a key one whether or not managers want it to be so. We cannot do without it, and we cannot meet our growth objectives unless it is performed effectively. Individual work by laborers is adequate to maintain primitive agrarian societies, but in modern industrial society neither labor, nor capital, nor government can provide needed goods and services without full use of business management.

As stated earlier, the managerial role is itself continually being redefined to gear it to new developments. Perhaps the largest area of

[9] See Roger Bellows, *Creative Leadership*, Englewood Cliffs, N.J.: Prentice-Hall, Inc., 1959; and Eugene E. Jennings, *An Anatomy of Leadership: Princes, Heroes, and Supermen*, New York: Harper & Row, Publishers, Incorporated, 1960.

[10] Bernard J. Bienvenu, "Is Business Developing the Right Kind of Manager?" *Personnel*, May–June, 1964, p. 17.

redefinition relates to the external environment and social responsibility thereto, as is being discussed in this book. But there are other areas of redefinition. The leadership role is being perceived as less autocratic and more participative. It is also less a matter of personality and more a matter of role behavior. Modern leaders are moving away from detailed task prescription toward goal setting which allows participants more latitude in task performance.

Similarly the role of system regulator is moving away from static emphasis on formal authority toward dynamic views of communication and decision making. The role of trustee is moving from custodianship of resources toward a responsibility to help resources grow and to use them nearer to their capacity. These are but a few of many role modifications happening. The managerial-role definition will not remain static.

Role performance over a period of time leads to what is called the *managerial mind*.[11] This kind of mind is committed to results through organizations. It is action-oriented and policy-oriented. It desires to seek and solve problems rather than avoid them. Tensions are used constructively toward action, rather than being perceived as a psychological ill. The managerial mind learns from experience and teaches what it knows to others. It is objective and realistic in decision making, working always within an environment of change.

MANAGERIAL VALUE SYSTEMS

Underlying all managerial behavior is each manager's own personal set of values. Values are different for each manager, but it is possible to make some generalizations about them as long as we understand that we are not talking about all managers. Additionally, these values develop into clusters which are reflected in particular schools of thought. Just as economics has its Keynesians and psychology its Freudians, business management has its economic individualists and its Machiavellians.

For each manager, values exist as a total system, with each value rubbing against other values, amending and restraining them, and in turn being amended and restrained. No one value independently determines behavior. There is little doubt, however, that value systems are at the root of managerial behavior. They affect behavior in a number of ways:[12]

1. They primarily determine what a manager thinks is good, right, beautiful, and so on.

[11] Charles E. Summer, Jr., "The Managerial Mind," *Harvard Business Review*, January–February, 1959, pp. 69–78; and David W. Ewing, *The Managerial Mind*, New York: The Free Press of Glencoe, 1964.

[12] Robert N. McMurry, "Conflicts in Human Values," *Harvard Business Review*, May–June, 1963, p. 131.

2. They provide norms on which he depends for guidance.
3. They chiefly determine his attitudes toward issues with which he comes into contact.
4. They influence the kinds of persons with whom he can be compatible and the kinds of social activity he can accept.
5. They largely determine the kinds of ideas he can understand and transmit without distortion.
6. They give him moral principles he can use to rationalize desired actions regardless of how realistic the actions appear to others.

All managerial values are related to a manager's perception of reality. When he looks across his desk into his office, his perception of what is there will be different from that of an associate alongside him with an almost identical physical view. He may see people wasting time, while his associate sees new furniture just purchased. Similarly, he will see something different from what his associate sees when both are looking at a balance sheet. The reality which is there is identical, but each person's perception of it is not likely to be fully correct or fully complete because each situation contains ambiguous factors and unknowns. Each selects by means of perception those factors which are meaningful to him in terms of his experience, values, and capabilities. In other words, order and organization are not in the physical stimulus, but in the observer. A man's behavior depends not on what is really there but on what he sees there.[13]

As a person matures, his perceptions change, and so does reality. This means that there is no one value system attributable to managers in general. And whatever values do exist are changing over time.

Businessmen recognize the importance of value commitment in achieving objectives. The chief executive of International Business Machines, one of the world's most vigorous businesses, attributes his firm's growth to three principal beliefs: respect for the individual employee and concern for his needs, dedication to customer service, and devotion to superiority in everything undertaken. He believes that no organization can survive without a sound value system on which to base policies.[14]

What are some of the values which business managers hold, particularly in advanced industrial societies? We shall discuss these values at two levels: the personal ethics of managers and the values they hold about business objectives.

Personal Ethics of Managers. Business leaders are people like the rest of us. This rather obvious fact is sometimes overlooked by commentators on business environment. They think that businessmen are moti-

---

[13] Mason Haire, *Psychology in Management*, 2d ed., New York: McGraw-Hill Book Company, 1964, pp. 51–59.
[14] Thomas J. Watson, Jr., *A Business and Its Beliefs: The Ideas That Helped Build IBM*, New York: McGraw-Hill Book Company, 1963.

vated by one purpose alone and that nothing else has any influence. Take the economic-man concept, for example. It assumes that businessmen are always guided by rational economic decisions which seek to maximize profits. Profit maximization is a useful assumption for exact theoretical analysis in a classroom, but it is quite unreliable in the world of reality because it ignores the fact that managers are people. It also ignores facts of history and research evidence. After studying this situation, Robert N. Anthony, of Harvard Business School, commented:[15]

> I have reviewed what I am told are the five largest selling economics texts, accounting for some 250,000 copies a year. All of them base their analysis of business decisions on profit maximization. . . . But I know of no study of general business practice that supports the profit maximization premise, and I shall mention later studies whose findings are inconsistent with it.

Business leaders do seek profits. There is no argument about this. The point is simply that rational profit maximization is not the sole value underlying their decision making. Rather, the businessman's whole value system is involved when he makes a decision. As a participant, not an observer, he experiences a personal involvement in every decision situation. The whole person decides, not a separate and abstract computer in his head. And the whole person has many ethical values, not one.

March and Simon suggest that businessmen make decisions which are merely satisfactory rather than optimal or maximal. The difference is that optimal decisions are based on criteria permitting *all* alternatives to be compared, then selecting the one *most* desired. Satisfactory decisions are based on criteria describing minimally satisfactory alternatives, and one which meets these criteria is selected. The difference is similar to that between looking for the sharpest needle in a haystack and looking for a needle only sharp enough for sewing. They comment: *"Most human decision-making, whether individual or organizational, is concerned with the discovery and selection of satisfactory alternatives; only in exceptional cases is it concerned with the discovery and selection of optimal alternatives."* [16]

Businessmen are thought to be pragmatists: if something works, it is good. But this is not quite the same as saying that if something works, it is best. Businessmen seldom claim that no decision could be better. They claim only that the decision they are making is satisfactory. They labor in a world of application and cannot wait for theoretical perfection before making a decision.

When the techniques of science were combined with pragmatism,

---

[15] Robert N. Anthony, "The Trouble with Profit Maximization," *Harvard Business Review*, November–December, 1960, p. 127.

[16] James G. March and Herbert A. Simon, *Organizations*, New York: John Wiley & Sons, Inc., 1958, pp. 140–141.

scientific management developed as a basic managerial value. By studying actual operations according to scientific principles, businessmen sought to develop better ways of work. Frederick W. Taylor fathered scientific management. Some of his followers, such as Frank Gilbreth, sought the one best way of work without regard to human differences and situational factors, but this engineering perfectionism soon generated opposition. Scientific management has now evolved to a search for better ways within the limits of practicality. It remains a basic part of most managers' value systems and is reflected today in motion study, operations research, job evaluation, and time study.

Since the days of Adam Smith, and even before, businessmen have valued market freedom. On the other hand, they have adapted to large amounts of market regulation when the need arose, and their adaptation has been efficient. They have been as law-abiding and productive under government regulation as any other group. This fact further supports the view that neither market freedom nor any other value is pursued to its maximum. Like a pail filled with a mixture from 100 bottles, a manager's value system is an equilibrium of many value inputs.

The quest for market freedom is not peculiar to business but is a general cultural phenomenon. Almost all groups seek autonomy, even though—like business—they are subject to regulation. The academic leader seeks academic freedom for his group so that ideas can be freely traded. The labor leader wants to make whatever demands he feels appropriate within a context of free collective bargaining without governmental restrictions. All three are brothers in their search for operating freedom.

More recently the works of Elton Mayo and his followers have brought greater emphasis on human values in business relations. Though Mayo's work concerned employees, the interest he generated has spread to all human contacts in business, including those with customers and vendors. Probably the human relations movement was an incentive and a key step toward broader-based values of social responsibility. It opened the eyes of businessmen to the fact that social values are a significant part of the business environment.

Concurrent with the rise in nebulous social values has been an increase in attention given to rational values of mathematics, economic theory, and science. In a kind of reverse pragmatism, some managers conclude: "If I can make this decision work in a mathematical model, it must be good." They overlook the fact that many of the assumptions underlying the model are merely estimates and predictions.

On occasion managers seek hedonistic values, acting so as to gain pleasure and avoid pain. A manager who avoids making a decision sometimes does so because the possibility of a wrong decision is so painful to his ego that he prefers to make no decision at all. On the other hand, that same manager at another time may rush forthrightly into combat, following Machiavellian values of divide and rule and "Do unto others before they do unto you." The pail filled from 100 bottles is indeed a varicolored mixture!

An opposite of Machiavellian values is the Golden Rule, "Do unto others as you would have them do unto you." Some managers at first glance thought this was the universal guide they needed, but when they tried to apply it in operating situations, they found it wanting. Moved from its spiritual context, it was unable to specify exactly which decision alternative to choose. The trouble was that other people did not want the same treatment a manager wanted. They were different. The precept applied spiritually because the spirits of men are assumed to be equal, but it could not provide a precise operational answer because the personalities of men are different. Therefore, the precept needed amendment to read, "Do unto others as you would have them do unto you *if you were as they are*." The original precept remains a basic one in managerial value systems, but it is not the simple cause-and-effect determinant of action that some persons expected it to be.

Values Concerning Business Objectives. Some managerial values are expressed as beliefs about the business function and business objectives. Overriding all beliefs is the confidence that business (commerce) is a useful function providing social goods and services. Because of their devotion to commerce, business leaders are understandably frustrated and impatient when advocates of welfare decision making belittle the role of commerce in human advancement. As stated by M. J. Rathbone, chairman of the board of New Jersey Standard Oil Company: "Most people would, I think, agree that business corporations are necessary, perform vital services, and are good for the country. Yet the attitudes often displayed toward business reflect the contrary. We who are associated with big companies feel especially frustrated by the attitudes we encounter." [17]

Within the concept of usefulness through service rendered, business leaders have usually emphasized three areas of output greater than input. These are public service through more and better goods and services, rewards to personnel, and returns to investors. Personal values supporting these three outputs usually apply to both private and public business operations, and many managers have shown the capacity to move from one to the other and perform effectively without modifying their value system about these three areas of payoff. For example, a government office must satisfy its citizen customers by producing services just as much as a private factory must satisfy customers by producing goods. Personnel services of the two institutions are even more similar. Likewise, the government office must in the long run provide an output for citizen investors, or else it will not receive capital for expansion or may be abolished. It

[17] M. J. Rathbone, quoted in Bienvenu, *op. cit.*, p. 15.

is true that measurement of investor return is slower and more indirect in public business, but it is there. Government offices do close and charities do go out of business when they inadequately use the resources society has invested in them. In fact, every time capital is allocated to one public business rather than another, society demonstrates its belief that one use of its resources provides a better return than another use.

From time to time business leaders emphasize one payoff group above the others. As discussed in earlier chapters, emphasis has been on investor profit. If you ask a private-business leader today what the main purpose of his business is, he is also likely to emphasize profit. If you question him closely, however, you will find that he has a broader view of profit than his historical counterpart. First of all, he looks further down the road toward long-run profit, compared with short-run return. Second, he tends to choose satisfactory profit as one of several necessary payoffs the firm must generate, rather than rationally choosing maximum profit according to earlier economic theory. His decisions are ". . . concerned with discovering courses of action that satisfy a whole set of constraints." [18]

Third, he recognizes the multiple uses of profit and evaluates it in different ways according to these uses. From an investor point of view, he sees profit as a motive for investment and a source of income. From higher management's point of view, it is a measure of how decentralized profit centers are meeting their objectives. It is also a matter of personal pride and status because it is evidence of successful performance. To the firm itself, profit is the basis of survival and growth. As stated by the president of E. I. du Pont de Nemours and Company:[19]

> Without profits, our system literally cannot be maintained any more than man can survive without oxygen. No one would argue that breathing is an objective of life. But no one could deny that, without it, no other objectives would be conceivable. And so it is with profit for a business. Without it, the business dies and takes with it any possibility of improving man's state of affairs.

For the firm, profits also serve as a device for internally allocating resources to their most efficient use. In the words of one manager: "Profit for us is a kind of traffic cop which directs the use of resources. . . ." [20] Beyond the firm in the whole society, profits are also a

[18] Herbert A. Simon, "On the Concept of Organizational Goal," *Administrative Science Quarterly*, June, 1964, p. 20.

[19] Lammot du Pont Copeland, "Building a Strong Economy" (speech before Investment Bankers Association of America, Nov. 27, 1962), Wilmington, Del.: E. I. du Pont de Nemours and Company, p. 7.

[20] John D. Lockton, treasurer, General Electric Company, "The Creative Power of Profits" (speech at Macalester College, Apr. 22, 1964), Schenectady, N.Y.: General Electric Company, p. 4.

basis for allocating scarce resources among almost unlimited demands according to the propositions of economics.

Probably the strongest argument for making profits primary is that they are necessary for survival, and in the rational order of things *survival must come first*. However, the president of du Pont in the quotation just presented deflates the survival argument by showing that an essential element of life does not necessarily become the primary objective of an organism. Under normal conditions the essential element is more of a precondition to the seeking of other useful values.[21]

More recently there has been strong support for consumer payoffs as the primary objective of business. Lyndall Urwick, who is active internationally in management, represents this view with his comment: "On the other hand, in a competitive and free economy the primary *social* function of the businessman, the entrepreneur, is to protect the interests of every man *in his capacity as a consumer*." [22] Others have said that the essential purpose of a business is to "create a customer" and have argued that profits are an academic question until a customer provides funds from which profits can be taken.

There is also support for making employee values primary in business. Usually the reasoning is that human values must come first in any value system, but this view begs the question, for investors and consumers are also people. However, it is true that employees tend to have a greater proportion of their investments tied up in a company because of their full-time association with it. The investor and customer have only part-time association with a company, and loss of this association may be less detrimental to them than to an employee. However, employee investment is not always larger than the owner's. Consider the case of a small business owner who has his life savings in his business, compared with a carpenter who works for him. Even by standards of humanism, the owner has the greater membership investment in this situation. If the carpenter is laid off, he usually can take his skill elsewhere. But if the owner goes bankrupt, as hundreds do every month, this may be a major personal and human loss for him and his family for a long period of time.

Each view of what should be the primary value system of business has its merits, but probably a more realistic view is that all three—customers, employees, and investors—are mutually dependent on one another and one of them cannot claim absolute priority over the others. The importance of all three is supported by data from an interview survey of 145

---

[21] For comments on survival needs, see Peter F. Drucker, "Business Objectives and Survival Needs: Notes on a Discipline of Business Enterprise," *Journal of Business*, April, 1958, pp. 81–90.

[22] Lyndall F. Urwick, "The Purpose of a Business," *Dun's Review and Modern Industry*, November, 1955, p. 53.

chief executives or their deputies. In response to the question "What are the aims of top management in your company?" profit, customer service, and employee welfare were the three aims most mentioned.[23] A French industrialist explains these three values as follows:[24]

> In any free economy, business enterprise has three major functions:
> Satisfy the public by producing the goods and services it needs.
> Support the personnel.
> Make a profit.
> None of these three pillars on which business enterprise rests is any more or less important than any other. While they are entirely different from each other, these three functions are absolutely interdependent.
> Without profits there can be no possibility of raising wages and no capital for modernizing the business.
> With unsatisfied personnel, good production is not possible.
> With poor production, the public goes elsewhere.

A deficiency in the model using three pillars is that public service is included in consumer services rather than being separately emphasized; that is, "Satisfy *the public* by producing the goods and services it needs." The modern model is developing into four pillars in which public service, or social responsibility, stands alongside consumer, investor, and personnel services in a manager's value system. A paper company vice-president expressed this idea as follows:[25]

> We in Crown Zellerbach believe that shareholders, management, and labor are all a part of the same team and that each plays a vital role in its success or failure. We also believe a company can progress only as the industry as a whole progresses, and that industry progress depends upon all the innumerable other factors that affect the economy. We further believe that a company must satisfactorily discharge its responsibilities to society if the desired progress is to be permanently attained.

SUMMARY

The managerial role is the main linking pin between business and its environment. Role defines expectations that others have concerning how

[23] James K. Dent, "Organizational Correlates of the Goals of Business Managements," *Personnel Psychology*, Autumn, 1959, p. 369.

[24] English translation of Rolf Nordling, Solitaire, SA, "La Simplification du Travail au Niveau de la Direction Générale d'une Entreprise," *CNOF—Revue Mensuelle de l'Organisation* (June, 1954), New York: General Electric Company, 1955, pp. 13–14.

[25] A. B. Layton, vice-president, Crown Zellerbach Corporation (speech to Security Analysts of St. Louis, Mo., Sept. 30, 1955), quoted in Stewart Thompson, *Management Creeds and Philosophies*, New York: American Management Association, 1958, p. 108.

a manager should act, and these claims do influence managerial behavior. Once a claim is perceived, a manager screens it for legitimacy and then integrates it with other claims that are influencing his behavior. He tends toward role action which brings outputs greater than inputs, as weighed by values he perceives. Managers around the world have similar perceptions of their role, subject to minor cultural influences. Perceptions are similar regardless of whether ownership control of the business is government, labor, or private capital.

Historically the managerial role progressed from a dynastic rulership to economic individualism to paternalism to career management. The role definition of career management emphasizes the following behavioral expectations: system regulator, innovator, productivity catalyst, trustee, boundary mediator, and leader. All six expectations relate to change; hence, we can say with reasonable accuracy that management is primarily the function of administering change through people. The managerial role itself will continue to be redefined.

Personal value systems underlie all managerial behavior because managers are participants, not disinterested observers. Values are dynamic, not static. They vary from manager to manager. No particular set of values can be attributed to managers in general; rather, their values range broadly. Personal value systems are configurations of many values mingled together. One value alone does not exclusively determine behavior.

With regard to business objectives, managers believe that business functions are a social good, providing services especially to investors, employees, customers, and the general public. In the next chapter we shall discuss how these values become expressed as business creeds, ethical codes of professional groups, standards offered by external advisory groups, and statements by business associations.

QUESTIONS

1. It is sometimes said that the managerial functions are planning, organizing, directing, and controlling. What is the difference between managerial functions and the managerial role?

2. Discuss similarities of managerial-role perceptions in different cultural environments.

3. Trace the development of the managerial role from dynastic rulership to career management.

4. What are the main expectations in the role definition of career management?

5. Interview a manager and report to your study group what personal value systems you think primarily influence his behavior.

6. Appraise the idea of the "three pillars on which business enterprise rests."

CHAPTER 6 BUSINESS CREEDS AND
CODES OF ETHICS

> In the last analysis, high ethical standards can be
> achieved only through voluntary effort.
>
> PRESIDENT JOHN F. KENNEDY[1]

> It is intended that no TIer shall ever be required
> to compromise high moral and ethical standards in the
> performance of his job, nor will Texas Instruments,
> upon fair determination, countenance compromises of
> high standards by any TIer.
>
> TEXAS INSTRUMENTS, INC.[2]

Business creeds are involved in a variety of situations illustrated by the
following incidents. On January 5, 1960, in a speech to a General Electric
management conference, Mr. Ralph J. Cordiner, chairman of the board
of General Electric Company, prophetically stated: "Every company . . .
that is operated on a basis of cartel systems is liquidating its present
strength and future opportunities."[3] On June 22 of that year his own
company was among those indicated in the United States District Court,
Eastern District of Pennsylvania, for alleged conspiracy with others in
price-fixing and restriction of competition, although no evidence was
ever presented that the alleged actions were known at Mr. Cordiner's
level in the corporation.

In 1961 the United States Secretary of Commerce convened a Busi-

---

[1] John F. Kennedy (statement at a meeting of the Business Ethics Advisory Council, Jan. 16, 1962), from A Statement on Business Ethics and a Call for Action, Washington, D.C.: U.S. Department of Commerce, 1963, p. 9.

[2] Ethics in the Business of TI, Dallas, Tex.: Texas Instruments, Inc., about 1963.

[3] Clarence C. Walton and Frederick W. Cleveland, Jr., Corporations on Trial: The Electric Cases, Belmont, Calif.: Wadsworth Publishing Company, 1964, p. 1.

ness Ethics Advisory Council to encourage voluntary improvement of business conduct as indicated by President John F. Kennedy's comment quoted at the beginning of this chapter. In 1963 the thirteenth International Management Congress met in New York City, and one of the principal issues at the congress was the ethical purpose and standards of business.[4] During all these years a number of companies were establishing standards of conduct. The second quotation introducing this chapter gives a summary sentence from a code of ethics published by one of these companies.

Whether business standards are consciously established or not, they exist in the cultural heritage of civilization. Whether written or not, they do guide actions of businessmen. The question, then, is not whether to have them; rather, it is how intelligently they are established and applied. In this chapter we shall discuss standards of conduct established in company creeds, ethical codes of professions in business, codes offered by advisory groups, and views of business associations.

COMPANY CREEDS

All businesses must meet certain standards of law and minimum cultural standards. All are further influenced by the general cultural milieu of their time. But in spite of these tendencies toward uniform conduct, there are important differences among businesses. Each has its own personality, as each human being does. These organizational differences do produce different results. Take the case of Avon Products, Inc. In 1964 it had the highest return on invested capital of any company on *Fortune* magazine's list of the 500 largest corporations, and its net income since 1954 had risen at a rate over 19 percent a year compounded. Why? Testimony from various sources indicated that its ethical orientation was unique and unusually strong. The board chairman stated: "We have this concept of people working, cooperating, liking each other." The president stated: "This is a very human business involving people with a desire to improve themselves by selling on commission. We never cheated or lied to them or tried to get rich quick." These views were confirmed by an industry observer: "They're folksy; they're terribly sincere." And an executive of a supplier stated: "They're cleancut and straightforward—they never give you a snow job." Even Avon's advertising style is unique, appealing to "innocent freshness," as they call it, rather than sex and passion. The outstanding results speak for themselves.[5]

Surveys of Conduct Standards. Surveys show that men in all types of organizations are concerned about ethical practice. A 1961 survey for

[4] *Proceedings of the Thirteenth International Management Congress*, New York: Council for International Progress in Management (United States), Inc., 1963.

[5] Seymour Freedgood, "Avon: The Sweet Smell of Success," *Fortune*, December, 1964, pp. 109–112.

the tenth reunion of the class of 1951, Harvard Business School, produced almost three hundred responses from people in different types of organizations. Eleven percent of this group felt that they were under pressure to behave in "ethically repugnant" ways toward others in their organization. Fourteen percent regarded as unethical some practice of their organization.[6]

At about the same time a more extensive survey was made of 1,531 readers of *Harvard Business Review*, 84 percent of them in management.[7] Sixty-eight percent of respondents felt there were "a few" or more unethical practices in their industry. When asked about the one practice they would most like to see eliminated, they stressed gifts and bribes, unfair pricing, and misleading advertising. When asked whether they favored a self-developed ethical code for their industry, 71 percent favored a code and only 10 percent opposed it. The largest benefits expected from an ethical code were a useful aid in refusing unethical requests (87 percent) and personal help by clearly defining the limits of acceptable conduct (81 percent). On the negative side, 11 percent believed the code might protect inefficient firms and retard industry growth.

Other results of the survey show that businessmen are alert to social responsibilities but that they disagree on what is the proper conduct in a specific situation. They recognize that there are no single, clear-cut answers. Generally they rate themselves as higher in ethics than the "average businessman," and they look to top management for leadership in improved practice. They feel religion has been lax in providing concrete guidance, and they would welcome more guidance from clergymen with thorough knowledge of business problems.

Another survey covered 323 managers in general management, marketing, production, personnel, finance, and purchasing. Concerning whether they thought their competitors engaged in unethical practices, 9 percent said "frequently," 62 percent said "sometimes," 24 percent said "seldom," and 3 percent said "never." Marketing managers had the lowest opinion of competitors, with 23 percent saying "frequently." Personnel men had the highest opinion of competitors, with 35 percent saying "seldom" or "never." The entire group said marketing and purchasing had the most unethical practices, and they designated pricing as the main problem area. The majority of respondents felt the public image of business practices was "not too high," and the majority also felt that more could be done to raise ethical practices. They particularly favored active discussions of business ethics among business people.[8]

---

[6] "A Positive Code of Ethics," *Business Week*, June 17, 1961, p. 166.

[7] Raymond C. Baumhart, "How Ethical Are Businessmen?" *Harvard Business Review*, July–August, 1961, pp. 6ff.

[8] Thomas F. Schutte, "Executives' Perceptions of Business Ethics," *Journal of Purchasing*, May, 1965, pp. 38–52. Even though this survey gave high rank to ethical

A survey of 186 manufacturing firms by the National Industrial Conference Board reported that seventy of them have issued written statements of ethical standards.[9] Most statements are concise, although they range up to a 100-page booklet. Among the means of distribution are employee handbooks, framed statements on walls, policy manuals, and bulletin boards. Smaller companies report that they have less need for formal written statements because mutual contact throughout the organization permits them to maintain standards informally.

Among names applied to written standards of conduct are "codes of ethics," "creeds," and "philosophies." Usually the latter two terms are more general, including basic philosophy and objectives as well as ethical standards. One survey of company creeds reported that the wording of the creed was usually drafted by the president (30 percent), by another senior officer (31 percent), or by committee (25 percent).[10] Less than 5 percent of the firms encouraged employees to participate in formulating the creed. The board chairman or president originated the idea of having a creed in 54 percent of the cases. Reasons given for developing a creed were:

1. To define the purpose of the company
2. To state moral and ethical principles underlying its actions
3. To establish a uniform climate within the business
4. To provide guides for managers so that their decisions would reflect the best interests of the business along with fairness and justice to all concerned

The same survey reported that 89 of the 103 creeds examined contain some reference to profit or return on investment. Most creeds also stated other objectives such as obligations to customers, the public, employees, suppliers, and society in general. What the creeds did not discuss was how these mutual and sometimes conflicting objectives could be balanced in actual operating conditions. Take a contemplated layoff as an example. Even though an executive implicitly knows he must consider employee responses and public attitudes concerning the layoff, along with its economic aspects, very little has been done to define explicitly how a manager weighs and balances these different values.

Written Statements of Creed. Let us review several business statements of creed in order to see what practices they cover and how they are

problems in the purchasing area, purchasing managers themselves gave low rank to ethical matters. When asked by a management training institute to "check those topics of greatest interest to you," they ranked ethics twenty-fifth among thirty-nine items. See William P. Stilwell, "Curriculum Planning for the Continuing Education of Purchasing Managers," *Journal of Purchasing*, August, 1965, p. 36.

[9] Sorrell M. Mathes and G. Clark Thompson, "Ensuring Ethical Conduct in Business," *The Conference Board Record*, December, 1964, pp. 17–27.

[10] Stewart Thompson, *Management Creeds and Philosophies*, New York: American Management Association Research Study 32, 1958.

phrased. First we shall review complete statements, and then we shall review statements on specific areas of practice, such as conflict of interest. Because of space limitations, the complete statements we have chosen are necessarily the shorter ones.

The following code of ethics of a metal stamping company illustrates the type of statement which emphasizes ethical ideals rather than business objectives. It states that business is a worthy vocation which serves society and that business can be conducted according to high standards of ethics.

CODE OF ETHICS OF A METAL STAMPING COMPANY

In the conduct of our business, day by day, our chief thought may well be directed to the acceptance of our due responsibilities and to the fulfillment of our varied duties in the hope that their accomplishment shall have helped to raise, in some measure, the level of human ideals and achievement. And to this end, it may prove helpful to us to hold before us these principles:

- That we consider our vocation worthy as affording us distinct opportunity to serve society.
- That we desire to improve ourselves, increase our efficiency, and enlarge our service, that by so doing we shall measure up to the highest standards of worth-while ambition.
- That the ambition to succeed is worth while, but that we desire no success that is not founded on the highest justice and morality.
- That the exchange of our product, our service, and our ideas for profit, is legitimate and ethical, provided that all parties in the exchange are benefitted thereby.
- That we believe that no success is legitimate or ethical which is secured by taking unfair advantage of certain opportunities which may be questionable.
- That we should so conduct our business that we may approach a perfect service, equal to or better than that of any competitor, and when we are in doubt, that we should give an added service beyond the strict measure of debt or obligation.
- That we believe in the universality of the Golden Rule— "All things whatsoever ye would that men should do unto you, do ye even so unto them"—and that so believing, its application to our daily endeavor shall prove helpful to us and of benefit to society.

SOURCE: Sorrell M. Mathes and G. Clark Thompson, "Ensuring Ethical Conduct in Business," *The Conference Board Record*, December, 1964, p. 18. Reproduced with permission.

It affirms that profit is legitimate ". . . provided that all parties in the exchange are benefitted thereby" but that taking unfair advantage of others is not a legitimate way to success. The Golden Rule is specifically offered as a guide in daily decisions.

Indeed, the stamping company code reflects a high standard of conduct compared with present standards in all types of organizations, both business and nonbusiness. In fact, if the word "profit" is amended to read something like "additional capital for growth," this code could apply to nonprofit organizations, government, community-service groups, and even religious organizations. All of them compete with regard to ideas, resources, and/or services, and they want that which they offer to be "equal to or better than that of any competitor." They also believe they are in a vocation which serves society.

The following creed of a small manufacturing company is limited to one paragraph. It stresses the Golden Rule and relates it to the three pillars of company service discussed in the preceding chapter—employees, customers, and investors.

FUNDAMENTAL PRINCIPLE OR CREED

Using the Golden Rule as a guide—to build an organization that will give *our associates* the best possible job opportunity, work satisfaction, happiness, and security; *our customers* a higher-quality product at a favorable price commensurate with good service before and after sale; *our stockholders* a reasonable continuing return on their investment—*and* conduct our affairs in such an efficient, capable, and friendly manner that everyone who comes in contact with us would be happy to become associated with us.

SOURCE: Stewart Thompson, *Management Creeds and Philosophies*, New York: American Management Association Research Study 32, 1958, p. 110.

The creed of management shown on page 110 gives more weight to company objectives as they apply to customers, investors, employees, and the community. It specifies services which the company expects to provide each of these groups. In its preamble it also affirms that the company exists to serve society through service to the groups mentioned.

Restraint of Trade. The creeds which have been presented give general standards for conduct; however, a number of other creeds are specific with regard to certain areas of practice. One of these areas is price collusion and restraint of trade. These acts are unlawful in the United States,

THE CREED OF MANAGEMENT

The goal of management is the optimum development of the opportunity to serve society, specifically the customers, the investors, the employees, and the community of the Charles Beck Machine Corporation.

To serve customers by:

1. Continually enhancing our knowledge of their and allied fields.
2. Analyzing their requirements, and providing products best adapted to their needs.
3. Producing products of maximum value, at the lowest practical prices.
4. Providing technical assistance and service facilities at all times in order to maintain maximum performance of our products.
5. Carrying on continuous research and development on new and existing products.

To serve investors by:

1. Obtaining highest profit potential.
2. Realizing over-all long-term growth, expansion, and diversification.

To serve employees by:

1. Encouraging and fostering individual advancement and high employee morale.
2. Giving each job meaning and dignity.
3. The appreciation that the employee's standards of living, security, and welfare are intimately linked with the welfare of the company.

To serve the community by:

1. Carrying the company's fair share of community financial responsibility.
2. Encouraging employee participation in worthwhile community endeavors and organizations.
3. Encouraging employee membership and participation in related technical and trade associations.

The attainment of these objectives will insure maximum realization of business leadership in a public trust.

SOURCE: Stewart Thompson, *Management Creeds and Philosophies,* New York: American Management Association Research Study 32, 1958, pp. 100–101. Reproduced with permission.

and also they strike at the philosophical heart of a free economic system. In the electrical equipment antitrust cases in 1961, Judge J. Cullen Ganey commented at the time of sentencing: "What is really at stake here is the survival of the kind of economy under which America has grown to greatness, the free enterprise system." [11]

The following code of ethics of Texas Instruments, Inc., an electronics manufacturer, is specific regarding price conspiracy. It also distinguishes between minimum standards of law and additional standards required by the company.

> It is unlawful in many countries and particularly in the U.S.A. to collaborate with competitors or anyone representing them for the purpose of establishing prices. TI's policy goes beyond the letter of the law and holds it to be unethical even to discuss prices with competitors at any time. Information that might affect prices must never be revealed to anyone outside of TI. Even within TI, such information must be limited to those with a need to know.
>
> It is also unethical and unlawful to collaborate with competitors or anyone representing them to restrain competition in other ways. Whenever one of us has any doubt as to whether a contemplated action may have the effect of restraining competition, he should consult TI legal counsel.
>
> SOURCE: *Ethics Is the Business of TI*, Dallas, Tex.: Texas Instruments, Inc., about 1963.

Appendix A at the end of this book gives the final report of the board of advice which Westinghouse Corporation employed to help it comply with law after price-conspiracy indictments in 1960. The report shows the immense effort which a large company must take to assure that its market activities comply with law. During fourteen months an economic and legal educational program directly reached 10,000 management persons. Many managers apparently need economic education because their background has not provided it. In our society of many technical and liberal arts graduates, persons frequently reach executive levels without ever having a course in basic economics or marketing, and most executives have never had a course in economics of competition. In spite of talk about a business civilization, our universities are not oriented toward providing most of their graduates with a strong foundation in economics. Consequently, when a manager faces complex market situations, he may not know the implications of his actions. And perhaps worse, his background in the philosophy of economic competition may be so weak that he does not support the law encouraging competition. In the case of Westinghouse, the board of advice recommended that the company plan and administer a

---

[11] "The Business of Business," *Industrial Management Review*, Massachusetts Institute of Technology, Cambridge, Mass., May, 1961, p. 3.

program of education "in the economics of competition" as explained in Appendix A.

Conflict of Interest. Another area having specific standards is conflict of interest. A conflict of interest arises when an employee, either management or nonmanagement, has an interest in a transaction or is a party to a transaction that is so substantial that it reasonably might affect his independent judgment in his acts for the business. Both purchasing and sales are special areas of sensitivity, but the situation could exist anywhere.

One area of conflict of interest is substantial financial investment in a supplier, customer, or distributor. Usually it is acceptable to hold a small percentage of stock in a publicly owned supplier, especially when it is listed on a public stock exchange. The permitted amount of ownership varies. In one company it is 10 percent of outstanding stock; in another it is one-tenth of 1 percent. Another criterion is what percentage of the employee's total investment funds is involved in this one investment. Some companies require key executives and purchasing agents to disclose outside business interests. One company's standard reads as follows: "Any member of management who has assumed, or is about to assume, a financial or other outside business relationship that might involve a conflict of interest must immediately inform his supervisor of the circumstances involved." [12]

Another possible area of conflict of interest is business gifts, particularly those which are of more than nominal value. Generally nominal advertising items with the donor's name imprinted thereon are excluded from regulation. One survey reported that over two-thirds of responding companies have policies restricting employee acceptance of gifts. One quite specific policy states:[13]

> Our employees may accept Christmas and other gifts from suppliers and others only when the gifts are
> 1. of nominal value, i.e., less than $10.00 retail value
> 2. not an intoxicating beverage
> 3. received from a supplier with whom there is an existing business relationship
> 4. received by an employee who has a direct relationship with the supplier
> 5. received by not more than two employees
> 6. not given oftener than annually in the absence of special circumstances
> 7. given under circumstances where the objectivity of a purchasing decision will not be influenced.

The giving of gifts other than nominal advertising-imprint items appears to be declining, especially in larger public corporations. The survey

[12] Mathes and Thompson, *op. cit.*, p. 21.
[13] *Ibid.*, pp. 23–24.

just mentioned reported that 60 percent of respondents give no gifts and that a number of others have reduced gift giving.[14]

Entertainment of customers and suppliers is usually defined separately from gifts and is a common practice in business. One company informally distinguishes entertaining from gift giving as follows: "If you can eat it or drink it on the spot, it's entertainment." According to this definition a ham dinner costing $10 at an expensive club is permitted entertainment, but a $10 ham given to an employee is a prohibited gift. Entertainment is generally controlled through expense-account policies and rules.

Another area of conflict of interest is the use of privileged information or one's official position to make transactions for personal gain. An example is the purchase or sale of real estate whose value might be affected by company activities.

In its totality, conflict of interest is difficult to control because of its many variations and dependence on personal interpretation. For these reasons, the most effective approach is self-discipline by ethically oriented individuals; however, management needs to provide a basic code to encourage uniform action and to provide follow-up to assure that a few unprincipled persons do not pull down the whole level of ethical practice. In the last analysis, a company's conduct can never be better than its people.

Considering creeds as a whole, one weakness is that they are sometimes stated for their public relations value and not really made an expectation in the company. One of the greatest limitations of creeds is that those who prepare them assume that the meaning and feeling shared at the time they are written can be transferred to others by distributing a document for others to read. This is not so. Ethical codes are too complex and full of values to be conveyed in a few written words. For this reason, businesses use participation in planning the code in order to build more understanding and commitment to it. In addition, reevaluations in which there is wide participation will help maintain standards. Equal in importance with participation is the necessity for higher managers to support the code by example, because the standards they set will tend to be the ones others use, regardless of what the written statement says.

ETHICAL CODES BY PROFESSIONAL AND ADVISORY GROUPS

Business standards are indirectly set by external forces. Occupational groups set codes of conduct for their members who work in business, and public groups pronounce standards which they wish business to follow.

Professional Codes of Ethics. As occupational groups professionalize, they tend to develop codes of conduct which support fairness, full disclosure, independent decisions free of influence, and other action in the

[14] *Ibid.*, pp. 25–26.

public interest. These codes govern the conduct of their members in business and thereby determine a minimum standard of conduct in their area of the business. Sometimes their codes spill over into surrounding functions and eventually become adopted by the whole business. The standards for buying and selling sponsored by the National Association of Purchasing Agents (NAPA), for example, surely encouraged the growth of companywide policies on gift giving and gift acceptance. The NAPA standards are shown below.

STANDARDS FOR BUYING AND SELLING SPONSORED BY THE NATIONAL ASSOCIATION OF PURCHASING AGENTS

Unnecessary sales and purchasing expense is an economic waste—a tax on legitimate industry. Its elimination will assure satisfactory profits to the producer, economy to the consumer, and greater efficiency in commercial relations.

We recognize that the concern which buys must also sell, that buying and selling are companionate functions, that sound commercial transactions must be mutually profitable, and that co-operation between buyer and seller will reduce the cost of purchasing, sales and distribution with consequent benefits to industry as a whole.

In furtherance of these principles, we subscribe to the following standards in our buying and selling:

1. To buy and sell on the basis of value, recognizing that value represents that combination of quality, service and price which assures greatest ultimate economy to the user.

2. To respect our obligations and neither expressly nor impliedly to promise a performance which we cannot reasonably expect to fulfill.

3. To avoid misrepresentation and sharp practice in our purchases and sales, recognizing that permanent business relations can be maintained only on a structure of honesty and fair dealing.

4. To be courteous and considerate to those with whom we deal, to be prompt and businesslike in our appointments, and to carry on negotiations with all reasonable expedition so as to avoid trespassing on the rights of others to the time of buyers and salesmen.

5. To avoid statements tending to injure or discredit a legitimate competitor, and to divulge no information acquired in confidence with the intent of giving or receiving an unfair advantage in a competitive business transaction.

6. To strive for simplification and standardization within the bounds of utility and industrial economy, and to further the development of products and methods which will improve industrial efficiency.

7. To recognize that character is the greatest asset in commerce, and to give it major consideration in the selection of customers and sources of supply.

8. To adjust claims and settle disputes on the basis of facts and fairness, to submit the facts to arbitration if a mutual agreement cannot be reached, to abide by the decision of the arbiters and to resort to legal measures in commercial disputes only when the preceding courses prove ineffective.

9. To provide or accept no gifts or entertainment in the guise of sales expense, where the intent or effect is to unduly prejudice the recipient in favor of the donor as against legitimate competitors.

10. To give or receive no bribes, in the form of money or otherwise, in any commercial transaction, and to expose commercial bribery wherever encountered for the purpose of maintaining the highest standard of ethics in industry.

With regard to conflict of interest, engineers generally have codes prohibiting practices of this type. Selected portions of the guide to professional practice of the American Society of Civil Engineers indicate how the code applies to conflict of interest:[15]

Article 1: (1) He [the civil engineer] shall not undertake any assignment which would create a potential conflict of interest between the engineer and his client or his employer. . . .
Article 2: It shall be considered unprofessional . . . to accept remuneration for services rendered other than from his client or his employer. . . .
Article 9: (3) He shall not create obligation on prospective clients or employers through extravagant entertainment, gifts, or similar expenditures. (4) He shall not engage in "fee splitting" or other distribution of fees for other than services performed and in proportion to the value of such services. . . .

Observe that the items shown, especially Article 9, apply to the civil engineer in the business role of seeking consulting contracts as well as in the regular role of professional engineering employee. In this manner business conduct is governed directly by codes of professional associations, as well as indirectly.

Advertising is another occupation where standards of practices have been established. This occupation has perhaps greater public visibility than any other business group. The Advertising Code of American Business, shown below, was developed jointly by the Advertising Federation of the West and the Advertising Federation of America. The code was ap-

[15] *Guide to Professional Practice under the Code of Ethics*, New York: American Society of Civil Engineers, 1964.

proved by both groups in 1964, and later in the year it was endorsed by the American Association of Advertising Agencies. The code deals specifically with a number of advertising practices in an effort to encourage advertising truth, responsibility, public decency, bona fide offers and guaran-

THE ADVERTISING CODE
OF AMERICAN BUSINESS

We hold that advertising has a responsibility to inform and serve the American public and to further the economic life of this nation. Believing this, the following principles are hereby affirmed.

1. **Truth**
   Advertising shall tell the truth, and shall reveal material facts, the concealment of which might mislead the public.

2. **Responsibility**
   Advertising agencies and advertisers shall be willing to provide substantiation of claims made.

3. **Taste and Decency**
   Advertising shall be free of statements, illustrations, or implications which are offensive to good taste or public decency.

4. **Disparagement**
   Advertising shall offer merchandise or service on its merits, and refrain from attacking competitors or disparaging their products, services or methods of doing business.

5. **Bait Advertising**
   Advertising shall be bona fide and the merchandise or service offered shall be readily available for purchase at the advertised price.

6. **Guarantees and Warranties**
   Advertising of guarantees and warranties shall be explicit. Advertising of any guarantee or warranty shall clearly and conspicuously disclose its nature and extent, the manner in which the guarantor or warrantor will perform and the identity of the guarantor or warrantor.

7. **Price Claims**
   Advertising shall avoid price or savings claims which are unsupported by facts or which do not offer bona fide bargains or savings.

8. **Unprovable Claims**
   Advertising shall avoid the use of exaggerated or unprovable claims.

9. **Testimonials**
   Advertising containing testimonials shall be limited to those of competent witnesses who are reflecting a real and honest choice.

tees, and fair-price claims. This code represents a strong move toward social responsibility on the part of the advertising profession.

It appears that preparation of codes of ethics by occupational groups, especially professional groups, is one of the best ways of developing higher standards of business conduct. Even though the influence of these codes is mostly indirect, it is becoming powerful. Since professional codes are developed democratically by those who must live by them, they earn strong commitment from members. Their image is favorable because they are a means to more status and public recognition for the occupation. Originating with many groups, these codes offer avenues for experimentation and variety in the search for better standards of conduct. They can work their way piece by piece into organizational life, proving their value as they go. Reformers would have businesses suddenly change into ethical models by edict from the president, but conversions of this type seldom stick. The democratic gradualism represented by professional codes of ethics will tend to be more lasting. These codes are not substitutes for internal codes within each organization, but they are an important adjunct to them. In a number of cases they serve as a stimulus to a business to develop better internal codes.

Codes Offered by Advisory Groups. External advisory groups also offer to business a variety of codes which they want it to adopt. There is a significant difference between professional and advisory groups. The professional groups are self-generating a code for their own self-control, both in business and out of it. They seek to raise *their* standards. Advisory groups, on the other hand, offer to raise the standards of *others*. They say to business: "This is the way we think you ought to live if you want to live better." Usually they do not offer evidence that they follow these standards in their own organizations, such as foundations, religious-action groups, and universities. And frequently their views represent special pleading for a certain philosophy.

The fact that advice arises externally does not make it improper or unwise. Much that is offered to business is useful, and businessmen would do well to heed it, but it is of a different order. It lacks the reality that being on the inside can bring. It lacks the personal commitment that self-generated standards for one's *self* can bring. Sometimes it has the taint of the ivory tower because it comes from the "sayers" not the "doers." And the sayers may be the last to adopt the code themselves, usually because they feel their situation is different. A foundation, for example, may object to economic layoffs, but when its own income drops, it makes layoffs, which it wants private business not to do. Or a social-action group which discovers a disloyal employee may dismiss him or drive him away, even though it does not want "business" to do so in a similar situation.

In this section we shall give a brief sample of the multitude of codes offered business in order to illustrate the variety of views involved.

Following the electrical conspiracy indictments of 1960, the United States Secretary of Commerce appointed a Business Ethics Advisory Council which convened for the first time on May 17, 1961. Its purpose was to explore "some approaches to the development of ethical guidelines that might be useful to the business community" and to encourage businessmen toward self-regulation. Strictly speaking, this council was not a group of businessmen working for self-regulation, for over half the committee consisted of educators, clergymen, and journalists. Some businessmen were on the committee. This council issued a call for better self-regulation and pointed out six areas for self-evaluation: general understanding of ethical issues, compliance with law, conflicts of interest, entertainment and gift expenses, customers and suppliers, and social responsibilities. The council offered a brief "Statement on Business Ethics and a Call for Action," which concluded as follows:[16]

> A weighty responsibility therefore rests upon all those who manage business enterprises, as well as upon all others who influence the environment in which business operates. In the final analysis, however, the primary moral duty to establish high ethical standards and adequate procedures for their enforcement in each enterprise must rest with its policy-making body—its board of directors and its top management.
>
> We, therefore, now propose that current efforts be expanded and intensified and that new efforts now be undertaken by the American business community to hasten its attainment of those high ethical standards that derive from our heritage and traditions. We urge all enterprises, business groups, and associations to accept responsibility—each for itself and in its own most appropriate way—to develop methods and programs for encouraging and sustaining these efforts on a continuous basis. We believe in this goal, we accept it, and we encourage all to pursue its attainment.

Economic research and educational groups are also important influences on business practice. One of the best known is the American Economic Foundation, established in 1939. It has been especially active in economic education about market economics and economic freedoms. It reports that during the twelve years ending in 1962, its materials were used in economic training programs for 3½ million employees. Here are two examples of basic principles it presents which tend to influence business values and practices:[17]

[16] Business Ethics Advisory Council, A *Statement of Business Ethics and a Call for Action*, Washington, D.C.: U.S. Department of Commerce, no date. See also Theodore L. Thau, "The Business Ethics Advisory Council: An Organization for the Improvement of Ethical Performance," in Arthur S. Miller (ed.), *The Ethics of Business Enterprise*, Philadelphia: The American Academy of Political and Social Science, *The Annals*, vol. 343, September, 1962, pp. 128–141.

[17] *The Ten Pillars of Economic Wisdom*, New York: The American Economic Foundation, no date.

In our modern exchange economy, all payroll and employment come from customers, and the only worthwhile job security is customer security; if there are no customers, there can be no payroll and no jobs. . . .

The greatest good for the greatest number means, in its material sense, the greatest goods for the greatest number which, in turn, means the greatest productivity per worker.

At the opposite end of the continuum is the National Council of the Churches of Christ, organized and primarily supported by the central offices of liberal Protestant churches. It holds conferences, supports study groups, and issues reports. It gives religious backing to certain views in a way that individual churches could not do because of differences in theology within their membership. Generally its work has criticized the free market and business practices. Orientation has been toward uniform ethical practice and general welfare, often idealistically bypassing economic realities. In its statements it is often interpreted in the public press as speaking *for* its member churches; however, it maintains that it speaks independently *to* them and to the public.[18]

Universities in their classrooms and publications also offer many ethical standards to business. Here is a brief code, offered by a faculty member, which drew favorable response at a business conference:[19]

The professional manager affirms that he will place the interest of his company before his own private interests.

He will place his duty to society above his duty to his company and above his private interest.

He has a duty to reveal the facts in any situation where his private interests are involved with those of his company, or where the interests of his company are involved with those of society.

He must subscribe wholeheartedly to the belief that when business managers follow this code of conduct, the profit motive is the best incentive of all for the development of a dynamic economy.

BUSINESS ASSOCIATIONS

Some business associations are organized in terms of a specific purpose, such as the Committee for Economic Development (CED). It is a select group of 200 business leaders, including some educators. It is nonprofit, nonpartisan, and nonpolitical. It seeks to unite scholarship with business judgment in analyzing issues and developing recommendations to

[18] An example of its work is *In Search of Maturity in Industrial Relations*, New York: National Council of the Churches of Christ, Department of the Church and Economic Life, 1960.

[19] "A Positive Code of Ethics," *Business Week*, June 17, 1961, p. 166, code presented by Robert W. Austin.

resolve economic problems. Since it does make concrete recommendations, it offers values to both businessmen and the general public. Generally its reports and recommendations are thorough and of good quality. They represent carefully developed viewpoints oriented toward general public benefit rather than partisan needs of business. The CED makes recommendations in all areas of economic life, including international business and public-policy issues such as economic growth.

The CED states its basic objectives as follows:[20]

1. To develop, through objective research and discussion, findings and recommendations for business and public policy which will contribute to the preservation and strengthening of our free society, and to the maintenance of high employment, increasing productivity and living standards, greater economic stability and greater opportunity for all our people.

2. To bring about increasing public understanding of the importance of these objectives and the ways in which they can be achieved.

The CED represents primarily a *managerial ideology*, the kind found among professional managers in larger businesses. It accepts Keynesian economics and government intervention in the free market.[21] It

. . . deemphasizes the traditional forces of supply and demand as determining prices in the competitive market and stresses more the composite group decision making of government, business, labor, and the public consumer. It argues that management is a trustee who serves the interest of all groups, taking account of more than just the concern of his own stockholders for profits.

Somewhat different from the CED is the National Association of Manufacturers (NAM). Representing most manufacturers, its membership is much larger than that of the CED; however, the CED represents a broader business segment because it includes nonmanufacturers such as bankers and insurance executives. Compared with the managerial ideology of the CED, the NAM ideology represents the *classical business ideology* of free markets with minimum interference by government and labor. It supports free competition, with individual producers and consumers determining economic activities by means of their aggregate decisions.

Because of the NAM's economic position, labor unions have usually chosen it as their whipping boy in union publicity and public speeches. To unions the NAM is the image of old-fashioned greed and avarice. Favoring a free market, the NAM would prohibit union activity which

---

[20] *The Committee for Economic Development*, New York: Committee for Economic Development, 1961.

[21] R. Joseph Monsen, Jr., and Mark W. Cannon, *The Makers of Public Policy: American Power Groups and Their Ideologies*, New York: McGraw-Hill Book Company, 1965, p. 47.

PRINCIPLES OF FREEDOM OF ACTION

Freedom of action is our way of life. Our progress has been founded on individual initiative, ingenuity, and freedom of action. A free competitive economy is based on individual ambition which is the most universal, reliable and powerful of human motives.

The principles of freedom of action recognize that individuals know their own wants best and that human dignity requires that free men should not have their wants dictated by others. Freedom of action is based, therefore, on individual decisions and voluntary agreements and not on commands and obedience. It recognizes that the individual producer is best qualified to make sound decisions concerning his business problems, and that the aggregate of such decisions as tested in the free market results in wiser solutions of the economic problems of society than would decisions imposed by any outside agency.

Nevertheless a Government of law is necessary to guarantee freedom of action, to encourage individual initiative and to settle conflicts. It is an essential condition of freedom of action that the methods of competition must be peaceful and honest.

We stand for a nation of free people, free to act, work and choose. We are opposed to monopoly in the fields of production and distribution, whether it be a monopoly of capital, of labor, or of government. A free society within a dynamic economy where the welfare of each citizen depends primarily upon his own ability, industry and thrift has been shown by experience to be the best way to create large real national income and to promote social, material and technological progress. A society built on these principles is eminently able to make adequate provisions for those of its citizens who through no fault of their own are unable to provide for themselves, in such a way as not to diminish the individual's sense of responsibility for his own welfare. This is the fundamental philosophy upon which our way of life was founded and adherence to its precepts constitutes our best guarantee for the future.

SOURCE: *NAM: 1964 Viewpoints*, New York: National Association of Manufacturers, 1964, p. vi.

tries to force persons to join unions, including boycotts and violence. This position prohibits closed and union shops and supports right-to-work laws. In further support of the free market and equal treatment before the law, the NAM believes that the Sherman Antitrust Act should apply to unions also. The statement of principles by the NAM, given above, accurately reflects its economic philosophy. The code of practice which it recommends to its members is shown below.

🔲🔲🔲🔲🔲🔲🔲🔲🔲🔲🔲🔲🔲🔲🔲🔲🔲🔲🔲🔲🔲🔲🔲🔲🔲🔲🔲🔲🔲

CODE OF BUSINESS PRACTICES

While there can be no question as to the right of American citizens to engage in private business under our Constitution and form of government, this right like all rights has accompanying responsibilities. Business organizations must serve the public interest, as separate entities and in the over-all sense, if this right is to be respected and maintained.

NAM and its member companies are committed to policies and practices which will strengthen faith in our free economy and inspire public confidence in our business enterprises and those who manage them.

All members of the Association are urged to subscribe to the official CODE OF BUSINESS PRACTICES adopted by the Board of Directors, which is as follows:

1. We will strive at all times to conduct the affairs of this company to merit public confidence in American business and industry and faith in our free private competitive enterprise system.

2. We will see that our employees are given every opportunity to progress with the company and are appropriately compensated for their work.

3. We will deal fairly with customers and suppliers and extend to them the same treatment we wish to receive ourselves.

4. We will compete vigorously to serve our customers and expand our business, but we will avoid unfair or unethical practices.

5. We will seek through sound management practices to produce the profit necessary to the continued progress of the business and so fulfill our responsibilities to our stockholders, employees, customers, community and nation.

SOURCE: *NAM: 1964 Viewpoints*, New York: National Association of Manufacturers, 1964, p. iv.

🔲🔲🔲🔲🔲🔲🔲🔲🔲🔲🔲🔲🔲🔲🔲🔲🔲🔲🔲🔲🔲🔲🔲🔲🔲🔲🔲🔲🔲

The association which represents more businesses than any other is the Chamber of Commerce of the United States. Its affiliated local chambers of commerce are active in most communities. Representing all businesses, it is concerned primarily with the general development of commerce in all its forms. It makes some policy declarations, and these usually stand between the views of the CED and the NAM.

There are hundreds of other business associations, usually representing a specific group of tradesmen, such as florists, retail druggists, or automobile dealers. We have given only a sample to represent the range of ideologies, for each has its own separate philosophy and standards. Research discloses that these associations develop and grow primarily by promoting the mutual interests of the groups they serve. They continue to flourish to the extent that they can keep their methods and objectives congruent with ever-changing psychological, sociological, and economic forces in society.[22]

Considered as a whole, the public image of business associations has been only fair. They have had minimal success in presenting to the public the advantages of a free market. While the public has tended to listen attentively to farm, educational, and labor groups when they present their ideas, the public has tended to label business views as "special interest" and partially to close them out. One reason is that business often fails to present its ideas in terms of the public interest. Another is effective negative labeling of its ideas by business critics. No other major public group has been subjected to as much negative labeling as business, such as "Robber Barons," "antiunion," and "self-interest." With regard to self-interest, there seems to be a popular assumption that businessmen always act in their self-interest but that few other people do! This hardly agrees with historical evidence or psychological research.

SUMMARY

Standards for business conduct exist in any culture; hence, the question is not whether to have them, but how to establish and apply them intelligently. Surveys show that people in business activities have an interest in ethical guides. Unethical activities most mentioned are gift giving, bribery, unfair pricing, and misleading advertising. Seventy-one percent of businessmen in one survey favored a self-developed code, and only 10 percent opposed it. Another survey reported that over 40 percent of businesses had a written code, usually originated by top management.

Business creeds emphasize basic ethical ideas such as the Golden Rule, and they include statements of responsibility to the claimants on business, especially employees, customers, investors, and the general public. They also make statements about certain practices such as price conspiracy, compliance with law, conflict of interest, gift giving, and entertainment.

Business standards have been helped by ethical codes of occupational groups. Being self-generated, these codes earn strong commitment and affect business both indirectly and directly. Codes originated by advisory groups vary widely in economic viewpoint. This variation plus their external origin reduces their influence.

Business associations also range widely in their views, rather than presenting a single business ideology. Considered as a whole, their public image is deficient. Reasons include failure to present ideas in terms of public interest and negative labels attached to their ideas by others.

[22] Desmond D. Martin, "The American Trade and Business Association: A Study of Its Growth, Structure, and Functions in the Emergent American Society," *Academy of Management Journal*, March, 1965, pp. 55–56. (Abstract.)

QUESTIONS

1. How do businessmen feel about having business codes of ethics or creeds? What reasons do they give for having one?

2. Discuss the kinds of ideas covered in business codes of ethics and creeds.

3. What is conflict of interest, and what aspects of it are covered in creeds?

4. Discuss the application of occupational codes of ethics to business. What is the difference between occupational codes and codes originated by advisory groups?

5. Compare the managerial ideology of the CED with the classical business ideology of the NAM.

6. Identify the following: National Association of Purchasing Agents; Westinghouse Corporation, Board of Advice; Business Ethics Advisory Council; Committee for Economic Development.

CHAPTER 7 THE INDIVIDUAL AND THE ORGANIZATION

> Oneness, they say, creates harmony. But with one-
> ness, flabbiness and decay may also come.
>
> WILLIAM G. SCOTT[1]

> *It is our hypothesis that the incongruence between
> the individual and the organization can provide the
> basis for a continued challenge which, as it is fulfilled,
> will help man to enhance his own growth and to de-
> velop organizations that will be viable and effective.*
>
> CHRIS ARGYRIS[2]

The contest between man and organization is as old as organized society. Man has a drive for freedom and self-actualization, while the organization needs coordination and control to unify effort toward objectives. From time to time in the history of society the pendulum has swung toward either man or the organization. In the first half of this century the trend was toward oneness in the organization, but as suggested by the first quotation introducing this chapter, oneness has its problems. The modern trend is more toward man, the aim being to produce a balanced relationship between man and the organization, as stated in the second quotation opening this chapter.

This chapter will discuss man's struggle to make his organizations viable and satisfying. It will cover the development of the organization

[1] William G. Scott, *The Social Ethic in Management Literature*, Atlanta, Ga.: Georgia State College of Business Administration, Studies in Business and Economics Bulletin 4, 1959, p. 98.

[2] Chris Argyris, *Integrating the Individual and the Organization*, New York: John Wiley & Sons, Inc., 1964, p. 7.

125

man, tendencies toward conformity in both formal and informal organization, and rights to privacy. It will also examine various business practices which tend either to develop organization men or to lead toward self-determination by each employee.

THE ORGANIZATION MAN

In 1956 William H. Whyte, Jr., published *The Organization Man*, which defined in modern terms the eternal struggle of man and his organizations. Whyte stated that a new social ethic had developed that rationalizes the organization's demands for wholehearted dedication and loyalty. According to Whyte:[3]

By social ethic I mean that contemporary body of thought that makes morally legitimate the pressures of society against the individual. Its major propositions are three: a belief in the group as the source of creativity; a belief in "belongingness" as the ultimate need of the individual; and a belief in the application of science to achieve the belongingness. . . . Essentially it is a utopian faith. . . . It is quite reminiscent of the beliefs of utopian communities of the 1840s.

The social ethic is, according to Whyte, an ideology provided by intellectuals, not by the organization. To take an example, one author states that the individual is really an "interchangeable unit of infinitesimal importance." He explains:[4]

Looked at rationally and from outside, that is exactly what he is, and from this point of view it seems positively absurd to go on talking about the value or meaning of the individual. Indeed, one can hardly imagine how one ever came to endow individual human life with so much dignity when the truth to the contrary is as plain as the palm of your hand.

Whyte goes on to state that it is the ideas of the intellectuals, not their goodwill, that he questions. Further: "The fault is not in organization, in short; it is in our worship of it." Man "is imprisoned in brotherhood." The people he is talking about "belong" to the organization. They are the ones ". . . who have left home, spiritually as well as physically, to take the vows of organization life." [5]

Whyte offered a powerful indictment of personality testing, bureaucracy, and conformity. He even offered an appendix entitled "How to

[3] William H. Whyte, Jr., *The Organization Man*, New York: Simon and Schuster, Inc., 1956, p. 7.

[4] C. G. Jung, *The Undiscovered Self*, translated from the German by R. F. C. Hull, Boston: Atlantic Monthly Press, Little, Brown and Company, 1958, p. 16. Jung merely states the viewpoint quoted; he does not support it.

[5] Whyte, *op. cit.*, pp. 3, 12, 13.

Cheat on Personality Tests." To Whyte, man's answer to the social ethic should be to fight the organization, but not self-destructively.

In 1957 Chris Argyris published *Personality and Organization*, which further defined the conflict between man and the organization. Argyris dealt particularly with psychological problems of work, such as alienation, frustration, and suppression of self-actualization. He contended that there is a lack of congruence between the needs of healthy employees and formal organization. They want independence; it wants dependence. The result of this conflict is frustration, a sense of failure, and loss of self-esteem. The waste of productive resources is bad enough, but what is worse from the point of view of social responsibility is the person's almost passive capitulation to destruction of his own drives and self-image. He finally comes to the point where he, too, defends organizational aggrandizement!

The basic philosophy in Argyris's own words is as follows:[6]

> An analysis of the basic properties of relatively mature human beings and formal organization leads to the conclusion that there is an inherent incongruency between the self-actualization of the two. This basic incongruency creates a situation of conflict, frustration, and failure for the participants. . . .

Interpreting the Organization Man. The views of Whyte and Argyris have sometimes been interpreted as a conflict for ultimate victory which either man or the organization must win. This interpretation is an erroneous extension of the Whyte-Argyris thesis. Neither they nor most others who write on this subject have advocated that mankind should return to cave civilization in order to live without organization. Nor do they reject organization and choose a sort of social anarchy. They recognize that the existing conflict is not an ultimate one, but simply a challenge toward better resolution of competing interests. Man needs the organization, and, with some exceptions, he comes to it voluntarily. Their plea is not to abolish it. They simply want the organization to serve man, rather than the other way around.

The organization-man thesis is often interpreted as an attack on business, compared with other organizations. This is not so. Business has no special problem. No evidence has been offered that business seeks or creates organization men more than the military, government, or even the slum street gang. The issue of the organization man is universal with regard to both type of employing organization and type of national culture. Whyte says: "This conflict is certainly not a peculiarly American development," and he adds with a flourish:[7]

---

[6] Chris Argyris, *Personality and Organization: The Conflict between the System and the Individual,* New York: Harper & Row, Publishers, Incorporated, 1957, p. 175.

[7] Whyte, *op. cit.,* p. 3.

Blood brother to the business trainee off to join Du Pont is the seminary student who will end up in the church hierarchy, the doctor headed for the corporate clinic, the physics Ph.D. in a government laboratory, the intellectual on the foundation-sponsored team project, the engineering graduate in the huge drafting room at Lockheed, the young apprentice in a Wall Street law factory.

Those who present the organization-man hypothesis deserve credit for bringing public attention to a significant problem. They usually, however, apply the rules of debate to present their own special views, without full disclosure of arguments on the opposite side. There is much evidence to limit or reject this organization-man hypothesis. It is filled with strong value judgments not proved by research.[8]

One erroneous value judgment is the assumption that men universally desire self-actualization and opportunity to create. Actually, men find fulfillment under all sorts of conditions. Some desire routine work which leaves their minds free to dream. Others like the challenge of heavy physical labor. Still others want the guidance of a firm authority because they feel more free to act when solid boundaries are set. Some, it is admitted, do need creative opportunities. "This is not to say that the individual does not have needs for creativity, independence, activity. It is saying that man may have equally strong needs for destructiveness, dependence, and passivity." [9] Whatever the extent of a certain man's creative needs, we invoke a value judgment when we say that he should satisfy those needs on the job. Work is not necessarily the central life interest of everyone. Some prefer to meet their creative needs through community work, family, social organizations, hobbies, and so on.

Another unproved value judgment is that the situation is getting worse, not better, and so an alarm must be sounded. It is true that modern man does have problems with organizations, but he is better off than he was in the days of feudalism or slavery or in an early English factory. It is also true that modern factories do routinize certain tasks, but these few tasks must be offset against the millions of jobs technology has made less routine, such as picking cotton or pulling oar in a galley. "In all probability . . . in modern society there is far greater scope for skill and craftsmanship than in any previous society, and . . . far more people are in a position to use such skills." [10] In addition, modern technology has created a host of new occupational roles, thereby expanding the quantity

---

[8] George Strauss, "The Personality-versus-organization Theory," in Leonard R. Sayles, *Individualism and Big Business*, New York: McGraw-Hill Book Company, 1963, pp. 67–80.

[9] Warren G. Bennis, "Leadership Theory and Administrative Behavior: The Problem of Authority," *Administrative Science Quarterly*, December, 1959, p. 279.

[10] J. A. C. Brown, *The Social Psychology of Industry*, Harmondsworth, England: Penguin Books, Ltd., 1954, p. 207.

of roles available to employees. Since each person is different, the expanded role choices provide a better chance for each person to find his special fulfilling niche at work.[11] And as a further fact, automation is decreasing routine jobs. Considering all these factors, man's alienation from the organization may be declining.

The value judgment that conflict and frustration are all bad is also in error. Man develops through challenge. His learning depends somewhat on frustration. The first sentence of this chapter refers to the "contest between man and organization" in order to bypass the negative implications of conflict. Certainly a contest can be healthful. It is the way democratic elections are held. And when two groups engage in a sports contest, both expect to benefit even though only one has the winning score. In other words, a conflict properly contained can be a challenge and a basis of growth, as Argyris points out in the quotation introducing this chapter. It is myth to assume that tension and frustration are undesirable. They are needed for challenge and growth, and through these they bring psychological rewards.[12]

A value judgment sometimes implied in the organization-man hypothesis is that bigness is at the root of the problem. It is assumed that if we could splinter organizations into small pieces, thereby diffusing authority, harmony would again prevail. With smaller organizations, man would be proportionately stronger, and power would be equalized. However, some analysts believe that big organizations diffuse power through decentralization to more than offset centralization of certain functions. One observer comments: "The result of bigness is actually a diffusion of the decision-making and decision-influencing process far beyond the wildest dreams of those worshipers at the shrine of Louis Brandeis, who wanted to keep power diffused by keeping the units of society small." [13]

Research discloses that the accusing finger pointed at bigness is actually pointing in the wrong direction. A survey of 1,916 managers reported that more organization men were in the smaller companies. They gave less emphasis to forcefulness, imagination, and independence, but more emphasis to caution and tact. In addition, emphasis on conformity came not from the executive suite but from lower management in these companies.[14]

Considering both sides of the issue, we see that the organization man is not an ultimate flaw likely to bring business crumbling down; instead,

[11] Keith Davis, "Individual Needs and Automation," *Academy of Management Journal*, December, 1963, p. 281.

[12] David W. Ewing, "Tension Can Be an Asset," *Harvard Business Review*, September–October, 1964, pp. 71–78.

[13] Harlan Cleveland, "Dinosaurs and Personal Freedom," *Saturday Review*, Feb. 28, 1959, p. 12.

[14] "Tracking Conformity to Its Business Lair," *Business Week*, Feb. 27, 1965, p. 74.

he represents one of many challenges. Intelligent resolution of the organization man's needs will bring positive payoffs for both man and the organization.

Conformity. Implicit in the organization-man hypothesis is the idea that man is required to conform to the organization, rather than the other way around. In reality, each adjusts to the other. Adjustment is reached through a fusion process defined as the ". . . *simultaneous* operation of the *socializing process* by which the organization seeks to make an agent of the individual for the achievement of organizational objectives, and of the *personalizing process* by which the individual seeks to make an agency of the organization for the achievement of his personal objectives." [15]

Recognizing that some conformity exists, it is then appropriate to ask how it arose and in what way it applies. Figure 7-1 presents a projected system of the legitimacy of organizational influence as typical employees might view it. The higher an item is in the system, the more probability there is that employees will question the right of management to influence them on that item. The system shows that some pressure for conformity arises externally from requirements of law and from community culture and that this is merely transmitted by business. But other pressures are originated by the organization. For these we need to ask whether they are simply required as a means toward group coordination or whether they are, indeed, more substantive. We are all acquainted with the traffic light, which does require a sort of conformity but the purpose of which is to create sufficient order to permit all to proceed toward destinations of their own free choice and along routes freely chosen.

Substantive conformity may be either of action or of thought. If of action, it may be on the job or off the job, as shown in Figure 7-1. For off-the-job conduct, the organization can attempt to influence by means of educational programs, hobby groups, and communications, but what about its right to use disciplinary power to enforce its desires? We can begin with the premise that it cannot use its disciplinary power to regulate employee conduct off the job; however, the line of separation is difficult to draw. What about a petroleum employee living on a company pumping site and on twenty-four-hour call? But even when an employee has departed company property and is not on call, the boundaries of employer interest are still not fixed. Consider the employee who waited until his foreman left the plant and then struck him several times in the presence of other employees. In cases of this type arbitrators have consistently upheld company disciplinary action because the altercation was job-related. In the United States at least, the organization's jurisdictional line is clearly functional, related to the total job system and not the property line.

[15] E. W. Bakke, *The Fusion Process*, New Haven, Conn.: Yale University, Labor and Management Center, 1955, p. 5.

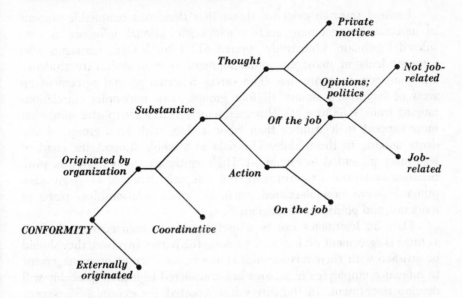

Key: The higher the item, the more likely the legitimacy of influence will be questioned

Figure 7-1 Legitimacy of organizational influence; projected value scale for typical employees.

One study of sixty-six arbitration awards found a number of ways in which off-the-job conduct could be involved in disciplinary action.[16] In addition to job-related fighting, just described, conduct which damages organizational reputation or business interests is subject to discipline. This factor has been significant in public-service employment such as bus driving and news editing where reputation is likely to affect customer acceptance. In other instances, off-the-job conduct may show that the employee is unfit for his present responsibility. In one case a plant guard pulled a gun in an after-hours fight, and this action was held to indicate lack of judgment in the use of firearms. In another case, however, discharge of an employee for public-welfare chiseling was not supported because the arbitrator reasoned that the employee's job did not require a large degree of trust. Discharge of political security risks has generally been supported if the risk is documented and if the employer is engaged in news publishing or in production vital to national defense. Disciplinary action has also been upheld in the case of employee wage garnishments, especially after repeated offenses. In summary, arbitrators generally tend to protect the worker's rights off the job, but they will sustain disciplinary action if acts are shown to be work-connected.

[16] Arthur M. Sussman, "Work Disputes versus Private Life: An Analysis of Arbitration Cases," *ILR Research*, vol. 10, no. 1, pp. 3–12, Ithaca, N.Y.: Cornell University, New York State School of Industrial and Labor Relations, 1964.

Limited research evidence shows that there is a reasonable amount of agreement concerning areas where organizational influence is considered legitimate. One study covered 812 labor leaders, managers who were students in management-development courses, university students, and managers in companies. The survey reported general agreement on areas of legitimacy among all four groups, with rank-order correlations ranging from +.88 to +.98. However, managers as a group gave somewhat more support to legitimacy than labor leaders, with both groups of students ranking in the middle. The data as a whole support the chart of legitimacy presented in Figure 7-1. High legitimacy items related to work behavior or attitudes toward work and company. Items of low legitimacy primarily were non-job-related, such as family relationships, place of residence, and political and religious views.[17]

Data on legitimacy can be a useful guide to management. As long as there is agreement on legitimacy among the parties involved, they should be satisfied with their relationship. However, an attempt by management to influence employees in an area not considered legitimate probably will develop resentment. In the survey just reported, for example, 55 percent of company managers believed it was legitimate to influence a subordinate's participation in noncompany public activities, but only 10 percent of labor leaders thought so. If a company attempted action in this area, it probably would be opposed by labor leaders unless they clearly understood the company's rationalization in this particular case.

Rights to Privacy. Figure 7-1 shows that areas of least legitimacy are private thoughts, opinions, and motives. Privacy refers to the employee's private person or psyche more than to his private (noncompany) activities. Employees believe that their religious, political, and social beliefs are part of their own inner self and should not be subject to snooping or analysis as a requirement for getting or keeping a job. The same view applies to personal conversations and to certain personal locations such as company rest rooms and private homes. Exceptions are permitted grudgingly, if at all, only when a job involvement is clearly proved, and burden of proof is on the company.

The Polygraph. As social science becomes more sophisticated, there is a tendency to use its discoveries to delve more deeply into a person's psyche. We have learned, for example, that conscience usually causes physiological changes when a person tells a significant lie. The polygraph (lie detector) is based on this principle. Used first in police work, it has now spread to public and private employment. With regard to public employment, a congressional hearing reported that in 1963, seventeen Federal agencies used 512 lie detectors to give 20,000 tests to employees. Private business uses the polygraph primarily to control theft. It is esti-

[17] Edgar H. Schein and J. Steven Ott, "The Legitimacy of Organizational Influence," *American Journal of Sociology*, May, 1962, pp. 682–689.

mated that employees steal over 1 billion dollars a year from employers. Supporting the seriousness of the theft problem, the Council of Polygraph Examiners reports that 30 percent of persons tested for positions of trust fail, nine-tenths of them on "their own admissions of serious criminal behavior."[18]

Employees claim that polygraph tests are being extended from theft investigation to investigation of drinking habits, marital life, political beliefs, and other nonjob subjects. Even when the polygraph is used only concerning theft, employees tend to resent it because they consider their conscience personal and they object to "being judged by a machine" over which they have no control. They especially object to having to prove themselves innocent, that is, take a test routinely even when no theft has been discovered or no evidence points to them as a thief. They object less to a specific test about a specific known theft of major proportions. In this situation they may welcome a test to take the pressure of suspicion off them.

In addition to theft control, management has other arguments favoring polygraph tests. In employment screening, management states that the polygraph protects *employees* from undesirable associates who might abuse their morals, reduce their work satisfactions, or take their personal property. Especially in decentralized retail operations, such as drive-in grocery stores, management states that polygraph tests permit the company to abolish various audits and controls that would otherwise be oppressive. This arrangement gives the employee more freedom from surveillance and leaves him free to work in whatever manner is most productive to him.

Regardless of need for the polygraph, its intrusion upon the psyche is evident and is causing it to be more tightly controlled. Organized labor is seeking to abolish its use, as well as all other forms of secret surveillance. By 1965 five states (Alaska, California, Massachusetts, Oregon, and Rhode Island) had outlawed use of the polygraph in employment situations. And in 1965, Akron, Ohio, became the first city to do so.[19]

Personality Tests. Equally at issue is the use and abuse of personality tests. Workers respond fairly well to tests of skill, but when their psyche is invaded by tests they are understandably rebellious. When one executive was asked on a test whether he was ever bothered with a feeling that someone was following him, he answered in derision: "No, I got rid of him before I came into the building to take the test!" Some psychologists admit that personality testing invades privacy, but they contend that an employer has a large investment in an employee, which justifies invasion of privacy, but only for information directly bearing on job per-

[18] "Unions Act on Threats to Privacy," *Business Week*, Mar. 13, 1965, pp. 87–88.
[19] *Ibid.*

formance. One psychologist states: "Tests in professional hands are perhaps the safest and certainly the least public invasion of privacy."[20] This view begs the question, however, for an invasion of privacy still exists even if it is "safest" and "least public."

Even if the psychologist handles his work perfectly, management is likely to require a report from him, and he has no control over how management may later misuse confidential data in his report. Reports on individual employees usually find their way into the employee's personnel files. In one instance these files were available to any personnel clerk. In another instance a small firm was absorbed by a larger company in a merger. Executives of the larger company 1,000 miles away called for the files. Without any personal knowledge of the situation or the people involved, they hurriedly used old test reports to decide what to do with the people they had acquired.

Personality tests can be faked by an employee to give results that he thinks the employer desires, making the effective use of these tests even more difficult. The test result is then a fiction, rather than a genuine reflection of the employee's personality. Over the years many studies by competent scientists have proved that a wide selection of personality tests can be faked. A recent study of a sales test reported: "Under directions to fake Checklist scores in the direction of selling, both salesmen and sales applicants show marked changes in their responses and in their scores on the various keys of the Checklist. Previous experience with the Checklist seems to make faking even more extreme."[21]

Even when personality tests are not faked, psychologists still have difficulty proving their validity as a selection device. One study of a personality test widely used in industry for years concluded: "It is felt that AVA has failed to demonstrate any practical utility as a *selection device* in industry."[22]

In spite of poor results with personality tests plus strong employee objections, more and more employers seem to be using them. Why? Sometimes employers are not aware of the evidence against tests. Other employers implicitly accept continued company growth or some other event as a validation of their tests, even though the connection is meager

[20] Roger Ricklefs, "How Companies Are Using Psychological Tests," *The Wall Street Journal*, Feb. 9, 1965, quoted in *Management Review*, April, 1965, pp. 46–47.

[21] Marvin D. Dunnette, Jean McCartney, Howard C. Carlson, and Wayne K. Kirchner, "A Study of Faking Behavior on a Forced-choice Self-description Checklist," *Personnel Psychology*, Spring, 1962, p. 23. This article reports studies verifying the fact that other personality tests can be faked.

[22] Edwin A. Locke and Charles L. Hulin, "A Review and Evaluation of the Validity Studies of Activity Vector Analysis," *Personnel Psychology*, Spring, 1962, p. 41. Similar results for other personality tests are summarized in Robert M. Guion and Richard F. Gottier, "Validity of Personality Measures in Personnel Selection," *Personnel Psychology*, Summer, 1965, pp. 135–164.

or entirely false. Others believe that test advantages outweigh any deficiencies.

Perhaps the two main reasons for continuing to use personality tests lie with the employer himself. In the intangible world of human personality, tests give him something concrete and scientific. He is assured that he is using the best science has to offer. Furthermore, the test somewhat absolves him of the awful responsibility of choosing men. He can lay the blame for selection on science and its impartial "truth," leaving his own conscience free. In other words, the test is for the higher manager's personal security as much as it is for company needs.

Often a manager continues to use tests simply because he has not thought through their long-run implications. Invasions of privacy imply by their existence that employers think employees live in moral squalor and must be regularly checked and coerced. This philosophy may be accurate, but it is largely a negative distrust of people rather than a positive support of them. It implies that observation of acts at work is not enough; hence, the mind must be invaded to determine proclivity to acts. Indeed, Big Brother *is* watching! The ultimate question must be asked: Are we sure Big Brother is any better than the people he is watching?

Another long-run danger is that personality tests may produce a standarized work group because the tests overemphasize conformity and fitting into the group. The creative individualist is likely to fail because he *is* different; hence, a firm may test itself into conformity and stagnation. Furthermore, are we really testing what we want to know? Every man has primitive, uncivilized drives as far as can be determined. The crucial question is: How well does he handle them? This we learn by observing his conduct, not by exploring his psyche.

Taken as a whole the history of personality tests in employment raises serious questions of social responsibility. Legislation may be expected to correct abuses, just as it came with polygraph tests, unless improvements are made. Perhaps an employee bill of rights may be necessary to guarantee the right of private motives, as distinguished from acts. One writer comments: "If the corporation assumes responsibility for raising 'mature individuals' (whatever that means) . . . it assumes a power and responsibility over private folly and uniqueness that goes beyond that demanded by even the family, the church, or the university."[23]

The dangers of conformity are especially grave. We think the modern goldfish bowl may make minnows of us all!

Determining Infringements on Privacy. Other items sometimes claimed to invade privacy are microphones, cameras, and one-way win-

[23] George S. Odiorne, "Management's Motivation Muddle," *Michigan Business Review*, March, 1965, p. 31.

dows. There are many situational variations, some of which probably constitute infringements on privacy while others do not. Four tests may be applied. First, does the device invade the psyche, such as polygraphs and personality tests, already discussed? Second, is the device secret? Companies are regularly using television cameras for various types of controls, but these are work observations that are not secret, so the employee has some opportunity to know whether he is being watched and, if he desires, to challenge the instrument. A third test is whether the purpose or use of the instrument is to observe the employee, as distinguished from some other use. Banks, for example, have hidden cameras for taking photographs during robberies or other emergencies. These photographs include employees, but this hardly seems an invasion of privacy provided use is confined to the original purpose. Fourth, is a private act or location being observed? According to this criterion, hidden cameras or microphones in locker rooms have been condemned. Similarly, a worker's clothes locker and toolbox are often considered private, not subject to management prying.

Sometimes novel questions of privacy arise. Women employees in a major English company recently persuaded management to remove from their rest room a loudspeaker on the regular paging system. This was not a case of snooping. They simply claimed that they were shocked to hear a man's voice in their rest room, and they demanded privacy therefrom! Indeed, privacy is a worldwide issue. As industrialization advances along with the technology of snooping, public and private employers must increasingly seek responsible behavior measured by criteria of the type we have been discussing.

RESPONSIBILITIES OF THE INDIVIDUAL
TO THE ORGANIZATION

The employment relationship is two-way. Without question, the organization does have responsibilities to the individual, but also—and again without question—the individual has responsibilities to the organization. This is a mutual relationship. As explained in an earlier chapter, a person makes certain membership investments in an organization, and he expects profitable payoffs in return. The organization also invests in the individual, and it, too, expects profitable payoffs. A relationship is profitable for either party when payoffs (outputs) are larger than investments (inputs) measured in a total value system. In the usual business relationship both parties benefit, just as they do in the usual social relationship. Both parties benefit because the trading exchange between them produces new values which exceed the investment each makes.

The profitable relationship deteriorates if either party fails to act responsibly toward the needs of the other. The employee can fail to act responsibly just as the organization can. Under these conditions if employees display shoddy responsibility toward organizations, they can expect organizations to respond by using tight controls and investigative procedures to try to maintain a viable operating system with adequate payoffs.

Take the matter of theft and consider it in public employment. If some government employees persist in theft from government when opportunity arises, then government employees may expect continued use of polygraphs. If polygraphs are banned because of undesirable features, then more sophisticated management controls and social science devices will be developed because the organization must keep viable. Overlook for the moment the moral-ethical aspects of theft. From the point of view of technology only, theft interferes with schedules and budgets. It causes reorders. It reduces output. It calls for more controls. In sum, it reduces both reliability and productivity of the technological system. This in turn reduces outputs available to employees, as well as those outputs needed by the organization. In this situation the organization must act to protect outputs for employees as well as for itself.

The polygraph would not be used if it were not discovering and preventing substantial theft. In fact, it is rarely used with groups such as professional accountants whose high standards of integrity and responsibility make it unnecessary. All employees could destroy the usefulness of the polygraph by similar conduct. In other words, the roots of the polygraph problem lie in employee conduct and not in the device itself. Just as the polygraph invades the privacy of an employee, so does theft invade the privacy of the organization. We deal with only half of the problem when we condemn the polygraph without also condemning the conduct which makes it useful. Theft was the original invasion which made a counterinvasion by the employer appropriate. This reasoning does not justify employer use of the polygraph, but it does recognize from the point of view of the whole social system the mutual responsibility that exists for its use.

The polygraph matter is an illustration of the larger issue of an individual's responsibility to his organization. In preparing this book, we searched business literature for studies of employee responsibilities to employers, and we found very little. We contacted prominent unions for materials on this subject, and the substance of their replies was that they had no materials on employee responsibility. Similarly, literature of social-action groups extolled employer responsibilities only. This general deficiency reflects a public failure to realize the mutuality of any social exchange and the importance of codes of responsibility for both parties.

In management books, employee responsibility is generally defined as "a fair day's work." However, other employee responsibilities are needed to reflect the whole social system at work. The main one of these is *support,* meaning that employee acts peripheral to job performance will support organizational objectives within established policies. This definition refers to employee acts, not beliefs. Employees retain their own private motives, but in accepting an employment relationship (a social exchange) they obligate themselves to support objectives of the exchange—just as the organization likewise is obligated. According to this criterion the employee is obligated to find and use better ways of work because this is supportive. On the other hand, theft is nonsupportive and an abdication of responsibility, regardless of its ethical rightness or wrongness. In other words, support is not part of an ethical model but belongs to an operating model based on responsibilities which arise from a social exchange relationship.

As a further example, release of trade secrets to a competitor is nonsupportive. In fact, acts of carelessness which fail to safeguard secrets properly are also nonsupportive. Under conditions of support, criticism which is directed internally toward corrective action should be welcomed in an organization. Wanton public criticism of organizational practices normally would be nonsupportive action. However, the concept of support does not demand loyalty, if we assume that loyalty is defined as emotional agreement with the organization's values. The individual retains his own emotions and value system. He may continue to work for the United States Internal Revenue Service, for example, even though he rejects the concept of a graduated income tax, provided his acts support his employer's objectives.

CONFORMITY TO INFORMAL ORGANIZATION

When conformity is mentioned, a person usually thinks of an autocratic boss, tight rules, and large organizations. He sees a bureaucracy, public or private, laying a heavy hand on insecure men and requiring obedience from them. In short, he sees a formal, official organization. Rarely does his mind picture one of society's greatest sources of conformity, the informal organization. This side of organization is so much a part of his everyday life that he has grown accustomed to it and hardly realizes it is there. It is a ghost organization structure, the one that is not on the organization chart.

Informal organization is a powerful influence upon people. It has reached into palaces to assassinate kings. It maintains juvenile street gangs. And it reaches into every office and station of business. Informal organization is the network of personal influence derived from social contacts. Informal power attaches to a person himself, compared with formal power, which attaches to a position and which a person wields only by virtue of his incumbency in that position. Informal power is personal, compared with the institutional nature of formal power.

By giving our attention to formal organization as the primary source of conformity, we may be "looking up the wrong tree for the bear." At least we have failed to see another large bear in another tree, for informal organization is a strong pressure for conformity. Informal employee conformity in restriction of work was documented in a pioneering study by Mathewson in 1931.[24] Over the years, rate-busters have undergone social isolation, have had trash put in their lunch boxes, and have been subjected to other types of harassment. Sometimes they have suffered physical injury. The power of informal organization in employee relations was further documented by Roethlisberger and Dickson in their report of research at Western Electric Company published in 1939.[25] There is also plentiful evidence of informal pressure for conformity in labor relations, including such strong practices as bombing and assault. Even though casual observers associate conformity mostly with formal organization, the actual facts are that much conformity is caused by informal groups within those formal structures. That is, the people themselves are a primary cause of conformity, rather than their employer.

A Natural Pull toward Conformity. Informal groups arise and persist because they satisfy wants of their members. Informal organizations perform four main functions for members, all of which pull toward uniformity and conformity rather than individuality.[26] One function is to perpetuate cultural values, thereby preserving the group's integrity by providing a commonality of values. Another is to give social satisfactions through association with others; however, this socializing process tends toward a uniform culture. A third function is communication, by which a commonality of information is maintained. The fourth function is social control, by which others are coerced and regulated according to group norms. Taken as a whole, informal groups do not want many differences within the group because differences threaten group norms; therefore, both social and physical sanctions are used to induce conformity.

In spite of their general tendency toward conformity, informal groups also can serve man's individuality through developing norms which encourage it. Through their award of status to persons, they can treat people differently. Also they tend to accord different roles to members according to individual capabilities. However, with the tendency

---

[24] Stanley B. Mathewson, *Restriction of Output among Unorganized Workers,* New York: The Viking Press, Inc., 1931.

[25] F. J. Roethlisberger and William J. Dickson, *Management and the Worker,* Cambridge, Mass.: Harvard University Press, 1939.

[26] Keith Davis, *Human Relations at Work,* 2d ed., New York: McGraw-Hill Book Company, 1962, pp. 238–244.

toward uniform culture in informal groups, individuality and uniqueness develop best only when members make a conscious, responsible effort to support these traits.

The principal problem with informal group conformity is not its dull uniformity—which is bad enough—but rather that members become subject to willful control of an informal leader who may manipulate the group toward undesirable ends. He wields great power without the official controls, weight of responsibility, and public regulation that formal leadership has. In this fashion the informal group can become an instrument of neurotic sowers of conflict or nonresponsible rabble-rousers using the group for their own selfish ends.

Confusion of Informal Interest with Public Interest. Further problems occasionally develop from a group "delusion of righteousness."[27] Members come to believe that what they seek must be in the public interest because it arose within the group rather than from formal authority. They equate their own interest with public interest, but the actual facts are that informal groups can be just as vindictive, covetous, and destructive as formal groups. Informal groups even may tend to have more of these negative characteristics because they are less subject to public control. At least, they have the same human frailties as other human organizations.

The following will illustrate how self-interest pressures by an informal group can disrupt the larger social organization. In one department of a factory all six positions eventually came to be filled by members of a racial minority group having only small representation in the community. An informal racial clique developed without management realizing what was happening. Sometime later, technical changes were made requiring jobs to be restudied in this department. The industrial engineering supervisor assigned his best man to the study, but this man immediately recognized the racial overtones involved and asked to be excused. He knew that he had a reputation of being the toughest time-study man, and he felt that his firmness might lead to charges of racial discrimination.

The supervisor finally assigned another industrial engineer who was known for his ability to work closely with people. He studied the jobs and determined a small reduction in rate. The day after the new rate was announced the six men through their union instituted a formal grievance charging racial discrimination. They gave no reasons other than the fact that the rate had been cut. The industrial engineering people were incensed at this emotional charge, and so were a number of workers in the plant. The grievance eventually went to arbitration

---

[27] Keith Davis, "Togetherness: The Informal Variety," in Donald M. Bowman and Francis M. Fillerup (eds.), *Management: Organization and Planning*, New York: McGraw-Hill Book Company, 1963, pp. 41–52.

and was lost by the men. But five years later, emotions were still strong about this particular event, and understanding between racial groups at work was strained.

The weight of evidence points toward informal groups as a major cause of conformity in business. Conformity in business—or in any other area of life—cannot be fully understood by looking only at formal organizations.

BUSINESS PRACTICES

A number of business practices have been developed which encourage employee individuality and reduce conformity. In this section we shall discuss a few of the principal developments.

Revised Organization Structure. One approach is to revise organization structure so that it is less autocratic. In engineering and scientific areas *matrix organization* has proved effective. It is also known as *program management* or *project management*. In matrix organization a project manager is established to direct all work toward completion of a major product contract, such as production of fifty missiles. Men from functional departments are assigned to the project manager and are subject to his general direction, even though they may remain in their functional departments for general supervision. In fact, one man may even have his time divided and assigned to two project managers in addition to being under the general supervision of his functional manager. The mix of each project group is tailored to fit that project, and when that project is completed, members are returned to their functional areas to be assigned later to other projects with a different mix of people.

Matrix organization disregards formal organizational levels and functions, superimposing its own structure on existing organization in accordance with project needs. For example, an engineer at the fourth level in the functional structure may operate at the second level in the matrix structure. In the functional structure he may be an operative performer, but in the matrix structure he is an adviser and consultant. Matrix organization gives people an opportunity to test their performance in different roles and to contribute according to their talents regardless of their rank in the functional structure. It is less hierarchical in structure and more democratic in function.

Although matrix organization is complex, occasionally causing frustration, it widens the scope of initiative and self-motivation for higher-level people who are ready and able to contribute. Research suggests that it improves communication, encouraging direct contact and reducing inhibitions that result from formal rank. One observer states: "The matrix approach, permitting a close exchange of information, benefits specialists and develops generalists."[28] Research shows that those involved in matrix organization understand the project manager's unusual role very well, which further suggests that good communication develops on the matrix team.[29] Matrix organization does not apply to all types of work, but where it does apply it proves to be psychologically more advanced than traditional work hierarchies.

Another organizational revision is nonstructured management. Striking success with this approach has been achieved by Non-Linear Systems, Inc., of San Diego, which produces complex electronic gear. The assembly line was scrapped, and independent production units of from six to seven workers each were established. Each group organizes work as it wishes. In some groups an individual worker builds the complete product, but in others the product is produced by two or more persons. After the change, three months was required to restore output to regular levels, but output then became 30 percent higher than it had been before the change. Morale increased greatly, rejects were virtually eliminated, and production flexibility improved. A similar structure was applied at staff levels with mixed results, and at the management level the idea was unsuccessful.[30]

An older form of organizational revision is decentralization. Although decentralization may still require "conformity" to policies, it does permit greater operating independence by opening decision making to more people. Total management authority is not reduced but is diluted among a larger group. Decentralization certainly seems to benefit the individual; however, some of its benefits to the organization, such as more flexibility and better information for decision making, have been challenged.[31]

Improved Personnel Practices and Human Relations. Instead of revising organization structure, the personnel environment may be changed to provide better fulfillment for each individual. Human relations practices such as improved communication, participation, and consultive supervision have these aims. The Scanlon Plan is a specific approach which helps each employee to participate and find his best way to contribute.[32] With regard to performance rating, some managers now

[28] D. B. Hertz, "The Management of Innovation," *Management Review*, April, 1965, p. 52. See also John F. Mee, "Matrix Organization," *Business Horizons*, Summer, 1964, pp. 70–72.

[29] Keith Davis, *Role Perceptions of the Job of Program Manager (Project Manager) in Technical Work*, Tempe, Ariz.: Arizona State University, College of Business Administration, 1965, pp. 1–47.

[30] "When Workers Manage Themselves," *Business Week*, Mar. 20, 1965, pp. 93–94.

[31] Mayer N. Zald, "Decentralization—Myth vs. Reality," *Personnel*, July–August, 1964, pp. 19–26.

[32] Fred G. Lesieur (ed.), *The Scanlon Plan*, New York: John Wiley & Sons, Inc., 1958.

help each employee to set his own goals instead of presetting them for him. Then his performance is appraised according to the standards he has set. Many other approaches to meeting employee needs at work are covered in the extensive literature on personnel management and human relations.

One personnel practice with both positive and negative virtues is sensitivity training, T-group training, or laboratory training. Its uniqueness is that it seeks to change the *person* rather than the environment. It seeks to give him better insights into employee feelings, thereby making him more responsive to needs of other persons. The training method, however, may require intense, emotional group sessions which lay bare a person's psyche to the group. Some persons feel that this approach is an invasion of psychological privacy if an employee is required to attend this training. Usually an employee is allowed to volunteer, but it is difficult to mark the fine line between real voluntary choice and coercive pressure to "volunteer." If sensitivity training becomes the route to special status and favors, and if people who lack it are bypassed for promotion, then they are being coerced to submit to what they perceive is an invasion of privacy.[33]

Trends. A number of persons have expressed the view that advancing civilization creates an ever-widening web of rules to limit man's freedom and that industrialization follows this trend by constantly extending control over him at work. Clark Kerr states:[34]

> The complex web of rules and the growth of large organizations tend to weaken the position of the individual and to set ever-narrower limits for his freedom of action. We cannot, of course, do away with the web of rules or with large organizations for they are inherent in the logic of industrialization. The realistic approach is to make sure that the costs in individual freedom which we pay for the many benefits of industrialization are kept as low as possible.

From the long view, all the evidence is not yet filed with regard to man's relationship to organizations. As history unfolds, a short-run pendulum of emphasis swings from man to organization and back again. Perhaps, in the manner of a solar system, there is another movement in a longer time dimension which eventually will permit greater individuality for men within organizations. Organizations could eventually swing almost full circle to make individual freedom and nonconformity the established culture rather than the exception. Perhaps organizations will

[33] A study by Robert J. House confirms the view that required sensitivity training is an invasion of privacy. See Robert J. House, " 'T-group' Training: Some Important Considerations for the Practicing Manager," *NYPMA Bulletin*, New York: New York Personnel Management Association, May, 1965, pp. 4–9.

[34] Clark Kerr, quoted in Philip Selznick and Howard Vollmer, "Rule of Law in Industry: Seniority Rights," *Industrial Relations*, May, 1962, p. 99.

become a type of joint venture among equals in the manner of some ancient trading ventures. We do know that organizations can be used to free men as well as to confine them. For example, the more sophisticated structure of republican government freed men from autocratic rule of kings. We may be approaching similar sophisticated developments in industrial organization and management practice. Matrix organization is a step in this direction.

SUMMARY

The contest between man and his organizations is as old as history. Their relationship challenges management to develop viable systems which serve the needs of both. The social ethic, an ideology provided by intellectuals, has given philosophical support to further subordination of man to the organization. The result is the organization man, who faces a number of problems, particularly with regard to conformity and rights to privacy. There are many types of conformity, some of which present no problem. When conformity involves acts off the job or private opinions and motives, serious questions of legitimacy arise. Informal organization also plays a major role in creating conformity.

Since the employment relationship is two-way, the individual also bears social responsibilities to the organization. The trading exchange between a man and his organization is not likely to be socially profitable for both unless each acts responsibly regarding the needs of the other. Under suitable conditions, the trading exchange between them produces new social values which exceed the investment each makes.

Business is attempting to improve the man-and-organization relationship by developing new organization structures, improving the personnel environment, and heightening men's sensitivity to the needs of others. In terms of long-run history, these actions may indicate a shift toward more self-determination for each person in the organization.

QUESTIONS

1. With regard to the relation of man and his organizations, what is the meaning of (a) the social ethic and (b) the organization man?
2. Explain some of the limitations of the organization-man hypothesis.
3. Discuss types of conformity and explain which of them present the main questions of legitimacy.
4. Appraise both favorable and unfavorable aspects of polygraphs for testing employees.
5. What is meant by the right to privacy of organization participants? Do personality tests invade this right? If so, is the invasion justified? Discuss.

6. Prepare a statement of employee responsibilities to organization, giving reasons for the responsibilities you select.

7. Explain how informal organization develops conformity.

8. What is matrix organization, and how does it improve the role of the individual in the organization?

CHAPTER 8 TECHNOLOGY AND INNOVATION

> For the old capitalists controlled only money; the new managers control science and technology, which are immensely more powerful than money itself.
> BENJAMIN M. SELEKMAN[1]

In the 1960s it was estimated that 90 percent of all the scientists who ever lived were still alive.[2] This figure suggests in an approximate way that society is now in the process of absorbing about 90 percent of the total technological change it has had. The result is that business is in the midst of a massive task of absorbing technology on a scale never before experienced. Because business has successfully absorbed new technology in the past, we expect it will do so again, but this expectation should not blind us to the magnitude and difficulty of the job.

Business is working hard at the task. It is estimated that business in the United States is spending 30 billion dollars annually for on-the-job training of workers. This figure equals all business profits after taxes in a normal year or the total investment in our formal educational system through college.[3] Business annually spends some 40 billion dollars more on new plants and equipment. Its expenditures for training and for plants and equipment are therefore 2⅓ times larger than profits derived from the conduct of business. The statement of Alice in Wonderland is almost

[1] Benjamin M. Selekman, "Call for Business Statesmanship," *Harvard Business Review*, July–August, 1962, p. 22.

[2] Billy E. Goetz, "Avoiding Managerial Obsolescence," *California Management Review*, Spring, 1965, p. 91.

[3] George S. Odiorne, *Personnel Policy, Issues and Practices*, Columbus, Ohio: Charles E. Merrill Books, Inc., 1963, p. 227.

a truism of technological society: "You have to run as fast as you can to stay where you are."

In this chapter we shall discuss the relationship of business and technology. Modern technology has given managers new powers, as indicated by the quotation beginning this chapter. It has also given them new responsibilities, such as translating technology into productivity, retraining employees, and managing the creative spirit. A major concern is the relation of technology to unemployment and management's responsibility in this situation.

ABUNDANT TECHNOLOGY

Throughout history technology has pressed onward like a glacier, overturning everything in its way and grinding all opposition into dust. Its unrelenting power has overcome all who tried to stand in its way. In eighteenth-century England, for example, a band of unhappy workers known as Luddites challenged the Industrial Revolution by roaming the countryside, smashing machinery and burning factories. From their narrow viewpoint, machines were enemies taking away jobs and freedom and harming mankind. But the Luddites were soon overcome by the benefits brought by the same machinery they opposed. They sank into oblivion, just as their more modern successors have done. And we know now that they were largely mistaken. Though the Industrial Revolution created new problems, it was a great advance in the history of man.

The glacier of technology grinds on toward progress because of man himself. Man, having tasted the fruit of knowledge, cannot suppress his desire for it. He forever seeks to expand knowledge of his environment. Once he discovers something, he wants to apply it in order to reap its benefits. At this point business becomes important because *business is the principal instrument which translates discovery into application for the public good.* Public symphony concerts, printing, education, and television are all dependent on business activities to make them work. Society depends on business to keep the stream of discovery flowing into useful goods and services for all mankind. Less-developed countries have learned that scientific discoveries mean very little to them unless they have competent organizers and managers to produce for their people what science has discovered. Developed countries have learned that their progress stops unless they operate a business system which contributes to discovery and uses discovery to produce for their people.

In further support of the role of business in technological development, a university study of 900 key inventions in this century reports that in most cases growing markets stimulated invention, rather than invention coming first and creating a market. In all but a few cases "market was the mother of invention."[4]

General Effects of Technology. Advancing technology creates a wave of effects throughout society. Some of the principal effects relating to business are complexity, change, demand for capital, larger investment units, higher skill requirements, adjustments to affluence, and unemployment (discussed in a later section of this chapter).

An evident effect of technology is complexity. The modern washing machine does a better job than the old washboard and tub, but when it breaks down, it requires a specialist for repairs. And it may break down more often because of its complexity. The same reasoning applies to a complex production system. In November, 1965, for example, an equipment failure on a power network in the Northeastern United States caused a power overload and opened circuit breakers nearby. In turn, a larger system became overloaded because of interties with other power systems. At once almost the entire Northeastern United States and part of Canada were gripped in a giant power failure which lasted throughout the night and into the next day. About 20 million people were affected. Gasoline stations could not pump gas, traffic lights stopped, elevators hung between floors, and so on. A localized problem on one circuit ballooned into a regional problem affecting other areas because of the intertie. Under conditions of this type, management is under great pressure to keep the whole system working all the time.

Also because of complexity, failure of one part in a system such as an airplane or a missile can abort the whole operation for the long run. The Nike missile system has over one million parts, and they all must work. Reliability of performance, therefore, assumes new significance in the business world. It is possible that technology eventually will lead to simplicity and small independent operational units, but that condition is far into the future. Meanwhile, more complexity in work and product systems is expected. Business is developing zero-defects programs in order to maintain reliability under these conditions.

A characteristic of technology is its geometric growth, which accelerates change in business. Throughout this book we keep returning to the subject of change because it is the dominant theme in a complex business civilization. As the technical order changes, the economic order alters to adjust to it. The business system and all other systems are caught up in this whirlpool of change because all systems are tied together.

Another effect of technology is its insatiable demand for capital. At the turn of the century, an investment of $1,000 for each worker was adequate in a factory, but today investments in pipelines and chemical operations exceed $100,000 for each worker. Capital needs become stag-

[4] "What Is the Key to Progress?" *Business Week*, May 16, 1964, p. 132.

gering when considered in terms of new jobs. Considering a moderate investment of only $10,000 for each worker and using forecasts of 20 million new jobs needed in the United States in fifteen years, 200 *billion* dollars of new capital is needed. This figure does not include expenditures for capital replacement to keep the existing labor force employed. These developments require business to generate large amounts of capital and engage in more long-range planning and budgeting for capital use.

Further, the magnitude of investment units is increasing. An old factory could increase production by adding units of one machine at $1,000 and one man at a time. A modern factory having an integrated production system may discover that expansion is possible only in system units having twenty machines and much supporting equipment costing 3 million dollars. The output potential of the system unit is likewise much greater than that of the one machine in the old factory. These conditions mean that expansion which permits idle capacity over an intermediate term is often technologically correct and in the public interest from a cost viewpoint. Expansion at the rate of consumer use, allowing no idle capacity, would be costly or not feasible technologically. Idle capacity, therefore, is not necessarily a social ill. During periods of business growth and technological change, wise use of resources requires investment in system units which will have idle capacity.

Another effect of technology is to upgrade the skill and intellectual requirements of a total work force. This effect is well known and evident from greater demand for college graduates in business. The day laborer becomes a craneman, the shop clerk becomes an accountant, and the laboratory technician becomes a Ph.D. chemist. A generation ago the typical factory had a range of skills approaching curve A shown in Figure 8-1. This curve was shaped more or less like the normal curve of intelligence among people. Being matched to people, it suggested that an adequate supply of labor would be available at all levels of business in the long run.

In modern business the curve has moved toward the right, higher in skill, as shown in curve B. And in many organizations the skill distribution has become bimodal, as shown by the second top on the curve. Many scientific and professional people are required in research, development, planning, and other specialized work, creating the secondary bulge toward the skilled end of the scale.

Curve C represents the skill distribution which is developing in firms oriented toward research and development or company branches engaged in government scientific contracting. Even though these firms manufacture products for sale, much of their effort is devoted to development and building prototypes. In some of these the number of engineers, scientists, and college-graduate specialists exceeds the total number of all other employees.

Affluent citizens with new wants are another result of advancing technology. Now supplied with the necessities of life, affluent customers spend more money on semiluxuries such as boats and country homes. Having the power to buy more things, they are not going to buy more of the same things. They want something different. Many of them are becoming independent, demanding adaptation of products to their unique needs. Already there are hundreds more models of cars and combinations of accessories than in the days of the Model T Ford. Demand is expanding even for custom semihandcrafted automobiles, and this market is being served by customizing shops, custom parts wholesalers, and specialized magazines. Society has come almost full circle from handicraft production to standardized mass-production items and back to semicustom production of some products, even though these custom items are constructed largely from standardized parts. The factory of the future may be like an organ console with a complex, integrated system, from which an operator produces an infinite variety of sounds. Business is reappraising its affection for standardized mass production of major products and services. In any case, business will be responsible for producing a greater variety of products in the future.

The affluent employee also adds new responsibilities because he is financially and emotionally more independent of his employer than he used to be. He insists on taking part of his productivity gain in the form of a shorter workweek. Then he becomes a moonlighter, working more than forty hours weekly between his two jobs, thereby avoiding overtime laws and complicating his and his employer's schedules and economic life. Even though he is more affluent, his wants increase at a faster rate than his ability to satisfy them, so if he does not moonlight, he lets his

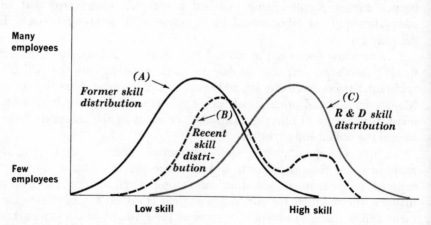

Figure 8-1 Changes in skill distribution in a business as required by advances in technology.

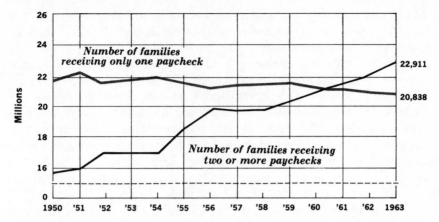

Figure 8-2 Families receiving two or more paychecks outnumber those receiving only one paycheck. (*Reprinted from U.S. News and World Report, Oct. 19, 1964, p. 85. Data from U.S. Census Bureau.*)

wife work. As shown in Figure 8-2, in 1961 for the first time the number of families receiving two or more paychecks from work exceeded the number receiving only one paycheck. At this time over twenty million women were employed.

Indeed, technology is creating all sorts of new situations to which people are reacting in unique ways. The technological revolution causes, perhaps with a time lag, an associated social revolution. The problem with technology is that it moves so fast that it creates problems before society is able to work out solutions. For these reasons business firms associated with technological change have been supporting public research on the subject in addition to their own private research. Notable is a ten-year study at Harvard Business School financed by a 5-million-dollar grant from International Business Machines Corporation. The project seeks ". . . to identify and analyze the primary and second-order impacts and effects of technological change on the economy, business, government, society, and individuals."[5] Another firm, U.S. Industries, has established the American Foundation on Automation and Employment in cooperation with the International Association of Machinists. The company supports the foundation by payments based on gross receipts from automated machines it sells or leases.[6]

In summary, we recognize that technology is changing the whole structure of industrial civilization. More competition is expected from distant geographical areas and from nontraditional fields. The life-span of many products will decline because of technological obsolescence.

[5] "A $5-million Search for Answers," *Business Week*, July 4, 1964, p. 84.

[6] John I Snyder, Jr., "Automation and Unemployment: Management's Quiet Crisis," *Management Review*, November, 1963, p. 17.

Many new and unusual business opportunities will develop, but it will be more costly to take advantage of them because of the effort required for research and development. Companies which fail to keep up technologically, shifting as necessary, will be wiped out by technologically superior firms. Traditional management will be inadequate for success unless it is coupled with technological progress. These conditions will increase risk and cause disturbing economic dislocations as industry shifts with technology. For these reasons, government will continue to play an overriding role in regulating technological change. And government itself will be personally involved in the same adjustments business is making. For example: "No automation equipment in history ever knocked out jobs as fast as the shift from bombers to missiles."[7]

Research and Development. As technology has advanced, research and development (R & D) has become a giant new function in business. Research concerns the creation of new ideas, and development concerns their useful application. Direct research and development expenditures in industry in 1960 were over 10 billion dollars, and it is estimated that these expenditures will exceed 30 billion dollars by 1970. These figures do not include billions of indirect expenditures such as planning and introducing new products. Much R & D work is supported by government contracts, but private industry is also risking large amounts of its own money. The National Science Foundation estimates that by 1961 industry investment in company-financed R & D had reached about 2 percent of its sales dollar annually. Electrical equipment manufacturers were spending over 10 percent of their sales dollar in R & D financed from all sources.[8]

Effective management of R & D is an important business responsibility because R & D brings social benefits through increased productivity. Comparative research among countries of the world shows that R & D investment is closely related to economic growth. This international study concludes: "It is suggested that the civilian economy will continue to benefit from further increase in the fraction of national income devoted to R & D, even if the increase is at the expense of more conventional uses of investment funds."[9]

R & D has become so important in some companies that it is ranked along with production and sales as a primary function, or "line function," of their businesses. No longer do they only produce goods and sell them. With accelerated technology, many companies now develop goods, produce them, and sell them. In some instances R & D becomes the primary

[7] James R. Bright, "Opportunity and Threat in Technological Change," *Harvard Business Review*, November–December, 1963, pp. 76–86.

[8] Hamilton Herman, "R & D Pathway to Progress," *Automation*, April, 1964, p. 66.

[9] Herbert K. Weiss, "Some Growth Considerations of Research and Development and the National Economy," *Management Science*, January, 1965, p. 393.

emphasis of an organization, with production only secondary. Research and development becomes the largest department, having more employees than either production or sales. Its salary budget is larger, and it assumes an active voice in the councils of top management. The traditional industrial order of priorities shifts from production to R & D. The assumption is that new products must be developed in order to keep abreast of competition and that if something useful can be developed, production and sales will develop normally. R & D, therefore, becomes the key to market leadership in many situations.

The changes that are occurring place new responsibilities on management to keep abreast of technology in order to be sure it is using investor funds in the best way. Further, management needs to reconsider organizational objectives to be certain they are broad enough. The wagon firm which looked upon itself as only making wagons has gone out of business, but the wagon firm which saw its objective as providing consumer transportation equipment could move into automobile manufacturing. The attrition of technology is evident from a comparison of lists of the 100 largest manufacturers in 1909 and 1959. Less than one-third of the 1909 firms are on the 1959 list. In other words, advancing technology initiates action on management requiring adjustment, just as much as it does in the more publicized cases requiring workers to adjust.

Some of the changes in technology have been striking. Nylon filament is extruded at 4,000 feet a minute, which is one-half million times faster than a silkworm produces silk. A good glassblower with a helper could make some fifteen hundred light bulbs a day, but a single machine today produces 132,000 bulbs *an hour*. Another dramatic example of productivity increase is the telephone system. It is estimated that if the telephone system of the 1960s depended on manual operation as used in the 1930s, every woman in the United States over eighteen years of age would be employed in telephone work to handle the volume of calls made in the 1960s.

With the new emphasis on technology, management faces the responsibility of reexamining all its organization forms and practices to see whether they apply to new conditions. The whole concept of staff is being reappraised.[10] New forms of organization are being developed, such as matrix organization, discussed in an earlier chapter. Decentralization came into vogue and then faced reappraisal as better computers made recentralization desirable for some functions. More emphasis is being given to process relationships and organizational influence, as distinguished from official authority and chains of command. The technological process itself becomes a determinant of how people organize and work together.

[10] Gerald C. Fisch, "Line-Staff Is Obsolete," *Harvard Business Review*, September–October, 1961, pp. 67–79.

Expansion of technology has placed new responsibilities on business for managing the creative spirit, sometimes called "maverick management." Historically, the scientist worked in a small laboratory at his own pace, usually in an academic setting, but more and more he is working for big organizations, both private and public. Most certainly he performs best in a work culture different from that of the assembly line.

Creative and intellectual workers expect relatively high job freedom. They are motivated by opportunities which offer a challenge for growth and achievement. They are less motivated by the expectations of higher formal authority than by their own professional interests and perception of opportunities. Their orientation is *cosmopolitan*, toward their profession and the world outside their organization, rather than *local*, depending primarily on the reward structure of the firm itself. Although they are a part of the company work culture, they are just as much a part of a separate scientific culture operating beyond their organization's boundaries. Under these conditions they have an organizational rootlessness and a tendency to move on to new opportunities.

Business is adjusting its supervisory practices to meet needs of intellectual workers. Some companies have established dual promotion ladders so that distinguished technical people can rise to ranks and receive salaries that are equivalent to those of managers. Flexible work schedules are allowed. Profit sharing is provided to give the creative person a financial stake in the ideas he creates and to discourage his rootlessness. Attendance at professional meetings and writing professional articles are supported. In further response to the intellectual worker's cosmopolitan interests, he is allowed to teach part time or is given special assignments. In fact, research covering industrial, government, and university scientists discloses that the more productive scientists are those who spend part of their time in teaching, administration, or other nontechnical work. In other words, the more productive scientists spend less than full time on technical activities. Although a cause-and-effect relationship is not proved, it appears that diversity in the scientists' work situations actually enhances their performance. Having broad and cosmopolitan interests, they thrive on variable conditions. At a minimum this research suggests that the more productive scientists have an expectation of broad duties and gravitate toward them. This research covered Ph.D.s in research and in development, non-Ph.D. scientists, engineers, and assistant scientists, and all five groups reported greater technical productivity when they had some nontechnical work.[11]

---

[11] Frank M. Andrews, "Scientific Performance as Related to Time Spent on Technical Work, Teaching, or Administration," *Administrative Science Quarterly*, September, 1964, pp. 182–193. For further details on managing the creative spirit, see the special issue on professionals in organizations, *Administrative Science Quarterly*, June, 1965.

Although there is room for improvement, business has been fairly successful in integrating scientific and intellectual workers into today's complex work systems. In the work environment which business provided, they have been productive. As we shall discuss in the next section, business has had more difficulty with automation because of its broad social effects.

COMPUTERS AND AUTOMATION

There have been three stages of the Industrial Revolution. The first was mechanization based on the application of mechanically powered machines to work. The second was mass production, a type of production organization which provided for standardized product flow through repetitive operations. The third is automation, an integrated operating system based on information processing and self-correcting control systems. This last stage appears to be of greater magnitude than the earlier stages. Certainly it has caught the attention and fired the imagination of workers, managers, and the public alike. Some persons see it as a blessing which will quickly achieve a world free from material want and grant all workers more leisure. Others see it as just another routine stage of the Industrial Revolution. Others display a *technophobia* in which they view automation as a great terror which will cast poorly educated workers into permanent unemployment and reduce all workers to obeisant servitude to machinery. They foresee a day when workers, having lost all their individuality, will drift uselessly under the care of giant machines. This wide variety of views is a normal result when people with different perceptions try to predict what an unknown social force will do at some unknown future time. As is usually the case, actual future events will probably range somewhere between the extreme views.

At the root of the automation revolution is electronic data processing by various types of computers. Their fantastic speed has temporarily overwhelmed business with more data than it now knows how to use. The result is "data indigestion"—a deluge of data but a dearth of usable information. An allied difficulty is psychological dependence on computers. They are so complex and so fast that managers, public leaders, employees, and citizens tend to defer to them. Engineers, for example, may depend on a computer to select a highway route by routine physical calculations but may not think to locate the highway where it will not compound ugliness. Regarding the computer, one observer comments:[12]

> I suspect that the feeling of being left out, being outside the decision-making party, as it were, is one of the causes of the malaise of our society.

[12] Sir Charles P. Snow, quoted in Henry A. Singer, "The Management of Automation," *Advanced Management Journal*, April, 1964, p. 5. See also Gilbert Burck, "Will the Computer Outwit Man?" *Fortune*, October, 1964, pp. 120ff.

I believe that the computer is a wonderful subject and a tool from which we can get great service, but if we let the individual human judgment go by default, if we give all the power of decision to more and more esoteric groups, then both the moral and intellectual life will wither and die.

A further issue with computers is that their data outputs are accepted without paying attention to the assumptions and estimates on which the outputs are based. For example, automation is an issue in the national growth rate and the employment rate, but small errors in these figures can result in very misleading guides to decision making. As explained by an economist-statistician, suppose the normal growth rate without error is 1.8 percent. Now: "Suppose gross national product for the second year is only plus 1 percent off and gross national product for the preceding one is minus 1 percent off (a total error of only 2 percent), then the growth rate is 3.9 percent. But if the signs of the errors are reversed, the growth rate is −0.2 percent!"

He adds that since these data cannot possibly be free of error, there is a ". . . question whether the computation of growth rates has any value whatsoever." He also comments with regard to monthly changes in the unemployment rate, say, from 5.8 to 5.5 percent, that ". . . statements of this kind are completely devoid of the meaning attributed to them." [13]

Considered as a whole, computers are a significant benefit to mankind provided that users are forewarned of their limitations and do not become psychologically dependent on them. It will be easy for a lethargic management to lapse into dependence on computer outputs, relaxing its own awareness of business environment and surrendering responsibilities for leadership. This condition is sure to develop a number of times in the future, but with a forewarned management it should be the exception, not the rule.

Automation and Employment. No other aspect of automation has developed as much controversy as its effect on employment. Automation obviously seeks to reduce labor costs, which means that fewer employees are needed to achieve the same output. Other persons, however, claim that automation does not reduce employment. The primary reason for these differences of opinion is that some people are looking at employment units within the economy, while others are looking at the economic system as a whole. They do not see the difference between eliminating jobs in individual circumstances and causing general unemployment in the whole economy. From the point of view of units within the economy, automation—and all technological change—causes skill dislocations and economic adjustments. The individual worker who thinks that automation may abolish the exact job he has now is probably correct. It is estimated

[13] Oskar Morgenstern, "Qui Numerare Incipit Errare Incipit," *Fortune,* October, 1963, pp. 144, 174.

that few people starting their work life today will be able to keep the same jobs all their lives even if they should want to do so. Their jobs will change, requiring relearning. Likewise, whole departments may be abolished because their work is made unnecessary by automation.

Looking at the whole economy, the view is different. The overwhelming weight of evidence is that automation is not a primary cause of unemployment in the whole economic system. Based on his study of employment statistics, the United States Commissioner of Labor Statistics concludes: "Technology as such does not result in a net loss of jobs in the economy." [14] The reason is that technology merely permits human labor to be allocated to more efficient uses, but it does not destroy the need for labor. If automation causes unemployment, then jobs should decline as productivity increases, but this does not occur. Figure 8-3 shows a steady rise in job opportunities as mass production and automation moved into the economy of the United States. India, on the other hand, has very little automation, but it has massive unemployment.

Studies fail to show any connection between automation and gen-

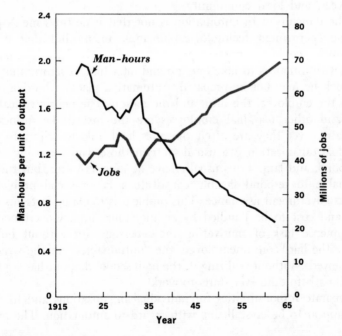

Figure 8-3 Comparison of man-hours per unit of output with number employed in the United States. (*Yale Brozen, "Putting Economics and Automation in Perspective," Automation, April,* 1964, *p.* 32.)

[14] Ewan Clague, "What Employment Statistics Show," *Automation,* April, 1964, p. 55.

eral unemployment. One study concludes: "We are also unable to find evidence that rapid technological change is directly implicated in the problem of persistent high levels of unemployment." [15] And a research study prepared for the Senate Committee on Labor and Public Welfare reports: "The great majority of professional economists today agree that we simply cannot have any such thing as permanent technological unemployment." [16]

From the broader view of international business, automation in one country may reduce its labor costs, thereby adversely affecting the trade of another country where automation is advancing at a slower pace. In this instance, automation helps the country where it occurs, indirectly penalizing another country which fails to use it. Automation becomes a worldwide pressure for productivity improvement.

Considering all the evidence, automation is a disturbing factor causing dislocations in labor markets around the world, but it is not a cause of permanent unemployment. Because of its wide effects, businessmen in making their decisions are required to evaluate it from different levels —international business, the national economy, and their own industry, employees, and local community.

The difficulty with automation is not that it destroys men's jobs for all time (permanent technological unemployment) but that it creates jobs which people are not yet prepared to fill. The bargain automation strikes with a man is to take one job and offer him in return another one for which he may not be prepared. Automation places a burden of training on the employee, the firm, and the nation. The poorly educated, the aged, and other marginal employees are the first to be dislocated by automation; yet they are often the ones least able to adjust to it. The individual organization can usually retrain those who are ready and able to respond, and large firms usually have done exactly this, but those who are unable to respond flexibly constitute a larger social problem that requires government assistance. This problem is too large in terms of both scope and cost to be handled by an individual firm. Government faces the immense task of motivating these persons, for without help they become the hard-core unemployed, the "untrainables," or the structurally unemployed. Without realizing it, the high school dropout has set his own job ceiling before he ever starts to work!

Separate responsibilities for individual organizations and for government appear to be crystallizing with regard to automation. The organiza-

[15] Robert L. Aronson, "Perspective on Automation," *ILR Research*, vol. 10, no. 3, p. 11, Ithaca, N.Y.: Cornell University, 1965.
[16] Charles C. Killingsworth, "Automation, Jobs and Manpower," in *Nation's Manpower Revolution*, Hearings before Subcommittee on Employment and Manpower, Senate Committee on Labor and Public Welfare, 88th Cong. 1st Sess., Washington, D.C.: Government Printing Office, 1963, part 5, p. 1461.

tion is becoming responsible for introducing automation at a pace that will permit it to handle internally whatever dislocations occur. Through transfer and retraining it adjusts those who are able to respond to normal personnel procedures. Those who cannot so respond become a primary responsibility of the community at all governmental levels. The employer may assist in these situations, but the primary responsibility rests with government. Society does not hold the employer responsible for a poorly educated employee. The Federal government is taking initiative in this area with its Manpower Development and Training Act of 1962, anti-poverty programs, employment assistance, aid to the handicapped and minority groups, and aid to education. State governments have also set up programs of their own.

Peter Drucker concludes that the principal source of employee insecurity really is not automation but the *education revolution*. Since the majority of young people seeking jobs today have a high school diploma, job specifications tend to call for these qualifications in order to upgrade the labor force for the future. Most of the older manual workers have less education, and consequently they are bypassed for promotion and other opportunities. Their job independence is also declining. Formerly the maintenance man decided how and when to service a machine, but now the plant engineer provides a detailed schedule. More and more the knowledge context of first-level jobs is being moved upstairs to be handled by an educated man. The result is that the production worker sees doors closing to him and his status slipping. The security of even skilled craftsmen is being threatened by new training procedures which show that a long apprenticeship is not necessary and that a young man can know more about a craft job in six months than an old-time apprentice learned his first six years. Drucker concludes: "No one in America—least of all the manual worker—would dream of repealing the educational revolution! . . . Yet its social and psychological impacts on the manual worker are serious—even though automation has very little to do with them." [17]

One further point is that businessmen are taking a harder look at projected savings from automation because they are becoming aware of its broad social and economic effects. Estimated savings are often not as large as they appear in the beginning. When all social costs are considered, economic savings dwindle, and the technological change appears to be unwise considered in its totality. For example, a petroleum company made an analysis of one of its regional offices handling credit-card accounts. This office employed 500 persons and handled 25 million dollars annually. An accounting study showed that the office could be abolished and all accounting done by a computer in the national office of the company at a saving of $75,000 out of an annual regional office cost of $500,000.

[17] Peter Drucker, "Automation Is Not the Villain," *The New York Times Magazine*, Jan. 10, 1965, p. 82.

This saving appeared to justify centralization; however, investigation disclosed other factors affecting the decision. If the change were made, mail contact with customers would be slowed three days by regular mail or one day if air mail was used at an additional cost. Since no other jobs were available at the regional office, it was estimated that 325 employees would need to be moved to other offices including the central office. These costs were not computed in estimating the saving. Some other employees would be laid off or retired, which would incur additional costs of dismissal or early retirement benefits. As a matter of fact, the central office was in a large city in expensive office space, and no further space was available. Space would have to be leased or new facilities built.

Furthermore, fixed costs resulting from equipment lease cancellations at the regional office were not counted. Also omitted was the necessity for simultaneous operation of both offices during the changeover period. The company personnel director also observed that salary costs were generally higher in the national office, and he predicted that persons who transferred would soon get sizable increases in order to bring their salaries into line with those of other employees and to allow for living costs in their new community.

Considering the total picture, management decided that the saving would be less than $10,000 and that in terms of total economic and social costs to the company, the change would be unwise. It was not made.

Organizational Influences. A number of automation's effects within a firm relate to business environment beyond the firm. Some of these areas of influence are the manager shortage, worker morale, and the shorter workweek.

It has been predicted that automation will reduce the status and number of middle managers, but this trend has not developed. In theory, advanced systems sometime in the future may centralize planning and controlling and reduce the need for middle managers. Meanwhile, research discloses that automation has tended to increase the load of middle management. The middle manager's job is more complex, he has more data to analyze in depth, he is using more experience and judgment, and the scope of his responsibilities is increased.[18] His work is more interconnected with other departments, increasing requirements for lateral communication. These conditions add to the demand for educated, professionally trained, mature managers, who are already in short supply because of economic growth.

Neither has automation reduced the proportion of managers in the labor force of automated plants. The labor saving of automation applies primarily to operative workers. They are the ones displaced by machines, while the cadre of managers remains the same or even increases. Assume,

[18] Donald R. Shaul, "What's Really Ahead for Middle Management?" *Personnel*, November–December, 1964, pp. 8–16.

for example, that a department before automation has ten managers and ninety workers. Its ratio of managers to workers is 1 to 9. As a result of automation ten workers are laid off, but the management cadre is not reduced. The ratio of managers is now 1 to 8. If one specialized manager is added, the ratio of managers increases to one manager for each 7.3 workers. This change in ratio can move fast. In one department of seventy employees the ratio of managers to workers was 1 to 35 before automation but 1 to 8 after automation.[19] Meanwhile, the new firms which are developing to hire displaced workers will also need managers for them. The result is that the proportion of managers in industrial society is inching upward, compounding the existing managerial shortage. If the proportion moved up only 1 percent for the entire United States labor force, about eight hundred thousand new managers would be required. This condition is one of the reasons business is giving more effort to management training internally, plus cooperating with external agencies in executive-development programs.

The manager shortage is likely to get worse before supply is able to catch up with demand. The business investment in training and education above the worker level is high and will continue to grow. Likewise the community investment will grow. Since management is a key factor in making other resources productive, it is beginning to receive priority in economic development. It, along with high-level technical manpower, constitutes a "takeoff" investment which enables other resources to be used more productively. However, as discussed earlier, modern technology requires higher training for all types of work. One study reports: "The proportion of national income devoted to human resource development is likely to rise in all countries that are growing." [20]

Advancing technology requires more *biprofessional managers*. These are men who are professionally trained in management and also in an intellectual specialty which they need in order to understand the environment they manage. Examples are physics and management and biochemistry and management. Usually this situation exists for first-level supervision and middle management. At higher levels, a technical specialty is less necessary because general business activities covering many functions are being managed.

Even triprofessionals are being sought. A pharmaceutical firm spent several months seeking a man who had degrees in both biology and advertising, professional training in management, and a Ph.D. They wanted this man to head their advertising program. They found him and paid the price required to move him from his present employer. The trend

---

[19] Otis Lipstreu and Kenneth A. Reed, "A New Look at the Organizational Implications of Automation," *Academy of Management Journal*, March, 1965, p. 26.

[20] Frederick Harbison and Charles A. Myers, *Education, Manpower, and Economic Growth*, New York: McGraw-Hill Book Company, 1964, p. 186.

toward biprofessionalism places even more responsibility on business to support education and training because the preparation of this kind of person is expensive. Fortunately, automation's greater productivity eases the burden of the costly education it requires in society.

Automation's effect on morale is variable. Workers who like to work with complex machines and manipulate systems, as a jet pilot does, will respond favorably to the challenge of automation. Others will be overwhelmed by its technology and will lose morale. Tension is heightened by the fact that the machinery is expensive and production is faster, so mistakes can be costly. Some employees are discomforted by the fact that they must relearn and retrain, while others accept the situation as an opportunity. There is general agreement that morale drops during changeover to automation because of difficulties in adjusting to the system. A study in one plant, using fourteen attitude questions, showed a negative shift on all questions, with eleven of the fourteen shifts significant at or below the .05 level.[21]

Low morale from automation affects the community image of an organization. It interferes with recruitment, reinforces public fear of automation, and causes public clamor for legal controls of automation. Because of these circumstances, management has a responsibility to pay the same attention to the human side of automation as it does to the technical side. Adequate planning and full use of existing knowledge about human relations should prevent major shifts in morale when automation is installed. There is no evidence that automation reduces morale permanently; therefore, the changeover period is the time when special attention is required.

Some persons have suggested that society should pursue automation fast without regard for worker satisfactions, letting workers get their satisfactions from the leisure time that develops from automation. One business observer speculates: "All this suggests the irreverent notion that *perhaps* the best use of our resources is to accelerate automation, shorten the work week just as fast as possible, forget about on-the-job satisfactions, and concentrate our energies on making leisure more meaningful." [22]

Man will undoubtedly take some of his productivity gains in the form of a shorter workweek. Even if we assume a near-term reduction to thirty hours weekly, work still remains a central feature of life and the consumer of much of man's time. If we ignore man's needs for satisfaction during this major block of his time, we may psychologically cripple him. And certainly he would object, perhaps in turn crippling the automated system

[21] Otis Lipstreu, "Automation and Morale," *California Management Review,* Summer, 1964, p. 87.

[22] George Strauss, "Some Notes on Power-equalization," in Harold J. Leavitt (ed.), *The Social Science of Organizations: Four Perspectives,* Englewood Cliffs, N.J.: Prentice-Hall, Inc., 1963, p. 52.

which depends on his cooperation. Therefore, this approach appears unworkable.

Furthermore, man expects psychological satisfactions from his activities, and there seems to be no good reason for making work an exception. When a person goes to work with an organization, he makes a psychological contract with it which includes an expectation of satisfactions. Employers cannot afford to ignore this expectation; consequently, automation will probably cause only a slow reduction in the workweek with full attention continuing to be paid to satisfactions at work. In a world where hunger still exists, a drastic reduction in the workweek is not expected.

As the workweek reduces we are likely to experience more moonlighting. Some of this will be work at a second job. More of it is likely to be what we call "public moonlighting," which is semischeduled, responsible assistance with public-service activities of the community. Usually five to ten hours a week is given without pay or with token payment for expenses, the person seeking to satisfy his idealistic drives. Being affluent, man feels he now can afford to give of himself directly to others. This delayed offer of help may not please the spartan idealists who think man should *first* give of himself to others, but man, being what he is, is likely to feather his own nest before he looks toward others. He feels a primary responsibility for himself. Examples of public moonlighting are devoting Saturdays to youth council work, providing social work ten hours a week in a hospital, or working eight hours a week on a city beautification committee.

Since automation does bring more productivity and the possibility of a shorter workweek, it releases employee time for pursuit of idealistic social objectives. It is not often recognized that many of the public-service activities which are found in the United States—activities which are not directly productive of basic goods—exist only because of wealth produced by a partly automated industrial society. An impoverished economy could hardly support well-equipped hospitals or aid for retarded children. Likewise productivity is essential to support mass cultural activities, such as community museums and symphonies, as distinguished from culture for a few elite. As these activities expand in society, some of them—such as a two-hour noon committee meeting—will conflict with work schedules. Additional responsibility will be placed on employers to support these developments by permitting flexible working hours. At the same time the complexity of automation will be pressing for full attentiveness to one's job without a break. One solution to this dilemma will be broadly trained men who are interchangeable on jobs within the system, in the same way they would interchange in case of sickness absence.

Assuming that factory workers do secure a shorter workweek of perhaps thirty hours, will others follow? What about managers, family physicians, shopkeepers, research workers, and teachers? Surveys show that most persons in these groups now work closer to fifty hours a week. In many instances they will find it difficult to reduce hours because of demands made on them or because of their personal enthusiasm for their occupation. The distinct possibility exists that *two* standards for hours worked may develop. Some occupations, especially intellectual work, may tend to hold a long workweek, while other occupations gravitate toward a shorter workweek. Those on the longer week may have schedule flexibility, compared with closely controlled schedules for those on a shorter workweek. Employees then would have a measure of choice concerning whether they wished to take the fruits of productivity in more pay or more leisure. Since there is no basis for assuming that all persons want a shorter workweek, this flexible arrangement permits some adaptation to different desires. It also burdens the organization with additional planning and scheduling responsibilities.

Viewing automation as a whole, it increases productivity but at the expense of greater complexity in work. Hans Christian Andersen in "The Nightingale" tells of an emperor who depended on a mechanized nightingale to sing its beautiful song. Its clockwork was so good that he banished the real nightingale. But eventually the clockwork failed and was discovered to be so complex that it could not be repaired. Again he came to depend on the real nightingale. Though automation is complex, like the mechanical nightingale, we expect that man will be able to keep it "singing" for his benefit without having to return to old production structures.

Viewing technology as a whole, its greatest impact is probably on education and training. Its tendency to create a surplus of underdeveloped manpower and a shortage of highly developed manpower will continue unless more educational investment is made in people. In economic terms, by requiring workers to be better prepared in order to contribute fully, it increases the marginal productivity of skilled and intellectual work, while decreasing the marginal productivity of unskilled and manual work. It puts the most strain on workers already marginally productive; therefore, employers face added responsibilities to help society retrain these people. Automation needs to be introduced with full regard for its effects on society.

SUMMARY

Business is the principal instrument which translates discoveries of science into application for the public good. Industrial society is absorbing technology at a fast pace, but not without side effects. Some of these effects are complexity, change, demand for capital, larger investment units, higher skill requirements, and adjustments to affluence. Research and development (R & D) has become a major new function. In some organizations it is considered a primary line function because it becomes the key to market leadership. In R & D and elsewhere, management faces new responsibilities for managing the creative spirit. Surveys show that more productive scientists spend less than full time on technical work.

Automation, a third stage in the Industrial Revolution, has captured the imagination of critics and supporters alike. The computer supports automated operations. Some people develop a psychological fear of it, and others develop psychological dependence on it, but most persons adjust to it successfully.

Automation in an organization leads to employee transfers, retraining, and even layoffs, but for an entire economic system there is no evidence that permanent technological employment can exist. Business helps those employees to adjust who are able to respond to normal personnel procedures, depending on society to handle more complex responsibilities of automation. The most difficult problem is educational upgrading and employment of marginal producers. Automation also affects the manager shortage, worker morale, and the shorter workweek. Public moonlighting may expand, and two standards for hours worked may develop.

QUESTIONS

1. Appraise the efforts business is making to adapt constructively to technological change. What are the main deficiencies in adaptation?

2. Discuss some of the ways technology is affecting business environment. Chart the changes in skill distribution which are developing.

3. What is meant by the statement that technology initiates action on management?

4. Define the following: cosmopolitan employee, technophobia, psychological dependency, biprofessional, and public moonlighting.

5. Discuss the difference between eliminating jobs in economic units and causing general unemployment in the whole economy.

6. Discuss the relation of automation to the shorter workweek.

CHAPTER 9 SOCIAL POWER AND

RESPONSIBILITY

> For the fact to be attended to in modern industrial society is not the location of ownership but the location of responsibility.
>
> JOHN F. A. TAYLOR[1]

> We should welcome the Gospel of Social Responsibility; . . . at a minimum, it has replaced the Free Enterprise campaign with a new cliché, and, depending on our response to it, may provide the basis for more flexible use of private enterprise in our mixed economy.
>
> EARL F. CHEIT[2]

During the last 100 years, from the time of the American Civil War through the Granger movement, the trustbusters, the Great Depression, labor reform, and now automation, business thinking and action have changed dramatically. Business practices of a century ago would not be accepted even by a backward firm today. The point is academic whether business initiated these changes or whether society pushed business into them. In actuality, progress was mutual; each initiated changes on the other, assisted by other institutions in the total social system. Business could not have come as far as it has without the help of society, nor could society have progressed to its present state without corresponding business progress. We have learned this latter point from the experience of underdeveloped countries. Some are mature and cultured, but their progress has been stunted by a lack of a progressive business system.

[1] John F. A. Taylor, "Is the Corporation above the Law?" *Harvard Business Review*, March–April, 1965, p. 126.

[2] Earl F. Cheit, "The New Place of Business," in Earl F. Cheit (ed.), *The Business Establishment*, New York: John Wiley & Sons, Inc., 1964, p. 192.

As society changes, there is a need for business to change in order for the business system to be maintained at a high level of service to society. A significant change sweeping business today is the interest in social responsibility. Historically an owner managed his assets and could be held directly responsible by society. Now that ownership and management are separating, questions arise concerning the location of responsibility, as stated in the quotation introducing this chapter. In response to this felt need, the concept of social responsibility is developing. Some welcome it, as indicated by the second quotation introducing this chapter. Others fear it as a parasite that will consume the whole business system.

In this chapter we shall explore further the development of social responsibility, including its background and the relationship of power and responsibility. We shall examine the socioeconomic and human values that are involved with social responsibility and discuss how constitutionalism becomes the instrument for crystallizing social responsibility. Finally, membership investments and payoffs will be related in a theory of distributive justice.

DECISION MAKING AND RESPONSIBILITY

In the first chapter of this book we defined social responsibility as a person's obligation to consider the effects of his decisions and actions on the whole social system. The importance of social responsibility derives from the fact that it may affect a businessman's decisions, along with technical, economic, and other values which he must weigh. Social responsibility is rarely the exclusive reason for a decision, but it is usually a participating influence in decision making.

Defining a Socially Responsible Decision. A decision can be made for strictly technical reasons and by chance also be in the public interest, but this chance connection is not usually considered evidence of social responsibility. The true test of social responsibility is whether issues of public interest are considered at the time a decision is made. If so, then social responsibility is involved.

A socially responsible decision does not necessarily guarantee results in the public interest. The decision may, because of poor judgment or unforeseen events, actually cause results against the public interest, but society expects the majority of socially responsible decisions to affect the public interest favorably. Actually, many business decisions start a series of developments some of which serve the public interest and some of which, considered by themselves, are against it. A discharge for cause, if the man's unemployment is considered by itself, is hardly in the public interest. The decision as a whole, however, may be in the public interest. The only realistic approach is to consider the net effect on the public interest expected from the whole decision, adding pluses and minuses together.

Finally, there is no precise way to determine what the "public interest" is, how to measure it, or how to serve it; hence, socially responsible decisions will always be made in a state of imperfection and uncertainty.

While it is true that only businessmen (rather than businesses per se) make socially responsible decisions, they decide in terms of the objectives and policies of their business institution, which over a period of time acquires social power in its own right. Thus each business institution and the entire business system eventually come to stand for certain socially responsible beliefs and actions. But in the last analysis it is always the businessman who makes the decision. The business institution can only give him a cultural framework and policy guidance.

The substance of social responsibility arises from concern for the consequences of one's acts as they might affect the interests of others. This idea exists in most religions and philosophies of the world. Quite frequently, however, there is a tendency to limit this idea to person-to-person contacts. Social responsibility moves one large step further by emphasizing institutional actions and their consequences on the whole social system. Without this additional step there is a tendency to divorce personal and institutional acts. A man can lead a model personal life but go to work and continue to justify his business's pollution of a river because no direct personal consequence is involved. He can consider river pollution a "public problem" of little concern to him. The idea of social responsibility, however, requires him to consider his acts in terms of a whole social system in which he is responsible for the effects of his acts anywhere in the system.

Social responsibility, therefore, broadens a person's view to the total social system. When a man's primary frame of reference is limited strictly to himself, he may be counted upon for antisocial behavior whenever his values conflict with the ones society has. If his values refer primarily to a certain group or organization, he tends to become a partisan, acting as the group expects. But if he thinks in terms of all society as a whole system, he begins to build societal values into his actions, even when they are for a certain organization. This is the essence of social responsibility.

Actions for the benefit of an organization may still be socially responsible. To require that all acts be only in the public interest is to deny the pluralism of society. Centers of initiative are many, and in order to maintain these centers, their goals must be served as well as the general welfare. But the price which public society exacts for this pluralism is that private organizational acts shall be taken with due concern for public responsibility. There is in pluralism a concurrent private freedom and public responsibility. Pluralism is expected to continue as a dominant

American philosophy because the American community has confirmed it decisively in its Constitution and its culture.

Actions taken by a person for his own benefit may still be socially responsible if they benefit others also. To require that all acts be only in the public interest is to deny the psychological fact that all men act in their own interest. Social responsibility does not try to remake man; it asks of him only that he consider the broader social system when he acts. In this kind of social exchange both he and his neighbors should benefit. As emphasized by George C. Homans: "Not all self-interests are selfish interests." [3]

We have indicated that this book concerns business decisions in all types of organizations such as government, private business, and nonprofit institutions. Social responsibility applies to all of them. A man is no less free of the consequences of his actions simply because he works for government or a foundation. The petty bureaucrat in government can deny social responsibility for his business decisions as easily as the petty autocrat in private business. And so can the committee member or consultant. Studies disclose, for example, that 38 percent of the enormous government funds granted to universities for scientific research and development in 1963 went to less than ½ percent of the nation's 2,100 universities.[4] This unequal distribution of funds, even though based mostly on scientific issues, was an economic allocation affecting community development and concentration of power. It was partly a commercial decision weighted with business social responsibility.

Reasons for Emphasizing Social Responsibility. There are several reasons for recent emphasis on social responsibility.[5] One is that society today is bound together in greater complexity, with each of its parts more dependent on other parts. There is a new *social dependency*. A century ago the acts of a businessman in India were of little significance to the United States. Today with the world tied together in technology, communication, and politics, and with United States firms operating in India, business developments in that country are significant. The same reasoning applies even more strongly to social dependency within a national economy.

A second reason is that society has more wealth and culture which it wishes to protect; therefore, it is less willing to risk the disruption that might occur from irresponsible acts. The climate of public opinion in-

---

[3] George C. Homans, "Bringing Men Back In," *American Sociological Review*, December, 1964, p. 816.

[4] Leo S. Tonkin, "The Government's Role in University Research," *Industrial Research*, April, 1965, p. 83.

[5] See especially Howard R. Bowen, *Social Responsibilities of the Businessman*, New York: Harper & Row, Publishers, Incorporated, 1953, chaps. 8, 9.

creasingly insists that actions by all institutions and persons be responsible. Businessmen recognize that more responsible action is desirable to maintain a viable public image. They also wish to avoid encroachment of public regulation. From the view of their own self-interest, therefore, it is wise to be more responsible.

A third reason is that businessmen share the attitudes and values of society as they did a century ago, but those attitudes have moved toward more responsible conduct today. Sharing these values in society, the businessman supports them in his actions.

Finally, and perhaps most important, ownership and control are more separated in modern society. The career manager takes the longer view over time and the broader view among claimants on the organization. The separation of owner and manager has not been required by law but has developed *de facto* by delegation because this arrangement worked best. But this arrangement also confuses the location of responsibility. When the owner managed, the acts of the firm proceeded from his initiative. The identity and power of the firm resided in him. In this situation the law could directly fix responsibility in him without confusion. But with the separation of ownership and management, normal legal channels of responsibility have eroded. No one is quite sure how much public responsibility managers have nor through what channels it is controlled. To illustrate this problem, ignore legal details for the moment and assume that a corporation's owners at their death give their stock to it so that it eventually owns itself! Probably none of its practices would change from what they are today. Then to whom would it be responsible, and how?

We must be cautious, however, that we do not overplay the *possible* separation of owner and manager, because *actual* facts still show considerable unity of the two parties. The unity is evident in smaller firms. With regard to larger firms, one study reported that in 141 out of 232 of the nation's largest industrial firms, ownership by the board of directors was sufficient to have working control. And shareholder attendance at annual meetings is reported to be increasing rather than declining. Furthermore, the personal stake of stock ownership by an executive may be large, even when he owns only a small proportion of the firm. In 1957, General Motors Corporation officers owned an average of 11,500 shares each. This number of shares is a tiny portion of General Motors stock, but it is a personal investment of ½ million dollars for the executive who has it. His ownership is major to him. He therefore behaves like an owner.[6]

In summary, there appear to be good reasons for considering the social-responsibility issue, but the situation is probably not as alarming as

---

[6] Cheit, *op. cit.*, pp. 172–178, quoting studies by Don Villarejo, American Society of Corporate Secretaries, and Gabriel Kolko. See also the excellent discussion of management accountability in Ernest Dale, *The Great Organizers*, New York: McGraw-Hill Book Company, 1960, chap. 6, pp. 175–216.

some have pictured it. One fact is certain; businessmen cannot withdraw into isolation and avoid the social-responsibility issue. Neither can they claim that business is amoral and exempt from considerations of responsibility. The simple fact is that business is a major social institution, and as such it is importantly involved in social values. This is to its credit— a mark of its status. If business were not importantly involved in societal value systems, this fact would be evidence that it was detached from the mainstream of society and of little significance. But business is in the mainstream of life and, hence, in the mainstream of value. As stated by one top manager: "We must sense and be responsive to the social demands of the public as well as the marketplace and recognize the social consequences of economic decision-making." [7]

A fundamental issue in social responsibility is whether we shall define it by law or depend on self-regulation. Business has shown some adaptability and responsiveness to public demands already. As the connection of owner and manager grows more diluted, career management with its semiprofessional standards has developed to fill the responsibility gap. On the other hand, society runs a risk if it depends on business to set its own standards of responsibility. In the past, society has needed to step in with laws, such as the Sherman Antitrust Act and the National Labor Relations Act, in order to set general standards of responsibility, leaving to business most of the operational details. This policy combines both legal standards and self-regulation. It appears likely that a similar approach will develop for new areas of social responsibility as they arise.

THE POWER-RESPONSIBILITY EQUATION

Most persons agree that businessmen today have considerable social power.[8] Their counsel is sought by government and community. What they say and do influences their community. This type of influence is *social power*. It comes to businessmen because they are leaders, are intelligent men of affairs, and command vast economic resources. The assets of the Bell Telephone System, for example, were about 30 billion dollars in 1963, making it the largest business in the world. Among manufacturing businesses General Motors and Standard Oil (New Jersey) had both assets and sales of over 10 billion dollars in 1963. The annual sales of General Motors Corporation were greater than the Netherlands' gross national product. The five hundredth manufacturer in size in the United States in 1963 was still a large company, with sales of 86 million dollars

---

[7] Laurence I. Wood, "Social Performance of Business," *Economics and Business Bulletin*, Philadelphia: Temple University, September, 1964, p. 18.

[8] Portions of this section are adapted from Keith Davis, "Can Business Afford to Ignore Social Responsibilities?" *California Management Review*, Spring, 1960, pp. 70–76.

and assets of 117 million dollars. Studebaker Corporation lost nearly 81 million dollars in the same year. At the end of the year it closed its South Bend, Indiana, plant after over one hundred years of continuous operations. The closure caused major economic dislocations in the South Bend area.[9]

In many ways businessmen speak for the important institution we call business. They speak for or against legislation, economic policy, labor relations policy, and so on, *in their roles as businessmen.* When they speak and act as citizens only, and those involved recognize this fact, then whatever social power businessmen possess is that of a citizen and is not directly attributable to business. In practice, however, it is often difficult to distinguish between these two roles, thereby further complicating the social-power relationships of businessmen.

Social Responsibility Goes with Social Power. To the extent that businessmen or any other group has social power, the lessons of history suggest that social responsibility should be equated with it. Stated in the form of a general relationship, social responsibilities of businessmen need to reflect the amount of social power they have.

The idea that responsibility and power go hand in hand appears to be as old as civilization itself. Wherever one looks in ancient and medieval history—Palestine, Rome, Britain—men were concerned with balancing power and responsibility. Men, being something less than perfect, have often failed to achieve this balance, but they have generally sought it as a necessary antecedent to justice. This idea has its origins in reason and logic. It is essentially a matter of balancing one side of an equation with the other. As stated by one philosopher: "The demand of the law in a well-ordered society is that responsibility shall lie where the power of decision lies. Where that demand is met, men have a legal order; where it is not, they have only the illusion of one." [10]

The idea of equal power and responsibility is no stranger to business either. For example, one of the tenets of scientific management is that authority and responsibility should be balanced in such a way that each employee and each manager is made responsible to the extent of his authority, and vice versa. Although this tenet refers to relationships within the firm, it seems that it would apply as well to the larger society outside the firm. As a matter of fact, businessmen have been strong proponents of balanced social power and responsibility in external society, particularly in their views on the responsibilities of labor leaders.

The logic of reasonably balanced power and responsibility is often overlooked by discussants of social responsibility. On the one hand, it is argued that business is business and that anything which smacks of

[9] "The 500 Largest U.S. Industrial Corporations," *Fortune,* July, 1964, pp. 179–198.

[10] Taylor, *loc. cit.*

social responsibility is out of bounds. An economist contends: "Few trends could so thoroughly undermine the very foundations of our free society as the acceptance by corporate officials of a social responsibility other than to make as much money for their stockholders as possible." [11] Another author speaks of the "frightening spectacle" of a powerful business group which in the name of social responsibility ". . . imposes its narrow ideas about a broad spectrum of unrelated noneconomic subjects on the mass of man and society." [12] He advocates a powerful democratic state to look after general welfare, leaving business to pursue its main objective of material gains within limits of everyday civility.

The objections to social responsibility are meaningful. There are indeed some dangers as business moves into untrodden areas of social responsibility. The fallacy of these objections is that they are usually based on an economic model of pure competition in which market forces leave business theoretically without either social power or social responsibility (a balanced-zero equation). In real life, however, the economic model cannot be divorced from its social effects. Modern businesses possess such large aggregates of assets that their market use does have social effects. In reality, therefore, the no-responsibility doctrine assumes that business will keep some of its power but not worry about responsibility.

At the other extreme, some persons would have business assume responsibilities as a kind of social godfather, looking after widows and orphans and assuming responsibility for public health, juvenile delinquency, or any other social need, simply because business has large economic resources. This position overlooks the fact that business operates in a pluralistic society which has other institutions available to serve people in the areas mentioned. Business is one of many centers of initiative in the social system; hence there is no reason to make it a monolithic Big Brother overshadowing the state as it solves everyone's problems. The total-responsibility doctrine also confuses business's function of *service* to society with *servitude* to society. Workers, investors, and others participate in a business as free men, not as slaves of society. They have their own lives to live, and the business is their cooperative venture for fulfilling their own needs while serving others.

Both the no-responsibility and the total-responsibility doctrines are equally false. According to the first doctrine, business keeps its power but accepts no responsibility, thereby unbalancing the power-responsibility equation. According to the second doctrine, responsibility far exceeds power, again unbalancing the equation.

[11] Milton Friedman, *Capitalism and Freedom*, Chicago: The University of Chicago Press, 1962, p. 133.
[12] Theodore Levitt, "The Dangers of Social Responsibility," *Harvard Business Review*, September–October, 1958, p. 44.

The Iron Law of Responsibility. It is true that if business's social responsibilities could be avoided or reduced to insignificance, business would be released from a heavy burden. Social responsibilities are difficult to determine and apply. Their relationships are complex. If the complexities of social responsibility could be avoided, business decisions would certainly be easier to make. But what are the consequences of responsibility avoidance? If power and responsibility tend toward a state of balance in the long run, then *the avoidance of social responsibility leads to gradual erosion of social power.* This is the Iron Law of Responsibility: Those who do not take responsibility for their power ultimately shall lose it. Its long-run application to man's institutions certainly stands confirmed by history.

As it applies to business, the Iron Law of Responsibility decrees that to the extent that businessmen do not accept social-responsibility obligations as they arise, other groups will step in to assume those responsibilities. This prediction of diluted social power is not a normative statement of what we think *should* happen. Rather, it is a prediction of what *will tend* to happen whenever businessmen do not keep their social responsibilities approximately equal with their social power. In support of this view a study of business's social responsibilities concludes: "And it is becoming increasingly obvious that a freedom of choice and delegation of power such as businessmen exercise would hardly be permitted to continue without some assumption of social responsibility." [13] A businessman states the idea more emphatically: "I am convinced that unless we do [accept social responsibilities], the vacuum created by our unwillingness will be filled by those who would take us down the road to complete statism and inevitable moral and social collapse." [14]

History supports the mutuality of power and responsibility in business. Take safe working conditions as an example. Under the protection of common law, employers during the nineteenth century gave minor attention to worker safety. Early in the twentieth century, in the face of pressure from safety and workmen's compensation laws, employers genuinely accepted responsibility for safety. Since then there have been very few restrictions on business power in this area because business in general has been acting responsibly. Accident rates have been reduced dramatically, until the work place is safer than most away-from-work areas.

For an opposite example consider unemployment. Business in the first quarter of this century remained callous about technological and market layoff. As a result, business lost some of its power to government, which administers unemployment compensation, and to unions, which restrict it by means of tight seniority clauses, supplemental unemployment benefits, and other means. Now business finds itself in the position of paying

[13] Bowen, *op. cit.*, p. 4.

[14] Ben Moreell, *The Role of American Business in Social Progress*, Indianapolis: Indiana State Chamber of Commerce, 1956, p. 20.

unemployment costs that it originally denied responsibility for but having less control than when it did not pay! Business power has drained away to bring the power-responsibility equation back into balance.

Consider also the equation in terms of a current problem, gainful employment of older workers. The plight of workers in the over-forty-five age bracket is well known. In spite of public pronouncements of interest in them and in spite of their general employability, many of them find job opportunities limited or even nonexistent. At this time the power of initiative is still substantially with business, but it is being gradually eroded by fair-employment-practice laws. Will management stop this erosion by taking more responsibility? We do not know, but in any case the power-responsibility equation gradually, but surely, finds its balance.

Balancing Power and Responsibility. In line with the foregoing analysis, proposals for a strictly economic function of business with no social responsibility lose some of their glamour because they mean substantial loss of business power. Historian Arnold J. Toynbee predicts this result when he speaks of business managers eventually becoming part of a "new world civil service," not necessarily working for government, but working under such stability and elaborate rules from both within and without that they form a relatively powerless bureaucracy similar to the civil service.[15]

It is unlikely that businessmen will concede their social power so easily because they are men of action who will not sit quietly on the sidelines of progress. They want to be in the midst of progress, offering their innovations in all areas. It is even unlikely that society would permit businessmen to concede their power because it is coming to recognize its need for them. The more probable outcome is that society will persuade businessmen to accept more social responsibility in order to balance the power-responsibility equation. In serious situations, such as developed with trusts in the 1880s, "persuasion" will take the form of legal force on policy matters, leaving operating initiative to independent business units. The paramount point is operating initiative. If business conduct is so irresponsible that operating initiative is assumed by government boards, then the business civil service may truly develop.

It appears that both business leaders and the general public are coming to accept the idea of balanced power and responsibility. When businessmen accept the logic of this idea, their next step is learning to apply it when making decisions. Granted that there are no pat answers, they still need some guides, or else each will take off in a different direction according to his own views. At this point, the ideas already stated begin to offer operating help. If social responsibilities of businessmen need to reflect their social power, then, in a general way, in the specific operating areas

[15] Arnold J. Toynbee, "Thinking Ahead: Will Businessmen Be Civil Servants?" *Harvard Business Review*, September–October, 1958, pp. 23ff.

where there is power, responsibility will also reside. And the amount of responsibility will approximate the amount of power. Consider the situation of two companies, each closing its plant in a different city. Company A is a major employer in a small town. It is moving its entire plant out of the community. Company B is moving its plant of the same size out of a large city, where it is one of many employers. Other things being equal, it appears that Company A needs to give more thought to social responsibilities in connection with its move because of its greater effect on its community.

Even accepting the greater responsibility of Company A, and some would not go this far, there is no measure of exactly how much more responsibility it has or of how it should adjust to its greater responsibility. Thus the equation of balanced power and responsibility serves only as a rough guide, but a real one. For example, do businessmen by their industrial engineering decisions have the power to affect workers' feelings of accomplishment and self-fulfillment on the job? If so, there is a balancing need for social responsibility. Do businessmen have power to determine the honesty of advertising? To the degree that they do, does not social responsibility also arise?

One matter of significance is that the conditions causing power are both internal and external to the firm. In the example of advertising honesty, power is primarily internal, being derived from the authority structure of the firm and management's knowledge of product characteristics. In the case of Company A, much of its social power is derived from the external fact that it is the only employer in a small town. Each case is situational, requiring operating appraisal of power-responsibility relationships each time a decision is made.

Constitutionalism. A primary device for equating power and responsibility in an official way is constitutionalism, which was introduced in Chapter 1. Constitutionalism is the establishment of standards which protect society from arbitrary and unreasonable use of organizational power and establish due process for all parties involved. The words "arbitrary" and "unreasonable" are significant because any organization must have power in order to attain its objectives. Constitutionalism does not destroy power, but rather it defines conditions for responsible use of power. Its dual purpose is to channel organizational power in supportive ways and to protect private interest against unreasonable organizational power.[16] Constitutionalism is used to balance the power-responsibility equation. Its emphasis is upon the responsibility side of the equation, primarily limiting whatever power exists. This relationship with power suggests that as

[16] An excellent discussion is provided in Richard Eells and Clarence C. Walton, *Conceptual Foundations of Business*, Homewood, Ill.: Richard D. Irwin, Inc., 1961, chap. 17.

more power is acquired by organizations, more attention must be given to constitutional channeling of that power.

The philosophy of constitutionalism arises from political government, but it is finding its way into other large organizations as a result of social pressures to assure that power is used justly. Selekman speaks of the "urgency of a framework of constitutionalism for the modern corporation" in order to enhance its compatibility with modern society. He recognizes the difficulties involved: "Indeed, the carrying out of social and moral responsibility in complex situations is hardly ever a tidy, roseate affair except in utopian narratives." [17]

Constitutional standards may be generated internally, as in the case of codes of ethical practice or a company judicial procedure established to resolve executive disputes. Standards more often are generated through agreement with an external pressure group. The most notable external sources are labor groups and government, both discussed in later chapters. The labor agreement is a constitutional document defining rights and duties of both parties. An example in another area is a manufacturing concern's informal agreement with city officials that it would use a fume-producing work process only during midday hours, when rising air currents would dissipate the offensive odors. If the process were used at night, odors would settle in the neighborhood for hours. And in another city domestic airlines agreed that jets taking off would pass a certain landmark before turning in order not to pass over the downtown area of the complaining suburb. In still another city domestic airlines agreed to schedule no jets between midnight and 7 A.M. because they flew over hotel and residential areas.

An important corollary of constitutionalism is *due process*, which defines the conditions for use of power and the conditions for appeal of its excessive use. In employee relations, for example, a foreman may be unable to discharge a man directly. He can only suspend the man and recommend discharge to a higher office or a board. This procedure notifies others who may check his action, and it delays action to prevent decisions based on emotion in the heat of an argument. If an employee wishes to challenge his foreman's action, due process may permit him to have a hearing if he requests it, before discharge can be finalized. Constitutionalism thus provides procedural checks and balances on power.

CLAIMS ON BUSINESS

A view of social responsibility is not complete without looking at it from the other side, that is, the claims which others have on business.

[17] Benjamin M. Selekman, *A Moral Philosophy for Management*, New York: McGraw-Hill Book Company, 1959, pp. 206, 219.

These claims are the expectations which business is trying to meet when it acts responsibly. At this point we shall relate these claims to social responsibility in a general and abstract way. Part 3 of this book will discuss claims of specific groups such as unions, vendors, consumers, and the community.

Balancing Value Systems. Businessmen in making decisions balance together a number of value systems. Some of these are:

Technical—based on physical facts, science, and logic
Economic—based on market values determined by supply and demand
Social—based on group and institutional needs
Psychological—based on personal needs of individuals
Political—based on general welfare needs of the state
Aesthetic—based on beauty
Ethical—based on what is right

A measure of all values must be taken when a decision is made, but ultimately all measures tend to come back to man. He creates the supply and demand on which economic values are based. He makes up the groups which determine social and political values. He interprets what is right and what is beautiful. Perhaps, then, the broadest social responsibility of all is for business to be sure that human values are served in the business process. The cold technology of production can never be an end itself, but only a means to human ends. And these human ends concentrate on the person. As explained by the chairman of the board of one of the world's largest oil companies: "Every problem we face, whether of economics or technology or whatever it may be, is truly significant only as it bears on our great underlying concern: the fullest development of the potential which is hidden in every human being." [18] The president of the American Management Association confirms that ". . . it is the function of business management to develop the individual (and this is so fundamental with me, it is a deep conviction)." He adds that this is also the purpose of the church, education, and government: "Every important segment of society is interested in developing either the spiritual, mental, physical, or economic welfare of the individual." [19]

Organizational Payoffs Required. What are the expectations of persons as they relate to organizations such as business? There are at least three organizational payoffs required for human fulfillment. None of them can be provided in the absolute, but a measure of each is necessary for viable organizational life. The more of each payoff that can be gained,

[18] M. J. Rathbone, *The Businessman and the Problems of Progress,* New York: Standard Oil Company (New Jersey), 1963, p. 15.
[19] Lawrence A. Appley, "Affirmative Action," *Management News,* January, 1965, p. 2.

other things being equal, the more successful organizational life will be for the person. These three expectations are:

Improvement—the psychological purpose of man's attachment to an
organization
Independence—the individual price required for cooperation
Justice—the social standard for membership in organizations

Improvement is the basic reason a person joins an organization. For his membership investment he expects a payoff which brings him closer to his goals. If there is no payoff, he will withdraw his membership if he is free to do so. Improvement is expressed in terms of the rewards he receives from organizational attachment including money, recognition, and his own personal development.

Independence is the basic demand that a person makes of any organization in return for his cooperation. Normally he does not give all of himself. He reserves something for his own initiative and self-determination. Within the organization he insists on some freedom of action. He seeks organizational forms and supervisory practices which give him more independence. In advanced working environments independence finds its expression in self-actualization, which is highest on man's need structure.

Justice is the standard of treatment which a man expects from an organization, and through society he *demands* it of his organizations. Justice makes group life tolerable. It is based on fairness, reason, and prudence in organizational acts. It gives substance and meaning to human dignity because it protects the person in his dealings with the group. Justice means compliance with the spirit of a relationship as well as the letter of it. Justice is what holds an organization together in voluntary cooperation. If a man has a measure of independence plus improvement in the direction of his goals *but* bears injustice, he will leave an organization. If he cannot leave it, he will withhold full measure of cooperation.

The justice which man seeks from organizations is essentially a distributive justice concerning ". . . the feelings of rightness or wrongness in the balance between environmental rewards and social investments. . . . Individual rewards, when compared with the rewards received by other group members, should be proportional to social investment." [20] Education, for example, is considered to be a social investment. When people offer it to the organization as a membership investment, they expect rewards in terms of status and income. When investments and rewards are not in agreement, people feel that the situation lacks justice. To them it is not fair. They express unhappiness, they complain, and they withhold their cooperation.

[20] Abraham Zaleznik and David Moment, *The Dynamics of Interpersonal Behavior*, New York: John Wiley & Sons, Inc., 1964, pp. 330, 400.

Justice is a social comparison with others; therefore, a change in what others receive can cause a person to feel injustice just as much as a change in what he receives. Assume that a business partner feels he has a satisfactory situation in a partnership. He then discovers when he examines yearly expense accounts that two other partners have been entertaining business clients more often and much more expensively than he has. If in his mind he can find no "rational" reason for the difference, he may feel that the situation is unjust, even though he did not feel so until this moment.

Justice has an historical basis. A person feels that there should be some relationship between what he has contributed in the past and received in the past and what he is contributing and receiving now. A physician, for example, makes major internship investments with low financial rewards; therefore, he expects justice to provide him with quick financial rewards when he finally reaches his productive years. His is a delayed payoff in relation to investment. A different situation is that of a construction superintendent who has had high pay and status in the past and who expects the same on his present assignment, even though his contribution on this job is not quite as great as usual because of external factors. The just organization relates each person's membership investments to payoffs, both in relation to history and in relation to the investments and payoffs of others.

SUMMARY

Social responsibility refers to a person's obligation to consider the effects of his decisions and actions on the whole social system. It applies to both public and private institutions. Reasons for recent emphasis on social responsibility are more complex social dependency, more wealth needing more responsible care, changing attitudes, and partial separation of ownership from management.

Business has social power. The power-responsibility equation suggests that business should develop a corresponding amount of social responsibility. Avoidance of social responsibility leads to gradual erosion of social power, thus bringing the power-responsibility equation into balance. This is the Iron Law of Responsibility. Historical developments in business reflect this balance of power and responsibility. More specifically, in the operating areas where power is, responsibility exists also—and in approximately the same amount. Social responsibility is expressed in law, custom, self-regulation, and constitutional agreements which define conditions for responsible use of power. There is a need for more business constitutionalism.

Human ends are the basis of all business decisions. Three significant payoffs which persons normally expect for their organizational investments are improvement, independence, and justice.

QUESTIONS

1. Discuss reasons for growing interest in social responsibility in modern times.

2. How do pluralism and social responsibility relate to each other?

3. Discuss both sides of the issue concerning how large the separation of ownership and management is today.

4. Discuss how the power-responsibility equation applies to the social power of business.

5. What is the relationship of constitutionalism to social responsibility? Select an area of business practice, such as advertising or employment tests, and prepare detailed statements of business responsibility in this area. Defend your statements in seminar discussion.

6. Discuss three important organizational payoffs expected by members. Could you defend one payoff as most important?

3. BUSINESS AND ITS PUBLICS

CHAPTER 10 BUSINESS AND

GOVERNMENT RELATIONS

> One thing is certain, I believe: that no modern,
> dynamic society can operate at all if either industry or
> government is to be straitjacketed by outmoded con-
> cepts concerning size and scope. What is wanted is
> more understanding of the needs of both; not less.
>
> Roger M. Blough[1]

Jack Smith grew up outside a small town in the forest country of the
northern United States. Like everyone else, he attended public schools. At
the outbreak of World War II, Jack entered the Army and served four
years. Upon discharge, he enrolled in his state university and received his
degree under the GI Bill of Rights.

After graduation, he moved to the Rocky Mountains and obtained a
job with a lumber company. Shortly thereafter he got married and bought
a home with a Veterans' Administration guaranteed mortgage. Jack was
smart and capable. He advanced rapidly with his company and was able to
save money. With the help of a Small Business Administration loan, he
built a sawmill and entered business on his own. He was, at the same time,
the successful bidder in a timber sale held by the Forest Service.

Because Jack was a veteran, he received priority in bidding on some
land which the Bureau of Land Management was selling at public auction.
He was successful in obtaining a small parcel of land and built a modest
home on it. His retired parents soon moved into the house, where they
lived quite comfortably on their social security checks.

As Jack became more firmly established in business, he became more

---

[1] Roger M. Blough, "The Real Revolutionaries" (address before the Whirlpool
Corporation Management Club, Benton Harbor, Mich., Sept. 25, 1963), New York:
United States Steel Corporation, 1963, p. 15.

interested in local and state development. Under a Federal program, he was instrumental in having his town declared a recreation area, which made it eligible to receive Federal funds to develop recreation. A park and swimming pool were built. He was also active in getting the government to build a large dam and irrigation project close to town. He was appointed to the State Planning Commission and was elected to the state chamber of commerce.

One day Jack wrote to his congressman: "I urge you to do everything in your power to curb increasing governmental give-away programs. Government's willingness to enter virtually every phase of private and business life is rapidly destroying the American heritage of individualism. In addition, high taxes which businessmen must pay to support these programs are rapidly destroying the profit motive and sapping the vitality of the business system. I demand that you exert all effort to preserve free competition and our laissez-faire tradition."

THE LAISSEZ-FAIRE TRADITION: A FICTION?

Like Jack Smith, thousands of businessmen today are deeply concerned about government-business relationships. Also, like Jack Smith, most of those same thousands of businessmen enjoy a vast variety of benefits which stem directly from government participation in our free enterprise economy.

John R. Bunting has pointed out that most businessmen are victims of dual economic ideology.[2] They are, according to Bunting, happily inconsistent, arguing on the one hand for a pure form of free enterprise and decrying unrestrained competition on the other. To illustrate, he contrasts two speeches given before a convention of businessmen.[3] In the first speech a businessman thoroughly denounced "price chiselers" and accused them of "leading us back to cutthroat competition." "The only way to ensure profits," the speaker continued, "is to stick together, keep prices high, and maybe push them higher." Bunting, then a Federal Reserve officer, followed with a speech entitled "Free Markets and the Federal Reserve System." In his speech Bunting explained ". . . how the Federal Reserve, by its decision to stop pegging government bonds, had helped to start a trend back to free-market principles." Although the speeches contradicted each other, the audience made no distinction. They agreed with both speakers.

Businessmen do appear to have a schizophrenic philosophy toward the roles of business and government in the national economy. The reason businessmen seem to be inconsistent is that modern business philosophies

---

[2] John R. Bunting, *The Hidden Face of Free Enterprise: The Strange Economics of the American Businessman*, New York: McGraw-Hill Book Company, 1964.
[3] *Ibid.*

are a blend of portions of classical economic models which best fit their needs. When a businessman says he believes in the free enterprise system and *laissez faire*, he does not mean that he accepts Adam Smith's *laissez faire* and pure competition. He is talking about something else. How a businessman feels about a particular act of government depends on how it affects him. Many New York businessmen who believe in free enterprise, for example, wholeheartedly supported efforts to prevent a large New York store from selling nationally labeled whiskeys at a price below that set by the state liquor control agency.

It is doubtful that businessmen ever really believed in perfect competition and pure *laissez faire*. While perfect competition stressed businessmen's pursuit of self-interest as the best way to national well-being, freedom of the market kept any individual from maintaining a competitive advantage. Similarly, laissez-faire philosophies viewed government as a passive body sitting weakly on the sidelines, performing only those functions which were inappropriate to the profit system.

Businessmen today have modified these theories to fit their needs. For the modern businessman, pursuit of self-interest means securing and holding a competitive advantage. *Laissez faire* means to him minimum interference with *his* pursuit of self-interest and maximum support of *his* endeavors. The modern businessman often views the problem emotionally, so that when he advocates cuts in government spending, he usually means in all areas or regions except his own. Or when he encourages free trade and cutting tariffs, he usually means in all areas except his own. For example, when a recent decision to close a number of military establishments in various parts of the country was announced, floods of letters poured into Washington from businessmen in the affected areas protesting the closing of *their* installation. Similarly, a few years ago, thousands of dollars were spent by various communities trying to influence the Federal government to select *their* community as the site for the Air Force Academy.

There is nothing wrong with such actions on the part of businessmen. On the contrary, they add strength and vitality to the economic system. What is important is that both business and government, as two major agents of society, agree upon what kind of competitive free enterprise system is best. Businessmen's thinking, reflected in their speeches and actions, appears to affirm their belief in monopolistic competition and rejection of a pure laissez-faire philosophy. On the other hand, government's actions often appear to emphasize a belief in a weakly modified form of pure competition. What is needed by each is an understanding of the other's basic philosophy. Failure to understand and respect the other's point of view will result in continued conflict. This chapter will discuss the roles of business and government in the American free enterprise system. We shall consider business's efforts to project a favorable social image and the various ways business and government relate to each other.

Finally, we shall discuss the separate and joint responsibilities for a strong national economy and the role of businessmen in politics.

THE BUSINESS IMAGE

Businessmen's concern over public views of business is nothing new. Indeed, businessmen have been fighting against an unfavorable public image for hundreds of years. People have held a distrust of the business system to one degree or another since the earliest forms of business emerged. Chapters 2 and 3 described some of the earlier public attitudes toward business. But people throughout the world and over time seem to have simultaneously held two opposing views of business. Since business has been the prime mover in economic development over the centuries, people have looked favorably upon economic results generated by business. Job opportunities, investment opportunities, and a constant flow of new and improved products have led a majority of people to accept and encourage business growth. On the other hand, a deep and persisting fear remains that too much economic power has been concentrated in big business. This fear is reflected in periodic waves of restrictive public policy directed toward the business system.

In America, public attitude toward business has been remarkably inconsistent, vacillating between support and encouragement of business growth and attacks on concentrations of economic power. These attitudes are, in turn, reflected in ever-changing public policy toward business which has left businessmen unsure of their economic behavior. Public attitudes toward business seem to be a function of national emergencies. Figure 10-1 shows the relationship, over time, between public confidence in and public suspicion of the American business system. During periods of national emergencies, such as war, when national security

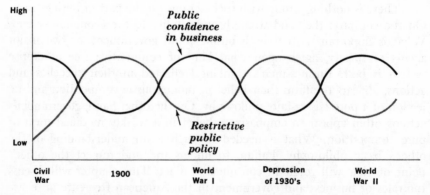

Figure 10-1 Historical relationships between public confidence in business and government restrictions on business.

depended upon performance of America's productive powers, public confidence in business has always been high. National need for production has always been accompanied by reductions in restrictive policies and emphasis on policies which favored business integration and increased capital accumulations. Noncrisis periods have typically brought forth increases in restrictive policies.

Obviously, it is in noncrisis periods that business must be most concerned with the image it presents. Aside from daily decisions concerning ethical behavior, business is becoming increasingly concerned with its image and is exerting considerable effort in many quarters to strengthen it. Economic education at all levels, including public schools, has been emphasized and encouraged in recent years. Support of community activities and projects has stressed corporate citizenship. In an effort to reach high school students, the American Management Association recently established a summer camp dedicated to showing boys what makes business tick. On another front, a group of successful New York executives have organized the Interracial Council for Business. By contributing their talents in the form of free consulting services to Negro businessmen, they see an opportunity to take a positive part in the civil rights movement.

Whatever form efforts take, it is clear that business needs continually to solicit public support of the free enterprise business system. As modern economy becomes more complex, greater concentrations of capital will be necessary to accomplish the economic tasks that lie ahead. Only with the fullest public understanding of the role of business and the resulting favorable public policy will it be possible for business to achieve national economic goals. It is also increasingly clear that business cannot accomplish national objectives alone. Government, along with labor, needs to develop stronger working relations with business.

HOW MUCH GOVERNMENT?

From the time the Constitution was written and signed, government has been active in one way or another in American business. The Constitution itself provides for certain government interventions in the business system. It specifically gives Congress the power to tax, to regulate commerce, to establish a mail system, to grant patents, and to provide for a common defense. In the history of America, there has never been a question (as many people would like to believe) of *whether* there would be government participation in business. Rather the questions have always been, and will continue to be: *How much* and *what kind* of government participation is appropriate?

Traditionally, business has been given major responsibilities for national well-being. Until the latter part of the nineteenth century, business bore these responsibilities practically alone. But experience gained during this period showed the undesirability of what Mund calls the "rule of the jungle."[4] The results of unbridled pursuit of self-interest in a no-rules, no-holds-barred sort of competitive game were the misuses of monopoly power discussed earlier in this book. Clearly, this was not the best way to achieve maximum social well-being. It was evident to society that rules were desirable and that a referee was needed to enforce the rules. Society empowered government to perform these functions.

Government intervention in business affairs has not stemmed the growth of business, as was prophesied by the nineteenth-century proponents of *laissez faire*. Business has continued to grow. A current gross national product in excess of 600 billion dollars is ample testimony of this growth. But as business has grown, so has government. The Federal government is the biggest spender, the biggest employer, the biggest property owner, the biggest tenant, the biggest insurer, the biggest lender, the biggest borrower, and the biggest customer in the free world.[5] It is also true that government exercises powers which many consider to be violations of individual liberties. Indeed, as Lammot du Pont Copeland observed: "The Federal government is a partner in every business in the country. For most of us . . . it has been a majority partner." [6]

There are many today who feel that in trying to escape the "rule of the jungle," society has gone too far in the other direction, and they point to the undesirability of the "law of the jail."[7] They condemn increasing authoritarian control by government with its restrictions and regulations. They contend that excessive government involvement in the private sector of our economy has a demoralizing effect which invites evasions of laws, destroys the American innovative spirit, crushes the profit motive, and therefore dilutes the strength and vitality of the economy. Many among this group cry for a return to the good old days of *laissez faire*.

Both business and government have grown tremendously, and they will continue to grow. Utopian pleas to return to the "good old days" will do little to develop proper business-government relationships. Rather, managers' jobs today are dependent upon finding ways to live and work with government. Both government and business are striving for the same end—greater social well-being. Businessmen need to get over viewing government as an enemy, bent on destroying them. Similarly, society

---

[4] Vernon A. Mund, *Government and Business*, New York: Harper & Row, Publishers, Incorporated, 1960, p. 520.

[5] Lammot du Pont Copeland, *It Takes Two to Make a Partnership Work* (speech before the New York Chamber of Commerce, Feb. 10, 1964), p. 5.

[6] *Ibid.*, p. 4.

[7] Mund, *loc. cit.*

(through the eyes of government) needs to stop looking at business as a hostile force, bent on destroying its well-being. Strong economic growth will be hampered as long as these attitudes prevail. Roger Blough expressed the relationship nicely when he said:[8]

> In this management task, one is continually confronted by the requirements, the proliferation and the constant growth and cost of government, both state and local [and Federal], which in the aggregate is enough to give anyone pause.
>
> But blind opposition to governmental growth and to the enlargement of governmental power can, I believe, be as disastrous to the progress of this economic revolution as the failure to guard our freedoms with discerning vigilance. For the idea that government must be the natural and irreconcilable enemy of the individual and his enterprises is—it seems to me—as anachronistic in this day and age as the outworn Marxist doctrine of eternal enmity between owner and employee.

In modern, complex society, there is plenty for everyone to do. Obviously, some jobs which are necessary to society's well-being can best be done by government. National defense, reclamation, and policing activities are traditional government jobs. Few would argue that government cannot perform these activities more effectively than profit-oriented businesses. On the other hand, there are a number of jobs that can best be performed by business. Product planning, product decisions, actual production, and innovation have traditionally been viewed as business responsibilities.

However, as our society becomes more complex, societal problems also become more complex, requiring joint attention from many social institutions. Business and government are increasingly sharing responsibilities for broad social problems. Business is, for example, playing a significant role in the antipoverty program.[9] Some large companies such as International Business Machines and Litton Industries have loaned executives to the program. Others have loaned economists and analysts to assist in analyzing job-stimulating policies that might be used in the future. Other executives have volunteered to serve on the Business Leadership Advisory Council for the purpose of promoting the antipoverty program in their communities and to develop jobs for Job Corps graduates. A number of businesses have volunteered to operate one or more job centers under the program.

Social problems of retirement and small-business failure also have lent themselves to joint solutions by government and business. To ease the pressures of forced retirement and at the same time provide much-needed business consulting service for small businesses, the Small Busi-

---

[8] Blough, *loc. cit.*
[9] "How the $1-Billion Will Be Split Up," *Business Week*, Aug. 15, 1964, p. 30.

ness Administration has organized the Service Corps of Retired Executives (SCORE).[10] The Association of Management Consultants is helping to guide the Boston project of SCORE and plans to continue to advise the Small Business Administration as new regions are organized.

Martin Marietta Company's unique approach to laying off valuable scientific personnel further illustrates how business can share responsibility in broad problems.[11] One problem which has continually plagued the aerospace industry and which has sometimes slowed both defense and space programs is dislocation of scientific personnel and middle managers. These dislocations occur because fluctuations of contracts often make it difficult for companies to maintain a stable work force. Loss of contracts, failure to obtain new ones, or completion of existing contracts often causes companies to cut back personnel. Other companies, at the same time, may find themselves short of qualified people because new contracts are obtained. Considerable cost is incurred in locating additional people. Industry estimates that it costs $2,000 to recruit a single middle manager. To alleviate the situation and to take the sting out of layoff, Martin Marietta hired a consultant to find jobs with other companies for 162 middle managers after their last personnel reduction.

It is, of course, impossible to answer precisely the question of how much government participation in business is appropriate. There are a number of answers to the question, depending upon who is answering it. It would be presumptuous to propose any set and fixed formula for business-government relations, and we shall not try. But, since government is probably the most important single public that business relates to, it is appropriate to examine briefly some of the relationships that exist.

AREAS OF GOVERNMENT ACTIVITY

Many relations between government and business are regulatory; others are supportive. But whatever the relation, they complicate businessmen's lives. In this section we shall examine some of these relations, not because we necessarily feel that they are right and appropriate, but because society feels that they are.

Regulatory Relations. Beginning with the Sherman Act, businessmen increasingly have been subjected to regulation and policing by government agencies. Economic profits normally are made by producing more and better goods and services. But unfortunately for society, more profits can sometimes be made (at least in the short run) by producing inferior goods, by misusing monopoly power, and by misleading or de-

---

[10] "Where Sick Companies Can Turn for Advice," *Business Week*, Aug. 15, 1964, p. 94.

[11] "Taking the Sting out of 'De-hiring,' " *Business Week*, Jan. 2, 1965, p. 78.

ceiving customers. In order to curb social evils and ensure maximum social payoffs, society has seen fit to impose controls and restrictions on a variety of business activities.

Most people, including businessmen themselves, agree that some regulation of business practice is desirable. Partly because of a genuine recognition of public need, and partly to avoid unrealistic regulatory action, businessmen often join public authorities in formulating regulations. A few years ago, a plant manager of a large Eastern company recognized the appearance of a strong demand for legislation on air and water pollution which would affect a large and highly concentrated manufacturing area. Instead of waiting for legislators to draft and introduce bills, he and his associates, with the help of their engineers and technicians, drafted what they considered an effective bill. It solved the problem and yet was a regulation they "could live with." The proposal was enacted into law to the satisfaction of all concerned.

In many other areas businessmen feel that regulations hamper their effectiveness and act as a damper on their ability to move the economy into high gear. These criticisms are true to some degree, but society has felt it necessary to establish rules. And as the economy becomes more complex, businessmen and government will need to work more closely than ever before and with greater understanding and appreciation of each other's needs. If business is to have rules and regulations which it can live by and which will encourage it to perform its economic task, it needs to take a more active part in developing and modifying regulations.

Antitrust Policy. The purpose of antitrust laws has been to preserve competition. Probably in no other area of regulation have businessmen encountered more confusion and frustration. The vagueness of the laws themselves and court inconsistencies in enforcing them have left businessmen uncertain as to what they can do. It has become increasingly difficult for them to conform to legal requirements and at the same time perform their economic functions as they perceive them.

At the center of businessmen's confusion are antitrust policies of the Federal government. It has been observed that the " . . . most important recent antitrust development from the viewpoint of managerial decision making is the tightening up of the prohibitions against corporate mergers and acquisitions." [12] In 1950, the Celler-Kefauver amendment to Section 7 of the Clayton Act made it clear that mergers would be illegal if they substantially lessened competition or created a monopoly. The rules which were laid down stated that (1) companies who are major competitors cannot merge under any circumstances; (2) companies can-

[12] Jesse W. Markham, "Antitrust Trends and New Constraints," *Harvard Business Review*, May–June, 1963, p. 85.

not merge if, as a result, they would control 30 percent of the market; and (3) if one company is already a giant, it cannot acquire another, no matter how small the share of the market is.

Considerable controversy exists over whether or not antitrust laws, as they are currently being administered, really do strengthen competition. The Justice Department's policy of "grow from within, not by merger," has been attacked as lessening competition rather than strengthening it. As a result of the Justice Department's blocking the merger of Mack Trucks, Incorporated, with Chrysler Corporation, one Mack official commented that "the Justice Department attitude itself tends to lessen competition, since it leaves small companies no way to grow and diversify in an industry dominated by giant corporations who themselves originally took the merger route. Ironically, the department is helping the giants by stopping mergers that would make others stronger."[13]

Justice Department officials are also facing other difficulties in administering their antimerger policies, and there is some evidence of need for softening the provisions. Justice officials seem to be considering social as well as economic ramifications of their decisions. Early in 1965 the Justice Department withdrew objections to the merger of electrical appliance maker Landers, Frary, and Clark with General Electric. The apparent reason for blocking the merger was that General Electric is so large that acquiring even a small competitor would violate the Clayton Act. However, two senators, fearing that Landers, Frary, and Clark plants in their states would be shut down, resulting in unemployment, if the merger were not allowed, asked the Justice Department to reconsider its decision. The Department reversed its decision, ". . . apparently on the theory that antitrust enforcement should consider other dimensions as well as competition."[14]

Businessmen increasingly are making demands for clarification and rewriting of antitrust laws. The need is apparent if one looks at the increased number of antitrust actions brought by the Justice Department and the Federal Trade Commission. From 1948 to 1962 the number of suits initiated by the Justice Department more than doubled, increasing from an average of thirty-six cases annually to an annual average of seventy-eight. Federal Trade Commission cases have increased even more. Presently, the Federal Trade Commission is processing approximately six hundred cases a year, as opposed to about one hundred 10 years ago.

But businessmen will not get the relief they need by sitting idly by. To get laws they can readily understand and more easily conform to, businessmen will need to increase their cooperation with government and

[13] "If You're Big, Grow from Within," *Business Week*, Aug. 8, 1964, p. 26.
[14] "Antitrusters Drop Fight on G.E. Deal as Senators Fear Closing of Plants," *Business Week*, Apr. 17, 1965, p. 36.

press for opportunities to participate in developing a workable set of clearly defined antitrust rules.

Government as a Customer. Government has always depended upon business to furnish a variety of goods and services needed to accomplish its functions. In 1790 government spent 14 million dollars. As America has grown and the economy has become more complex, government expenditures have steadily increased. In 1914 total government expenditures were 735 million dollars, and by 1945 they had climbed to over 12.5 billion dollars. In 1964, however, government spent about 17 billion dollars for research and development alone, and it is most likely that research and development outlays will reach 20 billion dollars by 1970.[15]

Government purchases an almost incomprehensible array of goods and services today. Purchases range from paper clips to space capsules, and from adding machines to huge electric generators. It buys the services and skills of thousands of people who perform the tremendous variety of activities it is engaged in. As government grows larger, it will become an even greater purchaser of goods and services.

Today government purchases of goods and services have become a major factor in national economic health. Major industries have developed since World War II that are almost wholly dependent upon government purchases; aerospace and defense industries are examples. Defense alone accounts for 9 percent of gross national product, directly employs 10 percent of the labor force, indirectly accounts for employment of thousands of other people, and finances approximately half of national research and development efforts.

While high rates of government spending for defense and space research contribute substantially to national well-being, there are some dangers and disadvantages. The major disadvantage is that the companies that have become highly efficient in specialized areas, such as aerospace, have become nearly wholly dependent upon one purchaser. For example, to accomplish space programs, companies often become so narrow and specialized (encouraged by government) that the products and skills they develop are salable only to government. McDonnell Aircraft sells 99 percent of its production to the government. Likewise, Raytheon Corporation depends on government to take 86 percent of its output; North American Aviation, 90 percent; and General Dynamics, 95 percent.

A high degree of interdependency has developed between government and business in the defense and aerospace industries. By allowing a dependency relation to grow, government must assume some responsibility for the companies' survival. However, government may have difficulties in properly exercising responsibilities to both captive suppliers

[15] "By 1970, a $20-billion Plateau?" *Business Week*, July 25, 1964, p. 64.

and society. On the one hand, withdrawal of purchases may cause a company to fail. On the other, government cannot continue programs that are not needed. But one thing seems certain: government cannot suddenly withdraw support from captive suppliers. Nor can government suddenly shrink special programs which have been directly responsible for industrial expansion. Unfavorable economic consequences would be too great. Rather, it seems clear that government needs to help these industries diversify. Government may find it necessary to reevaluate its stand on mergers and acquisitions if transitions from defense and aerospace activities to civilian production are to be strengthened rather than stifled. To help defense and aerospace companies diversify, government has suggested several areas where defense technology could be utilized. One high official in the Defense Department suggested that systems-oriented companies sell their scientific and manufacturing skills as a problem-solving service. Three areas frequently mentioned that could benefit from application of defense technology include "advanced urban mass transit systems, improved air and space travel, improved communications and weather forecasting, and more reliable air and highway traffic control systems." Also suggested have been "mining the ocean floor, sea farming, revitalizing the merchant marine, air and water pollution control, urban renewal, educational aids and technical assistance to underdeveloped countries."[16]

But there are other dangers of a broader nature inherent in selling to government. Government, in its role as a buyer, has had tremendous influence on business policies. Its purchasing power is sufficient to allow it to dictate terms of purchase, and as a result, management decision and control have been narrowed. So great has government influence been that hundreds of companies have found it necessary to modify policies in the areas of pricing, products, marketing, financing, and labor.

Government as a Competitor. Government does not purchase all goods and services from the business sector of the economy. Indeed, it has become a substantial and not always welcome competitor of private business. Government produces a wide variety of goods and services, some of which society views as public enterprise. Publicly operated enterprises, such as the mint, postal service, and the highway network, are reserved as appropriate governmental activity. But the government is engaged in a variety of activities that compete directly with private business.

Competition with private industry by government agencies has been an issue since the early 1930s. Aggravated by economic dislocations and increased needs during World War II, government moved into many areas which directly conflicted with private businesses. There is no accurate measure of the true amount of government competition. In 1960 the Budget Bureau reported 14,100 industrial-commercial activities en-

[16] "What Will Take up the Slack?" *Business Week*, July 18, 1964, p. 55.

gaged in by the Federal government. However, of this total, 8,000 activities were small custodial operations for government buildings, and 3,900 were grain storage bins. No dollar valuation was assigned to any of the activities.

Nevertheless, businessmen feel that government competition is substantial, and they continue to press for government withdrawal from commercial and industrial activities. Over the years, government has responded by disposing of such varied activities as a tin smelter, coffee roasting plants, a Mississippi River barge line, scrap metal processing plants, paint production facilities, auto repair shops, and shipyards.[17] But in spite of these divestitures, the government continues to produce vast quantities of goods and services that compete directly with business.

Through agencies such as the Small Business Administration, the Commodities Credit Corporation, and others, it loans money in competition with conventional lending agencies. Power produced by the Tennessee Valley Authority competes with privately produced power. The Veterans' Administration insures lives, and farmers can obtain crop insurance from the government. Insurance industry spokesmen expect the Medicare program to preempt most of the health insurance for superannuated persons. Most insurance companies are preparing to discontinue their health insurance for the aged because they cannot compete with the government. Some three hundred military commissary stores sell annually about 800 million dollars in foods, and military post exchanges compete with local merchants in the sale of consumer goods. In other areas, the government operates the largest single employment agency, competes with printers, builds and repairs ships, installs and operates microwave radio systems which compete with private telephone companies, makes false teeth, and provides a wide variety of consulting services which compete with private consulting firms. It has recently been suggested that all patents stemming from government-supported research become the property of the government, rather than belonging to the firm doing the research.

In an attempt to help solve the problem and ease competitive pressures on private business, President Johnson recently instructed the Budget Bureau to revise the 1959 guidelines on when and how the government can provide products and services for its own use. After seeing the draft of the new proposal, many businessmen doubt that they will receive much relief. The Wall Street Journal reports:[18]

> The new draft, like the old order, provides lots of reasons why the presumption in favor of private enterprise can be ignored: A need for

---

[17] "Uncle Sam, Inc., Drive to Cut Rivalry by U.S. with Business Makes Little Headway," The Wall Street Journal, Apr. 27, 1965.
[18] Ibid.

secrecy or for experience in meeting some mobilization emergency, a need for a service in a remote geographical area or for a product so specialized that industry won't produce it—plus substantially higher costs of purchase from private firms.

But the new order does spell out in detail a specific procedure that a Federal agency must conform to in order to enter into any new industrial or commercial type of activity. One businessman commented: "It may be that the most help we get from the new order will come in keeping the government from starting new things, rather than getting it out of things it's already doing."[19]

RESPONSIBILITY FOR A STRONG ECONOMY

Business is typically viewed as the prime mover of the economic system. Society depends on business to produce an ever-increasing flow of goods, jobs, and investment opportunities. However, during the prolonged Depression which followed the crash of 1929, there was a diminishing public confidence in the ability of the business system alone to maintain a strong and viable economy. There was a growing belief that government and business should jointly assume responsibility for national well-being. In 1936 Arthur Burns suggested: "All efforts to deal with unsatisfactoriness of the outcome of the present organization of industry lead in the end to the acceptance by the state, in some form or other, of responsibility for participating in the exercise of economic power."[20] John Maynard Keynes also expressed doubts that a free enterprise market system could maintain full employment without assistance from government spending.[21]

There seemed to be two ways in which government could contribute to economic strength. "First, . . . excessive concentration of business power should be eliminated. Second, insofar as the economic system appeared incapable of self-adjustment, it would become the direct function of government to restore the economic balance and to underwrite continuing high production and employment."[22] Regulation of business power through antitrust legislation has been discussed earlier, and we shall now consider government participation in economic growth through supportive public policy.

Most businessmen today accept a joint responsibility with govern-

---

[19] *Ibid.*

[20] Arthur R. Burns, *The Decline of Competition: A Study of the Evolution of American Industry*, New York: McGraw-Hill Book Company, 1936, p. 529.

[21] John Maynard Keynes, *The General Theory of Employment, Interest, and Money*, New York: Harcourt, Brace & World, Inc., 1936, pp. 30–31, 378.

[22] A. D. H. Kaplan, *Big Enterprise in a Competitive System*, rev. ed., Washington, D.C.: The Brookings Institution, 1964, p. 30.

ment for an expanding economy. However, they view the proper role of government as supportive rather than active participation. They perceive the government role to be one of providing a climate which will encourage business to exercise its full talents to the greatest degree. Government, according to businessmen, should not introduce restrictions that will hamstring business's economic efforts. Although businessmen do not always approve of specific governmental actions, they generally approve of the public policy of maintaining a stable economy. Peter Drucker observed:[23]

> That government is best that gets the necessary and fundamental things done—the foundations in education, transportation and monetary and fiscal policy we need; the foundations of predictable and equal justice for all and of law and order for all; the capacity to defend one's territory against aggression and one's civil peace against usurpation and internal strife—in short the classical duties of government which have not as much changed over the millennium as they have become increasingly more complex, increasingly more demanding.

Internationally, as well as domestically, government and business share responsibility for business success. International business will be discussed in greater detail in later chapters, but it is appropriate here to point out that business success abroad depends in large measure on government's foreign policy. Conversely, foreign policy in many cases can be strengthened or undermined by actions of businessmen operating in foreign countries.

Regarding government's responsibilities to generate and maintain an expanding economy, M. J. Rathbone suggested the following public policies toward business:[24]

> First, within the sensible and humane limits . . . indicated, government must give less emphasis to protecting outmoded jobs, skills, and business from the salutary effects of improved technology—whether domestic or foreign—and place more emphasis on spreading to all our people the benefits of efficiency in the form of lower prices, wider markets, and ultimately, more jobs. In short, government should promote efficiency, not discourage it.
>
> Second, government should see that none of its policies or laws puts American investments abroad, and especially American business operating abroad, at a disadvantage in world competition. It should recognize that foreign investment has an important role to play in our economy.

[23] Peter F. Drucker, "Government and Business as Partners in Economic Development" (speech before the Fifth Inter-American Management Conference, Lima, Peru, Nov. 8–14, 1964), p. 3.

[24] M. J. Rathbone, chairman of the board and chief executive officer (retired), Standard Oil Company (New Jersey), "Three Men in a Boat" (speech before the Harvard Business School Club of Washington, D.C., Nov. 28, 1962), pp. 9–10.

Third, government should use its influence to achieve a reasonable balance of power between labor and management, and to help both sides see their interests in broad terms compatible with the national interest. As this is done, need for direct government intervention in labor-management disputes will tend to diminish.

Fourth, tax reduction remains an urgent item. This will provide an immediate stimulus. It will create new demand, promote new investment, and thereby accelerate the rate of economic growth.

Fifth, government must find a way to become more efficient and cut costs. For it is only in this way that, in the long run, taxes can be cut and stay cut. I think it is a safe bet that there are at least as many obsolete skills within our government as there are in industry. What I urge is that government be as stringent in attacking its own efficiency and unnecessary functions as we in industry must be.

Lastly, looking to the future, one doesn't need to let his imagination wander very far before he sees new products—and in fact new industries —growing out of the vast governmental expenditures for research, space and the military. I suggest that when this occurs they be turned over, just as fast as possible, to the private competitive economy to be developed for civilian use. It is encouraging to see that, despite opposition, we have already done this in some cases. Let us not slow down this process by attempting to invoke governmental control.

BUSINESS'S PLACE IN POLITICS

A great deal has been said in recent years about businessmen's place in politics. Strong arguments have been advanced criticizing businessmen for becoming involved in politics *as businessmen*. Arnold Maremont comments:[25]

It is my conviction that business ought, for its own good, to stay out of politics.

I favor the widest possible participation in politics on an *individual* basis, for when it becomes the province of the elite few our system is in danger. It is when corporations begin running political classes, conducting political schools, and urging that their executives enter the political arena to expound the corporation viewpoint that I become deeply fearful of the consequences.

Equally strong arguments are made encouraging businessmen to be active in politics both as individuals and as businessmen.[26]

How to become active in politics is a question to which few busi-

[25] Arnold H. Maremont, "The Dangers of Corporate Activity in Politics," *Business Topics*, Winter, 1960, p. 7. Also see Michael D. Reagan, "The Seven Fallacies of Business in Politics," *Harvard Business Review*, March–April, 1960, p. 68.

[26] Willard V. Merrihue, "The Business Leader's Role in Politics," *Business Horizons*, Summer, 1960, pp. 38–44.

nesses have found a satisfactory answer. They often resist having their executives and/or employees become active participants in party politics for three main reasons. First, employees of a corporation who rise to high places in a political party or who campaign for political office while still in the employment of the company are likely to generate severe public criticism of the company itself. Even though the individual and the company may be unselfishly motivated, skeptics are likely to consider such a person a "tool of business" with special interests and therefore a poor public servant.

Second, from a personal standpoint, many individuals may not be willing to make the necessary sacrifices. Movement into public office from private employment often demands that the individual face a substantial financial loss.

Third, loss of a key individual from the organization may impose serious hardships on a company's operations. A policy of leaves of absence for political activity creates an even greater dilemma. Few businesses could operate effectively if they were unsure, from election to election, which employees would remain and how many would return.

Although business and labor relationships will be discussed in a later chapter, another main point is that labor is in politics *as labor*; therefore, business must be in politics *as business* in order to balance the equation. Otherwise, labor's political power will become dominant, destroying pluralism. Therefore, it is essential for business to enter politics to preserve political balance of power.

It is becoming increasingly clear that businessmen need to become more concerned with governmental processes. Because of the growing complexity and interdependence of the government-business relationship, businessmen can ill afford to stand silent. Just as business needs support of government in order to do its job, so also government needs participation by business in formulating public policy. It needs advice and information from business leaders in making policy decisions, and this is true at the local and state levels as well as at the Federal level.

A 1964 survey showed increased interest in, and enthusiasm for, more political activity by businessmen.[27] Table 3 shows an increase since 1959 in actual political activity taken by businessmen. It also shows that executives participating in the survey believed that business should further increase political activity. Nearly 70 percent believed that their firms should encourage employees to register and vote. Many companies, according to the survey, believe that they should be active in formulating trade-association policy on political issues and also that they should belong to organizations whose objectives are to influence the political

[27] Stephen A. Greyser, "Business and Politics, 1964," *Harvard Business Review*, September–October, 1964, pp. 22ff.

TABLE 3   Opinions on company political activities

"In Which of the Following Activities
Does/Should Your Company Engage?" *

	1959	1964	
	Does	Does	Should
Urge employees to register and vote	70%	68%	73%
Belong to organizations designed to make the political climate more favorable to business	44	50	59
Participate actively in formulating trade association policy on government issues	25	48	55
Belong to organizations designed to improve the efficiency of government operations	36	40	64
Encourage employees to participate actively in campaigns	21	31	47
Urge executives to serve as elected officials in the city where plant is located	16	29	45
Take stands on specific political issues	22	24	39
Encourage campaign contributions by employees	15	21	31
Allow candidates to come into the plant and meet employees	14	21	29
Invite elected officials to meet with the management group	13	21	46
Have top managers make talks on important issues	14	20	38
Employ specialists to deal with elected officials	13	20	20
Carry articles on current public issues in the company paper	15	19	37
Give employees time off to work on campaigns	12	14	20
Perform services for politicians	12	12	9
Invite elected officials to talk to employee groups	6	12	35
Consider political activity in recommendations for promotions	3	5	7

* Question did not include "should" in 1959.
source: Stephen A. Greyser, "Business and Politics, 1964," *Harvard Business Review*, September–October, 1964, p. 177. Reproduced with permission.

environment of business or to improve government efficiency. Executives also believe that government officials should meet with management representatives on critical problems and be invited to talk with employees.

Table 4 indicates the types of political activities executives think are right and wrong for businesses to engage in. Providing government officials with businessmen's views on selected political issues leads the list. Ninety-eight percent of those executives surveyed thought this activity was proper. Substantial numbers felt that businessmen should give executives

TABLE 4   Percentage of respondents rating selected company
political activities as "proper"

	1964	1959
Company X offers cash to those politicians who will take it	7%	5%
Company X's representative writes a legislator to explain the firm's position on pending legislation	98	96
Company X invites campaigning politicians into the plant	56	54
Company X hires legislators as consultants	14	14
Company X gives executives time off to work on a campaign	64	71
Company X makes available a few jobs which selected legislators can give to constituents	3	5
Company X's president endorses a candidate in a newspaper advertisement	55	52
Company X provides legal and other specialized services to politicians	13	15
Company X's representatives take legislators to lunch on company funds	57	60
Company X gives presents or vacation trips to legislators	1	2
Company X contributes to candidate's political campaigns*	52	—

* This statement was not included in 1959.
SOURCE: Stephen A. Greyser, "Business and Politics, 1964," *Harvard Business Review*, September–October, 1964, p. 177. Reproduced with permission.

time off to work on political campaigns, invite campaigning politicians to the plant, publicly endorse candidates, and take legislators to lunch on expense accounts.

While few businessmen move directly into political offices, they are becoming increasingly active in the day-to-day processes of government. In many ways, business and government are working together to solve problems. Early in 1964, for example, the Committee for Economic Development issued a report on improvement of management in government.[28] Among other things, the Committee recommended establishment of a separate office of executive personnel in the White House, stronger and broader management-development programs, and substantial salary increases for many top executives.

In other areas, too, businessmen are participating in both day-to-day problems and policy formulation. For example, in reviewing a six-year-old oil import law, the Interior Department invited executives from the oil industry to participate in the hearings. Over five hundred executives attended three days of hearings. At a somewhat higher level, the Business

[28] "CED's Plan to Nourish the Top Bureaucrats," *Business Week*, July 25, 1964, p. 70.

Advisory Council (an organization made up of top corporate executives) is periodically invited to discuss with top government officials important current government activity affecting business.

Whatever the method used, both business and government need to understand each other's needs. Strength and growth of the national economy depend upon cooperation, and as the economy grows more complex, the needs for understanding and cooperation will become more important and demanding.

SUMMARY

One hundred years ago, businessmen were only mildly concerned with business-government relationships because businessmen and society in general believed that the role of government should be limited to performing those functions which are inappropriate for a profit-oriented market system to perform. As business became stronger and more aggressive, as business organizations became larger and more powerful, and as monopolistic competition replaced pure competition, society began to reevaluate the roles of both business and government. Loss of public confidence in business resulting from actions of "big business" during the latter part of the nineteenth century led to public demands for more government participation in the economic system.

Over the years, government participation in business has taken two forms, one supportive and the other restrictive. Legislation and public policy seem to fluctuate between these two forms. When public confidence in business is high, public policy favors supportive legislation. When public confidence is low, restrictive policies seem to prevail.

As society becomes more complex, it seems clear that national economic performance depends on both a strong government sector and a strong business sector. Neither can function effectively without the other. If the complex social and economic problems of the future are to be met and solved, greater trust and understanding will be needed between business and government. This will mean more participation in government by businessmen—not necessarily through running for public office but through participating to a greater degree in the day-to-day workings of government. Businessmen need to make their points of view heard. They need to participate with government in solving social problems— many of which have been compounded by business activities. And they need to be sensitive to the needs of government.

QUESTIONS

1. Why do businessmen sometimes appear to have a schizophrenic philosophy toward the role of government?

2. Starting with the Civil War, compare dates of various pieces of legislation

affecting business with dates of national emergencies such as wars and depressions.

3. In what ways do government and business relationships today differ from those of one hundred or so years ago?

4. In what ways are government and business mutually dependent in attaining national goals?

5. Compile as many arguments as you can, both pro and con, on the question: Should businessmen be active in politics?

CHAPTER 11 OWNERSHIP CLAIMS

ON BUSINESS

> Management responsibilities to shareholders should
> be defined with reference to shareholders' legitimate
> expectations, a reflection of goals of passive investors
> rather than those of co-owners in a business enterprise.
>
> DAVID B. WEAVER[1]

Peter Drucker, in *The Practice of Management*, tells us that the first
duty of a business is to survive.[2] To survive, it must operate at a profit.
One hundred or so years ago there was little question that the sole
function of profit was to provide reward for entrepreneurial risk. Today,
in our complex society, many social groups make strong demands on
business which tend to dilute profits. Each group, including stockholders,
feels that it has a vested interest in business firms, and each in its own
way tries to maximize satisfactions of its demands.

Relationships between managers and owners have changed during
the last 100 years. As indicated by the quotation at the beginning of
this chapter, stockholders in widely held corporations perceive themselves as passive investors rather than co-owners of a business. Under
these conditions, traditional legal controls by stockholders break down
and become unrealistic, thus placing on managers the responsibility of
making choices between alternative demands of claimant groups. As a
further complication, managers must also make decisions concerning
present versus future demands.

---

[1] David B. Weaver, "The Corporation and the Shareholder," in Arthur S. Miller
(ed.), *The Ethics of Business Enterprise*, Philadelphia: The American Academy of
Political and Social Science, *The Annals*, vol. 343, September, 1962, p. 84.

[2] Peter F. Drucker, *The Practice of Management*, New York: Harper & Row,
Publishers, Incorporated, 1954, p. 46.

In this chapter we shall discuss conflicts between owners and managers occasioned by changing relationships between the two groups, legal responsibilities of management to stockholders, and finally the "management-trusteeship" concept of management responsibility to stockholders.

MANAGEMENT-OWNER RELATIONSHIPS

In every business there are two separate and distinct functions which must be performed. It should be emphasized at the outset that we are not talking about functions in the organizational sense of marketing, production, and finance. Rather, we are making a distinction between the functions of ownership and management.

Every business must have a supply of money with which to acquire production resources in quantities necessary to achieve business objectives. Businesses are owned by those who provide the necessary capital. In the ultimate sense, then, the sole function of ownership is to provide capital. Separate and aside from the function of ownership is the function of management. Management is charged with the responsibility of operating the business. Questions of how a business should be operated, for whose benefit it is operated, and the purpose of a business in our society have led to conflict between owners and managers. Their points of view are different.

Separation of functions and conflict of viewpoints between ownership and management exist regardless of whether the business is organized as a single proprietorship, a partnership, a corporation, or a government business. Where owners and managers are the same person, as in a proprietorship, a partnership, or a small, closely held corporation, owner-managers play two roles which are in conflict with each other. But the very fact that owners and managers are the same person aids in resolving conflicts. In publicly held corporations conflict is more severe because owners and managers are two separate groups.

Conflict in Viewpoints. What are the responsibilities of managers to owners? Answers to this question depend on whether one takes the managers' viewpoint or the owners' viewpoint. Owners perceive management's responsibilities to be the operation of the business in a way that (1) provides the largest possible return on their investment and (2) causes the value of their ownership shares to appreciate. Both emphasize the concept of maximum profits. Both emphasize priority of ownership demands upon the firm.

There is an increasing tendency for managers to view their responsibilities as being primarily to the firm, rather than to owners. They perceive themselves to be (1) responsible for economic survival of the firm; (2) responsible for perpetuating the firm through product innovation, management development, market expansion, and other means; and (3) responsible for balancing the demands of all groups upon the firm in such a way that these demands do not hinder the achievement of the firm's objectives. This viewpoint emphasizes optimization of profits within various constraints imposed by societal groups. It emphasizes satisfactory rather than maximum profits. It emphasizes the idea of a "socially profitable business" and considers owners to be one group among many. Concerning their specific responsibilities to owners, managers today often express the belief that "what is good for the business is good for the owner."

The heart of owner-manager conflict lies in arriving at a common definition of profit. Differences of opinion arise over what items should be deducted from gross revenue to arrive at a profit figure. What are the unavoidable costs of doing business? What are "legitimate" expenditures of company funds? Speaking from the managerial point of view, Drucker observes that profit serves three purposes:[3]

> It measures the net effectiveness and soundness of a business's efforts.
> It is the "risk premium" that covers the costs of staying in business.
> Finally, profit insures the supply of future capital for innovation and expansion.

To Drucker, "costs of staying in business" cover a wide range of expenditures including (in addition to the usually accepted costs) contributions to a variety of social costs. He summarizes by saying:[4]

> None of these three functions of profit has anything to do with the economist's maximization of profit. All the three are indeed minimum concepts—the "minimum" of profit needed for the survival and prosperity of the enterprise. A profitability objective therefore measures not the maximum profit the business can produce, but the minimum it must produce.

Profit Maximization versus Security Maximization. Most managers learned long ago that emphasis on short-run profit maximization is a shortsighted approach to operating a business. Businessmen today speak of long-run profit maximization and acknowledge their obligation to "make a dollar for the owner." But even the concept of long-run profit maximization is unsatisfactory. Businessmen today do not maximize profits (as the classical economists defined maximization) in the long run.[5] Rather, they maximize security and survival. Managers have learned that they cannot ignore demands made upon business by various societal groups such as consumers, labor, suppliers, etc. Emphasis on profits (short run or long run) at the expense of one of these groups (either by individual firms or by the business system as a whole) has always resulted

---

[3] *Ibid.*, pp. 76–77.
[4] *Ibid.*, p. 77.
[5] Robert N. Anthony, "The Trouble with Profit Maximization," *Harvard Business Review*, November–December, 1960, pp. 126–134.

in pressures that threatened survival. Exploitation of the above-mentioned groups in the last half of the nineteenth century resulted in restrictive legislation. For example, refusal to recognize demands of labor brought forth the Wagner and Taft-Hartley Acts, wage-and-hour legislation, and economic harassment by unions.

Examples of firms maximizing security can easily be found. When a manager of a nonunion firm raises wages above union scales, he is often doing so to keep the union out rather than because of profit maximization. When a firm in an oligopolistic industry refrains from merging with other companies or from absorbing supplementary business in order to integrate forward or backward, it is undoubtedly trying to avoid future antitrust action by the government. When managers voluntarily allocate money to develop means of controlling factory smoke or odors, they are trying to avoid community ill will. In short, all managers in the examples just given were maximizing security and survival by making expenditures that would prevent certain groups from exerting pressures that would restrict the firm in attaining its objectives.

Conflict between owners' views and managers' views is most apparent in the area of financial policy. Owners, in their role as owners, of course, favor financial policies that will provide the most return on their investment. They favor policies which emphasize that business should be run for the benefit of the owners. Expenditures which may reduce the amount available for distribution to owners at the end of the year are often questioned. This kind of policy implies strongly resisting pressures from other groups. Managers, in their role as managers, favor policies which emphasize the idea that business should be run for the benefit of a large group of claimants. Expenditures which may reduce the profit picture at the end of the year but which enhance survival of the firm appear quite justifiable in the managers' eyes. The job of today's manager is to formulate financial policy that will resolve the owner-manager conflict.

In single proprietorships and partnerships, the management problem of balancing demands of owners with those of other groups is less severe than in the corporate form of business. At least the manager is in a position to resolve owner-manager conflict concerning expenditures of current income. Decisions are made jointly because owners and managers are the same people. Even in proprietorships and partnerships, however, managers must guard against the temptation to emphasize short-run profits at the expense of long-run survival and long-run profits. In his role as an owner, it is difficult for the manager not to give priority to his economic payoff *as an owner* and subordinate claims of other groups to ownership demands. For example, expenditures for plant beautification are often weighed heavily against projected year-end profits, or there may be a temptation to use needed working capital to pay "traditional" dividends.

Managers of closely held corporations are, in general, subject to the same pressures as managers of proprietorships and partnerships for precisely the same reason. Decisions are made jointly by owners and managers because they are the same people.

OWNERSHIP AND POLICY FORMULATION

Public corporations impose pressures on managers which are different from those inherent in proprietorships, partnerships, and closely held corporations. The problem remains the same, but owners and managers are two separate and distinct groups.

Separation of Ownership and Control. Stockholders as a separate group—aside from, and external to, the actual business—are a relatively new development in American business. Prior to 1900, the majority of corporate securities in existence were held in large concentrations by only a few individuals. The objective of holding stock, for these people, was ownership and control. As nineteenth-century firms expanded into today's industrial giants, new issues of stock were dispersed over a wider range of buyers. Many old stock concentrations were broken up and spread over a greater number of people through inheritance or sale on the market. As stock ownership became more diversified and as greater numbers of people held smaller amounts of stock, their reasons for holding stock changed. Few small shareholders today equate their ownership with corporate control. Rather, they view themselves as investors and are primarily concerned with returns on investment, not control.

As David Weaver points out, "the distinction is one of attitude," [6] but this is an important distinction. As corporations have matured and grown in size and wealth, there has been an increasing separation of management and ownership and the growth of a professional management group. Dispersion of shareholdings has diluted or destroyed internal ownership control on management decision making and transferred the power of decision to the management group, who may or may not hold stock in the corporation.[7] Owners of large corporations (with the exception of those stockholders who are also corporate officers) do not make decisions. Rather, the small stockholder, in his role as an investor, depends upon professional managers to make corporate decisions.[8] Stockholders, at least in the large and socially powerful corporations, have been removed from

[6] Weaver, *op. cit.*, p. 90.

[7] For a complete discussion of this thesis, see Adolph A. Berle and Gardiner C. Means, *The Modern Corporation and Private Property*, New York: The Macmillan Company, 1932.

[8] Discussions of implications of growth of professional management groups are presented in Adolph A. Berle, Jr., *Power without Property*, New York: Harcourt, Brace, & World, Inc., 1959; and Edward S. Mason, *The Corporation in Modern Society*, Cambridge, Mass.: Harvard University Press, 1959.

decision-making centers and emerge as an external force exerting pressures on professional managers.

WHO ARE STOCKHOLDERS?

After World War I, the public at large became significant holders of corporate stock. Today over eighteen million people have direct ownership in our great corporations.[9] That is, they own stock of one or more companies. People from practically every occupational group own stock. Professional people, farmers, teachers, workers at all organizational levels, merchants, public-service workers, housewives, and children of preschool age represent a few groups that own stock. Other millions of people have indirect ownership in corporations through mutual funds, union funds, retirement funds, insurance policies, savings accounts, and other holdings. In recent years there has been an increasing amount of stock held by institutional buyers. While insurance companies, savings and loan companies, and banks seem to emphasize holding preferred stock or bonds, they do hold some common stock. Mutual funds, union funds, and private pension funds, on the other hand, have substantial holdings of common stock.

As owners have increasingly changed from active participants in business to absentee owners who view themselves primarily as professional investors, relations between owners and professional managers have also changed. The approach to corporate financial policy varies considerably between these two groups. Managers use different yardsticks from those which stockholders use to measure financial performance. Table 5 illustrates different approaches by managers and stockholders concerning four types of financial policy decisions. Management yardsticks emphasize security, while stockholder yardsticks emphasize priority of stockholder claims.

To complicate management's job, a balance among different groups of stockholders must be achieved. Investment objectives differ between the groups. Small stockholders emphasize short-term dividend return and capital gains, while institutional stockholders tend to emphasize predictable and stable long-run returns because they have fixed long-term commitments.

WHAT DO STOCKHOLDERS OWN?

It is commonly accepted that stockholders "own" the company in which they hold stock. But what do they really own? Do they own property? Do they own certain rights which are attached to private property?

[9] John C. Clendenin, *Introduction to Investments*, 4th ed., New York: McGraw-Hill Book Company, 1964, p. 42.

Or do they own merely pieces of paper whose value is determined in the stock markets? One author explains it this way: "A share is just what the word implies, a fractional interest in a whole of undefined size—not a claim for any fixed amount payable at any stated time." [10] However, answers to these and similar questions depend on whether one approaches

TABLE 5 Different yardsticks used by management and stockholders

TYPES OF DECISIONS	MANAGEMENT'S YARDSTICKS	STOCKHOLDER'S YARDSTICKS	SAMPLE AREAS OF POSSIBLE CONFLICT
Measuring financial performance	Anticipated changes in specific cash flows in the fore-seeable future—amount, certainty, and timing	Anticipated changes in property values as measured by trends in earning per share (E.P.S.) and dividends	Ranking of invest-ment alternatives; depreciation policy; stock options; ac-quisition of sub-sidiaries
Investment proposals	Internal rate of re-turn which existing management is ca-pable of achieving —as indicated by past performance	External as well as in-ternal investment opportunity rates, including compet-ing business organ-izations of compa-rable risk	The cutoff rate on acceptable invest-ment opportunities and amounts com-mitted to perpetu-ate existing invest-ments
Sources of funds	Preference for (a) re-tained earnings, (b) long-term debt, and (c) new com-mon stock—in that order	Preference likely to be for (a) debt, (b) retained earnings, and (c) new com-mon stock—in that order	The extent of use of these sources in fi-nancing growth
Assumption of voluntary risk	Risk standard in terms of preserving the individual cor-porate entity and management's goals	Risk standard in terms of a port-folio of investments over many com-panies	Diversification of products and mar-kets; debt/equity proportions

SOURCE: Gordon Donaldson, "Financial Goals: Management vs. Stockholders," *Harvard Business Review*, May–June, 1963, p. 121. Reproduced with permission.

them from a legal viewpoint or the viewpoint of what seems to be reality.

Stockholders do not own property in the sense in which we usually think of property ownership. That is, they do not have title to company property, nor can they control its use in the same way that a single proprietor can control his property. A corporation, according to law, is an artificial person empowered by the state to own and use resources neces-sary to accomplish corporate objectives. Property is owned by the corpora-

[10] Weaver, *op. cit.*, p. 85.

tion, not by the stockholder. The board of directors determines how corporate property will be used. Stockholders have no direct claim on corporate property except in the case of business failure and liquidation of assets. Even in this case, stockholders' claims are subordinate to the claims of many other groups, such as creditors, bondholders, and holders of preferred stock. In other words, common stockholders get what is left after all prior claims have been satisfied. From this point of view, then, stockholders own an undivided share of the company net worth on any given date. Since stockholders do not own company property, they can control its use only to the extent that they can influence corporate policy. Stockholders who hold significant numbers of shares are in a position to influence corporate policy through the veto power of their votes, but the small stockholder who owns only a few shares individually has little influence.

From another point of view, since the small stockholder does not have a specific claim against the corporation for any fixed amount, he is likely to look to the market to determine the value of his ownership share. From this viewpoint he is likely to perceive that he owns merely certificates that derive their value from the marketplace. Inability of the small stockholder to influence corporate policy encourages him to take this point of view and focus on his role as an investor. From this viewpoint he loses identity with the corporation and becomes apathetic.

Regardless of which view is taken, stockholders have certain rights which must be respected by professional managers. Among these is the right to good management, management which will protect shareholders' interests and preserve their claims upon the enterprise.

Legal Rights of Stockholders. While the law grants wide latitude of decision and action to corporate officers, it does not relieve them of their fiduciary responsibilities. However, the law does not define exactly what the corporate responsibilities should be nor to whom the corporation is ultimately accountable.

Specific rights of stockholders are established by law. Legally, stockholders can influence corporate policy through the voting mechanism or, if necessary, by challenging actions of corporate officers in the courts. Stockholders have the following legal rights (and these vary somewhat between states):

1. To share in the profits of the enterprise—*if dividends are declared by directors*
2. To elect directors
3. To receive annual reports of company earnings
4. To inspect the corporate books
5. To hold directors responsible for their acts—by lawsuit if they want to go that far

6. To vote on mergers, consolidations, changes in the charter, and bylaws

7. To dispose of ownership certificates

It is, however, difficult for small stockholders to exercise these right other than in a perfunctory manner. If stockholders are dissatisfied with actions of directors, they have three alternatives. First, they may replace corporate officers by voting the old regime out and new officers in. Second they may sue the corporate officers for misuse of power. Third, they may sell their stock. The first two alternatives may be all but impossible for the small stockholder to exercise. In reality these alternatives have lost their significance as devices to protect small stockholders' interests.

Annual stockholders' meetings are held by law for the purpose of discussing corporate business and electing directors. Each year a portion of the corporate directors are elected. Sometimes all are. Terms of office are defined by law and vary between states. Most states limit the term for which directors may hold office to three years, but, of course, they may be reelected for additional terms. Where corporations are small and local in nature or where they are closely held, annual meetings work very well. It is relatively easy to assemble a majority of the stockholders, there is a true representation of stockholders' interests in elections, and corporate business is considered and acted upon personally by at least a majority of stockholders. But for the large, publicly held corporations with hundreds of stockholders, annual meetings are not so satisfactory for accomplishing legal objectives. The number and wide geographic dispersion of stockholders have altered the character of annual meetings. Typically few stockholders attend in person, and only a small proportion of total shares is personally represented.

Annual meetings theoretically offer an opportunity to shareholders to approve or disapprove past actions of directors. Approval is expressed by reelecting the directors, and disapproval may be shown by refusing to reelect present directors and replacing them with new ones. But to unseat existing management in modern corporate society usually requires a proxy fight—an expensive process which most small stockholders are ill equipped to engage in. Most small stockholders have purchased stock not to have a voice in the operation of the company but to reap financial returns from their investment. Therefore, they have little knowledge of, or interest in, contests for control. It is easier for them to express dissatisfaction by selling their stock.

Even if they were so disposed, few small stockholders are equipped financially to initiate and wage a fight for control with existing management. To unseat present management requires gathering enough voting power by proxy to outvote the incumbents. This can be a difficult and expensive undertaking. To illustrate, it is reported that in 1939, Robert R.

Young spent over 1¼ million dollars gathering sufficient proxies to enable him to gain control of the New York Central Railroad.[11] In proxy fights, the odds for success are heavily weighted in favor of incumbent management. It is not easy to stir a group of apathetic stockholders to join the opposition. Lack of knowledge concerning issues typically leads small, uninterested stockholders to cast their lot on the side of management. Financially, too, present management has the upper hand. It may, and typically does, use both corporate personnel and corporate funds to gather proxies which it may vote in its own support. Financial competence necessary to overcome these odds does not lie with the small stockholder.

Just as it is difficult for small stockholders to engage in proxy fights, so is there little to encourage them to engage in stockholders' suits. Certainly, under law, dissatisfied stockholders may sue the corporation, but this right has been substantially diluted by limitations placed on instituting this kind of suit. Attempts to prevent harassment through the courts and to ensure pursuit of genuine complaints have led to serious impairment of small stockholders' rights to bring suit. In New York, for example, a stockholder-plaintiff who brings suit must own 5 percent of the shares, or if he does not he must be joined by others whose combined holdings equal or exceed 5 percent. In addition, the combined shares must have a market value in excess of $50,000. If the plaintiff does not own or control stock in the required amount and value, he may still be allowed to sue, but he must post sufficient security to cover litigation costs of defendants if he is unsuccessful in his suit.

Small stockholders also have little or no financial incentive for initiating and engaging in lawsuits against directors of the corporation. Assuming that they are successful, they can get no direct cash benefit. Cash benefits recovered from directors go to the corporation—not directly to the stockholder. The most small stockholders can expect is an unknown increase in future dividends, and they are not even assured of that.

The Texas Gulf Sulphur Case. Government may, however, step in to fill the gap. Where stockholders cannot protect their own interests, the government, through the Securities Exchange Commission (SEC), may do the job for them. The SEC has, for a number of years, had authority to protect stockholders from "inside dealings," that is, the ability of corporate officers to profit from inside knowledge. But what the SEC asks, in its civil suit against the Texas Gulf Sulphur Company, may well set precedent for years to come if it is eventually successful.[12]

The suit traces back to 1959, when exploration near Timmons, Ontario, showed signs of a rich deposit of copper and zinc. In 1963, test drill-

[11] J. A. Livingston, *The American Stockholder*, Philadelphia: J. B. Lippincott Company, 1958, p. 44.

[12] "Texas Gulf Suit Opens New Door for SEC," *Business Week*, Apr. 24, 1965, pp. 24–25.

ing confirmed preliminary reports and verified a large body of high-grade ore. To keep the find a secret, the drilling rigs were moved off, trees were planted around the drill hole, and a worthless core was left at the site. In the suit, thirteen "insiders" (officers, directors, and employees of the company) are alleged to have used this inside information about the company's rich Canadian ore strike to obtain profits from stock purhcases before the knowledge of the discovery was made public.

Between the time the Canadian drilling showed promise of a rich find and five months later, when the find was made public, the defendants are alleged to have bought outright 9,100 shares of Texas Gulf, to have bought call options on 5,200 shares, and to have received stock options for another 14,700 shares. During this period the stock rose from $17 to $34, and later, after public announcement, it rose further to $71.

The SEC demands go far beyond what has been previously viewed as the normal scope of regulation of inside dealings. In the past, the agency has largely been content to seek injunctions, but in the Texas Gulf Sulphur case the SEC is demanding that the defendants make up losses of individuals who sold Texas Gulf stock to defendants or associates. If the suit is successful, the defendants will have to sell stock back to those who sold stock during the period between November 12, 1963, when test drilling indicated the extent of the find, and April 16, 1964, when the findings were made public. They will also have to return to the company all profits obtained from stock options issued during this period. Furthermore, three defendants, even though they purchased no stock, will be required personally to pay damages for stock purchased by those to whom they gave information.

For all practical purposes, then, small stockholders have only one way to influence corporate policy, and at best it is weak and ineffective. They can sell their stock. Large stockholders are often part of management and therefore participate in the formation of corporate policy. Small stockholders, on the other hand, are dependent upon policy, rather than in control of it. If, however, the SEC suit against the Texas Gulf Sulphur Company is successful, small stockholders may have a powerful ally in the Federal government.

MANAGEMENT TRUSTEESHIP

The point has been made, very convincingly at times, that American stockholders are virtually at the mercy of professional managers.[13] Corporate law seems to support this position. According to legal rules of thumb, "directors are said to owe loyalty not to stockholders, as such, but

---

[13] Livingston, *op. cit.*

only to the corporation. . . ." [14] This leaves unanswered the important and interesting question: Who is the corporation accountable to? Large corporations carry great power with their size. The results of their actions are widely felt, not only by stockholders but also by many other societal groups.

Relationship of Stockholders and Professional Managers. Today, corporate directors and officers are generally considered to stand in a fiduciary relationship not only to stockholders but also to society as a whole. In establishing corporate policy, officers are increasingly guided by the philosophy of "what is good for the corporation is good for the stockholders." Courts seem to uphold this philosophy.

For example, consider the case of the *A. P. Smith Manufacturing Company v. Barlow.*[15] On July 21, 1951, the directors of A. P. Smith Manufacturing Company, wishing to exercise what they considered to be corporate public responsibility, donated $1,500 to Princeton University. Certain stockholders challenged management's right to dispose of corporate funds in this manner on the grounds that it was a misappropriation of corporate money and was, in fact, an *ultra vires* act. The stockholders contended that the directors of a corporation had no power to use corporate funds for any purpose other than those set forth in the corporate charter.

Through its president, the company argued that it considered the contribution to be a sound business investment. By contributing to educational institutions, it was argued, corporations were assuring a supply of properly trained people for future employment. It was further argued that the public expects corporations to support such institutions and that by doing so they gain goodwill in the community. Several highly respected business leaders supported this position by their testimony. Frank Abrams, chairman of the board of Standard Oil, testified that it was good business to accept "obligations of citizenship in the social community." Irving S. Olds, former chairman of U.S. Steel, commented that such expenditures were necessary for a company ". . . in protecting the long range interests of stockholders, its employees, and its customers."

Both the trial court and the appellate court upheld the corporation and its directors and agreed that "anything that tends to promote with the public a company's good will is a reasonable measure toward the

[14] Jacob Weissman, *Law in a Business Society*, Englewood Cliffs, N.J.: Prentice-Hall, Inc., 1964, p. 39.

[15] 13 N.J. 145, 98 A.2d 481 (1953). Appeal to the New Jersey Supreme Court found in 26 N.J. Super. 106, 97 A.2d 186 (1953). Appeal to the United States Supreme Court found in 346 U.S. 861 (1953). A complete review of this case may be found in D. R. Forbush et al., *Management's Relationships with Its Publics*, Evanston, Ill.: Northwestern University Press, 1960.

corporate objective of earning a profit." The United States Supreme Court dismissed the case for lack of a Federal question.

The Trusteeship Concept. With the growth of large corporations has come growing support of the "management-trusteeship" concept. This view deemphasizes management's primary identification with ownership and emphasizes the social-responsibility concept. It recognizes that business, in modern society, has responsibilities to many social groups. It is a concept of plural trusteeship. Under this concept, ownership interest must take its place alongside vested interests of other social groups. Management, then, becomes an arbitrator in balancing conflicting interests of all groups.[16] In the final analysis, business is accountable to society, not to any one social group.

The trusteeship concept, however, is not universally accepted as being the correct approach to management-stockholder relations. Those opposed to the concept[17] see it as establishing managers in authoritarian roles whereby they apportion shares of corporate income according to their own personal value systems. Shares are dictated on the basis of personal morals and ethics, rather than according to economic concepts of returns to factors of production. It is argued that acceptance of the trusteeship concept alters the nature and purpose of corporate enterprise and undermines the foundations of private property.

Even the most ardent proponents of management trusteeship would not contend that management has no responsibility to stockholders. On the contrary, it has very real and definable responsibilities. As Eells and Walton have expressed it: "It is one thing to say that the risk-bearing stockholder has little function; it is quite another to say that he deserves little respect." [18] It is generally conceded that management is obligated to preserve and protect the interests of stockholders—to operate the company in a way that does not waste corporate resources and thus endanger or threaten stockholder investment. Management decisions that result in large losses for the company always make management competence suspect, in the eyes of both stockholders and society in general. Ford Motor Company's debacle with their Edsel and General Dynamic's fiasco with the Convair 880 and 990 are cases in point. Unsound management practices endangered stockholders' interest as well as public interest in both cases.

The Edsel Case. Within the four years and seven months from the time the Edsel program was started until it was discontinued, Ford spent

---

[16] Berle and Means, *op. cit.*, p. 356.

[17] Among those opposed to the management-trusteeship concept are David McCord Wright, Theodore Levitt, and others.

[18] Richard Eells and Clarence C. Walton, *Conceptual Foundations of Business*, Homewood, Ill.: Richard D. Irwin, Inc., 1961, p. 151.

some 350 million dollars on the new Edsel project.[19] Why was the venture a failure? It is difficult if not impossible to focus the blame at any one point. A combination of several factors is probably the real answer. Poor timing has been suggested as a major reason. The Edsel, a medium-priced, medium-sized car, was offered at the precise time that compact cars were becoming popular. Second, motivational research used to design the car did not provide the right kind of information. Third, the intense pre-introduction advertising based upon suspense and mystery had the public so worked up that they expected a radical dream car. When the car proved to be fairly traditional, disappointment turned to resentment. Fourth, the car was introduced at the beginning of the 1957–1958 recession. Fifth, the design, while not wholly traditional, was not sufficiently different to motivate people to buy. Sixth, it has been suggested that the name Edsel conveyed the wrong image to the public. Last, heavy mechanical failure among the first cars along with considerable unfavorable press coverage destroyed public confidence.

While some of the above circumstances such as the 1957–1958 recession were difficult to forecast, others could have been avoided. In actual fact, the results were not as catastrophic for the company or its stockholders as might be imagined. Strength of the other Ford divisions allowed the corporation to absorb the huge losses. But potential dividends were lost, and market prices of stocks tumbled. Those stockholders who held their stock survived, but those who lost confidence and sold lost heavily.

The Convair Case. Even more severe were General Dynamics Corporation's losses through Convair Division's attempt to enter the market for commercial jet aircraft.[20] General Dynamics lost 490 million dollars on its jet program. In effect it lost 90 percent of its assets on one venture. Again a number of managerial errors combined in an exponential progression to result in the debacle. Poor cost analysis, unsound pricing, wrong forecasting of market needs and market potential, underestimating competition, and poor contract negotiation all contributed to the staggering losses. Death of a strong autocratic president who closely controlled the far-flung divisions left a gap in top management with no strong replacement. Lack of information and control at the corporate level occasioned by a highly decentralized organization let danger signals go unheeded. All these errors pointed General Dynamics squarely for the bankruptcy courts. Only putting strong controls into the hands of an executive committee of seven directors and imposition of severe financial restrictions by the banks has saved the corporation.

[19] John Brooks, *The Fate of the Edsel and Other Business Adventures*, New York: Harper & Row, Publishers, Incorporated, 1963.

[20] Richard Austin Smith, "How a Great Corporation Got Out of Control," 2 parts, *Fortune*, January, 1962, and February, 1962.

In retrospect, one senior vice-president of the company summed up by saying: "It's a grave question in my mind as to whether General Dynamics had the right to risk this kind of money belonging to the stockholders for the potential profit you could get out of it. All management has to take a certain risk for big gains. But I don't think it's right to risk so much for so small a gain." [21]

Need for Communication. In addition to protecting stockholders' financial interests, many professional managers feel an obligation to keep stockholders informed about company activities and financial position. To some degree this attitude stems from legal requirements concerning annual financial statements. To some degree it stems from external demands to revive a genuine "shareholder democracy" [22] and shareholder control through refinements of SEC rules governing proxy solicitation. And to some degree this attitude stems from a genuine desire on the part of management to gain more positive stockholder involvement, to convert negative attacks on past managerial performance to positive involvement and support.

In an attempt to overcome apathy and create closer stockholder identification with the corporation, elaborate stockholder relations programs have been created by some managers. These attempts have taken two basic forms: more elaborate annual reports and encouragement to participate in annual stockholders' meetings.

Many managers have felt it necessary to expand and upgrade the annual report. A quick glance at some of the reports prepared by larger companies reveals a trend to beautify as well as enlarge them. Few large companies are content to limit contents to financial statements but, rather, feel a necessity to emphasize gains, apologize for losses, and, above all, justify expenditures—expenditures that are really shares of corporate earnings allocated to various claimant groups.

Dissatisfactions with annual meetings as a device for discussing corporate business have led some managers to try to modify the meetings and encourage more stockholder participation. In an attempt to increase stockholder identification and participation, some companies have experimented with holding throughout the year numerous geographically dispersed stockholders' meetings.

There is no question that management has the responsibility of protecting stockholders' investments in business, but it also has responsibilities to other claimants. As was mentioned in Chapter 1, many social groups invest in American business in one way or another. Failure on the part of management to be genuinely concerned with claims of various other

---

[21] *Ibid.*, February, 1962, p. 187.
[22] F. D. Emerson and F. C. Latcham, *Shareholder Democracy*, Cleveland, Ohio: Press of Western Reserve University, 1954; and Lewis D. Gilbert, *Dividends and Democracy*, Larchmont, N.Y.: American Research Council, 1956.

groups may keep it from honoring its commitments to stockholders. It cannot emphasize stockholder claims at the expense of other claims, lest other groups through social pressures make their claims a threat to business survival.

NONPROFIT AND GOVERNMENT BUSINESSES

So far in this chapter, we have discussed business in a narrow sense. We have limited our discussion to private enterprises, but there are many other kinds of businesses, and people invest in them in various ways.

In Chapter 1 we said that we were going to use the term "business" to include more than private enterprises. In our broad use of the term we include all economic and commercial activities of organizations such as opera companies, philanthropic organizations, government agencies, and others. All these organizations engage in business activities in one way or another, and the fact that they are not based on a monetary profit motive has little or no meaning.

Nonprofit businesses depend on resource inputs just as profit-oriented businesses do. People invest in nonprofit organizations in a variety of ways. They contribute time, talent, effort, financial support, and other inputs necessary for the business to function. Like investors in private enterprises, they depend on management to use these resource inputs wisely and to give the payoffs these investors seek. For example, the large symphony orchestra association or the large civic theater association is supported financially by contributions and ticket sales. Others invest time and talent. But the investors have little to say about how the resources are used. These decisions are made by a professional manager who is hired by the investors, and they depend on him to provide culture and a better community, which are their payoffs.

The same applies to many government activities. For example, national parks are purchased or developed with tax funds and hence are "owned" by citizens. But ownership does not carry control with it. Only in a remote way do citizens control the way national parks are run. They depend upon managers to run the parks for their benefit. And the "owners" pay fees for their use just as a nonowner (noncitizen) does. Or consider a municipally owned sewage disposal plant bought by citizen investment. Citizens, or investors, depend on professional managers to run the plant and, except through occasional elections, have little direct control.

Ownership in nonprofit and government institutions is somewhat different from ownership in private enterprises. Owners do not own title to property. They do not even own certificates which they can sell in the market. Ownership in these institutions is really only an "investorship." Investors enjoy the right to use the benefits of their investment, but when they leave the area covered by the investment (for example, a city) they have no marketable shares to cash in.

In other words, the investor-manager separation prevails everywhere, not just in private enterprise, and the responsibility of managers to investors is the same whether we are talking about a private enterprise, a nonprofit enterprise, or a government enterprise. Managers are trustees for all the groups which make claims against the enterprise. Opera companies and national parks must bargain with labor, deal with suppliers, anticipate consumer demand, provide investor returns, and relate to other groups in much the same way that enterprise does. And they must depend upon managers to fulfill these responsibilities.

SUMMARY

In the ultimate sense, the functions of ownership vary widely from those of management. Owners, in their role as owners, furnish capital and assume entrepreneurial risk. Managers, in their role as managers, must operate the enterprise. Inherent in this distinction is a conflict concerning the question: For whose benefit should the enterprise be operated? Owners feel that the business should be operated in a way that will provide maximum returns to them on invested capital. Managers, on the other hand, feel primary allegiance to the firm—not the owners. They realize that they must balance the demands of owners with demands of other claimants. Managers, therefore, do not emphasize maximum profit but concentrate instead on security and survival of the firm.

As stock ownership has become widely dispersed among large numbers of individuals, motives for owning stock have changed. Small stockholders see themselves only as investors and have little inclination to participate in control of the corporation. They have emerged as an absentee owner group exerting pressures on a group of professional managers for social and economic payoffs.

With increased separation of management from ownership has come an increased acceptance of the management-trusteeship concept. Because results of business decisions are so widely felt, not only by stockholders but by other groups as well, management is increasingly considered to stand in a fiduciary relationship not only to stockholders but also to the rest of society. Increasingly, there has been an acceptance of the philosophy "what is good for society is good for the stockholder." Increasingly, management has come to view stockholders as one of several groups whose demands of the firm must all be properly balanced. Stockholders have the right to demand that management properly safeguard their investment in the enterprise, but so do other social groups.

Even in nonprofit and government enterprises, the separation of management and ownership or investorship prevails. The trusteeship concept also prevails here. Investors in nonprofit and government enterprise have little or no direct control over policies or operations. They depend on professional managers for their payoffs.

QUESTIONS

1. What, ultimately, are the functions of business ownership? Of management?

2. Concerning responsibilities of managers, how do viewpoints of owners and managers differ?

3. What is meant by a "minimum concept of profits"?

4. Explain the difference between profit maximization and survival maximization.

5. How have stockholders' perceptions of themselves changed over the last one hundred or so years? Why have they changed?

6. What are the legal rights of stockholders? Why have many of these rights become ineffective?

7. What is meant by the management-trusteeship concept?

8. In what way do the Edsel and Convair cases demonstrate lack of management trusteeship?

9. Does the management-trusteeship concept apply to nonprofit and government enterprises as well as to private enterprises? Explain.

CHAPTER 12   BUSINESS AND
CONSUMERS

> Modern civilization is dependent for its existence
> absolutely upon the proper functioning of the industrial
> and business system.
>
> HENRY L. GANTT[1]

In the eighteenth and early nineteenth centuries the United States was primarily an agrarian nation with relatively simple needs and wants. The bulk of its population lived in rural areas. Those who lived on farms produced a substantial portion of the goods they consumed. Even many of those who lived in cities and towns produced domestically much of what they wore, ate, and used. Businesses were small for the most part. Merchants dealt mostly in either luxury goods or basic items which could not easily be produced at home. Manufacturers, likewise, concentrated their efforts on basic items which were difficult, if not impossible, to manufacture at home. Crude iron, gunpowder, and firearms, for example, found a ready market. Similarly luxury items (for the times) such as china, silverware and pewter ware, and high-quality clothing found a market among the wealthy. For the most part, then, consumer reliance on business was limited.

As the nation became increasingly industrialized and urban concentrations grew, consumer dependence on business also increased. New products appeared, and old products became more refined and more complex. People in cities no longer had ready access to raw materials. And the United States increasingly became a nation of specialists, dependent in turn on other specialists for the assortment of goods and services neces-

[1] Henry L. Gantt, *Organizing for Work*, New York: Harcourt, Brace & World, Inc., 1919, p. 3.

sary to live in an increasingly complex economy. Rather than each citizen being a rugged individualist, independent and capable of providing for his own needs, citizens today are highly dependent both individually and collectively upon others for their well-being. The individual no longer grows or preserves his own food, makes his clothing, provides his own transportation, or makes his own tools. Nor does he attempt to make or build the hundreds of others items that go into making his life pleasant.

Dependency is one side of the coin. On the other side is responsibility. It follows, then, that since citizens as consumers are dependent upon business to satisfy their material needs, business must have responsibilities to consumers. In this chapter we shall examine business's relation with consumers.

THE MISSION OF BUSINESS

The quotation at the beginning of this chapter expresses the idea that the business system is the *key* system in our modern society. While this may not be true in the strictest sense, the economic well-being of modern industrial society depends heavily on the proper functioning of business. But businessmen should never be viewed as the leading group in society because there are many groups all interacting with one another. On the other hand, businessmen do "play a central organizing role in a private-enterprise economy." [2] But what is this central role that business plays?

Paul Samuelson points out that every society must answer three fundamental questions: [3]

1. *What* commodities shall be produced and in what quantities?
2. *How* shall goods be produced?
3. For *whom* are goods to be produced?

Businessmen play a key role in answering these questions in the free world. They decide, on the basis of their interpretation of consumer wants, what commodities should be produced in what quantities. And they bear the risk of wrong decisions. A decision to produce 100 million bars of unscented soap may be unprofitable for both the company and society if society wants scented soap. Businessmen also decide how goods shall be produced and how factors of production shall be combined so that products may be produced at the lowest cost and thereby offered to consumers at the lowest price. Businessmen also make decisions concerning for

[2] George L. Bach, *Economics: An Introduction to Analysis and Policy*, 3d ed., Englewood Cliffs, N.J.: Prentice-Hall, Inc., 1960, p. 6.

[3] Paul A. Samuelson, *Economics: An Introductory Analysis*, 5th ed., New York: McGraw-Hill Book Company, 1961, p. 17.

whom goods shall be produced. Decisions to produce high-quality and high-priced articles limit the number of consumers who can obtain the commodity. Businessmen, then, have a considerable voice in determining what the gross national product will be and how it will be distributed. In 1923, Oliver Sheldon summed up these ideas by saying:[4]

> Industry exists to provide the commodities and services which are necessary for the good life of the community, in whatever volume they are required. These commodities and services must be furnished at the lowest prices compatible with an adequate standard of quality, and distributed in such a way as directly or indirectly to promote the highest ends of the community.

In a planned economy such as Russia's, answers to the basic economic questions of what commodities to produce, how they shall be produced, and for whom they shall be produced are provided by a central planning agency. Russian businessmen are relieved of much responsibility to consumers. But businessmen in a free economy need to be consumer-oriented. They can best accomplish the mission of business as outlined by Sheldon and answer the questions posed by Samuelson by obtaining guidance from consumers.

Businessmen in free economies have no place to turn for answers except to consumers, who hold a veto power over business decisions. Businessmen can determine how best to serve society only by reviewing consumer votes in the market, that is, by noting what consumers buy or do not buy. Willingness to buy, in turn, depends upon how well products satisfy consumer needs.

Obviously, not all businesses serve the same consumer groups. Some businesses, such as General Dynamics or Motorola's military division, concentrate on government agencies as their customers. Others, such as Fisher Body, produce for the automobile industry. Still others, such as General Mills, produce items for general public consumption. Many companies produce for a variety of markets. But whatever consumer group a business concentrates on, whatever market it tries to claim, it must first look to consumers for survival and vitality. As Peter Drucker tells us: "There is only one valid definition of business purpose: *to create a customer.*" And later he expands his idea by saying: "Because it is its purpose to create a customer, any business enterprise has two—and only these two—basic functions: marketing and innovation. They are the entrepreneurial functions." [5]

[4] Oliver Sheldon, *The Philosophy of Management*, London: Sir Isaac Pitman & Sons, Ltd., 1923, chap. 8. Reprinted in Harwood F. Merrill (ed.), *Classics in Management*, New York: American Management Association, 1960, p. 300.

[5] Peter F. Drucker, *The Practice of Management*, New York: Harper & Row, Publishers, Incorporated, 1954, p. 37.

THE SYSTEM CONCEPT OF BUSINESS

From a functional standpoint it has been traditional to view marketing departments as being responsible only for activities concerned with the movement of goods and services from producers to consumers.[6] Marketing and production were seen as two separate and unrelated activities. But this view fails to recognize that production and marketing are both part of the same entrepreneurial function of satisfying consumer needs. To discharge its responsibilities to consumers properly, business needs to recognize and build upon the interdependence among all functional specialties. The business enterprise is a total system whose basic purpose is to satisfy consumer wants.

Difficulties with a System Concept. There are two reasons why it has been difficult for businessmen to integrate marketing and production activities. First is a general misinterpretation of the economist's term "production." Production, to the economist, means creation of form, time, place, and possession utilities. In economic theory, the production process includes all activities necessary to create a product *and put it into consumers' hands.* Economic theory clearly recognizes the necessity for a system approach in defining business purpose. But practitioners—businessmen themselves—have historically viewed production as being concerned only with creation of form utility. A typical attitude was that the sales department should sell whatever was produced in the plant.

Today, many businessmen are shifting emphasis away from production per se and focusing upon responsibilities to consumers. No longer is the preceding definition of marketing sufficient. Phelps and Westing suggest: "It needs extension backward toward product planning and forward toward responsibility for the product subsequent to sale."[7]

Consumer Orientation. The second reason why it has been difficult for businessmen to view the enterprise as a total system is the historical view of selling as a base and ignoble activity. In early chapters we discussed how social attitudes toward commercial activities were shaped by Aristotle's teaching and by Christian dogma. Although business activity in general has lost much of its social stigma, selling, as a specialized activity, has been slower to attain full respectability. Fifty or so years ago marketing and selling were viewed as synonymous, and because selling lacked respectability the entire marketing function was generally deemphasized. Because seventy-five or one hundred years ago consumers were so starved

[6] "Report of the Definitions Committee," *Journal of Marketing,* October, 1948, pp. 202–217.
[7] D. Maynard Phelps and J. Howard Westing, *Marketing Management,* rev. ed., Homewood, Ill.: Richard D. Irwin, Inc., 1960, pp. 1–2.

for factory-made goods, whose shortage was sometimes aided by monopoly conditions in many industries, it was relatively easy to dispose of any commodities that provided reasonable satisfaction of consumer needs. Production decisions could be made with only the broadest concern for consumer preferences because consumers were presented with a narrow range of choices. A philosophy of *producer sovereignty* rather than *consumer sovereignty* was popular among businessmen. The philosophy of producer sovereignty embodied the idea that producers knew better than consumers what products would best satisfy consumer needs. Therefore, producers frequently made unilateral decisions about what, how, and for whom goods should be produced.

But as monopoly power of producers diminished and was replaced by monopolistic competition, the philosophy of producer sovereignty became inappropriate. As ranges of choice among products increase and competition for consumer votes becomes keener, it is increasingly important that producers turn to the consumer himself for production decisions. This means finding out what customers want *before* goods are produced, rather than producing and waiting for consumers to apply their veto power or accept the product. In this way producers can best exercise their responsibility to provide goods at the lowest possible price consistent with adequate quality. Wrong decisions are expensive and add to total costs of operating a firm. Losses in one period must be recovered in the next if the firm is to survive, and losses can be recovered only at the expense of higher prices.

The primary responsibility which business has to consumers is to identify their needs. Only after needs are known can a producer hope to find ways of satisfying them. But identification of consumer needs is a major task in itself. Often consumers cannot define their own needs because they do not recognize that needs change over time. In order to do a better job, Boyd and Levy suggest that production decisions be made in terms of *consumption systems*, that is, ". . . the way a purchaser of a product performs the total task of whatever it is that he or she is trying to accomplish when using the product—not baking a cake, but preparing a meal. . . ." [8]

BUSINESS AS AN INSTRUMENT OF CHANGE

Business is a major instrument of change in our society. Remembering that we are including the business side of nonprofit organizations and government agencies in our definition of business, it is not inappropriate to say that business is the major instrument of change.

Because we live in a capitalistic economic system, we have grown

[8] Harper W. Boyd, Jr., and Sidney J. Levy, "New Dimension in Consumer Analysis," *Harvard Business Review*, November–December, 1963, p. 130.

used to change. Indeed, we have come to expect it, for capitalism itself is an evolutionary process. Competitive forces at work within our capitalistic economy center around finding better ways of performing the mission of business, that is, providing more and better goods and services for consumers at lower prices. In short, we expect the economic system under which we live to provide a rising standard of living, and "the fundamental impulse that sets and keeps the capitalistic engine in motion comes from the new consumers' goods. . . ." [9] As the agent of consumers, business has the responsibility of producing a never-ending flow of new and different goods and services, thereby contributing to increased consumer well-being.

Consumers, then, have delegated to business certain responsibilities for their well-being, and increasing consumer well-being depends upon change. When a consumer thinks of improvement in standards of living, he usually thinks of new products that have become available. But business responsibility for innovation goes much further and includes not only improvements in form utility but also improvements in time, place, and possession utility. Whether a company produces goods or services makes little difference. Responsibilities remain the same.

But how can business enterprises provide the kinds of goods and services demanded by consumers? How can business enterprises know what consumers want or need? The answer seems simple: Ask them. But in reality the answer is more complex. Consumers rarely know what kinds of products will best satisfy their needs. But they can and do define the need itself. For example, a few years ago women could not have told du Pont that they wanted nylon stockings. But they could and did express their need for stockings which were as sheer as silk but which were more durable, held their shape better, and were easier to launder. Once the need was identified, a product could be developed that would satisfy the need.

Similarly, a few years ago not many home insurance buyers could define "comprehensive homeowners' policies" as we know them today, but they recognized the convenience of combining their insurable risks and dealing with just one company. The companies that pioneered nylons and homeowners' policies were consumer-oriented. They were sensitive to the needs of the consumers *from the consumer point of view.* Examples of product innovation which has satisfactorily met consumer needs are numberless. Garbage disposals, television, electric garage doors, new techniques in vascular and heart surgery, computers, nuclear energy, new metal alloys, jet engines, plastics, and automobile and equipment leasing are a few examples of product research and innovation.

[9] Joseph A. Schumpeter, *Capitalism, Socialism, and Democracy*, New York: Harper & Row, Publishers, Incorporated, 1942, quoted in Edwin Mansfield (ed.), *Monopoly Power and Economic Performance*, New York: W. W. Norton & Company, Inc., 1964, p. 30.

Innovative responsibilities go much further than just product research. They extend to creation of all types of utility. Businessmen are responsible to consumers not only for producing new and improved products at lower prices but also for improving ways consumers gain possession of products (that is, marketing innovations). Thus, they need to be ever alert for new and improved ways to store merchandise, new and improved transportation methods, and new and improved ways for consumers to buy.

The following developments illustrate marketing innovation. Not many years ago consumers could enjoy orange juice only when the fruit was in season. Today, however, as a result of processes for concentrating fruit juice, quick-freezing techniques, refrigerated trucks and railroad cars, and "deep-freeze" display cases at the point of sale, consumers can enjoy orange juice at any season. Fresh lobster is available for the dinner tables of inland cities because of air transportation and improved packing techniques. Large assortments of goods are available to consumers because of new packing and storage methods. Furthermore, people can today obtain products easily because of innovations in consumer credit. It is much easier for most people to buy through monthly payments than on open account or by paying the total price in cash.

In order better to exercise innovative responsibility, businessmen have learned to encourage and develop upward communications from consumers. They are beginning to listen to customer complaints and to encourage customer suggestions, and more research is being done to identify consumer needs. Only when consumer needs are understood can business properly exercise its innovative responsibility—its responsibility to be creative in the consumer interest.

RESPONSIBILITY FOR PRODUCT INFORMATION

Understanding consumer needs and producing goods and services to satisfy those needs do not complete business's responsibility to consumers. Consumers need a variety of information about products, and business is the organization best able to provide this information. Communication of product information is accomplished through advertising.

There has been, over the years, considerable controversy over both the economic justification and the legitimacy of advertising. It has been argued that advertising is economically undesirable because it serves no useful economic purpose. Further criticism also centers around truthfulness. These criticisms need examination from the social-responsibility viewpoint.

Product Information and Consumer Well-being. Advertising is a key to any society's standard of living because that standard depends upon both production and consumption. Mere physical existence of manufactured items does not benefit anyone. Production, by itself, only adds to producers' inventories. It becomes economically meaningful only when ownership of goods can be transferred to consumers. But before consumers will or can consume, they must know that the product exists, how it will satisfy their needs, and how they can obtain it. It is true that some product information reaches consumers by word of mouth. But word of mouth has limited usefulness. For one thing, it is usually slow. For another, it is most effective in limited local markets. For rapid dissemination of product information over a wide area, advertising through the mass meda is much more effective.

In addition to acquainting consumers with new products which are continually being introduced, one author calls attention to the following economic services performed by advertising.[10] Product information helps develop and expand markets. In our dynamic economy, markets are not fixed but have shown a remarkable ability to expand. As population has increased and purchasing power has grown, advertising has played an important part in developing expanded markets by creating consumer demand, which in turn has encouraged mass production. Increased scale of production, in turn, results in lower unit costs, which become available to the producer in the form of increased profits or which may be passed on to consumers in the form of lower prices. Long-range results of increasing scales of production have usually been favorable to consumers. To be sure, instances of monopolistic pricing resulting from product differentiation may be directly attributable to advertising. But these are exceptions rather than the rule. By calling consumers' attention to the variety of substitutable products which are available, advertising tends to increase competition rather than lessen it, and competition along with production economies tends to lower prices.

Advertising is not reserved for the use of private economic enterprise. It is used by virtually every enterprise. Government agencies certainly advertise. Appeals by the Treasury Department to buy defense bonds depend heavily upon advertising. Local health departments advertise to encourage people to get chest X rays or polio immunizations. The Bureau of Land Management and the Forest Service advertise occasional disposal of public domain. Similarly, local public-service organizations such as symphony orchestras or theaters advertise. Universities advertise for graduate students and to sell tickets to lecture and concert series. These activities, like the advertising activities of private business, have as their objectives dissemination of product information and increased consumption.

While criticisms of economic waste are still occasionally directed against advertising, they seem to occur less frequently and with less intensity than they did a few years ago. This may very well reflect a more

[10] Robert V. Zacher, *Advertising Techniques and Management*, Homewood, Ill.: Richard D. Irwin, Inc., 1961, pp. 582–586.

sophisticated understanding which accepts advertising (*as an activity*) as both socially and economically desirable.

Responsibility for Truthfulness. More severe and persistent than questions of economic justification are criticisms of untruthfulness in advertising—misleading statements, half-truths, and failure to disclose full information about products. Closely akin to these are the criticisms directed at improper appeals to sex, prestige, physical prowess, and other like human needs. But these criticisms are directed against the *use* of advertising, not against the concept of advertising. Responsibilities of business to provide full and truthful information are clear. Consumers are fully dependent upon producers for product knowledge. Therefore, adequately to fulfill its responsibilities in its trading exchange with customers, business needs to provide as much truthful information as possible. Consumers seek confidence that the product will do what is claimed for it.

Not all businessmen have seen fit to assume their responsibility for advertising accuracy. Nor is this situation peculiar to the present. Much advertising of a generation or two ago would be distasteful if repeated today. Consider some of the early advertising claims of one prominent company. In reviewing early U.S. Borax Company advertising, one observer comments:[11]

> There is little doubt as to how the sophisticated customer of today would react to the optimistic selling pitch of one of the company's first advertising booklets: 20 Mule Team Borax was recommended as an aid to digestion; to keep milk sweet; as a complexion aid ("Don't wash your face in ordinary lake water"); to remove dandruff; and for the bath ("Use half a pound of powdered borax to the ordinary family bath of twelve gallons of water"). . . . And as a final fillip, Borax, claimed the advertisement, was also "excellent for washing carriages" and useful in curing epilepsy and bunions.

While there are few advertisers today who would make such broad claims for their products, many current advertising practices are frowned upon. It is not so much the blatant untruths that cause the trouble as the half-truths and the subtle deceptions. Untruths are relatively easily detected and controlled. Subtle misrepresentations and deceptions are much more difficult to control because they are subject to debate. In order to provide some standards against which to make judgments about the propriety of advertising claims and to protect consumers, Congress in 1938 passed both the Food, Drug, and Cosmetic Act and the Wheeler-Lee Act. The purpose of the Food, Drug, and Cosmetic Act is to prohibit movement in interstate commerce of adulterated and mislabeled food, drugs, and cosmetics. It is the law that controls what information may and may not appear on labels and packages. The Wheeler-Lee Act em-

[11] Velma A. Adams, "Why the Old Products Last," *Dun's Review and Modern Industry*, April, 1965, p. 112.

powers the Federal Trade Commission to prevent the use of false and misleading advertising of goods moving in interstate commerce. The law covers not only specific representations about products but also the extent to which material facts are *not* revealed.

But passing legislation does not solve the problem. In one way it only complicates it, for legislation encourages businessmen to focus on legal boundaries of advertising behavior rather than on ethical considerations. In considering this question one author polled New York City managers in seventeen different industries. He reported:[12]

> In personal interviews, time after time these executives told me, "It's for Legal to decide," when they were asked whether there were any special ethical, moral, or public relations considerations in those particular marketing areas heavily concerned with "consumer interest." Only 3 out of 31 executives could see any such relationship.

We are not suggesting here that the Food, Drug, and Cosmetic Act and the Wheeler-Lee Act be repealed, nor are we questioning the usefulness of these acts. We are suggesting that legislation is not enough. This fact is evidenced by increasing demands for more power to be vested in the Federal Trade Commission and by proposals of additional legislation to control advertising. The Advertising Federation of America reported that as of April, 1965, there were fifty-seven pieces of proposed legislation on advertising before the United States Congress.[13]

There will always be needs for legislation, but there should be a minimum of legislation, not a maximum. What is needed is not a flood of new legislation but a new kind of thinking among businessmen. President Johnson emphasized this idea in his remarks announcing the establishment of top-level consumer representation in the White House. He said: "The remedy for errors of taste, poor judgment and disorder in our economic life is not to be found in the legislatures or the courts but in the leadership of those who care." The entire problem, the President said, is ". . . a matter for corporations and organizations dedicated to the public interest." [14] This thinking does not focus on legal boundaries of advertising but rather is sensitive to consumer demands and complaints. A straightforward approach to evaluating advertising decisions concerning consumer interest has been suggested by Hopkinson.[15] He suggests that businessmen evaluate a decision in terms of questions such as:

Is this fair?
Is this ethical?

[12] Tom M. Hopkinson, "New Battleground: Consumer Interest," *Harvard Business Review*, September–October, 1964, pp. 98–99.
[13] *Washington Report*, Washington, D.C.: Advertising Federation of America, Apr. 20, 1965.
[14] *The New York Times*, Feb. 6, 1964, quoted in Hopkinson, *op. cit.*, pp. 97–98.
[15] Hopkinson, *op. cit.*, p. 102.

Would *I* like to be treated in this way?
What would *my* wife think about the labeling on this package?
Do I want *my* children to watch this kind of T.V. program?

RESPONSIBILITY FOR WARRANTY AND SERVICE

Consumers expect products to perform in the way producers claim they will. Advancing technology makes consumers increasingly dependent on producers for full and accurate product information. Most products are no longer simple, familiar to consumers, or easy to inspect. Rather, they have become so complex and technical that consumers in most cases are no longer competent to judge either their quality or their operating characteristics. This lessening of consumer ability to judge products places responsibility for product performance more squarely than ever before on the shoulders of producers. Consumers have no place else to go. They must depend heavily upon producers' information when they make buying decisions.

Concern over problems of fraudulent claims for products and shoddy merchandise has plagued consumers for generations. Aristotle (384–322 B.C.) was concerned with the problems of value of exchange.[16] St. Thomas Aquinas (1225–1274) in his *Summa Theologica* showed considerable concern over selling defective merchandise.[17] Both English and American common law are full of breach-of-warranty cases. While most of the early cases were concerned with express warranties, today's concepts of product liability increasingly focus on warranties implied through advertising claims. The philosophy of *caveat emptor* (let the buyer beware) is being replaced by the philosophy of *caveat vendor* (let the seller beware).

Warranty. Because buyers today are so heavily dependent upon producers' information in their buying decisions, problems of misleading information, fraudulent information, implied safety of use, and shoddy merchandise are receiving more attention than ever before.

For the first time consumer interest groups have direct representation in the White House. Early in 1964, President Johnson created a special White House assistant for consumer affairs who heads the new Committee on Consumer Interests. To educate consumers how best to protect themselves against unfair and misleading advertising, the committee (composed of top-level representatives of nine government agencies and twelve private members) has been conducting a series of regional consumer conferences.[18]

[16] Aristotle, *Politics*, quoted in Arthur Eli Monroe, *Early Economic Thought*, Cambridge, Mass.: Harvard University Press, 1951, pp. 13–22.

[17] St. Thomas Aquinas, *Summa Theologica*, quoted in *ibid.*, pp. 56–62.

[18] "Mrs. Peterson Named Consumer Advisor to LBJ," *Advertising Age*, Jan. 6, 1964, p. 1.

Consumer complaints, pressures in the courts, and a growing awareness of social responsibility have combined to make businessmen more sensitive to problems of product liability.

Businessmen are increasingly being encouraged by lawyers, design engineers, insurance executives, and business consultants to provide extensive and truthful information. They are being encouraged to avoid exaggerated claims of safety, quality, and durability. And they are being encouraged to indemnify purchasers against faulty products.

Heavy pressures from courts have emphasized business responsibility in the area of warranties. Recent decisions have stressed the point that since producers have done everything they can through advertising to convince consumers that their products are suitable and safe for a specific use, they must be liable for product performance. In a landmark case in 1960, a plaintiff sued both the manufacturer and the dealer when a new car ran off the highway because of defective mechanism. The driver was injured and the car damaged. The plaintiff won a jury decision "on the grounds of breach of express and implied warranty that the car was safe for its intended use." [19]

Expansion of the concepts governing product liability has been incorporated into uniform-commercial-code laws by twenty-eight states. The uniform code holds that "a manufacturer is open to suit by anyone using his products who claims injury, even if the claimant is not the original buyer." [20] For example, the court decided in favor of the plaintiff when a toy gun advertised as absolutely harmless set a child's clothes on fire, and again when a driver was blinded by a rock crashing through a "shatterproof" windshield.[21]

Businesses are liberalizing their policies on repair of faulty products, cash refunds, and exchanges of unsatisfactory products. There is an increasing trend to formalize and strengthen warranties. Most electrical appliances now carry with them express warranties for one year. Not many years ago the usual warranty on a refrigerator was three months; now a five-year warranty is normal. The Federal Housing Authority requirements of a one-year guarantee by builders on houses to be sold under FHA mortgages has set a precedent for general contractors. Chrysler Corporation has pioneered in the automotive field with the five-year, 50,000-mile guarantee. In the retail field, Sears, Roebuck led the way with their unconditional money-back guarantee. Much of Sears's success has been attributed to consumer confidence built in this way.

Service. Because many products are so complex, consumers also depend more heavily on producers to provide service in case of product

[19] "Consumers Sue for Defective Products," *Consumer Bulletin*, November, 1964, p. 43.
[20] *Ibid.*, p. 43.
[21] *Ibid.*, p. 17.

failure. Few consumers today can repair their own refrigerator, washing machine, lawn mower, or automobile. As products become more complex and technical, producers have an increasing responsibility to provide parts and service. Manufacturers of farm machinery and automobiles have long recognized their responsibility in this area and have maintained market-wide service organizations and local inventories of parts.

While many manufacturers cannot afford to maintain large service organizations, this does not relieve them of responsibility for service. Most reputable manufacturers have recognized this responsibility and have accepted it by maintaining stocks of parts, authorizing and training private service enterprises to service their products, and/or standing ready to repair items at their factories.

RESPONSIBILITY FOR SELF-REGULATION

Under ideal conditions the business system would be a self-regulating system in regard to consumer responsibilities, particularly for product information. Ideally, every firm should recognize its responsibilities to consumers and willingly exercise these responsibilities to its fullest ability. But this is a utopian approach which has little meaning in the real world of business. Because business behavior in the area of product information revolves heavily around ethics, it is difficult to obtain general agreement on proper ethical behavior. There are differences of opinion between consumers and producers concerning what is proper behavior.

Chapter 4 emphasized that if a social institution does not serve society so as to provide suitable social payoffs, society will replace or modify the institution. Society, then, controls various institutions by setting standards of performance. In the realm of product information, society sets minimum standards of performance and defines ethical behavior which business must follow. Business has little choice but to accept and conform to these standards. However, it does have two choices of *how* to conform. It may voluntarily regulate its own performance, or it may submit to forced regulation by society through legislation.

Business has not always taken the initiative in establishing high ethical performance standards for product safety and product information. This lack of leadership has encouraged minimum legal standards, such as those set by the Food, Drug, and Cosmetic Act and the Wheeler-Lee Act. On the other hand, much effort has been devoted by individual firms and entire industries to encourage high ethical behavior.

Basically there are three reasons why business tries to regulate and police its own activities. First, and the most often proposed reason, is to avoid government action. This reason reflects defensive thinking on the part of businessmen and focuses on minimum compliance with society's standards. It emphasizes the legal performance boundaries beyond which business cannot go without interference. Review of relations between the Federal Trade Commission and the cigarette industry over the years indicates that the establishment of an office to review and approve cigarette advertising was largely an effort to avoid legislation.[22]

The second reason for self-regulation is for status. In an attempt to "professionalize" an industry, businessmen sometimes submit themselves to self-administered policing under government procedures. For example, in many states contractors must be registered and licensed before they can operate. Contractors themselves often are quite active in establishing criteria for both registry and licensing and in formulating criteria for withdrawal of registry or license.

A third reason for self-regulation is a growing belief on the part of both industries and individual firms that "what is good for society is good for business." These beliefs are reflected in the authority given to some trade associations and in company codes of ethics. Rather than focusing on minimum performance, firms that hold this belief often choose to exceed society's standards.

Historically, fear of government interference and regulation has been the prime force motivating business toward more responsible behavior. Businessmen for the most part have taken a defensive position based upon the concept that any action not specifically declared illegal is legal and therefore appropriate. But judging actions solely on the basis of legality is not enough. Since legislation reflects public displeasure with actions, it defines only minimal conditions, leaving to business the responsibility to go beyond legislation. The prime responsibility of business to consumers is to understand and predict how it can best serve consumers, to view itself as existing for consumers—not the other way around.

RELATIONS WITH SUPPLIERS

Business itself is a consumer—a very specialized type of consumer, buying the vast multitude of materials, supplies, and services necessary to produce the products and services which it, in turn, will merchandise to its customers. These may be final consumers or other intermediate customers in the total business system. But three things distinguish the business consumer from other consumers. First, business purchases generally involve a much longer planning horizon and execution time. Second, they generally involve relatively permanent commitments—the business buyer cannot switch easily from one supplier to another. Third, business purchasers generally are much more sophisticated and knowledgeable regarding buying decisions.

[22] Dascomb R. Forbush, *Management's Relationships with Its Publics*, Evanston, Ill.: Northwestern University Press, 1960, pp. 105–127.

The importance to the firm of good supplier relations cannot be overemphasized. The sheer amount of dollars spent by the purchasing department of a firm generally makes it the largest single dollar-expenditure area over which management has control. A recent survey indicated that in the 100 largest nonfinancial firms in the United States in 1962, 54.3 percent of the sales dollar was spent for "goods and services purchased from others"—over twice as much as the 24.9 percent consumed by the next largest expenditure area—"wages, salaries, and employee benefits." [23] This same survey in 1957 showed only 48.3 percent of sales income spent for purchases.[24] And as the trend toward automation continues, the percent of sales income devoted to purchases undoubtedly will grow. Of course, reference to corporate annual reports will show that the percent of sales income channeled to purchases varies widely. A railroad, a utility, or an integrated petroleum company which owns its principal raw material may spend only 20 or 25 percent of its sales dollar for purchases. On the other hand, a meat-packer or a cotton cloth manufacturer may spend 70 to 90 percent of its sales dollar on purchases.[25]

Good supplier relations have a substantial effect on a firm's competitive position. If dollars are spent wisely, production costs are lowered, enabling it to price its products competitively. Additionally, the purchasing department, because of its external information sources, can keep management apprised of new methods, processes, and materials which might offer the company a competitive advantage.

Many times the effects of superior, or inferior, supplier relations are not easily detected, for they appear in other areas. For example, if material shortages occur, a production facility may be closed. Enforced idleness is quite costly, in terms of damage to customer relations and lost sales. Also, if purchased goods delivered by suppliers are of inferior quality, this can result in excess scrap and spoilage rates, costly rework, and damage to customer relations if an unsatisfactory product gets out into the market.

Objectives of Purchasing. Responsibility for supplier relations usually lies primarily with a company's purchasing department. While the purchasing department of a particular company will have a long list of objectives, some peculiar to that firm and its competitive and operating situation, there are three broad, major objectives which will be embraced by almost any well-run department.

The first broad objective is to provide for the uninterrupted supply of materials, supplies, and services to support operations. A cardinal sin

[23] "Annual Report on the 100 Largest," *First National City Bank of New York Monthly Letter,* June, 1963.

[24] *Ibid.,* September, 1958.

[25] The 1963 annual report of Armour and Company shows that every working day they spend over 5 million dollars for raw materials and supplies—a total of 1½ billion dollars a year. Sales in 1963 were reported at slightly over $1,810,000,000, meaning that purchases accounted for approximately 73 percent of the sales dollar.

for almost any purchasing department is to run out of a key material, commodity, or good, since fixed costs go on regardless of whether or not operations continue.

The second objective is to gain maximum value for each dollar expended for items and services procured. Because of its direct effect on the profit account, it is essential that purchase cost be minimized, consistent with meeting the quality requirements of material users.

The third and last major objective is to keep inventory investment and inventory losses due to obsolescence, deterioration, and theft at a minimum, consistent with adequate protection of supply needs. Inventory is a costly asset to maintain (cost per dollar invested, in money costs, storage, insurance, deterioration, and theft, may run upward of 40 percent annually, although 20 to 25 percent is an average figure); therefore, this asset must be controlled closely.

A close examination of these three objectives reveals that a company's suppliers are a vital "key" to their satisfactory attainment. With good suppliers, their realization is within reach; in the absence of competent suppliers with whom adequate long-term relationships have been developed, they are completely unattainable.

The job of developing good supplier relations is a never-ending and often complex task. In sheer numbers alone, the medium-sized firm may have several thousand suppliers.[26] And the very large firm well might have over twenty thousand suppliers. Monitoring relations with each of these vendors requires constant attention and action by responsible purchasing managers.

In one sense, the supplier's production line can be thought of as merely an extension of the buyer's production line—backward vertical integration, so to speak. Yet the supplier's production line cannot be controlled directly, although many indirect control measures may be used. Perhaps the best indirect control which can be exercised is the development of a partnership philosophy between vendor and buyer. Both are interested in developing a satisfactory long-term relationship and must realize that the success of one is dependent in large measure on that of the other. "Sharp trading practices" by either party can exist only in the short run, for they make it impossible for the other party to realize its goals, causing a dissolution of the "partnership."

Advantages to Buyers of Good Supplier Relationships. Advantages to suppliers of good vendor-buyer relationships are self-evident—a stable, profitable account, which hopefully will grow in importance over time. Although advantages to buyers of developing good supplier relations may

---

[26] For example, AiResearch Manufacturing Company of Arizona, which employs approximately thirty-four hundred people, spent over 30 million dollars with 2,602 vendors in 1963. This amounted to approximately 40 percent of the total value of products shipped. See *AiReporter*, February, 1964, their employee house organ.

not be quite as obvious, nevertheless they are quite real. The principal advantages are as follows.

Product Research. Frequently research done by a vendor can be used profitably by buyers in developing product innovations. Often a supplier engages in extensive research, both basic and applied. If the supplier has had a good long-term relationship with a buyer, he may make such research results available to him, perhaps giving him an edge on his competitors in new product introduction. Additionally, unnecessary and costly duplication of research efforts can be avoided. Buyer and seller firms in the chemical industry long have used such research trade-off arrangements to good advantage.

Price and Market Information. Success often depends upon a firm's ability to gauge accurately supply-demand-price trends in the markets in which it deals. Suppliers often have advance knowledge of the changing forces which will affect these markets and can make such information available to their customers. This enables the buyer to better adjust his present actions to the projected future market situation.

Financial Aid. It is not unusual for a firm to run into temporary financial setbacks. Such situations can be quite embarrassing to the firm and may damage its future credit standing. If good long-term supplier relationships have been developed, it may be possible to persuade suppliers to provide temporary financial support, either through an outright loan or by deferring payment on materials furnished until the goods produced with these materials have been sold and the money received.

Technical Assistance. Aggressive companies are always attempting to devise means of reducing total manufacturing cost, through either product redesign or manufacturing process changes. This is referred to as the *value-analysis–value-engineering approach,* in which cost is compared with function or result. The objective is to find alternative means of achieving the same function or result, but at a lower total cost. The supplier typically is more knowledgeable regarding his products than the buyer and can make this expertise available. Results often can be spectacular; North American Aviation recently reported a $144,000 savings from substituting a different manufacturing method for brackets being used to fit onto vapor tanks. Their supplier assisted in devising the substitute manufacturing method.[27]

Special Delivery Arrangements. When a buyer enters into a purchase agreement with a seller, it is expected that the supplier will live up to the purchase terms, including the specified delivery date. Yet it is the unusual firm that from time to time does not have an abnormal delivery requirement. This may necessitate cancellation of an order because of an unexpected change in the buyer's customer needs. If good relations have been

[27] James C. Tanner, "Purchasing Agents Play Rising Role in Holding down Corporate Costs," *The Wall Street Journal,* June 23, 1964, p. 1.

developed with the supplier, an equitable cancellation settlement easily may be reached. Otherwise, the supplier may insist on completion of the contract, which could lead to extended litigation. On the other hand, the buyer suddenly may need to raise the quantity of the purchase or to ask the supplier to give special treatment to an order to meet some emergency early delivery requirement to satisfy an unusual customer requirement.

Protection against Strike Shortages. Vendor work stoppages create difficult problems for the buyer unless he has anticipated and adequately prepared for them. With good vendor relations, the buyer can expect his vendors to assist him in avoiding such difficulties. An example of such supplier-buyer cooperation is the arrangement which the Yardney Electric Corporation of New York City has with its suppliers. A simple check system has been devised whereby suppliers accept the responsibility of keeping Yardney informed of their current and anticipated labor situations.[28] Also, the supplier may agree to carry a larger-than-normal inventory of raw materials to protect the buyer against interruptions in the supply of items made from these materials. For example, when a steel strike is threatened, suppliers often agree to increase their steel stocks to protect the buyer.

In recent years, companies have become increasingly aware of their relationships with suppliers. Suppliers and buyers are joined together in a mutuality of interest and dependence. Each must satisfy his basic objectives through the relationship for it to continue to be profitable, in the long run, for the other party.

SUMMARY

Every society must answer the questions of what commodities shall be produced in what quantities, how they shall be produced, and for whom the goods shall be produced. In the free world, businessmen play a key role in answering these questions. However, in giving business the power to make these decisions, society expects them to be socially profitable ones. In other words, business must produce commodities that customers need, want, and can afford to buy. This imposes responsibilities on business. Business is first responsible for generating and maintaining a flow of new and improved products. Closely related is the responsibility of finding new and better ways of shipping, storing, and helping consumers buy.

Business also has the responsibility of disseminating truthful and complete product information. As consumer products become more varied and complex, consumers find it increasingly difficult to make intelligent buying decisions. Since the average consumer today does not have sufficient knowledge, he must rely more heavily than ever before upon statements made by the seller concerning quality and product performance. Businesses

[28] "Don't Get Caught Short by Strikes," *Purchasing*, July 29, 1963, p. 45.

are finding it necessary to provide and honor warranties on their products. Also because of the complexity of modern products, businesses are finding it increasingly important to provide parts and service.

Business itself is a very special type of consumer. It must buy materials, supplies, and services in order to produce products and services for the ultimate consumer. In order to exercise its responsibilities to consumers properly, it needs to accept the responsibility of creating good relations with its suppliers. Advantages gained from concentrating on favorable supplier relationships help businesses exercise more effectively their responsibilities to ultimate consumers.

To perform the economic function allocated to business by society, business needs to increase its consumer orientation and self-regulation. Only by policing the type and quality of its products, its advertising, and its warranty and service policies can business continue to maintain its key position in society.

QUESTIONS

1. What part do businessmen in a free enterprise economic system play in consumer well-being?

2. What are the entrepreneurial functions of business, according to Peter Drucker? Do you agree that business has only these functions?

3. What innovative responsibilities does business have to consumers?

4. What major criticisms have been directed against advertising? Are these criticisms justified? Why or why not?

5. What responsibilities to consumers does business have for product information?

6. How do you explain the continued consumer demand for legislation against advertising?

7. Is it the proper function of government to set minimum legal standards for business? If so, do you feel this function of government applies to all other major social groups also?

CHAPTER 13   BUSINESS AND LABOR

> New relationships are in the making today among
> business, government and labor in America. All three
> of these great centers of decisions in our economy face
> a set of unfamiliar and potentially dangerous forces
> which won't spare the slow-witted or the fainthearted.
>
> M. J. RATHBONE[1]

As suggested by the introductory quotation, organized labor has become a
major power group in industrialized society. In discussing national economic problems, organized labor is usually accorded a place beside business and government. Seldom are problems of productivity or economic
growth discussed without considering the roles, contributions, and relationships of these three social institutions.

In large part, growth of union power has been based upon social considerations. Society has been willing to confer power on organized labor
because it felt unions needed power to promote the welfare of working
people—a responsibility which society perceived had not been met by business alone.

Some observers feel that organized labor is now in the most critical
period of its development. Many feel that labor has largely achieved its
social objectives of improving wages, hours, and working conditions and
must now concentrate on social responsibilities which are commensurate
with its size and power. Others feel that social objectives remain but have
changed form. But few would contest the fact that organized labor has
become a potent economic and social power in the industrial scene. Much

[1] M. J. Rathbone, chairman of the board and chief executive officer (retired),
Standard Oil Company (New Jersey), "Three Men in a Boat" (speech before the
Harvard Business School Club of Washington, D.C., Nov. 28, 1962), p. 1.

243

criticism leveled at labor today revolves around the concept of balance of power and responsibility. While business is held economically and socially responsible for its decisions and actions, it is often argued that labor is not. As social and economic problems become more complex, labor, like business and government, may need to broaden its vision and look at itself as a partner rather than an antagonist of the other two.

In this chapter we shall discuss growth of the labor movement in its social setting and how it has altered the environment of business. We shall also consider changing roles of organized labor, changing business-labor relationships, and the question of responsibilities each may have to the others. Finally, public interest in collective bargaining and its effectiveness will be discussed.

THE GROWTH OF ORGANIZED LABOR

Labor unions, in one form or another, have been an integral part of American national development. Activities of American workers who banded together for some specific purpose date at least as far back as 1636, when a group of fishermen appealed to authorities to help collect unpaid wages. In New York in 1676 cartmen refused to remove dirt from the streets. Journeymen tailors in New York struck in 1768 for higher wages. Similarly, printers in New York struck in 1778 for the same reason.

Government intervention in problems of business-labor relations also dates back to early colonial settlement in America. Shortages of skilled labor and the concurrent high demand for it led Massachusetts, in 1633, to attempt wage controls by legislation.

Organizations of workers were generally unstable and short-lived prior to the Civil War. Nevertheless, unions had, by 1830, introduced most devices used by modern labor unions. Pressures on employers through strikes occurred in America at least as early as the seventeenth century. Between 1800 and 1810, strike activity to raise wages was common. Early unions also used collective bargaining. In 1799 employers and the Philadelphia Journeymen Cordwainers negotiated a compromise of a wage dispute. Strike benefits, too, received attention of early unions. As early as 1786, Philadelphia printers pledged money to support journeymen who lost jobs because of refusal to accept wage cuts, and in 1805 the New York Shoemakers established a permanent strike fund. Demands for and attempts to maintain closed shops were also relatively common by 1830. According to Taft: "The demand for the exclusion of the unorganized man from employment coincides with the beginning of trade unionism. In fact, control over the supply of labor was characteristic of many of the first organizations. A charge that appears in almost all of the labor conspiracy trials is that trade societies sought to compel all craftsmen to affiliate." [2] Thus, the environment of conflict between business and labor is nothing new to modern businessmen.

Business and labor also are no strangers on the political front; however, unions remained weak politically throughout their early development. Most early union leaders were opposed to political activity and stressed business unionism, but unions have, from time to time, entered politics.[3] As individual citizens, workers have always been concerned with political questions, but until recently, labor as labor (that is, an organized pressure group) has never been a major factor on the political scene. With the exception of one experiment, the Working Men's party in the early 1830s, there has been no effort to organize a labor party in America. Labor has been content to influence major political parties as best it could.

In the decades between the panic of 1837 and the Civil War, labor as a social institution moved in two separate and distinct directions. Some of labor continued to pursue the objectives of improving the lot of working men through economic pressures on individual employers. In large part, however, labor turned to intellectuals for leadership and became involved in supporting various utopian socialist schemes. One historian commented that "many union members looked to utopian experiments of the day for their economic salvation and became supporters and members of cooperative colonies established by the followers of the British industrialist and dreamer, Robert Owen, the French Utopian Socialists, etc." [4] Another observed: "When the foundation for labor's bargaining power was lost, many workers became more interested in the more ambitious projects to restructure the entire organization of the economy. The intention was not to secure a 'fair day's pay for a fair day's work' within a labor market, but rather to eliminate the labor market." [5] In retrospect, those unions who refused to waiver from principles of business unionism remained strong and viable. Those who became involved in social reform disappeared.

As business became more active during the latter part of the nineteenth century, so did labor. The thirty years from 1870 to 1900 was a period of labor violence in which the public became aware of the seriousness of the labor problem. As the labor movement grew in size and power,

[2] Philip Taft, *Organized Labor in American History*, New York: Harper & Row, Publishers, Incorporated, 1964, p. 8. The conspiracy trials were the result of applying the English common-law doctrine of "criminal conspiracy" to strike activities of labor organizations.

[3] The term "business unionism" means union objectives of improving wages, hours, and working conditions through economic coercion of employers as distinguished from objectives of social reform through political action.

[4] Harry W. Laidler, "A Brief Labor History," *Current History*, July, 1954, p. 2.

[5] Paul E. Sultan, *Labor Economics*, New York: Holt, Rinehart and Winston, Inc., 1957, p. 102.

its public visibility increased. It has been observed: "Heretofore the labour question had forced itself upon the attention of the public merely for brief moments and then invariably in a catastrophic setting. . . . Since then the labour question has held the public stage practically without interruption, though the interest it has aroused has of necessity fluctuated." [6] Just as society had become distrustful of an unrestrained business system, it began to look upon labor also as an institution which needed restraint, even though its social objectives were admirable. Public concern over demonstrations of union economic power, along with willingness of courts to support business in disputes with labor, kept business in a dominant power position during the late 1800s and early 1900s.

However, with the Great Depression of the 1930s came a massive change in public opinion. Failure of business to generate economic recovery—accompanied by declining public confidence in business, mass unemployment, and wage-level declines—opened the door for widespread legislative action.

With the passage of the Wagner Act and its subsequent ratification by the Supreme Court, the whole environment of business as it is affected by labor relations was changed. Heretofore, bargaining relations between business and labor had existed in an informal atmosphere in which business was free to negotiate or not negotiate with labor as it saw fit and as the economic powers of one or the other prevailed. The Wagner Act forced business to recognize labor organizations and bargain collectively with them. In addition, it did much more than that. By the passage of the Wagner Act, American society officially recognized American labor as a major social institution and conveyed upon it by legal decree powers commensurate with its social position.

Supported by public opinion and government sympathies, labor made substantial progress prior to World War II. Business was learning to live with its changed environment, and lulled by marked gains in economic activity, it was for the most part complaisant. After the war, however, the environment changed. Labor, mostly inactive during the war, reformulated Samuel Gompers's objectives of "more and more" and pressed for economic gains on virtually every front. Vigorous and militant actions by labor led to serious questions concerning its power and responsibilities. McGuire comments on social attitudes toward labor as follows:[7]

> The end of World War II produced an environment which was completely different from that which existed in 1940. During the war American business had redeemed itself through its productive efforts. Franklin D. Roosevelt, the great champion of organized labor, was dead.

[6] John R. Commons and associates, *History of Labour in the United States*, New York: The Macmillan Company, 1918, vol. II, part 2, pp. 527–528.

[7] Joseph W. McGuire, *Business and Society*, New York: McGraw-Hill Book Company, 1963, p. 117.

Many labor leaders had acted capriciously during the war and in the immediate post war years. People were tired of conflict. They were opposed to strikes, which came with mounting frequency in 1946. They were prosperous and wanted to be able to purchase goods immediately, and they couldn't understand why labor held up production. Labor obviously was no longer the underdog it had been in the 1930's; now the public considered it arrogant and dictatorial—almost un-American.

In many cases it was obvious that unions had misused the power granted them under the Wagner Act. Unions often resorted to practices which a few years before they had labeled unfair in the hands of management. People became concerned that the Wagner Act had "loaded the dice" too heavily in favor of labor. They became concerned that society had conveyed to labor great social and economic powers without exacting equal responsibility or accountability.

The Labor-Management Relations Act (Taft-Hartley) of 1947 and the Labor-Management Reporting and Disclosure Act (Landrum-Griffin) of 1959 were attempts to reverse the pendulum of power and bring the power relations of business and labor to equality.

THE CHANGING BUSINESS-LABOR ENVIRONMENT

An integral part of the philosophy of the American Federation of Labor and Congress of Industrial Organizations (AFL-CIO) has always been that there is strength in numbers. Growth, then, is an important key to future union success, but growth has been disappointing to labor leaders in the recent past. From 18,500,000 members in 1955, membership in *all* unions declined to 18,100,000 in 1962.[8] Membership as a percentage of the labor force has also been slipping. As a percentage of the labor force, union membership rose from 12 percent in 1930 to 36 percent in 1945, fluctuated between 1945 and 1955, then declined to 32 percent in 1962. The trend has continued downward.

Successful unionism in America has, in the past, emphasized a "bread-and-butter" approach to union activity. Long experience taught union leaders that little was to be gained by attempts at social reform through political activity. Based upon concepts of business unionism which stressed improvements in wages, hours, and working conditions, labor has made significant gains. The eight-hour day and forty-hour week are common. In some cases labor has been successful in reducing the length of the workweek even further. The Electrical Workers in New

[8] Edward T. Townsend, "Is There a Crisis in the American Trade-union Movement? Yes," in Solomon Barkin and Albert A. Blum (eds.), *The Crisis in the American Trade-union Movement*, Philadelphia: The American Academy of Political and Social Science, *The Annals*, vol. 350, November, 1963, p. 3.

York have had a thirty-five-hour week for some time. Standards of living for American workers are at the highest level in history, and social barriers between blue-collar and white-collar workers are rapidly disappearing. Additionally, the climate of violent warfare between business and labor is rapidly disappearing. To be sure, the public is often painfully aware of conflicts between labor and business, but it fails to consider that approximately 98 percent of the contracts which are negotiated by business and labor are arrived at peaceably. It is the other 2 percent that reach public notice.

In view of the economic gains which unions have made for their members, it has been suggested that the labor movement has largely fulfilled its objectives as stated by Samuel Gompers and that its objectives need to be reevaluated in the light of contemporary national social and economic problems.

There is little doubt that the business-labor environment is changing. Although many of the old problems remain, they are less intense. Many have changed form. Demands for increased wages still remain prominent in contract negotiations today, but they are being overshadowed by security issues such as retirement, seniority, negotiated unemployment benefits, and guaranteed hours.[9] However, as unions gain economic and social power, they increasingly find themselves confronted with problems of a much broader nature than heretofore. Problems of automation, inflation, foreign competition, national productivity, unemployment, and retraining (to mention a few) are increasingly occupying the attention of labor leaders.

Charges have been made by many writers (Paul Jacobs, Sidney Lens, Solomon Barkin, Paul Sultan, and others) that labor is in the middle of a crisis of survival. The main theme running through writings of these authors is that the entire labor movement is in danger because it has failed and continues to fail to adjust to new problems and new challenges which confront it. Labor leaders themselves recognize and admit the dilemma they find themselves in today. A survey of thirty-eight union presidents and forty-seven union staff personnel indicates that many of them are aware of, and concerned over, this crisis.[10] They perceive their main problems to be automation, unemployment, unfriendly legislation, weakness of union structure, increased management power, and unsympathetic public opinion.[11] Benjamin Masse adds the problems of the cold

---

[9] Millard E. Stone, "Emerging Concepts in Labor Relations," *Personnel*, March–April, 1965, p. 37.

[10] Solomon Barkin and Albert A. Blum, "Is There a Crisis in the American Trade-union Movement? The Trade Unionists' Views," in Barkin and Blum, *op. cit.*, pp. 16–24.

[11] *Ibid.*, p. 16.

war, inflation, and foreign competition. Problems of productivity and profitability of individual firms might well be added to the list.

The dilemma facing labor today is one of philosophy and ideology, which may well occasion a shift from business unionism to social unionism. Problems facing labor today no longer lend themselves to solution by earlier union methods. Under concepts of business unionism the three major problems of wages, hours, and working conditions were largely autonomous problems which did not necessarily have any relation to one another. They were solved on the basis of individual bargaining between one firm and one local union, and results had little impact elsewhere in the economy. Problems facing unions today are no longer isolated and mutually exclusive. Rather, they are dependent one upon the other and will need to be solved as a series of simultaneous equations. No longer are unions involved with questions which affect only one employer and one local, but with problems the solution of which has significant and widespread impact on the American economy. To complicate the unions' dilemma, the problems confronting labor are also, for the most part, the same problems which are confronting business. They do not lend themselves to solution by militant action and unilateral demands. They are broad social problems of national scope whose solution depends upon cooperation between the major social institutions of business, labor, and government.

In addition to the charge that unions are experiencing a crisis, there is the more serious charge that labor is doing nothing to ease the crisis. Critics point to losses of union membership as a sign of deterioration. A few critics go further and suggest that labor has outlived its usefulness. We do not attempt here to justify or refute these observations. However, it does appear that if labor is to perform adequately its responsibilities in a pluralistic society, it needs to overcome many of the ideologies and philosophies of the past and recognize its changing role in society. Suggestions have been made that the labor movement needs to stress "responsible constitutionalism" and "collective cooperation" if it is to survive.

In many ways, development of the labor movement parallels the development of business. Labor today faces many of the same problems of maturing that business faced seventy-five or so years ago. Just as business at the turn of the century found itself with inescapable responsibilities which it did not ask for and did not want, labor today finds itself in much the same position. Unwise use of power and failure to accept responsibility have led to parallel results also—unfavorable public opinion, leading to restrictive legislation.

The new posture of unions, if there is to be one, will not be easily attained. Rather than discard all the old goals and objectives, as some would have unions do, it seems more realistic that they retain them but pursue them within limits set by broader social considerations. At the same time unions need to formulate new objectives and pursue these within the framework of the extensive social responsibilities which they have.

LABOR AS A MATURING SOCIAL INSTITUTION

Few observers of the American industrial scene would deny that the labor movement is beset with numerous problems. Many of these are problems of an immature social institution. In this section we shall discuss some problems which unions need to overcome in order to emerge as a mature and responsible social institution in dealing with business and the general public.

Labor's Image. First and foremost among these problems is the image of the trade-union movement. The growing unfavorable public attitude toward labor which now exists revolves, for the most part, around issues of union power. Beginning with the General Motors strike in 1945 and the steel strike and the railroad strike in 1946, public sympathies began to shift away from labor. For the first time people far removed from the scene of a labor dispute became aware of labor's economic power. The public often blames labor for high prices, low quality, and shortages of consumer goods. Furthermore, union's use of tactics and practices, which had been declared unlawful for management under the Wagner Act, contradicted the public sense of fair play. Legislative hearings and investigations which exposed corruption and Communist activity within the union movement have also added to public distrust of unions.

High-level labor leaders are becoming increasingly concerned over the image of trade unionism and are attempting to do something about it. One major strategy is to get labor representatives, along with business and professional representatives, on every committee dealing with overall community problems. Concerted effort is exerted to participate actively in problems dealing with civil rights, medical care, child welfare, urban renewal, education, alcoholism, and even drug addiction. The objective is to portray union members and leaders as conscientious citizens, concerned with the progress of the entire community and not just with their own selfish demands. One recent study showed, however, that unions have had more success in becoming involved in community-service committees than in securing elected positions in one industrial community.[12]

Other top leaders attempt to improve labor's image by working to prevent unwise local strike activity. But because they lack direct control

[12] William H. Form, *Organized Labor's Place in the Community Power Structure*, East Lansing, Mich.: Michigan State University, Labor and Industrial Relations Center, 1959.

over locals, this is not always effective. For example, imprudent use of strike power by a Philadelphia teamsters local drew stiff penalties recently for the union and its leaders. The walkout caused a shortage of food and other products and idled some ten thousand other workers in the city. It ended only after a judge found the local guilty of contempt of court for violating an injunction he had issued earlier barring the strike.[13] Such blatant disregard for the law contributes to labor's image of arrogance and irresponsibility. Declarations by union leaders in high office that the national union did not sanction such a strike do little to improve the image. Similarly, recent incidents of election rigging in steelworkers' and electrical workers' elections have further contributed to the image of corruptness.

Labor's image is the key to many of its other problems. Changing its image will not be easy. Change will come only with demonstrations of responsibility. Instead of being an antagonistic element in the environment of business, it needs to show a spirit of willing cooperation and joint participation in solving common problems. There will always be differences in the viewpoints of business and labor, but as President Johnson has suggested: *"It is possible to disagree without being disagreeable."* This phrase is the key to a successful pluralistic society and is at the heart of mature business-labor relations.

Unfriendly Legislation. Legislation unfriendly to the labor movement has centered largely around the question of unions as monopolies and the use of monopoly power. There is little question that unions are monopolies in the technical sense of the word. Arthur Goldberg, at the time he was counsel for the steelworkers, clearly recognized the monopoly position of unions. He observed: [14]

> Technically speaking, any labor union is a monopoly in the limited sense that it eliminates competition between working men for the available jobs in a particular plant or industry. After all, all unions are combinations of working men to increase, by concerted economic action, their wages, i.e., the price at which the employer will be able to purchase their labor.

Society has reacted to unions' misuse of monopoly power much as it reacted to business's misuse of monopoly power in the period prior to passage of the Sherman Act. Results, too, have been similar. Dissatisfied with social payoffs it received from labor's activities, society has moved to constrain union practices. Both the Taft-Hartley and the Landrum-Griffin Acts were designed to restore a balance of power between unions and business and to provide a more favorable environment for business than existed under the Wagner Act.

[13] *The Wall Street Journal*, June 28, 1965, p. 5.

[14] Arthur J. Goldberg, *AFL-CIO: Labor United*, New York: McGraw-Hill Book Company, 1956, p. 157.

The legislative problem is not one of eliminating labor power—or business power—but rather of establishing an environment in which both have relatively equal power. Many suggestions for balancing power have been made. These range from compulsory arbitration to making unions specifically subject to antitrust laws. To date, no satisfactory solution has been found. It is doubtful that the problem can ever be fully solved by legislation. Full solution to the problem can come only with responsible action by both parties, actions which generate an environment of mutual trust, respect, and problem solving.

Union Organization and Structure. Another problem facing labor and business in the ever-changing arena of industrial relations is union structure. Old trade-union structure with high degrees of specialization is rapidly becoming obsolete. Increasingly in today's modern plants, workers need to be generalists, capable of performing several operations. Jobs are being enlarged, and most workers today in automated plants need a number of high-order skills and the ability to move freely among them. A manager of a Southwestern oil refinery explained his company's requirements this way: "When we pick a man to do a repair job, we expect him to do it *all*. There's no calling back for an electrician or a plumber while the carpenter sits on his tool box. Not any more." [15]

Industrial unions face much the same problem. Because jobs are being upgraded and enlarged, there is no place for many modern workers in the old-style industrial-union structure. Unions have found it difficult, in many cases, to attract new-style technicians, craftsmen, and maintenance men. Upward attrition through job improvement has often been viewed by labor as a deliberate effort by business to weaken unions. Perhaps such charges are justified in some cases, but inability or refusal to modify union structure appears to be the main difficulty. Whatever the cause, union frustration often leads to conflict.

While the problems just discussed are problems of the labor movement, they are also important to business because they influence business and labor relationships. If business and labor are ever to work together cooperatively on problems of national importance, labor must overcome business's distrust of its motives. While some businessmen advocate elimination of the union movement, others are hopeful that it will truly mature into a dynamic and responsible agency willing to shoulder a portion of the burden of national well-being.

EXAMPLES OF BUSINESS-LABOR COOPERATION

The previous sections of this chapter have described labor as partly failing to accept economic and social challenges in a responsible man-

---

[15] "The Blue Collar Elite," *Dun's Review and Modern Industry*, March, 1964, Special Supplement, p. 122.

ner. On some fronts this is undoubtedly true. On others, labor has risen admirably to participate with business in national problems. In support of labor's increasing maturity, one industrial observer commented: [16]

> It is necessary to remember that union members are not a breed apart. They are citizens, taxpayers, consumers—and often also stockholders.
>
> Over the years . . . some American labor leaders have shown a growing awareness of the national interest. They have done valuable work here and abroad; in combating communism, in giving technical assistance to workers in new nations, and recently in supporting the Trade Expansion Bill. All these are areas in which they have seen the parallel between their own interests and those of the nation as a whole. Thus they have interest not only in good wages but also in even prices, lower taxes, high productivity and adequate profits.

Automation. Automation and technical change have been discussed in a previous chapter, but it is appropriate to discuss them further here because of their impact on collective bargaining and labor relations. Many social issues facing business and labor are made more difficult by changing technology.

Automation has changed the nature of factory work and thereby altered business's labor environment. In several ways it has weakened labor's position and strengthened management's position in bargaining.[17] As mentioned earlier, upgrading skills and job enlargement have taken a substantial number of workers out of traditional bargaining units. Shifts from production to technical and professional occupations have resulted in more white-collar than blue-collar workers. In 1950, for example, there were 21.6 million white-collar workers and 24.3 million blue-collar workers. By 1960 the relation had reversed: there were 28.7 million white-collar workers and 26.9 million blue-collar workers. The trend is continuing with increased automation.

New factory construction also tends to weaken bargaining units. Automation destroys work groups by reducing the number of workers performing a particular job. Furthermore, workers are dispersed more widely throughout the factory, thereby reducing physical contact among workers. Jobs, too, differ widely among workers, making it difficult for one worker to understand the work problems of another. Group solidarity and loyalties therefore deteriorate, and loyalties to employers tend to be strengthened.

Physical environments in newly automated factories also tend to circumvent the union's role of securing improved working conditions. Superior working conditions are a necessary by-product of most automated

[16] Rathbone, *op. cit.*, p. 10.
[17] James L. Stern, "Automation: End or a New Day in Unionism?" in Barkin and Blum, *op. cit.*, pp. 25–35.

processes. Cleanliness, air conditioning, superior lighting, and temperature control are often mandatory for automated processes to function properly. Improved washrooms and lunchrooms and physical attractiveness are routine considerations in modern factory design.

Automation also reduces the attractiveness of strike activity for union members. The strike, as an economic weapon, has lost much of its strength in automated industries. Reduction in the number of production workers, along with increases in the number of supervisors and technicians, makes it relatively easy to maintain production during a strike. One highly automated Texas oil refinery employing some twenty-one hundred production workers found that it could maintain production with approximately nine hundred supervisors.

Demands for wage increases also have lost intensity as bargaining issues in automated plants. Emphasis has shifted to issues of job security. Workers in automated plants and industries, because of higher skill levels, are more highly paid than their counterparts in nonautomated plants and industries. Wage increases are less important to them than threats of reductions in number of jobs through continued automation. For example, the United Mine Workers (UMW), under the guidance of John L. Lewis, has for a number of years encouraged automation in the mines in return for increased wages. But in doing so, the union also has had to accept elimination of jobs. There are one-fourth as many miners in the coal industry now as there were fifteen years ago. Concerned with this trend, the union is now asking for a job freeze to assure between 80,000 and 100,000 jobs in the bituminous-coal industry.[18] To justify this request, unions point to increased production over the past years. Similarly, I. W. Abel and his predecessor in the steel industry are pressing for "total job security."

But the problem of automation is not simply one of relations between one union and one employer. It produces problems of national importance requiring the cooperative attention of business, labor, and government. Problems relating to automation have been receiving joint attention for some time. In 1961 the President's Advisory Committee on Labor-Management Policy (made up of business, labor, and public leaders) reported to President Kennedy their views on technical change and automation. The consensus was that they "are essential to the general welfare" but that they must be made "without the sacrifice of human values and without inequitable cost in terms of individual interests." [19] Since then numerous suggestions have come from the Committee. Among the suggestions have been advanced planning and reporting on future manpower needs which could reveal training needs ahead of time—requiring

[18] "UMW Seeks Job Security, Safety," *Business Week*, Jan. 4, 1964, p. 68.
[19] "Easing the Stress of Job Losses," *Business Week*, May 30, 1964, p. 87.

advance notice of automation changes, changing from earlier retirement to later starts of working lives accompanied by a fourteen-year minimum in public schools—and increased in-plant training.

While no single solution has emerged, both unions and business are experimenting, and unions are joining management in some areas. For example, both the AFL-CIO and the business community in Arizona participate in a concerted campaign to prevent high school dropouts. In other areas, both management and labor are working jointly with government to develop programs such as in-plant training programs and orderly transfer of dislocated employees.

The real problem of technological change and automation is not so much the change itself as the speed with which change is occurring. Skill levels cannot be upgraded fast enough or in sufficient quantities to keep pace with ever-increasing demand. Responsibility for orderly adaptation to change lies primarily with business and labor, but government also can do much to aid in the transition. The Committee for Economic Development (CED) has suggested several areas of government activity that will facilitate operation of the labor market and adaptation to technical change. It has suggested that the government should: [20]

1. Make every effort to maintain high levels of employment and purchasing power (objectives of The Employment Act of 1946).
2. Improve the Federal-State system of unemployment compensation to make benefits available to those seriously engaged in retraining.
3. Make efforts to encourage movement of labor out of areas of chronic distress.
4. Expand the amount of information about job openings and job applicants.
5. Improve facilities for retraining experienced workers.
6. Share out-of-pocket moving costs for workers moving to new locations.

Fear of automation by union members has produced an uncertain bargaining environment for both business and labor. Recent rejections by rank-and-file union members of contracts negotiated by international officers and top management suggest that although union leaders are willing to face the broad pressures of automation and take responsible positions in trying to arrive at workable solutions to complex problems, membership may insist on protecting job rights. In 1964 and 1965, Walter Reuther, of the auto workers; David McDonald, of the steelworkers; and Thomas Gleason, of the longshoremen all experienced member rejections of contract provisions they had negotiated. One reason for mem-

[20] *The Public Interest in National Labor Policy*, New York: Committee for Economic Development, 1961, pp. 126–127.

bers' refusing to ratify the agreements was dissatisfaction with job-security provisions. Actions such as these will certainly test the ingenuity of all concerned if the national interest is to be maintained.

Unemployment and Poverty. Problems of unemployment and poverty go hand in hand. Business, unions, and government are all affected by unemployment. For business, unemployment means reduced demand for consumer goods; for unions, it means fewer members; and for society, it means governmental support of public charges. Some problems of unemployment are related directly to technical change and automation, but others are not. When one starts to explore the various reasons for unemployment and poverty, he is often amazed at the number of sub-problems that exist. Some statistical findings by the President's Council of Economic Advisers provide clues to the complexity of the problem. They reveal that a family is likely to be poor if the head of the family is not white, if he is more than fifty-five years old, if he is less than a grade school graduate, if he is a farmer, or if the family head is a woman.

When considering unemployment and poverty, two groups need to be examined. One group is comprised of those who are not capable of working, such as those who are in poor health or who are too old to be gainfully employed. The problem of coping with this group is not the problem of either business or labor. This is primarily government's job. Theodore Levitt makes this point forcefully when he comments: "Welfare . . . [is] not the corporation's business. Its business is making money, not sweet music. The same goes for unions. Their business is 'bread and butter' and job rights. In a free enterprise system, welfare is supposed to be automatic; and where it is not, it becomes government's job." [21]

The other group which must be considered consists of those who are unemployed but want to work and those who are employed in sub-standard jobs. Both business and labor have responsibilities regarding this group. For business this latter group represents potentially useful employees and consumers with more dollars to spend. For unions these people represent potential members to add to their strength. But even here, both business and labor need the help of government. And they are receiving it. Or perhaps it would be more accurate to say that government is receiving the help and cooperation from business and labor that is imperative in a successful fight against unemployment and poverty. Participation in the national antipoverty program, at both the advice and the planning levels, and also at the action level, will be necessary. Unions can contribute by opening membership to all qualified workers and by assisting in educating and training those who are not qualified. Business can contribute by developing economically depressed

---

[21] Theodore Levitt, "The Dangers of Social Responsibility," *Harvard Business Review*, September–October, 1958, p. 47.

areas, by supporting education and training, and by providing advice and counsel to small businesses.

There are also many other areas of joint cooperation which have not been mentioned, such as employee safety, fair employment practices, and community charity drives.

TOWARD MORE SOPHISTICATED COLLECTIVE BARGAINING

A decrease in the number of man-days lost because of strikes since 1960 seems to be evidence of a marked change in the environment of collective bargaining. Effects of technical change on collective bargaining in automated industries have been referred to earlier. But the pressures of automation are not altogether responsible for the more mature and sophisticated bargaining climate which exists today.

One factor which has contributed to greater labor peace is the realization that bargaining is a day-to-day process, rather than a once-a-year controversy. Negotiations are given more time, and communications between labor and management are much improved. Contracts in some industries have been extended to three years, and in a few cases to five years. Following the example set by the steel industry, with their human relations committee, many companies have found that bargaining issues which once would have been withheld and presented at the annual bargaining session can be better resolved informally in day-to-day continual bargaining.

Another factor contributing to more responsible bargaining is that unions and management have learned to live together. Bargaining has become largely professional, and the fact that the same men face one another across the bargaining table on many different occasions has led to mutual respect and understanding. Although professionalism is open to some criticism, it has caused better preparation for bargaining, which in turn has led to more responsible action by both sides.

A growing realization that business and labor have much in common has led to an increased awareness by both sides that they have a joint role in the national interest. Strikes today can lead to heavy economic losses for both parties, as well as the nation, and often bring government into the bargaining process. Few in either management or labor welcome an increased government role in labor relations.

While substantial progress has been made in labor-management relations over the past few years, there is still room for improvement. As mature social institutions, both labor and business have inherited broad social responsibilities, whether they want them or not. By subordinating their self-interests to broader social interests and by learning to work together, they will produce the social payoffs expected by a free enterprise society.

LABOR IN POLITICS

Prior to the Depression of the 1930s, there was little place in union philosophy for political activity. Historically, when unions have become involved in social reform or political issues such as public education or the greenback controversy, their power has been dissipated and eventually they disappeared. When Samuel Gompers rose to power in the American Federation of Labor, his was a policy of business unionism. Union philosophy centered around direct relations between business and unions. For Gompers, political activity was appropriate only when labor failed to make gains through pressures on business. This philosophy is partly responsible for failure of a labor party to emerge in America.

Not only is political activity an integral part of union philosophy, but it also has become one of labor's major activities. Historically, business has been more dominant than labor in the political arena, except for the period of Roosevelt's administration. Today, labor is in the political arena *as labor*. It has become one of the major lobbying groups at all levels of government. As an organized voting block, labor has also arisen to considerable prominence. In the 1964 election, for example, nearly three-fourths of the labor-supported candidates were elected to office.

There are certain social dangers attached to labor's increasing political power. The danger is not that labor will obtain more power, but that it will become dominant. Just as business dominance of political power nearly a century ago threatened to produce a monolithic social system, labor's efforts to dominate political power today stand as a threat to pluralism. Balanced power among the major social institutions is a prerequisite to a strong free enterprise system. Balanced power will mean cooperation rather than dominance, and only through cooperation and joint effort can America's free enterprise system produce the social payoffs necessary for national growth.

SUMMARY

Labor, as an environmental factor in the world of business, is nothing new. Businessmen have related to labor, in one way or another, throughout America's development. Traditionally, labor has been an aggressive and militant factor in the environment of business, demanding (and getting) improvements in wages, hours, and working conditions.

As labor has gained in strength and been more successful in obtaining economic concessions from business, many have come to believe that it is on the threshold of a new role in society and, further, that the future of the labor movement depends upon how well labor exercises its new role as a mature and responsible social institution.

In its new role, labor is forced to assume a portion of the responsibility for the national well-being. To accomplish this, labor must cooperate and work with both business and government to an ever-increasing degree. Just as businessmen in many cases have found it necessary to subordinate their self-interest to national interest, so must labor do the same.

Neither labor nor business can exercise proper social responsibility in a militant collective-bargaining climate. Strikes are costly for both sides as well as for society in general. Social pressures for labor peace have done much to encourage a more sophisticated bargaining climate. There is considerable evidence of willingness on the part of both labor and business to solve their problems peacefully within the framework of each other's needs. And both seem increasingly willing to view their problems within the context of the national well-being.

QUESTIONS

1. Discuss briefly the effects on business-labor relations of the Great Depression of the 1930s. Of the Wagner Act. Of World War II. Of the post–World War II boom.

2. Compare or contrast differences and/or similarities between the development of American business and that of American labor.

3. Differentiate between business unionism and social unionism. What are the business-labor relationships likely to be under each concept?

4. In what ways have automation and technical change benefited business in collective bargaining?

5. In the light of continued militant activity by some unions, can you substantiate the view that collective bargaining is becoming more sophisticated?

6. Cite as many examples as you can of business and labor cooperation on common problems.

CHAPTER 14   BUSINESS AND

THE COMMUNITY

> One thing seems clear, the corporation cannot oc-
> cupy the publicly accepted leadership roles of our
> business-oriented culture in the local community and
> wash its hands of the responsibility that occupation
> implies.
>
> NORTON E. LONG[1]

The community discussed in this chapter is an organization's area of
local business influence. It often includes more than one political community, for political boundaries do not necessarily follow economic and
social boundaries. A major company in a metropolitan area might have
as its community the central city and nine satellite cities. Another company might be located in a rural area having three surrounding cities as
its community. A public utility has a separate community for each of
the local economic areas it serves. In all cases both company and community have a mutual dependence which is significant economically and
socially. The following situations show how this mutual relationship is
expressed in practice.

Residents in one city prepared to go before the city council to prohibit factory trucks from using streets in a nearby residential neighborhood as a regular thoroughfare. Plant officials responded by rerouting
the trucks.

In another city during a coal strike the principal factory supplied
two carloads of coal to the local hospital, even though the factory supply of coal was very short. During the same strike a factory manager in

---

[1] Norton E. Long, "The Corporation and the Local Community," in Arthur S.
Miller (ed.), *The Ethics of Business Enterprise*, Philadelphia: The American Academy
of Political and Social Science, *The Annals*, vol. 343, September, 1962, p. 127.

another city rejected a civic organization's plea for coal for a recreation hall. He silenced requests with the comment: "Which is more important, to assure work for several thousand men or to continue a recreation program?"

During a local recession in another city, a corporation found it necessary to lay off several hundred women assemblers. After consultation with local leaders, it made an exception to its regular policy of layoff by seniority. Women who proved. they were the sole breadwinner in a family were not laid off, regardless of seniority.

Business affects the community in three important areas: personal services of businessmen in community projects, business giving, and regular commercial activities of business. All three will be discussed following a general introduction covering community relations.

COMMUNITY RELATIONS

The involvement of business with the community is called *community relations*. Two characteristics distinguish the modern corporate community's relations from those of the community of 100 years ago. One is *urbanization*. Migration to great urban centers has changed community life and has created new stresses for business and community. It is estimated that urban population (persons living in a city of 20,000 or more) increased from 22 million in 1800 to over ½ billion by 1950. Urban population is expanding even faster today.

The second characteristic is greater interdependence of business and community. Urbanization is a partial cause of interdependence, but so is technology, for it requires communities to become much larger in order to maintain self-sufficiency. Ancient communities could be self-sufficient with a farm and a few artisans. But a modern industrial community needs a college nearby to support lifelong learning, recreational facilities, public utilities, specialized service facilities, urban transportation, capital sources, and a host of other services. Business depends on these services in greater variety than ever before. Just as a rocket can fail because of some tiny malfunction, so can a community experience difficulty because of indirect effects of some isolated event. There is no escaping general community interdependence today. Business cannot remain detached from the community.

Small and Large Businesses Compared. Another feature of community relations, substantially unchanged over the years, is that small companies are vitally involved in setting general community standards. The conduct of home builders, used car salesmen, and retail proprietors is a significant influence on the business image in a community, regardless of what United States Steel Corporation does at the national level. If these small businessmen let downtown go to seed, take advantage of their customers, and oppose civic improvement, the community climate will be poor. If they take an opposite approach, the climate is likely to be good, regardless of what industrial giants decide to do nationally.

We can speak of the small businessmen as Lincoln spoke of the common people: "God must have loved them because he made so many of them." Approximately 95 percent of all business firms have less than twenty employees. Even more startling is the fact that the number of small business firms is increasing faster than the general population. The number of firms per 1,000 persons in the United States increased between 1900 and 1960. A total of 1.6 million firms in 1900 provided twenty-one firms per 1,000 persons. In 1960, 4.7 million firms provided twenty-six firms per 1,000 persons.[2]

In a community there are so many small businessmen that diverse viewpoints may be expected. This fact sometimes stymies unified effort for civic improvement. It is difficult to get them all going in the same direction. But most of all, because they control individually their business practice, their personal ethics are much more involved than is the case with managers in large firms. The large organization makes decisions based on policy, but the small one usually decides according to the proprietor's personal views. As explained by one author: "The family farmer can and will cheat where the vast corporate farmer will not. Altruism is a scarce good, and [large] corporations may help society economize on its use." [3]

On the other hand, the large business has its negative aspects also. Though its business practice may be more consistent, its community interest is frequently more detached. There are two reasons for this detachment. First, the larger firm's sales area usually extends far beyond the community, even though its only office is in the community. In contrast, the small retail or service business depends on the community as its primary market.

Second, many large firms are decentralized, giving them a local interest in several communities, rather than one. Although they have many centers of operation, they have only one headquarters where top management can be directly contacted for major support of community projects.[4] In the branches, managers come and go as they move through the promotion ladder of the total organization. It is difficult for them to

[2] A. D. H. Kaplan, *Big Enterprise in a Competitive System*, rev. ed., Washington, D.C.: The Brookings Institution, 1964, pp. 62–72.

[3] Paul A. Samuelson, "Personal Freedoms and Economic Freedoms in the Mixed Economy," in Earl F. Cheit (ed.), *The Business Establishment*, New York: John Wiley & Sons, Inc., 1964, p. 207.

[4] Warner reports that two-thirds of the headquarters of the 700 largest corporations are located in the ten largest metropolitan centers. W. Lloyd Warner, *The Corporation in the Emergent American Society*, New York: Harper & Row, Publishers, Incorporated, 1962, p. 27.

have the same interest in their community that a small retail proprietor has because their relationship to the community is different. Therefore, their decisions have to be based more on policy than on personal interest, and that policy is centrally determined, often without recognition of the peculiar needs of a certain community. This condition places heavy responsibilities on decentralized companies to give their local managers broad leeway to make community-related decisions. Even when these decisions seem to be exceeding the bounds of reason policywise, there may be justifiable local reasons for a certain decision.

The decentralized firm has special responsibilities for dealing with community rumor about its operations. Since some of its decisions are made in headquarters, the local operation is a natural subject for rumors, such as "leaving the community" or "won't help," every time a local problem arises. Following World War II, for example, automobiles were in short supply. Rumors started near an Eastern seaboard branch of an automobile manufacturer to the effect that it was withholding automobiles to create an artificial shortage. The rumor was based on the fact that several thousand cars were stored in fields near the branch assembly plant. When the corporation learned of the rumor, it issued news releases explaining that these cars were designed for export, had steering wheels on the wrong side, and were awaiting shipping space. The rumor soon subsided.

Offsetting the personal detachment which decentralized executives may have is the fact that they do represent additional resources brought to a community from outside. They also can call upon headquarters for specialists to aid in civic planning. They can even call for economic support in special cases, beyond what a local business might be expected to contribute. They bring to communities a high quality of leadership which may be in short supply in depressed localities. Perhaps more important they bring a steady stream of new leaders with fresh ideas. The decentralized managers have broad experience and a viewpoint far beyond local provincialism. They can expand community horizons and help a community adjust to changing world conditions. As a whole they counterbalance community provincialism.

The net balance of all these competing advantages and disadvantages appears to be favorable. Communities usually seek the help of branch executives and use them effectively. The possibility of transfer during a term of civic service is usually ignored. After all, small businessmen leave communities too.

The Pittsburgh Experience. An example of business initiative in a major community development is the Pittsburgh Renaissance.[5] Lo-

[5] Edward C. Bursk, "Your Company and Your Community: The Lesson of Pittsburgh," in Dan H. Fenn, Jr. (ed.), *Business Responsibility in Action*, New York: McGraw-Hill Book Company, 1960, pp. 29–54.

cated in a soft-coal area and having much heavy industry, Pittsburgh, Pennsylvania, has always been smoky and dirty. As early as 1840 Charles Dickens called it "hell with the lid off." Even in the 1940s lights sometimes had to be burned at midday because of the stygian pall of smoke that obscured the city. The city came out of World War II with a bleak outlook. It had smoke, dirt, and few civic improvements. Urban blight had overcome its downtown Golden Triangle. Vigorous younger people were beginning to move elsewhere.

In this depressing situation, a group of business leaders formed the Allegheny Conference on Community Development to initiate a bold improvement program. Their first effort was smoke control because the smoke was destroying beauty and lowering morale in the community. In determining to control smoke, businessmen were in effect deciding to control *themselves* as well as homeowners with soft-coal heating systems. Working closely with local government, they overcame vigorous opposition from homeowners, politicians, and those within their own ranks. Through smoke-control ordinances and voluntary effort, smoke was eventually reduced 90 *percent*.

With this victory the group tackled the Golden Triangle to convert it from a slum to a community showcase. One large improvement required nine major companies to sign twenty-year leases for space before ground could be broken. Since only the top executive in a firm could make this kind of decision, Pittsburgh was fortunate to have home offices of a number of major corporations. There was also opposition to the Golden Triangle project. Legal battles about some improvements were carried eventually to the United States Supreme Court. Finally, however, the Golden Triangle was rebuilt into a beautiful area. Although the primary objective of the Allegheny Conference was economic rejuvenation, cultural improvements followed once the morale of the city was restored. The conclusion from the Pittsburgh experience is that business-government-citizen cooperation can restore blighted communities. In Pittsburgh the initiative came from business; in other cities initiative might arise elsewhere.

Community Responsibilities to Business. In the business-community relationship we cannot ignore the responsibility of community to business. If citizens, labor, and government abuse business or take advantage of it, then cooperation for improvement becomes more difficult. As stated by one businessman: "It's difficult to cooperate with a community which discriminates by taxing business property at one rate and other property at a cheaper rate." A retailer added: "Business should be friendly and courteous, but what about the customers? Some are so suspicious and irritable that no one likes to serve them." A manager of a used-car firm spoke up: "You should see the 'lemons' the customers trade to me without revealing defects. I could sue some of them for fraud, but what would that do to my business?" A grocery store proprietor added: "I accidentally caught one of my regular customers putting butter in a margarine box in order to cheat me of a few pennies." If a business relationship is to be viable, then mutual responsibilities are required.

A notable example of how community restrictions increase business costs is the experience of the Museum of Modern Art, in New York City, as a consequence of which it had less funds to spend for culture in the community. It planned an award for Buckminster Fuller, noted designer, for his design of radar radomes, and it felt one should be assembled in the museum. The military radomes were designed to be erected in Arctic cold by untrained Eskimos in six to twelve hours. Because of labor restrictions and community controls in New York City, it cost over $5,000 and took over thirty days to erect one radome! [6]

BUSINESSMEN IN CIVIC AFFAIRS

In a pluralistic society, multiallegiant man has interests in many organizations. The businessman is no exception. Two of his allegiances are to his business and to his community. It is difficult to generalize about either allegiance because there are perhaps as many varieties as there are businessmen. Some businessmen were born and reared in their community, coming from its blue-blooded aristocrats. Others moved to their community when they graduated from college. Others may be transients merely seeking to make a "fast buck" and move on. Still others are young corporate experts more interested in their profession than in their community or company.

As with all pluralism, conflicts of allegiance sometimes develop. As a representative of the corporation, the businessman must be detached and objective about community demands. But as a family man and a member of a social group within the community, he is also intimately tied to community affairs. As described by a political scientist: "The corporate manager, like many other power-holders in history, is asked to serve two masters—the corporation and the local community. The service is difficult." Also the manager is an "implicit servant of the national and general economy," further dividing his responsibilities.[7]

Managers, however, do not seem to shirk participation in civic affairs simply because conflict of allegiance may arise. Used to resolving conflict in organizational affairs, they feel at home in a similar civic environment. Nearly every museum board, development committee, or other civic group has business managers well represented among its mem-

[6] Arthur Barber, Deputy Assistant Secretary, U.S. Department of Defense, quoted in *Management News*, October, 1964, p. 5.

[7] Long, *loc. cit.*

bers. One survey of 129 top managers reported that 80 percent played a responsible role in community- and public-service work. Nearly all of them used company facilities such as business machines and secretarial service in their civic work, and they permitted their employees to do likewise. For 44 percent of the executives, public service was time-consuming enough to intrude on the time they devoted to their businesses. Others admitted that their civic work intruded on their family life. Regardless of time intrusion, they continued their civic services because they believed it is a responsibility of good citizenship. Many of those whose businesses sold primarily to the local market also believed that public service improved their business.[8]

Community Power Structure. In their activities businessmen become part of the *community power structure.* Power is not in the man himself, but flows from the role he plays in the social system. It is dynamic and cannot be viewed apart from the community itself. If a businessman moves to another community, he is in a new system, and his power does not transfer. In fact, *within* the community the power structure varies with the problem being considered. In a New York town having about six thousand persons, five major community decisions were studied. Thirty-six leaders were involved, but twenty-two of them participated in only one of the five decisions. Only eight leaders were involved in two decisions; only four were involved in three decisions; only two were involved in four decisions; and no leader was involved in all five decisions. Businessmen's participation depended on the subject being considered. Flood control and the municipal building were determined by political leaders, and specialists determined the school bond issue. Decisions on the new hospital and new industry were dominated by businessmen.[9]

There are three main methods of studying community power. The positional method studies those holding official leadership positions in the community. The reputational method studies those named and ranked by informants as the real decision makers (leaders). The decisional method traces the actions of leaders regarding specific issues to determine situational power in decision making. Research results tend to vary, depending on method. Even using the same method, results still vary, a fact which suggests the general conclusion that there is no standard power structure in communities. Power varies depending on hundreds of factors, such as community history, degree of industrialization, and type of problem being considered. Businessmen do participate in the total power structure, but not necessarily in every major civic

[8] "Top Management and Public Service Activities: A Survey," *Management Review,* December, 1964, pp. 45–47.

[9] Robert Presthus, *Men at the Top: A Study in Community Power,* Fair Lawn, N.J.: Oxford University Press, 1964, pp. 92–100.

decision. Usually businessmen are influential, and they may also dominate. Some investigators believe that businessmen frequently dominate decisions. On the other hand, one investigator concluded that politicians actually initiated policy choices and that businessmen merely rubberstamped them after decisions were made.[10]

Of special interest is the manner in which labor leaders view the community activities of businessmen. A study of Lansing, Michigan, an industrial city, showed that labor leaders felt that businessmen dominated community decision making as a whole. However, when labor leaders named the ten persons they thought most influential in the community, they named only four businessmen. Only one of these, a newspaper publisher, was in the top five; therefore, the labor leaders' selections did not support their general conclusion of business domination. Others in the top five were the mayor, a Catholic bishop, the superintendent of public schools, and the president of the Labor Council. Labor leaders generally but not wholly supported the idea that businessmen are " . . . interested, hardworking citizens who act openly and responsibly for the good of the community." [11]

Status and Prestige. With regard to status of businessmen, one study of occupational status reports that the highest-ranked business occupation is that of banker, ranking tenth. Next is member of the board of directors of a large corporation, ranked eighteenth. The first three status occupations are those of United States Supreme Court justice, physician, and state governor, in that order.[12] Studies of the prestige of industries show only one business-oriented industry in the top five. It is banking, which ranks fifth. The order of the first four is medical services, universities, research laboratories, and atomic energy activities.[13] Viewed as a whole, businessmen are men of power and status in the United States, more so than in most other countries of the world, but they are not at the top. They tend to be extroverted leaders willing to enter into affairs of the community, especially where business interests are involved. Effects have been both negative and positive. There has been interference and occasional autocratic control. On the other hand,

[10] Charles M. Bonjean and David M. Olson, "Community Leadership: Directions of Research," *Administrative Science Quarterly*, December, 1964, pp. 278–300. This article provides an excellent summary of the literature. Comparative studies cited in the article show that two Mexican cities and one British city were less influenced by businessmen than ten United States cities.

[11] William H. Form and Warren L. Sauer, "Labor and Community Influentials: A Comparative Study of Participation and Imagery," *Industrial and Labor Relations Review*, October, 1963, pp. 18–19.

[12] Carroll L. Shartle, *Occupational Information*, 3d ed., Englewood Cliffs, N.J.: Prentice-Hall, Inc., 1959, p. 56.

[13] Robert E. Campbell, "The Prestige of Industries," *Journal of Applied Psychology*, February, 1960, pp. 1–5.

communities have in this way gained the assistance of some of society's most competent leaders.

BUSINESS GIVING

Since 1936 the Federal government, through its income tax law, has encouraged corporate giving for educational, charitable, scientific, and religious purposes. Corporations are allowed to deduct contributions which do not exceed 5 percent of their taxable income.[14] If this deduction were not allowed, corporations would have to pay taxes and then give gifts from the residue of net income, thus requiring them to earn about $2 in order to have $1 to give away. Since the 1936 tax law, corporate giving has increased steadily. By 1948 it had reached 239 million dollars, and by 1958 it was about 550 million dollars. Giving is expected to exceed 1 billion dollars by 1968.

Average corporate giving exceeds 1 percent of net income before taxes. A number of businesses, especially larger ones, have established foundations to handle their contributions. This approach permits them to administer their giving program more uniformly and objectively. It also provides a central group which handles all requests. This procedure is usually not used for minor local contributions in order to avoid red tape and permit some local autonomy. Examples of foundations are Shell Companies Foundation, Esso Education Foundation, General Electric Foundation, and the Maytag Company Foundation. A survey reports that about 40 percent of corporations with 1,000 or more employees have foundations or trusts for making gifts. Another survey indicates that companies with foundations give a greater proportion of their income, probably because they have a more carefully defined policy and more definite commitments behind it. The survey reported that twenty companies having foundations gave 1.59 percent of their net income, while twenty-three companies without foundations gave 0.70 percent of their net.[15]

Although average giving is only about 1 percent of net before taxes, some firms give the 5 percent maximum allowed for tax purposes. There is pressure to increase the percentage allowed, particularly from smaller companies whose leaders want more flexibility to meet special situations.

Reasons for Business Giving. There are several rationalizations to support business giving. Business giving is frequently justified as an *investment* which benefits the business in the long run by improving the community, its labor force, the climate for business, or other conditions affecting a particular business. A gift to a hospital building fund is ra-

---

[14] Gifts given by business partnerships or proprietorships are governed by individual income tax laws, which normally permit gifts up to 30 percent of adjusted gross income.

[15] John A. Pollard, "Emerging Pattern in Corporate Giving," *Harvard Business Review*, May–June, 1960, pp. 103–106.

tionalized in this way because it should create better health in the community. Gifts for education are viewed as improving the labor market or expanding the economy, thereby increasing a firm's potential market.

Another basis for giving gifts is to consider routine local ones as an *operating expense* of doing business. Gifts of this type are often thought to provide public relations or advertising returns and are treated like any other public relations expense. Examples are gifts of money to a local charity, literature to a high school, or milk to a church supper.

Both the investment and the expense philosophies are directly related to business objectives. Some of these gifts can be rationalized as supporting profit in the long run, if not in the short run. Others, such as general aid to education outside the plant community, have no direct connection with profit, but they are relevant indirectly because they affect the general economic and social climate of business.

A third philosophy assumes that a corporation is a citizen of the community as a person is, except that it has greater resources than most citizens. As a citizen it has a duty to support *philanthropy* without regard to its self-interest in the same way that a private person does. This approach can open a Pandora's Box of giving. Unless it is governed by carefully formed policies, it may bind the corporation to support requests without careful screening simply because it has no policy reason to say "no." Since the corporation has money in the bank and philanthropy is one of the noblest qualities of civilized man, how can it refuse its needy brother? This kind of reasoning can lead to imprudent waste of funds in the trusteeship of management and thus be irresponsible action rather than a display of responsibility. A number of observers consider this philosophy dangerous for a corporation;[16] yet, it undoubtedly is a philosophy which influences business giving. As we have said before, businessmen are human and are likely to act that way. They do feel concern for their community and are partly motivated by philanthropic ideals.

Another assumption is that some corporate gifts take on the characteristics of *taxes*. Since it is the prevailing opinion that corporations should be good citizens, helpful neighbors, and human institutions, the community comes close to imposing some types of gift giving on the corporation as a kind of informal taxation. The gifts are a cost of doing business. They are given to retain public approval for the business.

Regardless of whether gifts are viewed as an investment, an expense, a philanthropy, or a tax, most of their costs are probably passed on to consumers, for giving in the long run becomes a cost of doing business. If this view is valid, then the business is acting partly as agent and *trustee* for the community, receiving funds and distributing them according to community needs.

[16] A strong statement of the dangers is given by Richard Eells, "Corporate Giving: Theory and Policy," *California Management Review*, Fall, 1958, pp. 37–46.

At any rate, a business which makes contributions needs a carefully thought out policy for its actions. Most firms concentrate their giving in selected areas in order to make an impact with a substantial gift, rather than spreading their resources thinly. Law prohibits political contributions. Companies often do not give to religious groups. Others prohibit gifts to groups with limited membership such as veterans' organizations and fraternal societies. Others confine their giving to their market territory or the community where their facilities are. But they need to be cautious about provincialism. If their branches are nationwide or worldwide, they cannot justify giving only within their hometown. In accordance with the Iron Law of Responsibility, if their power is nationwide, their responsibility is nationwide also.

Business giving has become an integral part of modern society. In a pluralistic society, giving is an effective way to support other free institutions such as private education and local charity. Without this support, the local initiative and voluntary action which characterize communities might collapse. This situation would surely endanger pluralism and lead to concentrations of power, which might in turn threaten free business institutions.

Support of Education. Of the approximately 1 percent of corporate profits which are contributed as public gifts, about 0.45 percent of that amount is for support of education. Most of this support goes to higher education in the form of scholarships, research grants, capital grants for buildings, endowed professorships, and outright grants for general expenses. Figure 14-1 shows that the percentage given to education has *quadrupled*, from 0.11 percent in 1950 to 0.44 percent in 1964. This large increase in proportion shows the serious interest business has in upgrading

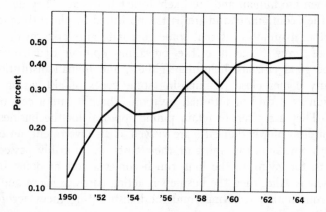

Figure 14-1 Percentage of corporate profits before taxes contributed to higher education. (*Business Week, Apr.* 3, 1965, *p.* 132. *Data from Council for Financial Aid to Education, Inc., and U.S. Department of Commerce.*)

the education of citizens and potential employees. (Educational payments for present employees are recorded separately as a fringe-benefit cost.) However, most of the increase in proportion of giving occurred between 1950 and 1958. Since that time the proportion has leveled off. One explanation is that business has reached a plateau which represents all it feels able or obligated to pay. Another is that Federal government support of higher education has caused businesses to feel that private help is no longer needed or wanted. Others probably feel that they are supporting education with their Federal taxes and that therefore they should not "pay twice" by making private gifts.

If higher education becomes almost wholly dependent on government funds, there are dangers that it will lose its capacity for free inquiry. According to President Robert F. Goheen, of Princeton University:[17]

> Increasing federal aid to higher education seems inevitable in view of the magnitude of our national educational needs. As it develops, it must not be allowed to take over the show, to restrict the independence and self-determining power of universities and colleges, to undermine our historic commitment to demanding standards and the cultivation of high excellence in the individual. Only continuing and enlarged support from all possible private sources can enable us to withstand these dangers. And —what I think is too often overlooked—private support will do this best if it helps strengthen universities and colleges at their centers—i.e., in their ability to sustain and develop their own programs, according to their own best judgment, carefully and consistently over time.

Corporate contributions to higher education rose from 43 million dollars in 1950 to 250 million dollars in 1964. The Council for Financial Aid to Education has set a goal of 500 million dollars for 1970. Surveys show that giving is concentrated in relatively few large businesses. Of the 200 million dollars contributed to higher education by business in 1962, more than one-third of it came from only 150 companies, each of which contributed over $100,000. In fact, increased giving by large corporations accounted for most of the total increase in corporate giving between 1960 and 1962.[18] There appears to be a significant difference in attitudes of larger businesses toward gifts to higher education, compared with attitudes of smaller businesses. Smaller companies participate in local charity drives and similar programs, but they are less likely to aid higher education. Perhaps one reason is that larger businesses tend to employ more specialized college graduates. Another is that small businessmen usually have no established policies of gift giving. Since there also

---

[17] "Corporate Support for Our Colleges . . . Let's Get It Soaring Again," *Business Week*, Apr. 3, 1965, p. 133.

[18] "Business Aid to Education: Let's Broaden the Base," *Business Week*, June 6, 1964, pp. 136–137.

is no planned campaign by those needing educational gifts, small business-men simply forget to give. Since local charity drives usually bring a knock at the door, there is more direct motivation to give in these circumstances. Small businessmen could benefit from planned giving according to policy just as much as larger businesses do. Otherwise the "squeaky wheel" gets the gifts.

Companies which are large enough to give substantial sums usually establish carefully developed policies, just as they would for any other expenditure. When General Electric Company developed its policy toward gifts to education, it took a four-page advertisement in a national magazine to explain the policy. The advertisement was written as an article rather than in the usual advertising style. At that time college graduates on its payroll numbered about thirty thousand persons from 760 institutions. The article began: "By now, most responsible people in industry are convinced that, both as individuals and as corporate citizens, they have some obligation to help American education solve its growing problems." Several principles for giving were emphasized, among them the "multiplication factor," which is that the company tends toward giv-ing to the need which probably will have the widest effect. "For example, in the choice between helping to pay a faculty member a higher salary, or assisting a student with a scholarship, the advantage lies clearly with the professor, whose improved teaching can influence a whole generation of students." [19]

Some employers give to both private and tax-supported institutions because they hire employees from both and feel that both have similar objectives. Other companies, while not prohibiting gifts to tax-supported institutions, give priority to private ones. They do so because the private institution depends on private society for nearly all its income, while tax-supported institutions can call upon government taxing power over the whole society, including the corporation. Further, aid to private insti-tutions keeps that sector of education viable in the face of encroachments from tax-supported higher education. Thus, private aid further supports pluralism in society.

Business aid to education is typically justified under the investment philosophy of giving. It is considered to be an investment in educated citizens (some employed by business), in advancing technology which business uses, and in a better public climate for business. All these ob-jectives can be demonstrably related to business's long-range well-being. In the words of Donald C. McGraw, president of McGraw-Hill, Inc.: "There are few, if any, financial operations that can pay larger returns in advancing the national interest, as well as the more immediate interest of the business community, than that of seeing our colleges and univer-

[19] "One Viewpoint on Corporate Aid to Education," Harper's, December, 1957, pp. 19–22.

sities receive steadily increasing financial support from more and more business firms." [20]

It seems certain that business aid to education will continue. It is founded on basic values of pluralism. First, there is support by one institution (business) for another institution (education) which provides useful services to business. Second, both business and education have a mutual interest in a free society (free business decisions on the one hand and free inquiry on the other). Third, regarding private educational institutions, there is the further point that one private institution wishes to help another keep viable in order to balance pluralistic interests better, especially to offset greater government control of education. Wherever businesses have examined policy implications of business giving to education, they have supported it. They are not, however, opposing tax-supported education. They recognize that the entire educational job is beyond their capacity, but they do wish to play a role in it to confirm their pluralistic interest therein.[21]

Support of Cultural Activities. A growing area of business giving is community cultural activities. Throughout the centuries, art has been heavily dependent on some form of patronage for support. Pharaohs, noblemen, the church, and the state have all provided patronage because the market cannot be depended on to support culture in the amounts sought by societal leaders. Traditionally in Europe, deficits are made up by state subsidies. In the United States wealthy persons have supported culture, but with greater tax restrictions on accumulation of wealth, this source has declined, requiring a broader base of support. Cultural organizations have sought support from business and in small amounts from today's more numerous middle class. Over 5 percent of the business gift dollar is now for cultural activities. The list of business donors to operas, art shows, symphonies, and ballets is gradually expanding. In Detroit, for example, twenty-six companies recently gave $10,000 each for a reorganization of the symphony. And 362 companies gave 9.5 million dollars to New York's Lincoln Center for the Performing Arts, with individual corporate gifts reaching as high as $450,000.[22]

Business justification for these gifts is based upon a better community image, upgrading culture and community satisfaction of employees, and aiding in recruiting. Companies say that a lively cultural environment is essential in recruiting today's sophisticated scientific and executive personnel. The business interest in art is worldwide. Italy's largest steel com-

---

[20] "Business Aid to Education: Let's Broaden the Base," *op. cit.*, p. 137.

[21] See Howard J. Samuels, "A Businessman's Plea for Government Investment in Education," *Business Horizons*, Spring, 1965, pp. 61–68. This article advocates a pay-as-you-*grow* plan of expanded debt financing.

[22] "Performing Arts Find an 'Angel' in Business," *Business Week*, Mar. 13, 1965, pp. 52, 55.

pany, a state-controlled business, has supported a distinguished program of art, even commissioning the best Italian artists to illustrate its publications.[23]

Concurrently with their gifts to culture, businessmen have discovered art as a means of creating a desirable in-company environment for employees and customers. Banks were among the first to move art from the museum to the office. Many banks and other offices today are, indeed, places of beauty with tastefully presented art collections that might even arouse envy in a museum director. By offering purchase prizes at art shows they add to their collections the best local works as they are produced.

A variation of business giving for community culture is Sears, Roebuck's program of bringing art to the community on a commercial basis. The world's largest retail merchant is buying original art around the world and presenting collections of it in its stores, with selling prices up to $10,000. The venture has created local interest in art and appears to be commercially successful. In the words of Vincent Price:[24]

> I do not divulge any business secrets when I testify that the Sears venture into art has paid big dividends. Not, perhaps, on the operation itself, though there is increasing optimism that, after all costs are met, the collection will ultimately show a profit. More important, at least in the short run, is the volume of store traffic generated wherever a show has been put on display. People who had never been inside a Sears store are now regular customers. . . .

Education and cultural activities account for over half of business giving; the other half is contributed mostly to charity. Business giving to charity is better known and therefore will not be discussed.

BUSINESS PRACTICES IN COMMUNITIES

Business practice has direct, significant effects on the community. These are not the effects of giving gifts or of volunteering time, but are the result of the way business conducts itself in the ordinary course of operations. Does business, for example, cause stream and air pollution? Are its plants an aesthetic asset or a blight? Do its policies encourage unfair competition and business conflict?

Both small and large companies affect communities in their own particular ways. Large national and international companies are significant because of their size and the fact that their policies originate externally to the community. Some large manufacturers upon entering a commu-

[23] "A Steel Company in the World of Culture," Fortune, October, 1963, pp. 138–141.

[24] Vincent Price, "The Sears Venture into Art," Business Horizons, Winter, 1963, p. 27.

nity have encountered zoning opposition from neighbors who have an image of factory blight and lowered home values and who must be shown evidence that a factory will be an asset. In response to these needs many factory sites today are genuine industrial parks, far more attractive than their surrounding neighborhoods. Their effect is to upgrade, rather than to blight, the neighborhood.

Community Influence. The success of a major community employer is inevitably tied to that of its community. If the employer fails economically, the community suffers. When Studebaker ceased making automobiles in South Bend, that community was set back economically for years. This situation was recognized by management, which worked closely with the community to encourage other companies to move into the sprawling Studebaker plant in order to maintain employment. In the long run, the adjustment actually may be desirable because South Bend is now less dependent on one industry.

The large resources of national firms permit major community improvements if business justification for improvement is strong enough. In the first decade of this century, Birmingham, Alabama, was menaced by serious health problems. Malaria, typhoid fever, and other diseases were prevalent because of unsanitary community conditions. This city was the site of a United States Steel subsidiary, Tennessee Coal and Iron Company, whose productivity was lowered by illness. Tennessee Coal and Iron organized a health department and hired a prominent specialist in the offending diseases from the Panama Canal Zone. In its first year of operation the health department spent $750,000 for draining swamps and improving sanitary facilities. This amount was thirty times the total health budget of the entire state of Alabama.[25]

Where large companies operate in suburban communities or small towns, they play an even greater role in community life. Early in industrial history many of these communities became virtual company towns, with the employer owning retail stores, the water system, and other public services. Historians have presented the difficulties with this kind of community. Primarily pluralism does not develop, and control becomes monolithic. There is dissatisfaction of all parties involved, regardless of their good intentions. Modern companies face the same need for a complete community that their forebears did, but they are taking a more sophisticated approach to getting it. Usually they initiate long-range planning and coordinate it with public authorities, but they leave development to others. They own and control nothing in the community but their own plant.

Burlington Industries furnishes an example of this more sophisticated approach. In Cramerton, North Carolina, a town of 3,200 persons, it

[25] Roger M. Blough, *Golden Anniversary*, New York: United States Steel Corporation, 1957, p. 14.

employs 1,700 persons in its factories. The town is 20 miles east of metropolitan Charlotte. Cramerton needs fuller community services and more modern housing, shopping centers, and recreational facilities. The company owns 1,600 acres of undeveloped land adjoining the community and is working with architects to plan a model community, including a country club, a marina on the lake, a shopping center, apartments, and homes. When completed in ten years, the new community will represent an investment of 100 million dollars. However, Burlington Industries will not develop the land or own any of it. It is performing the planning only, after which it will work with county zoning authorities to get the plan incorporated into county zoning regulations. Then it will sell the land to developers in whom it has no interest. They will develop and resell parcels according to the master public zoning plan, thus creating a model community with pluralistic ownership and interests. In case any part of the plan proves defective, public zoning can remedy it.[26]

Water and Air Pollution. Pollution of streams and air is another area of community interest. Although local in origin, these problems become regional or nationwide because of the flow of streams and air currents. With regard to water pollution, municipal sewage plants share with industry the responsibility for this condition. Sewage effluent and industrial wastes have made many lakes and streams unfit for swimming or water use. Fish are being killed. Figure 14-2 shows a map of the principal streams in the United States with pollution problems, including the ones where cleanup has started. Stream cleanup depends on the cause of pollution. On the Potomac, for example, pollution is largely municipal in origin, but on the Missouri pollution is caused by many types of industry including meat-packing, refining, chemicals, soap, and stockyards. Cleanup is slow and costly. It is estimated that it will cost 75 billion dollars in the next generation.[27]

The following experience of Mobil Oil Company with its Ferndale petroleum refinery illustrates the difficulties of pollution control:[28]

> To combat air pollution Mobil engineers designed many refinery units in a way that minimized emission of mist, sulfur dioxide, petroleum vapor and other chemical compounds. A special incinerator was installed to convert smelly compounds to less objectionable materials. A smokeless flare and blowdown system was provided to insure that all hydrocarbon releases were properly burned. Oil storage tanks with floating roofs were

---

[26] "Avoiding the Curse of the Company Town," *Business Week*, Aug. 22, 1964, pp. 48, 52.

[27] "Billions to Clean up Rivers," *Business Week*, Apr. 24, 1965, p. 50.

[28] "Ferndale Refinery: Profile of a Good Neighbor," *Mobil World*, February, 1965, p. 7.

Key:

━━ Rivers where cleanup has been started

── Rivers where conditions warrant immediate action

Figure 14-2 Principal interstate rivers with pollution problems in forty-eight states of the United States. (*Business Week*, Apr. 24, 1965, *p.* 50.)

selected to minimize evaporation losses. These and more design innovations put a tight clamp on air and plant pollution.

Control of water pollution turned out to be an even tougher nut to crack. . . .

The men who designed Ferndale planned six separate sewer systems to handle different types of waste. Expensive—but effective. These systems separately accommodate oil process waste, sanitary waste, phenolic process waste, normal storm drainage, emergency storm drainage and ship's ballast discharge.

"We even have educated 'bugs' to help us decontaminate the first three types of waste water" [said a process engineer].

Ferndale's bugs are fussy. Once they get accustomed to a certain concentration of phenol, they die or quit eating if served up a different diet of phenol. The waste water that goes into their tanks is, therefore, carefully controlled, and a reserve supply of sludge is always maintained just in case the main floc overeats. . . . When they're through, phenol in the water is nil.

Better Business Bureaus. We have discussed community development, water pollution, and air pollution as they involve business *with the community as a whole.* Another area of community relations is direct business contacts *with customers* in a particular transaction. Here a gyp, a "con man," or a fraudulent operator may quickly harm the community image of business. There may also be honest misunderstandings about transactions in which mediation will help. The most effective community device for meeting these needs is the local better business bureau.

Better business bureaus are nonprofit, public-service organizations created by private business for self-regulation. There are about 150 better business bureaus located in most large metropolita.. areas of the United States. There are also bureaus in Mexico, Canada, Israel, and Venezuela, indicating a gradual international expansion of better business practice through self-regulation. In the words of President John F. Kennedy:[29]

> By serving the public as a clearing house of factual information about business practices affecting the consumer, the Better Business Bureaus throughout the country effectively express the business community's sense of responsibility for high ethical standards and integrity, in trade practices and business-consumer relations.

The unique and effective idea of better business bureaus is that they reach the customer directly, receiving his complaints and inquiries. There is no charge and no disclosure of names. This approach gives customers confidence that business genuinely seeks fair business practice and will aid customers in exposing rackets and gyps. The bureaus are well used, as shown by the fact that they receive about 2½ million inquiries annually. They investigate inquiries or complaints and make factual reports to the inquirer. They also bring any illegal action to the attention of law-enforcement groups. With regard to advertising, they maintain programs to encourage advertising copy which is truthful, informative, and constructive. They also hold trade-practices conferences to aid the setting of voluntary standards for advertising and selling. When an unfair or misleading practice is encountered, they strenuously try to discourage it, even using paid advertising warning the public, as shown in Figure 14-3. The better business bureau idea is as follows:[30]

> Legitimate business firms . . . don't want gyps to get your money, which would cause you to question *all* business. Business concerns and individuals are jealous of their reputations, integrity, and the confidence you have in them. That's why business maintains the Better Business Bureau . . . and why its services cost you nothing.

The better business bureau approach to self-regulation has been successful and should continue to expand internationally. It does not solve all business-community problems, but it is effective in its area of work.

[29] *Facts You Should Know about Your Better Business Bureau*, New York: Better Business Bureau, Educational Division, p. 16. Other data presented are from this pamphlet and other publications of the National Association of Better Business Bureaus.

[30] *Why There Is "No Charge,"* New York: National Association of Better Business Bureaus, Inc., 1945, p. 4.

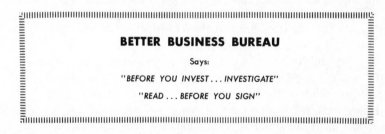

BE SURE . . .
BEFORE YOU BUY ANY
PRE-ARRANGED FUNERAL PLAN

PROTECT YOURSELF! Before You Invest

In Any Pre-Burial Plan, Contact

- YOUR ATTORNEY
- YOUR FAMILY FUNERAL DIRECTOR
- THE BETTER BUSINESS BUREAU

Under the laws of this state, it is improper for a funeral director to employ or otherwise engage agents to solicit business. The law further requires that all money paid for a pre-arranged funeral be deposited in a bank and held in trust. A person purchasing a plan should make sure that it provides for these deposits and that later, when the funds are needed, they will be available.

Be sure you fully understand the contract: that it complies with the state laws; all blanks have been filled in; and you have a copy of the contract before you sign.

BETTER BUSINESS BUREAU

Says:

"BEFORE YOU INVEST . . . INVESTIGATE"

"READ . . . BEFORE YOU SIGN"

Figure 14-3 A better business bureau newspaper advertisement. (*The Arizona Republic, May* 8, 1965, *p.* 12.)

SUMMARY

The community is an organization's area of local influence, rather than the political unit in which an organization is located. As a possessor of community social power, a business cannot remain aloof from its community responsibilities. Small and large businesses, local and national, all affect their communities, but in different ways. There are also community responsibilities to deal with business fairly and without discrimination, as it would a citizen.

Businessmen are an active group in the community power structure, but are not necessarily the leading power group. Positional, reputational, and decisional studies of community power structure reveal different structures changing to meet particular needs.

Business giving amounts to about 1 percent of net profits before taxes. It is encouraged by corporate income tax laws. Business giving may be justified as an investment, an operating expense, a philanthropy, a tax, or an apportionment by business acting as a trustee for the community. Some 45 percent of business gifts are for education, mostly higher education, in which business has a strong interest. An area of increasing support is community cultural activities.

Business also affects its community by its conduct in the ordinary course of operations, concerning such matters as land development, air pollution, water pollution, and fairness in dealing with customers. Two useful approaches to voluntary self-improvement are long-range planning in cooperation with community agencies and use of better business bureaus.

QUESTIONS

1. What are some of the principal ways business influences a community, and vice versa?

2. In a complex world of big business and frequent mergers, how do you explain the increase in number of firms per 1,000 persons from twenty-one in 1900 to twenty-six in 1960? Discuss some of the different community interests and effects of large firms compared with those of small ones.

3. Contrast the roles and contributions of the "native" business leaders and the branch plant "transient" managers in a community power structure.

4. Discuss the justifications for business giving in a community. Particularly, what do you think of the emphasis given to support of education?

5. How do you feel business should divide its support between tax-supported educational institutions and privately supported ones? Discuss.

6. Have you ever used a better business bureau? Survey a sample of citizens and offer your opinion of how effective better business bureaus are.

4. BUSINESS IN AN INTERNATIONAL WORLD

CHAPTER 15 INTERNATIONAL BUSINESS

> Managers of international companies, if they are
> to do their jobs well, must not only be technically
> competent in their field of work but they must also
> become deeply involved with the ideas and feelings of
> the people around them.
>
> DAVID A. SHEPARD[1]

Modern business relationships have become worldwide, flying on the wings
of jet aircraft, radio, and universal needs for the goods and services which
business provides. Expansion beyond national boundaries is much more
than a step across a geographical line. It is also a step into different social,
political, economic, and managerial environments. Supply lines are length-
ened, and control becomes more difficult. It is hard enough to run a business
in one language and one culture, but when there are two, three, four, five—
or seventy—languages and cultures, difficulties are compounded. Complex
businesses of this type push men's organizational skills to their limits.
The best of men's intellectual capacities and goodwill is called upon in
order to make these organizations workable.

Consider, for example, Japan, with a culture much different from
that of the United States; yet the businesses from one which enter the
other have the same needs for productivity and economic success. Ethiopia's political environment is unlike that of the United States, but a
United States company which enters Ethiopia is expected to have the
capacity to succeed there just as in the United States. The business adjustments required in different countries are almost as great as those the

---

[1] David A. Shepard, "Statism, Nationalism and American Business Abroad," *The
Lamp*, Winter, 1962, p. 2.

lion would have to make if he lived part of his life flying over the ocean, or the fish if it had to feed upon prairie grass. Great adaptability is required in order to support viability.

In the next two chapters we shall explore the international environment as it affects business, and vice versa. In the current chapter we shall discuss some of the conditions which complicate international business. These conditions are reflected in different business practices, which may be studied as comparative management systems. Finally, we shall analyze some of the more unique ways in which business is discharging its international responsibilities.

INTERNATIONAL BUSINESS CONDITIONS

The people of the world are organized into communities and nations, each in its own way according to its resources and cultural heritage. There are similarities among nations, but there are also significant differences which define the boundaries of business practice in each nation. Some nations have a customer-oriented economy, while others have a centrally planned economy, and there are various shades of practice in between. Some are economically developed, but others are just now developing. Some are a political dictatorship; others are more democratic. Some are socially advanced, while others have minimum literacy and social development. And in each case the managerial conditions of work are different because of different expectations from participants. Let us examine these social, political, economic, and managerial conditions as they affect business. We shall discuss these conditions in terms of a United States business entering other countries; however, it will be evident that a business from any nation which enters another nation will find most of the same conditions either to a greater or a lesser degree.

Social Conditions. One obvious characteristic of less-developed nations is the scarcity of human resources. There are major shortages of managerial personnel, scientists, and technicians, and these deficiencies limit business's ability to employ local labor productively. Needed skills are temporarily imported, while vast training programs prepare native workers. In fact, the lending of trained people to a country may be of more lasting benefit than the lending of capital because of the multiplier effect by which these people develop others. These others then become the nucleus for developing more nationals, in an ever-widening arc of self-development. Economic and social—and business—growth is difficult until human resources have been developed.[2] As stated by an economist:[3]

[2] Harbison and Myers spell out the needs for, and strategies of, human-resource development in Frederick Harbison and Charles A. Myers, *Education, Manpower, and Economic Growth,* New York: McGraw-Hill Book Company, 1964.

[3] Theodore W. Schultz, "Investment in Human Capital," *American Economic Review,* March, 1961, p. 1.

Although it is obvious that people acquire useful skills and knowledge, it is not obvious that these skills and knowledge are a form of capital, that this capital is in substantial part a product of deliberate investment, that it has grown in Western societies at a faster rate than conventional (non human) capital, and that its growth may well be the most distinctive feature of the economic system.

Shortages of trained people and community-supported facilities cause large social overhead costs when a business moves into a developing area. When Indonesia's Gresnik cement plant was built, for example, a village had to be constructed to house imported scientists and administrators and also native skilled workers. Schools and recreation facilities were built, police and fire protection established, and a bus system started for transporting workers. Ocean dock and oil storage facilities were required, a diesel power station constructed, a bag factory built, and railroad equipment added. The cost of these social overhead items was nearly 15 milion dollars. This sum was approximately the amount by which the cost of the Gresnik plant exceeded the cost of a similar plant in the United States.[4]

A key social condition is the variation in culture among countries. This creates different business practices and work problems, and is discussed in a subsequent section on comparative management systems.

Political Conditions. Social and political conditions are closely intertwined. A number of countries tolerate foreign firms, but are not friendly to them. A survey in France and Germany reports that 58 percent of the French and 49 percent of the Germans oppose encouraging in their homelands new firms from the United States. They fear exploitation and are concerned that the new firms might disregard customs of their society.[5]

Many nations have strong nationalistic drives. The people want their nation and their economic system for themselves without interference by foreign nationals. In Burma, for example, a visiting professor presented a case problem where there was conflict between a British shipmaster and a Burmese crew. Expecting a human relations discussion, the professor was surprised when his class focused on how to train Burmese to take over from the British master so that they would not have to deal with him.

When a foreign company does enter another nation, it has a wide variety of licenses, foreign exchange rules, and sanctions applied by government. These are complicated by the fact that the government itself is sometimes unstable, inconsistent, and bureaucratic, though well-

[4] Leonard A. Doyle, "Some Problems of State Enterprises in Underdeveloped Nations," *California Management Review*, Fall, 1963, p. 27. See also Leonard A. Doyle, *Inter-economy Comparisons: A Case Study*, Berkeley, Calif.: University of California Press, 1965.

[5] Leon C. Megginson, "Lessons from Europe for American Business," *Southwestern Social Science Quarterly*, June, 1963, p. 7.

meaning. Decisions are made on a political basis with little thought given to business needs. There is often much central planning. In France, for example, the economic growth rate is determined by the government after consultation with economic interest groups. This rate is translated by tripartite commissions into specific targets for each sector of the economy. Then fiscal and monetary pressures are brought on private business to conform to the plan. Similar planning exists in other European nations. At the thirteenth International Management Congress an Italian industrialist explained the situation this way: "While in the United States the 'homoeconomicus' is still nowadays the protagonist of economic events, in Europe he has somewhat faded and has been replaced by a type of economic subject who practically acts as the main character in a play written by the state." [6]

In many nations, particularly with regard to basic industries, the government will insist on being a partial owner in a foreign business which it admits. In other cases it is a full competitor, owning and operating a business selling the same type of product. The market may be allocated with a certain portion going to the state and another portion to the foreign business, as is the case with retail petroleum sales in Chile. The general conclusion is that in nearly all countries outside the United States, the government is more involved in business than is the case in this country. Businessmen in these nations have to be actively interested in government affairs in order to operate successfully. Sometimes they must give political considerations priority over economic and technical values when they make decisions.

The various types of government involvement in business may be summarized as follows:

1. Government ownership of an industry; other firms not allowed
2. Government ownership of a firm in an industry having private firms in competition with government
3. The arrangement described in item 2, with the market allocated
4. Partial government ownership of a private foreign firm
5. Government economic planning with sanctions applied to private industry to assure compliance
6. Routine government licensing and control only

In most nations there is also heavier government involvement in social welfare than exists in the United States. This affects a foreign business in a number of ways. Fringe-benefit costs as a proportion of wages will be high, running as much as 50 percent of wage costs. Layoffs of employees may be restricted and made expensive. And taxes are likely

---

[6] Guido Zerilli Marimo, "Management and the International Arena," *Proceedings of the Thirteenth International Management Congress*, New York: Council for International Progress in Management (United States), Inc., 1963, p. 416.

to be high to support government welfare payments. In fact, excessive welfare costs beyond a nation's economic capacity have been one cause of economic chaos and inflation in South America and elsewhere.[7]

Economic Conditions. A common economic condition in many parts of the world is inflation. In the United States, which has mild inflation, the value of the dollar was cut more than half in the generation from 1940 to 1965, but in other parts of the world currency has been cut to one-hundredth or even *one-thousandth* of its value since 1940, as reflected by cost-of-living indexes. What used to cost one unit of currency now costs 1,000 or more. In terms of dollar currency, the 10-cent ice-cream cone now costs 10,000 cents, or $100! In Brazil in 1963–1964 the increase in cost of living was running at about 100 percent annually, meaning that an item which cost 10 cruzeiros last year costs 20 cruzeiros this year.

With high inflationary conditions, such matters as inventory policy, sales policy, and cash discounts are guided substantially by the state of inflation.[8] Interest rates run as high as 5 percent monthly, which is 60 percent yearly; yet borrowing can be economical if the inflation rate runs higher, such as 8 percent monthly, permitting the debt to be repaid with cheaper money. An entire year's profit can be wiped out by a currency devaluation or some other development external to the firm. Typical "good management" through long-range planning is very difficult, and even regular operations become unsettled.

Just as business operations are unsettled, so is the worker's economic life. He must spend quickly lest his money lose its value. Savings payable in fixed currency units become meaningless because they lose their value; hence, he seldom plans for his own security, as workers do in the United States. He develops more dependence and more anxiety, and he becomes more volatile with social unrest. Usually the lower and middle economic classes bear the burdens of inflation more than the wealthy, who can afford careful management of their wealth to avoid losses. In Chile, the official cost-of-living index rose 2,972 percent between 1945 and 1957. "This inflation hit the lower and middle classes hardest, and sparked a series of riots in Santiago in April, 1957. . . . Real wages . . . dropped from an index of 163 in 1944 to 105 in September, 1954." [9]

Although some economists say that "mild" inflation can encourage economic growth, high inflation so upsets business operations that growth is deterred, leading to further social unrest. Table 6 compares inflation

[7] Frederick Harbison and Charles A. Myers, *Management in the Industrial World: An International Analysis*, New York: McGraw-Hill Book Company, 1959, especially p. 172, concerning Chile.

[8] James W. McKee, Jr., "Operating in an Inflationary Economy," in William D. Falcon (ed.), *Financing International Operations*, New York: American Management Association, 1965, pp. 45–52.

[9] Harbison and Myers, *Management in the Industrial World: An International Analysis*, *op. cit.*, p. 172.

and economic growth in South America. Although many factors affect the growth rate, it is evident that the four nations with extreme inflation, as shown by the average annual rise in cost of living, suffered the lowest growth rates. The growth rate of Bolivia, which has the highest inflation, was less than one-seventh of the growth rate of Venezuela, which has

TABLE 6   Relation between economic growth and inflation in
South America

COUNTRY	RATE OF ANNUAL GROWTH OF DOMESTIC PRODUCT, 1945–1959	AVERAGE ANNUAL RISE IN COST OF LIVING (INDEX UNITS), 1945–1959	1962 MONEY SUPPLY, 1953 = 100
Venezuela	8.3%	4	173
Ecuador	6.1	13	184
Brazil	5.4	57	1,372
Peru	4.3	26	261
Colombia	4.2	19	388
Uruguay	3.4	27	407
Chile	3.1	340	598*
Argentina	2.6	185	580
Paraguay	2.6	381	385
Bolivia	1.1	1,257	3,390

* 1955 = 100.
SOURCE: Herbert V. Prochnow, *Economic, Political and Social Trends in Latin America,* Chicago: The First National Bank of Chicago, 1964, p. 28.

the lowest inflation. High inflation tends to perpetuate underdevelopment and a low growth rate because it creates massive economic and social dislocations which interfere with business efforts to develop productivity. This is almost a social Law of Persistent Underdevelopment, Inflation, and Social Unrest. If a high growth rate ever could be established, it might help hold inflation in check, but with the interferences caused by inflation, a low growth rate is self-perpetuating—unless major outside help is available.

In further support of the Law of Persistent Underdevelopment, inflation in an underdeveloped country causes capital to flee the country for one with a more stable currency. This condition increases the capital shortage and further limits business growth. An interesting sidelight is that it makes check cashing easy for visitors from countries with stable currencies. A merchant is willing to risk accepting a stranger's check because he can send the check for deposit to his account in a foreign bank and get currency out of his country that way. It is estimated that the capital needs of many Latin-American countries could be met if their expatriated capital could be returned, but this is not likely to happen until each country's economic and social system is more stable. Again, the Law of Persistent Underdevelopment applies.

Nearly all nations have special restrictions for foreign business entering their country, and in some of them there is a coolness toward foreign business and imported capital. They fear loss of economic and political control. They object to different operating and wage practices, remoteness of decision making, and using expatriates in key executive positions. These objections are sometimes shortsighted, for the greatest benefit of foreign capital often is the cadre of managers and technicians imported to make the capital productive. They generate progress toward a higher level of human capital in the host country.

Managerial Conditions. Developing countries attach special importance to the managerial role of innovator, which was described in the role definition of management in an earlier chapter. As mentioned at that time, role emphasis is upon innovation rather than basic creativity. Innovation is developmental; it puts ideas to use. Let us take Lebanon as an example. Although it is a poor country, it has had fairly successful economic development. A study by a Lebanese economist reported that the innovating role of Lebanese managers was more important than their creative role. The innovators, instead of being spectacular operators, made "modest innovations" on an ever-widening front. They emphasized management, ranking as their two most important functions "conception of the idea of business" and "designing the organization." [10]

Not only must an international business live up to different standards in each country, but it also must be prepared to meet these standards with more perfection than native businesses in each country are expected to do. As an interloper from afar, its public visibility is greater than that of local businesses. Nationalism, love of one's own people, and desire to protect native business make local citizens more sensitive to the effects of an international business. They know that its whole loyalty —or even its primary loyalty—is not to their economy and their people. They are quick to condemn its indiscretions and hesitant and faint in their praise of its benefits.

Of equal importance is the tendency of critics, when they observe an indiscretion of a foreign business, to generalize therefrom to condemn all businesses from that same country. Native businesses are not subject to

[10] Yusif A. Sayigh, *Entrepreneurs of Lebanon: The Role of the Business Leader in a Developing Economy*, Cambridge, Mass.: Harvard University Press, 1962.

this kind of generalization. A country in Asia serves as an example. When one of its native businesses acts in a way considered contrary to the national interest, it is merely regarded as a bad citizen. But when a German subsidiary misbehaves according to those same standards, its record is used to condemn the whole group of German businesses in that country. Managers who make decisions in this climate of public visibility must actually pay more attention to native standards and national objectives than purely local businesses need to do.

Insight into all these nuances of social conduct is difficult for even the best-qualified manager. He needs to be broad in his thinking and have high sensitivity to political and social trends. If he comes from outside the host country, he cannot by himself sense all the fine points that should bear on his decisions; therefore, he depends on the counsel of native associates who are loyal and communicative. If they understand that above-average behavior is required because the business is an international one, they can be quite helpful in counseling toward responsible decisions. Unless they do see the situation broadly, they may for reasons of native pride be hesitant to help an "outside" business conduct itself better than native businesses do.

In mixed economies where government is an owner of business, foreign business managers are sometimes hesitant to assume major leadership, make heavy investments, or take risks because of fear of nationalization. The result is a self-fulfilling prophecy. Their action slows down private industry and in turn induces government to forge ahead in order to achieve economic growth. Nationalization does occur because of a vicious cycle fostered by fears of it. Extractive and basic industries are especially vulnerable. To avoid this vicious cycle, it is incumbent on management of a foreign business to assume leadership, thus proving that well-managed private industry is more productive. At the same time it serves as a model for improving native business, thus justifying its role both economically and culturally in the host country.

International Enterprise. Different forms of international enterprise are being explored in the hope of bringing about better adjustment to the great variety of business conditions in other nations. One of the simplest arrangements is to organize a wholly owned subsidiary operating as an independent profit center in a foreign nation. As quickly as possible the subsidiary employs only nationals. In time the home office serves essentially as consultant to the subsidiary, sending experts, capital, and technical guidance as needed and receiving profits as its consulting fee. Eventually, from an operating point of view, the subsidiary becomes a native business, even though it still is a foreign capital investment.

Since nationals do feel concern about substantial direct foreign investment, a number of firms are adopting a policy of *multinational enter-*

prise, which shares ownership with host countries. The firms establish joint ventures or other arrangements which have substantial native ownership, even more than 50 percent. Then the business is looked upon not as an intruder but as a part of the native country's business system.

A variation is to acquire overseas subsidiaries by giving stock in the central corporation. Natives then become *international* owners, reaping dividend benefits based upon the whole business's success internationally. This approach is rather different from that of having natives share ownership in the success of the subsidiary alone. A subsidiary could fail or be manipulated by the central corporation, but international stock ownership brings to owners the full security of the whole company.

It is likely that international ownership of corporations will continue to spread. A few firms, such as Nestlé International, have already developed an international image. It sells in most countries and manufactures in many. Although it is controlled by local citizens, it has many foreign shareholders.

The next step will probably be the *transnational enterprise,* in which ownership and management are not dominated by any single nation.[11] Being truly international it will overcome many of the problems caused by today's strong forces of nationalism. Royal Dutch-Shell and Unilever are two firms which closely approach the transnational concept today. Both are owned jointly by British and Dutch holding companies and operate internationally with a management cadre drawn from many nations. For a firm to be truly transnational, it should have ownership, operations, markets, and managers truly diversified, without primary dominance of any of the four by any one nation. Its managers should look at the world as an economic unit and be capable of managing in more than one culture.

Perhaps a further development, not yet in existence, will be the *supranational enterprise,* chartered and controlled by an international organization such as the International Bank. It would be a private business enterprise without direct national obligations. With its integrative view it should be able to draw the economic world closer together.

Whether it is a simple international enterprise or a more advanced multinational, transnational, or supranational enterprise, international business has proved itself an effective instrument to bring advanced technology and goods and services to the world. Some persons believe it also will spread, by example, ideals of mutual cooperation and constitutional government throughout the world. In the words of one observer: "It seems inevitable that international economic integration, satisfactory in-

---

[11] Donald P. Kircher, "Now the Transnational Enterprise," *Harvard Business Review,* March–April, 1964, pp. 6ff.; and Robert H. Cojeen, "Resentment toward U.S. Direct Investment Abroad," *Michigan Business Review,* January, 1964, pp. 28–29.

vestment climates, and constitutional government will follow. . . . These concepts can be transmitted most effectively by socially responsible business enterprise. . . ." [12]

COMPARATIVE MANAGEMENT SYSTEMS

Comparative management involves the relating of management practice to other variables such as the degree of industrialization or the national culture in which management operates. It improves understanding of how management adjusts to different external constraints and helps determine what combinations of factors are most workable and efficient.

Industrialism. Harbison and Myers in their studies of industrialization distinguish three types of management which have developed.[13] These are patrimonial, political, and professional management. These studies are interpretative rather than experimental, but they are based on years of international research by teams from major universities. They have added much to our understanding of management systems in society's developing industrialism. The term "industrialism" is defined as social organization in which industries, especially large-scale ones, are a dominant force.

Patrimonial management is the common first stage in a nation's march toward industrialization. It is management in which ownership, the major policy-making positions, and other key jobs in the business are all held by members of one extended family. In this manner they control the business, and its goals are oriented toward their interests and aspirations. In Europe, India, Brazil, Japan, and many other countries patrimonial management continues to be active. It does have its advantages. In developing industrial cultures where forms of industrial organization are not sophisticated, it encourages teamwork, loyalty, and mutual interest. Where controls are not well established, it provides some trustworthiness in handling finances and protects trade secrets from prying outsiders. In a society where education is scarce, it is likely that sons of prosperous businessmen will have much of the advanced education in the country; therefore, they are in many cases the best qualified to manage.

Patrimonial management can be dynamic and effective, but it usually runs into difficulty in the long run. Heirs tend to lose interest, lacking the personal commitment of founders. They tend to become conservative with their acquired assets, not willing to take the entrepreneurial risks

[12] Richard D. Robinson, *International Business Policy*, New York: Holt, Rinehart and Winston, Inc., 1964, p. 222.

[13] Harbison and Myers, *Management in the Industrial World: An International Analysis, op. cit.,* chap. 4.

that they once did. With advancing industrialization they sometimes lack the capacity to grow in their technical and organizational skills. And as the business grows it becomes too large to be staffed with one family, even including distant cousins. The house of Mitsui, in Japan, for example, finally expanded its patrimonial group to eleven families very loosely defined. Even these were not enough as the firm grew, so it started hiring outside managers. Because of the limitations of patrimonial management, it usually tends to adapt toward career management as industrialization advances.

Political management is often a second stage in industrial development, although it is less common than patrimonial management and some nations essentially bypass it. It is management in which ownership, the major policy-making positions, and other key jobs in the business are all held on the basis of political affiliations and loyalties. Access to leadership is dominated by political considerations, and management decisions are colored by political goals. Political management is commonly associated with government operation of enterprises. India, European countries, and others have political management in state-owned enterprises. Russia is an extreme example of political management. In the 1930s not only were party members established in key managerial positions, but they also shared power equally with purely political commissars who were in each plant to assure political obedience. The inefficiency of this system finally forced its abandonment, but party membership and loyalty are still important criteria in Soviet management.

Political management has approximately the same hazards as patrimonial management, with the additional hazard of diversion of resources and interests toward political goals rather than economic goals. Loyalty to an abstract party is also harder to maintain than the personal family loyalty of patrimonial management. For these reasons Harbison and Myers believe that political management is even less workable than patrimonial management. They comment: "Political management . . . is simply incapable of coping successfully with the intricate tasks which must be performed in modern, large-scale industry. In this respect, it is even less viable, in our judgment, than patrimonial management." [14]

Advanced industrial societies move toward *professional management*, in which major policy-making positions and other key jobs are held by leaders on the basis of competence. It is similar to the term "career management," which we have been using. Unlike patrimonial and political management, the location of ownership is of no consequence in professional management. Ownership may continue to reside in a family, state, or other group, but if managers rise to leadership by competence and make decisions free of external domination, then professional management exists. It is a distinct career requiring advanced training and continuing

[14] *Ibid.*, p. 75.

self-development. It will thrive in various economic and political systems, as evidenced by its success in Great Britain, Germany, Japan, Russia, and the United States. Professional management is the direction in which advanced industrial nations find it necessary to move in order to maintain their productivity. It is the only one of the three types of management which can deal successfully with the complexities of advanced industrial civilization.

Kerr, Harbison, Dunlop, and Myers have classified five types of elites which may assume social power in leading a nation toward industrialization. They seldom exist as pure types, but they do represent the dominant social and political leadership at any point in a nation's history. Each elite uses the three types of management systems differently. The *dynastic elite* in aristocratic societies tends to support patrimonial management. The *revolutionary intellectuals* support a monolithic state and are strong for political management. The *colonial administrators* also represent political management; this is a less monolithic elite, but it is external to the native society. The *nationalist leaders* in emerging countries are ambivalent. They ". . . may encourage the development of any or all kinds of management as the occasion demands." [15] The rising *middle class* is the one elite which tends to introduce professional management quickly, although all elites tend toward it as industrialization becomes more advanced.

Cultural Comparisons. Management systems may be further understood by comparing their operation in different national cultures. In this way adaptations which have been successful can be generalized for possible use in other cultures. This kind of knowledge is especially useful for training managers to prepare them to enter another country. Comparisons may cover the culture as a whole or some special part of it such as economic differences in a comparison of United States and Russian management systems. There are many studies of cultural differences as they relate to management. We shall mention a few recent ones in order to illustrate their range.

An Egyptian study provides a useful analysis of business management in a new socialist economy compared with business management in a private enterprise economy.[16] Beginning in 1961 Egypt nationalized all industry of any substantial size or influence. The study showed that a number of institutional and personal barriers have developed that are slowing down economic development. Socialist leaders suspect manage-

[15] Clark Kerr, Frederick H. Harbison, John T. Dunlop, and Charles A. Myers, "Industrialism and Industrial Man," *International Labour Review*, September, 1960, p. 244. See also by the same authors, *Industrialism and Industrial Man: The Problems of Labor and Management in Industrial Growth*, Cambridge, Mass.: Harvard University Press, 1960.

[16] Harold Q. Langenderfer, "The Egyptian Executive: A Study in Conflict," *Human Organization*, Spring, 1965, pp. 89–95.

ment of having different goals from those of the socialist regime; consequently, managers are afraid to take independent action. They try to diffuse responsibility through collective action. Political bureaucracy has not developed competent managers as fast as industry has, so it is cumbersome, slow, and uninterested in business problems. There is a lack of unifying national objectives. Standards for judging and rewarding progress are almost nonexistent. The net result is that management is having great difficulty performing its role of economic development in Egypt.

Studies of Russia provide comparisons with a more mature socialist economy. Richman found that "problems of inefficiency, waste, and opposition to innovation in production are serious, widespread, and as yet unresolved. . . . So far the Soviets have not been able to devise a system that effectively combines central planning with local decision-making and initiative." [17] Soviet managers are therefore more interested in making quotas than in producing goods and services for use. They resort to "storming," which is a mad rush to fill quotas in the last days of a month or quarter. They are dubbed in slang as "heroes of the twenty-ninth day" because most of their output is shipped in the final hours of the month. Richman believes that the lack of market standards, local initiative, and reward systems, as well as other factors, is a major deterrent to management effectiveness. The system used will not be effective in advanced industrialization. He concludes that proper reform in the external environment of business would greatly improve Russian productivity. The restrictive external environment is the central productivity problem, rather than untrained managers and workers.

Other studies compare cultural differences of economically developed and underdeveloped cultures. Their general conclusion is that the underdeveloped nations' concepts of management are as underdeveloped as their economies. According to the Law of Persistent Underdevelopment, they are caught in a self-perpetuating circle of low development, as shown in Figure 15-1. Cultural factors, represented by the larger circle, and economic factors, represented by the smaller circle, operate in tandem to perpetuate underdevelopment. As shown by the larger circle, in the beginning an underdeveloped culture leads to low educational attainment, which causes an inadequate supply of management, resulting in ineffective leadership, which perpetuates the underdeveloped culture. In the economic sphere a similar perpetuating chain exists. The scarcity of capital causes low efficiency, which leads to low return on investment, causing low savings, which perpetuates the scarcity of capital.

A country which is caught in these self-perpetuating tandem chains requires large economic and cultural inputs to generate a takeoff force which will break the circle and head it toward a more advanced society.

[17] Barry M. Richman, *Soviet Management, with Significant American Comparisons*, Englewood Cliffs, N.J.: Prentice-Hall, Inc., 1965, p. 253.

Business managers are a key factor in this takeoff force because they provide leadership to overcome inefficiency and cultural lag. By making their society productive enough to pay better wages to those who qualify themselves, management motivates citizens to upgrade their skills and education. Without advancement opportunities provided by successful business, citizen educational lethargy persists. People seek education as a result of self-motivation, not because of public exhortation to become educated.

A study of Mexico shows how job opportunities and educational level go together. Excluding the federal district in which Mexico City is located, the industrial state of Nuevo Leon has the highest percentage of population with twelve or more years of education. This percentage is over ten times that of several less-developed states. There is immense variation in the quality of management systems among Mexican states. Business development is by region, rather than being general throughout the nation. Generalizing for the benefit of other nations, the study suggests

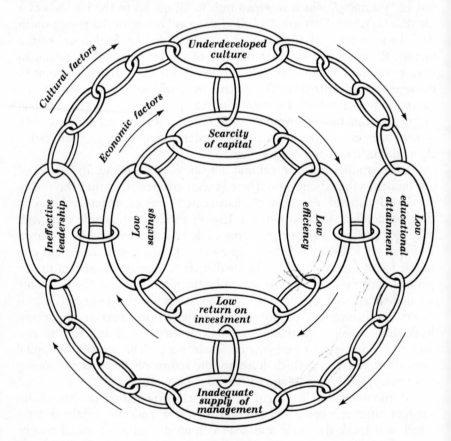

Figure 15-1 Tandem cultural and economic chains perpetuate underdevelopment.

that efforts to develop all Mexican states equally will spread resources so thin that underdevelopment will persist. The "only feasible procedure" for getting the very poor states developed ultimately is to concentrate limited resources in the advanced regions where management is already productive. This procedure will temporarily widen the contrast between states, but it will produce a growing surplus which then can be applied to bringing up the less-advanced states.[18]

Management systems may be different even in relatively advanced countries with similar economic systems. A number of studies show significant differences in management systems between Europe and the United States.[19] Generally, United States management looks toward mobility, informality, abundance, quantity, and tight organization. In contrast, European management looks toward stability, convention, necessity, quality, and diversity. Different views of organizational control are charted in Figure 15-2. European management imposes a minimum amount of order (that is, it allows diversity, represented by point A), thereby encouraging self-motivation (represented by point B). The result-

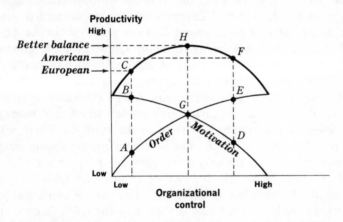

Note: The heavier line is the sum of values for order and motivation

Figure 15-2 Different management philosophies concerning amount of organizational control in Europe and the United States in relation to productivity. (*Adapted from Otto H. Nowotny, "American vs. European Management Philosophy," Harvard Business Review, March–April, 1964, Exhibit II, p. 108.*)

[18] Charles Nash Myers, *Education and National Development in Mexico*, Princeton, N.J.: Princeton University, Industrial Relations Section, 1965, p. 147. Statistics are from p. 27.

[19] Otto H. Nowotny, "American vs. European Management Philosophy," *Harvard Business Review*, March–April, 1964, pp. 101–108; and Fremont E. Kast, "Management Concepts and Practices, European Style," *Business Horizons*, Winter, 1964, pp. 25–36.

CHAPTER 15

ing balance produces a good level of performance, represented by extending line AB to the parabola, which is the sum of the order and motivation curves. Management philosophy in the United States, on the other hand, imposes tighter organizational control (point E), which holds down self-motivation to point D. Productivity (point F) is better than Europe's, but could be even higher if order and self-motivation were balanced at point G, causing productivity to rise to point H on the apex of the parabola. Other areas of practice are subject to similar balancing with the possibility that productivity would improve.

Just as management systems differ among nations, they may differ also among industries within a nation. Retail stores, electronics firms, and railroads are unlikely to manage in the same way or to be equally productive. Each industry has developed its own way of dealing with its environment. And, in fact, practices will also be different among firms within an industry.

Management Efficiency. Farmer and Richman have developed a model for comparing managerial efficiency in different nations.[20] They reason that efficiency is substantially affected by constraints imposed on management by the external environment (macromanagerial structure). That is, if the external environment does not permit and encourage internal efficiency, it will not be forthcoming. Constraints are grouped into four classes: economic, sociological, educational, and legal-political. Each class is divided into weighted subclasses which are rated for each nation to determine that nation's total constraints. A high constraint score indicates that external constraints are giving high support to efficient management.

Sociological constraints will serve as an example. Their maximum weight is 100 points out of 500. The subclasses and maximum weights are as follows: view of managers as an elite group, 10; view of scientific method, 40; view of wealth, 10; view of rational risk taking, 10; view of achievement, 20; and class flexibility, 10. The sum of constraint scores is the constraint index. This index is related to the nation's gross national product and its growth rate during the last decade in order to determine an efficiency index. The index expresses the efficiency with which a country converts its inputs into production outputs. Efficiency indexes for five nations are as follows: Saudi Arabia, 20; Mexico, 38; United Kingdom, 178; Russia, 273; and the United States, 405. This type of analysis also pinpoints reasons why a country is low in efficiency because a low score on a particular constraint shows that it needs improvement in order for there to be a gain in efficiency.

[20] Richard N. Farmer and Barry M. Richman, "A Model for Research in Comparative Management," *California Management Review*, Winter, 1964, pp. 55–68; and Richard N. Farmer and Barry M. Richman, *Comparative Management and Economic Progress*, Homewood, Ill.: Richard D. Irwin, Inc., 1965.

BUSINESS RESPONSIBILITIES INTERNATIONALLY

In our time the central international responsibility of business is to extend its productive capacities throughout the world to upgrade developing countries. The problem is not so much the shortage of capital as the need for productive use of capital. If management can employ capital productively with reasonable stability and protection of investment, capital will be forthcoming from many sources. The external environment of business is, however, a key factor in determining productivity. It is an input into the production system. It must be "industrialized" gradually in each nation in order to enable business to operate productively. All countries seek more goods and services for their people, and industrialism appears to be the only course available which will achieve these goals. Business, as the principal operator of industrialism, constitutes a strong pressure for more education, social development, law and order, rational cooperation, and other conditions of industrialism. Improvement in these environmental inputs is necessary for continued growth in outputs of goods and services, both material and cultural.

This input-output relationship of environment and productivity in the social system has been proved countless times when technologically advanced businesses entered underdeveloped countries. A well-equipped plant is not enough. The whole society needs to be upgraded in terms of education, health, respect for contracts and obligations, view of quality, and so on. The following experience of one of the authors brought home this relationship of environment and productivity in an underdeveloped country. Visiting that country's modern rayon plant, he noticed that sheets of cellulose (the main raw material) were made in Canada, 9,000 miles away. He asked why this was so because he knew that the underdeveloped country had vast forest reserves and some cellulose plants. The reply was: "We haven't yet been able to get our workers to make cellulose of a good enough quality for it to work in this modern plant."

There is, however, no simple formula to economic and social development. Each country, region, and industry is different. There are widely varied stages of development, with an infinite variety of cultural backgrounds. The only fruitful approach to these varying conditions is to work step by step to solve specific needs, and this is the kind of role in which business management has proved historically that it does contribute greatly. In fact, it leads in this role because of its singular focus on making things work.

International Management Groups. Business is approaching its international responsibilities in a number of unique ways. At the International Management Congress in 1963, David Rockefeller suggested a managerial task force of volunteers from business. These volunteers, on leave from their companies, would enter countries by invitation to assist them with difficult projects. This International Executive Service Corps gives business a stake in world development and permits countries to call upon competent business specialists *outside their company roles* when needed.[21]

Businesses have established in the United States the Council for International Progress in Management (CIPM). Membership consists of management associations (such as the Academy of Management), corporations, and universities. It works with management groups in other countries through the international management association Comité International de l'Organisation Scientifique (CIOS) to further management ideals of productivity and rational cooperation throughout the world. Its lucid statement of objectives is shown below. It has been very effective in cementing international business goodwill. Government and nonprofit managers are active participants in the international management movement.

CIOS and its national management affiliates have been active in supporting international executive-development programs which draw their participants from many countries so that no nation's executives dominate.[22] This kind of program is entirely different in focus from a local executive program dominated by natives of one country. Individual business enterprises have also been instrumental in creating international management-development programs. One of the most successful is the IMEDE program in Switzerland established by Nestlé International along with other business associates.

ꙮꙮꙮꙮꙮꙮꙮꙮꙮꙮꙮꙮꙮꙮꙮꙮꙮꙮꙮꙮꙮꙮꙮꙮꙮꙮꙮꙮꙮꙮꙮꙮ

STATEMENT OF OBJECTIVES

The Council for International Progress in Management in advancing the management movement at the international level, seeks to:

Develop understanding of strength of management movement

1. Develop widespread understanding that the management movement, based on sound moral, ethical and spiritual prin-

---

[21] David Rockefeller, "Managerial Work and Human Progress," *Proceedings of the Thirteenth International Management Congress*, New York: Council for International Progress in Management (United States), Inc., 1963, pp. 2–5; and "International Executive Service Corps," *Organizzazione Scientifica*, December, 1964, pp. 255–257.

[22] Details of many types of programs are reported in the special section "The Development of Managers: The World-wide Effort," *Proceedings of the Thirteenth International Management Congress*, New York: Council for International Progress in Management (United States), Inc., 1963, pp. 270–344. See also Arthur M. Whitehill, Jr., "Needed: A New Internationalism in Management Development Programs," *Business Topics*, Summer, 1963, pp. 27–32.

ciples, as well as professional and scientific knowledge, is one of the most powerful forces in maintaining and advancing the interests of mankind.

Continue contributions of scientific management to basic ends of society

2. Indicate conclusively that professional and scientific management will continue to contribute materially to:
—improvement in living standards
—conservation and proper utilization of natural resources
—a sense of common purpose, to the end that all parts of society may cooperate in increasing the results of human effort, or productivity, in which all share in proportion to their voluntary teamwork, self-discipline, honesty and recognition of the dignity of their fellow man.

Promote management in the public interest

3. Move always in the direction of creating understanding of the free society and of the constructive role management can play therein in the interests of all people.

Recognize scope of responsibilities of individuals in management

4. Stress that society will profit most through proper management action by individuals. Therefore, individuals in management everywhere are encouraged to accept their individual responsibilities:
—to the owners of their respective enterprises
—to the employees under their management at every level
—to their customers who act as the great regulator of a free enterprise system
—to the vendors and suppliers
—through "living what is right," and teaching by example what is right, to encourage those in business, voluntary associations and government to do the same.

Apply tested management principles

5. Inspire management groups and individuals to utilize basic management principles already discovered, developed, tested, and codified.

Stress measurement in management and respect views of others

6. Promote the acceptance of the fundamental principles of management by free and honest presentation of the facts; and by striving always to find better ways to measure management efforts and results objectively and refrain from trying to impose a predetermined point of view on others.

Use research to extend management principles

7. With the aid of research into all phases and functions of management, encourage individuals and groups in management to think through and come to their own conclusions about the best methods of enlarging and improving the management movement, and through it encourage the widest possible, and growing, understanding and application of sound and progressive management principles and practices.

Acquire and project new ideas

8. Acquire new knowledge so as to actively project available knowledge, so that its members and other managements can:
   —benefit from new ideas
   —understand others even when their aims are not the same
   —appreciate why methods can be successful under one set of conditions but not another.

Continue to pioneer in the management movement

9. Encourage management to use new methods and technological advances to improve productivity and widen the distribution among all people of its benefits, to advance the art of management, to learn by experimentation and to bring together and make available the new findings. Specifically encourage management to sense the impact of ever-multiplying and inter-locked scientific developments and technologies on many frontiers of knowledge, to keep the management movement always in tune with such pioneering advances. And encourage management to do so both by boldly using the new tools which technology thus makes available to management and also by steadily developing the profession of management itself so as to be able to cope adequately with the growing requirements for management skills and ability which are successively called for by such an increasingly complex social, economic and political environment.

Cooperate with government constructively

10. Advance the understanding, acceptance, and practice of professional management with, or in behalf of, governmental agencies when the voluntary cooperation of a large number of management leaders is required.

Widen areas of agreement internationally

11. Determine, recognize, and widen, wherever possible, the areas of agreement between men of different countries, first as to aims, then as to principles . . . keeping in mind that common purposes in management objectives, as in other scientific objectives, are less difficult to establish than political or economic agreements, but may be as effective a bridge to understanding.

Participate in CIOS

12. Participate actively and imaginatively in the activities of the management movement at the international level as a member of the International Committee for Scientific Management (CIOS).

In summary, the Council seeks to help management in all countries to understand what professional management can do in improving the conduct of all kinds of enterprise involving organized effort, including government, educational institutions, business enterprises, labor unions, and non-profit institutions. The

Council believes that such understanding, followed by action, will open up new vistas of human opportunities and welfare throughout the world.

Helping Develop Local Business. One way to aid a country is to encourage more locally owned, progressive businesses. Sears, Roebuck and other firms have actively encouraged local suppliers to develop when they move into a country. Sears's program has been especially successful in Latin America, leading to the establishment and growth of hundreds of companies. In the beginning, Sears could purchase within a country only a small percentage of the merchandise it sold there, but now in Latin-American countries, such as Mexico and Brazil, over 90 percent of its merchandise is made within the country.

The United Fruit Company encourages local owners and suppliers through its Associate Producer Program. This program helps develop native supply services and tries to bring natives into partnership in various aspects of the banana business. Company properties—farms, stores, restaurants, bakeries—are gradually being sold to natives. United Fruit helps arrange financing, provides technical help, and otherwise assists native producers. The far-reaching effect of this program is shown by the fact that all United Fruit's commercial banana acreages in Colombia, Ecuador, and the Dominican Republic have been sold to natives.[23]

In addition to encouraging suppliers and commercial associates, businesses may also work directly to develop new enterprises in unrelated business areas, thereby helping upgrade the general community in which they operate. In Venezuela, Creole Petroleum Corporation has formed a subsidiary investment firm to supply new risk capital to stimulate local investment and expand opportunity. Creole limits its interest to less than 50 percent to make clear that its purpose is to support local enterprise rather than dominate it. Other Standard Oil affiliates are taking similar steps in other countries.[24] The purpose is strictly to supply risk capital in new areas of business. This objective is entirely different from the common practice of forming a joint venture with a native firm for business purposes in product areas where the two firms normally conduct business.

International Trade Policy. A sticky issue of responsibility is East-West trade policy. From the business point of view, businessmen welcome the additional markets which would be opened by trade with the Communist bloc, and yet there are dangerous political implications in this

[23] Thomas E. Sunderland, "Foreign Trade and Foreign Policy: An Uneasy Co-existence," *Michigan Business Review*, May, 1965, pp. 2–11.

[24] Robert H. Scholl, *International Business and the Community*, New York: Standard Oil Company (New Jersey), 1963, pp. 1–10.

course of action. There are also nagging questions of whether Communist countries would use these trade relationships to weaken private business in the long run for political purposes. In other words, is it possible to deal with Communists on strictly a business basis, free of anti-private-business political objectives? The Committee for Economic Development, which we have indicated usually represents a managerial ideology, issued a statement in 1965 favoring expansion of East-West trade with numerous exceptions such as strategic goods. It opposed trade with Red China and Cuba, so the favorable views in its report apply primarily to Russia and its European satellites.[25]

In instances where trade licenses have been approved by the United States government, individual firms have had to wrestle with their own consciences in deciding whether to accept Communist purchase orders. In 1964 Goodyear Tire and Rubber Company refused Romanian proposals to purchase from it a 40-million-dollar synthetic rubber plant using its process, even though the United States government had approved the sale. Goodyear said that the sale would not be in the best interests of the United States. It stated that the sale would permit Romanians to use its trade secrets to produce a rubber which competed with natural rubber, enabling it then by market manipulation to disrupt national economies in Southeast Asia and Africa.[26] In 1965 Firestone Tire and Rubber Company terminated negotiations on a similar offer.[27] Many other companies, however, trade with Communist nations whenever it is permitted.

On a number of occasions government asks business firms to cooperate voluntarily in implementing a particular public policy. A notable request was that of the United States Secretary of Commerce in 1965 with regard to the United States deficit in its balance of payments. Although the balance of payments on business transactions was already producing a surplus, businesses were asked to expand "their contribution toward balancing our foreign accounts" by making a 15 to 20 percent improvement in 1965, compared with 1964 results. The less-developed countries and Canada were largely excluded from the request, meaning that it applied primarily to trade with developed countries. A quarterly reporting system was established for firms with investments of 10 million dollars or more in developed countries at the end of 1964 or with exports of 10 million dollars or more in 1964. The Secretary's letter to the approximately six hundred companies in this reporting group is reproduced in Appendix B of this book.

[25] *East-West Trade: A Common Policy for the West*, New York: Committee for Economic Development, 1965.
[26] *Akron Beacon Journal*, Oct. 23, 1964.
[27] *Business Week*, Apr. 24, 1965, p. 116.

SUMMARY

Major business enterprises are moving rapidly into worldwide operations which are so complex that they challenge men's intellectual capacities. Different social, political, economic, and managerial conditions in each nation affect business practices. Human resources are frequently scarce, along with economic capital. There are social overhead costs and various restrictions on business. Public visibility requires above-average conduct. Substantial inflation is a hazard in many countries. To adjust to international conditions, businesses are moving toward multinational and transnational forms of enterprise. The supranational enterprise may be forthcoming.

A study of comparative management systems aids business adjustment to international conditions. Three types of management have developed in the march toward industrialism: patrimonial, political, and professional (career). Cultural studies show that highly centralized political planning operates as a deterrent to production efficiency. It reduces flexibility, lacks market standards, confuses reward systems, and superimposes political values on operating decisions. Comparative studies also reveal that the concepts of management in the less-developed nations are as under-developed as their economies. They require large inputs to generate a takeoff force toward a more advanced society. Often it is advisable to concentrate limited resources in the more advanced sections of a nation where management is already productive in order to generate a quick surplus. Constraints causing low efficiency may be discovered by rating economic, sociological, educational, and legal-political factors according to the Farmer-Richman efficiency index.

Business's general responsibility internationally is to employ total resources productively. This obligation requires business to work for reduction of limiting constraints in the environment as rapidly as possible. Special evidences of responsibility are the International Executive Service Corps, the Comité International de l'Organisation Scientifique, development of local suppliers in other nations, subsidiary investment firms to encourage new ventures, East-West trade policy, and business assistance in improving the United States balance of payments. The next chapter will discuss management's international role in cultural change and productivity.

QUESTIONS

1. Discuss some of the international social, political, economic, and managerial conditions which affect business productivity.

2. What are some of the social effects of inflation on the business environment?

3. Distinguish multinational, transnational, and supranational enterprise. Comment on their usefulness in meeting modern needs.

4. Discuss differences in patrimonial, political, and professional management. Which of the three would a revolutionary intellectual elite tend to support?

5. Compare management in Russia, Egypt, and the United States.

6. In aiding a less-developed economy, how could you rationally justify *increasing* the economic and social spread beween its poorer and its more developed areas? Would the Law of Persistent Underdevelopment help you justify your view?

CHAPTER 16 CULTURAL CHANGE

AND PRODUCTIVITY

> The success or failure of a change agent's project
> will ultimately depend on the motivation of individuals;
> therefore it is worth considering what makes individuals
> desire an innovation.
>
> CONRAD M. ARENSBERG AND
> ARTHUR H. NIEHOFF[1]

As mentioned in an earlier chapter, a key part of management is the role of innovator, or change agent. This role is especially important in less-developed countries where management finds it necessary to introduce drastic changes in order to move the work culture rapidly toward better productivity. Impatient society will no longer wait for slow, generation-by-generation acculturation of people, like the slow drip-drip of a cavern stream forming a stalagmite. In its concern for others and for "progress," society is in a hurry—perhaps too much so for its own good. Nevertheless, it wants progress now and material goods now. It is depending on management to introduce quickly and effectively most of the changes that it wants.

Since less-developed countries provide the most difficult conditions for business change, this chapter will discuss how cultural change and productivity can be developed in these types of situations. First, we shall discuss the broad requirements for integrating different social systems. The technology and work systems of the new business need to be fused with the culture of its host country. Then we shall discuss the processes of introducing change, communicating it, and motivating less-developed cultures to respond to it. We shall not attempt to survey the entire theory

[1] Conrad M. Arensberg and Arthur H. Niehoff, *Introducing Social Change: A Manual for Americans Overseas*, Chicago: Aldine Publishing Co., 1964, p. 101.

307

of introducing change, but rather we wish to highlight the management responsibilities concerning change which apply especially to international business.

To illustrate the complexities that may arise as different cultures are mixed, consider the following incident.[2] In a South American nation a consultant from the United States was called in to study why the West German machinery in a cellophane plant owned by South Americans was not operating properly. (This single preliminary sentence reveals that already three different cultures were involved in the incident.) When the consultant arrived, he studied the situation for several weeks. His conclusion was that there was nothing at all wrong with the machinery. It was of excellent quality and in perfect adjustment. The raw materials and other supporting factors were entirely satisfactory.

The real problem, in the consultant's opinion, was the supervisors, to whom the patriarchal mill manager was a father image and who were unable to make operating decisions without his approval. They deferred to him as their elder and superior. When something in the mill went wrong, they waited indefinitely for his decision before they would correct the problem. Since he had other business interests and was frequently out of the mill for part of the day, or even for two or three days, they permitted the continuous-production machinery to produce scrap cellophane for hours or even days because of some minor maladjustment which they could have corrected. The mill manager tried to delegate decision making on these control matters to his supervisors, but neither he nor they were able to overcome this custom of deference to authority which existed in their culture. As the consultant finally summarized it: "The problem is the men, not the machines."

The cellophane machinery was built to operate in an advanced industrial culture, but in this instance it was required to operate in a less-developed culture. Neither the machinery nor the supervisors could be quickly changed to meet this new situation. Reengineering of machinery would be costly and time-consuming, and in this case, it might reduce the machinery's productivity. Training of supervisors to change their culturally determined attitudes, even if this were possible, would likewise be time-consuming. The solution offered by the consultant was an effective compromise. He advised the manager to appoint one person as "acting director" during his absence, give the acting director an imposing office, and work closely with him to build up his image of authority with the supervisors. Then there would always be someone at the plant to make decisions quickly.

    [2] Portions of this chapter are adapted from Keith Davis, "Encouraging Productivity in International Management," in Karl E. Ettinger (ed.), *International Handbook of Management*, New York: McGraw-Hill Book Company, pp. 334–341.

INTEGRATING SOCIAL SYSTEMS

International business offers many new situations of the type just mentioned. These situations require a blending of various cultures and new adjustments by all persons involved. A manager who enters an under-developed country to install advanced technological equipment and get it operating will have to make adjustments in leadership techniques which he employed in the advanced country from which he came. Also, native employees in this new installation will find that they can no longer follow the ways of their old, less-productive culture. In other words, both the manager and the employees must change. There must be a fusion of cultures in which both parties adjust to the new situation of seeking greater productivity for the benefit of both the enterprise and the citizens of the country in which it operates.

Understanding Social Systems. The overriding factor in all international business is that it operates within a different social system. This social system affects responses of all persons to business. For example, imported foreign managers tend to judge conditions in a new country according to standards of their homeland. Although this way of perceiving conditions is very human, it will thwart understanding and productivity. In order to integrate the imported and native social systems, a foreign manager will need cultural empathy for local conditions. Having this empathy, he must then be adaptable enough to integrate the communities of interest of the two (or more) cultures involved. But cultural adaptation is not easy. A ten-year study by International General Electric Company of overseas personnel failures reported that 60 percent resulted from poor cultural adaptability.[3]

In spite of the evident need for expatriate managers to have social empathy and to be adaptable, a manager often arrives unprepared at his new post. Selection may have been based solely upon his performance in the home country, with little regard for the fact that he will be doing business with people whose traditional beliefs are different from his own. He may not know the native language and may have little interest in becoming a part of the local community. Frequently he is not given any cultural training before departure. One survey of seventy large United States corporations reported that only three of them gave their overseas personnel predeparture training.[4]

Entering another country without preparation, a manager occasionally

---

[3] Richard B. Blomfield, "The Importance of Foreign Language to a Career in Business," *Journal of the American Society of Training Directors*, October, 1961, p. 35.

[4] Francis X. Hodgson, "The Selection of Overseas Management," *Business Topics*, Spring, 1963, p. 53.

suffers from "cultural shock." His surroundings appear to be behavioral chaos. He becomes disoriented and retreats into isolation or returns home on the next airplane. But a different culture is not behavioral chaos; it is a systematic structure of behavior patterns, probably as systematic as the culture in the manager's home country. It can be understood if the manager has a receptive attitude. But there *are* differences, and these differences strain a person, regardless of his adaptability. One observer comments about United States managers in Europe as follows: "Some operate in a continuous, though mild, state of shock—at how the market systems, distribution, and thought patterns they must deal with differ from those in the U.S. Almost all Americans in Europe work in a state of frustration at the different pace of business they meet there." [5] What an expatriate manager soon learns is that it is irrational to expect workers in the host culture to act "rationally"—that is, according to his standards of rational conduct.

Differences among Cultures. Compared with the United States, many cultures attach less importance to work. They also tend to have more respect for their elders. The result in some African areas is that there is high absenteeism among younger workers. When a young worker is told to perform some task by a village elder, that assignment seems more important to him at the moment than showing up for his job. Managers from the United States—and Europe also—have a different cultural background and are baffled when dealing with this kind of absenteeism.

On other occasions, social customs interfere with understanding. In the United States, a manager feels that a man to whom he is talking should look him in the eye. In fact, if an employee evades his direct glance, a manager judges that the man is "shifty" and may be trying to hide something. In some countries, however, it is a long-established custom for a person never to look an elder or a supervisor in the eye. To do so is considered impertinent. Consequently, a manager from the United States who tries to deal directly with his men in this manner may find that he cannot establish effective relations with them.

Similarly, culture in the United States emphasizes face-to-face thrashing out of differences. Hence, companies in the United States have been able to develop bargaining systems which in most industries are built around local, face-to-face negotiations by the persons directly involved. In Latin America, where status differences and authority are more significant, it is more difficult to deal directly with an employer. Hence, bargaining is more dependent upon an intermediate role by government. Workers have no difficulty telling an intermediary—government—how they feel about management, but they are not culturally prepared to tell management directly.

[5] Edward A. McCreary, "Those American Managers Don't Impress Europe," *Fortune*, December, 1964, p. 187.

One study of thirty-four technical advisers from the United States judged that twenty-six of them lacked cultural insight about the country in which they were working and that only eight had a reasonable amount of insight. The customs which frustrated them the most were those which were substantially different from practices in the United States. The three customs mentioned most frequently were orientation of the people toward life, nature, and behavior (mentioned ten times); lack of individual responsibility and initiative (ten times); and concepts of time and punctuality (nine times). Examples of "lack of individual responsibility and initiative" are failure to accept blame, reluctance to face facts, avoidance of work by educated men, and hiring people to work without training them. The men adjusted by trying to change themselves, trying to change the situation, accepting the situation, retreating from it, or marking time. The first two types of change were attempted most.[6]

William F. Whyte believes that cultural preparation for foreign responsibilities tends to be overlooked because it is a vague, nebulous concept and not subject to measurement. He comments: "Those factors for which measurements are not readily available tend to be neglected."[7] Regardless of the cause, it is evident that more attention needs to be given to cultural preparation of expatriate managers. Eventually a cadre of managers with cross-cultural sensitivity needs to be developed in businesses with large international operations. These men will be truly international managers who adapt readily to a variety of different cultures.

Once a manager is on location in a host country, his attention needs to be directed toward integrating the advanced technological culture with the native culture. Where local practices that interfere with production cannot be changed, perhaps they can be bypassed temporarily or integrated into a modified production plan. If, for example, a one-hour siesta must be accepted, perhaps siesta hours can be staggered so that equipment can be kept operating. If there is patrimonial management, which is the common first stage in a country's march toward economic development, members of the patriarchy can be given intensive training in productivity so that they can use their influence to sell productivity throughout the organization.

INTRODUCING CHANGE

With today's international markets, industrialization can move rapidly into a country under special circumstances. Libya is an example. In 1955 exploration for oil began in Libya. Four years later, in 1959, the first oil

[6] Francis C. Byrnes, "Assignment to Ambiguity: Work Performance in Cross-cultural Technical Assistance," *Human Organization*, Fall, 1964, pp. 196–209.

[7] William F. Whyte, "Culture, Industrial Relations, and Economic Development: The Case of Peru," *Industrial and Labor Relations Review*, July, 1963, p. 583.

discovery was made at Zelten, deep in the desert. The pace of petroleum development quickened, and by the end of 1963 foreign oil companies had invested 800 million dollars in Libya. They employed some ten thousand people in a country whose total industrial employment prior to oil development had not been much more than that. Before oil development the Libyan government's total annual revenue was about 30 million dollars, but by 1963 oil revenues alone provided about 65 million dollars to the government.

The Social Nature of Change. Whether the changes required are large or small, the work culture of a nation tends to change slowly, and in so doing, it gives stability and security to society. This is an advantage. However, there is an offsetting disadvantage, for culture makes changes more difficult to initiate. The international manager's job is to try to retain in his management practices the essential elements of both old and new cultures so that his group may work with the security of some old practices, but also with greater productivity than the old culture has normally accomplished. As we have learned from both experience and research, change is a social problem as well as a technological one. The technological part of change is usually solvable by the logics of science, but the social part is dependent on effective leadership.

The following incident, which occurred when air conditioning was new in the United States, indicates how change may be made acceptable through a simple adjustment. At the beginning of World War II, one of the first blackout aircraft factories was constructed on the plains of Texas. As was the pattern in those days, this factory had no windows or skylights, making possible its operation at night without showing lights to attract enemy aircraft. The building was air-conditioned by the latest equipment to control temperature, humidity, and air circulation. Since the ceiling was over 50 feet high, most of the air exits were high on the walls and ceilings.

As soon as the first group of employees started work, they began to complain about inadequacy of the air conditioning—it was too humid, too hot, and too close-feeling. Air-conditioning engineers were called to check the equipment and the temperature, humidity, and circulation of air throughout the building. They reported that the air conditioning was excellent—providing exactly the air conditions that scientific studies showed the human body needed. Still the complaints persisted. In fact, they grew worse, until they were definitely undermining morale and productivity.

Finally, one alert manager recognized the problem. He reasoned that most of the workers were rural people who were new to both industry and air conditioning. They were used to an outdoor life and felt restricted in a windowless plant where they could neither feel a breeze nor see it blowing. Since the vents were too high for employees to *feel* the air, they needed to *see* that it was stirring. This manager simply had tissue streamers tied to the ventilators high on the walls. Anyone who felt uncomfortable could look up to see the paper fluttering in the breeze and be assured that he was getting plenty of air. The result was that employee complaints soon became negligible. That which was technically right was finally made humanly right.

The paper-streamer device was later used around the world wherever air conditioning was new. It is rarely seen today in the United States because people are adjusted to air conditioning, but it can be seen in other parts of the world. In 1960, for example, a professor teaching in a South American executive program mentioned the paper-streamer incident to participants. A few days later, the group visited a new factory and observed the streamers in use. They asked why and were told that employees claimed that there was insufficient fresh air in the new building and that foreign consultants had advised management to use the streamers to demonstrate that there was fresh air. This action was a simple application of good international management—a recognition of the social factors in a technological change and an effort to apply social tools to achieve a workable result.

Encouraging Support for Change. Since management initiates most changes, it has the primary responsibility for handling them in such a way that there will be satisfactory adjustment. Although management initiates change, the native employees control the final decision to accept it or reject it, and they are the ones who actually accomplish it. Under these conditions, employee support becomes essential. Rather than trying to get employees to "accept" change, management really wants employees to join in producing it.

Management has developed a number of ways to encourage employee support of changes. One of these is to set up various pledges to protect employees from economic loss or from decreases in status and personal dignity. Each worker needs to feel that he personally will not suffer from change or, better yet, that he will gain from it. In fact, if workers can be assured that they will share the benefits of a particular change, this will be their positive motivation toward acceptance.

A foreign manager also reduces resistance to change by preventing trivial and unnecessary changes which are not central to the productivity he is trying to achieve. Individuals can tolerate only so much change, and if they are bombarded with irritating small changes, they will be less apt to accept major ones that occur later. It is not necessary to require that the natives *live* like the people in the manager's home country in order to produce like them. Only those practices which significantly restrict productivity should be emphasized.

Since change requires unlearning of old habits, some attention needs to be devoted to removing old habits instead of simply adding new ones on top of them. Take the situation of a native supervisor who is taught by an overseas management new ways of leading employees. What sometimes happens is that he retains most of his old approach also, so that now he has a strange mixture of newer, positive practices which are substantially offset by holdover practices from his old habit patterns. As a consequence, there is little net benefit from his new practices. If he does not substantially believe in these new practices, he tends gradually to return to his old ways of doing things because these ways are more secure. Even when he does believe in his new practices, he may become frustrated because his old habits (and those of his manager) interfere.

Old habits can be changed only through long-run creation of new conditions rather than by short-run temporary adjustments in management effort. This point is illustrated by the smoking habits of a man who usually smokes two packs of cigarettes a day. Sometimes, however, he smokes less, such as near the end of the month, when he is running short of money to purchase cigarettes, or when he reads a news article or receives a warning from his doctor about the possibility that cigarettes will cause cancer. At other times he smokes more, such as when he is nervous or worried. However, generally he returns to his old habit of two packs a day. These temporary pressures have not been effective in changing his long-run habit patterns. Neither will a single lecture or reprimand by an expatriate manager be effective in changing natives' long-established habit patterns. There must be a long-run effort based upon new long-run conditions.

Most people in less-developed countries are not accustomed to the rigid and taxing demands of an industrial system. They are not prepared for the rigorous timing and discipline, precise division of labor, rational forms of action, and impersonal styles of supervision and control that prevail in advanced work systems. And they cannot be so prepared by a speech or two and a few haphazard instructions from a supervisor. Long-run environmental forces are required to establish cultural changes of this magnitude.

Ways to Introduce Change. There are many ways to introduce change. Most frequently, probably, change is introduced through the formal authority and power of management. Another way is to have experts use their rational arguments and theoretical frameworks to convince others. Staff people in business especially apply this approach. Another way is to develop incentives which reward changed behavior such as greater output. Also procedures may be established which incorporate certain changes as a normal part of their sequence. Another way used by all management is communication of ideas, views, and problems. Finally, participation and group discussion are encouraged so that persons will themselves recognize the need for change and initiate it. This method is especially used with native managerial cadres.

Warren Bennis concludes that the last way mentioned is the most successful in achieving organizational change.[8] This approach pivots on *interpersonal* and *group relationships,* but it recognizes the centrality of work rather than merely seeking good relationships for their own sake. Bennis identifies three subtypes within the interpersonal-group approach. The first, an *equilibrium* subtype, is represented by the work of Jaques and others.[9] It assumes opposing forces which reduce energies available for the primary task of work, and it seeks through group discussion to reduce role conflicts, communication distortion, and other problems.

The second subtype is an *organic model,* used by Blake and others. It presents a "managerial grid" showing approaches to management and then focuses on problem-solving activities and laboratory training to achieve conflict resolution.

The third subtype, represented by the work of Argyris, is the *developmental model.* Using feedback from consultants and laboratory training, it works toward some particular goal of self-development or improvement.

All three subtypes are complex and depend upon assistance from social scientists. They have a number of limitations revolving around their overemphasis on the "people" side of a work system. Certainly it is not recommended that more traditional methods of accomplishing change should be tossed out and replaced by these methods. Yet, these new subtypes are being used successfully by large international businesses, and their use will probably grow as business learns more about social systems at work. Even though a manager does not use one of these subtypes, he can employ in his regular practice many of the ideas and techniques used in these change programs.

The British refinery of Esso Petroleum, a subsidiary of Standard Oil Company (New Jersey), has successfully used the interpersonal-group approach to achieve a major change in work rules. Working with the union, a joint consultation committee, and a consultant from the United States, major changes in archaic rules were made which increased efficiency substantially. For example, overtime was abolished, tea breaks and cleanup time were reduced, and the system of three mates (craftsman's helpers) for each five craftsmen was abolished.[10]

[8] Warren G. Bennis, "A New Role for the Behavioral Sciences: Effecting Organizational Change," *Administrative Science Quarterly,* September, 1963, pp. 125–165.

[9] Publications describing the three subtypes are, respectively, Elliot Jaques, *The Changing Culture of the Factory,* New York: The Dryden Press, Inc., 1952; Robert R. Blake and Jane S. Mouton, *The Managerial Grid,* Houston: Gulf Publishing Company, 1964; and Chris Argyris, *Integrating the Individual and the Organization,* New York: John Wiley & Sons, Inc., 1964.

[10] "How to Change Work Rules," *Business Week,* Mar. 31, 1962, pp. 50–52.

COMMUNICATING THE IDEA OF PRODUCTIVITY

In achieving work change in less-developed nations it is especially difficult to communicate the real meaning of "productivity" to the people involved. The modern industrial concept of productivity is not really understood in many cultures of the world. Simple social communication between people of different cultures is difficult enough, but when one steps up to the level of abstraction involved in the idea of productivity, effective communication is almost impossible.[11] The image which the sender transmits is not likely to be what the receiver interprets because he will see the image from his cultural point of view. In terms of the famous fable of the blind men and the elephant, the sender may perceive the trunk, while the receiver perceives the tail. Communication is made even more difficult by the fact that a foreign manager's communication with workers is usually secondhand through a native supervisor who may attach his own values to what is being transmitted.

Cultural Restrictions on Productivity. Even when the image received is accurate, it is difficult to get action on the basis of that image. Although natives are able to talk about productivity in an intelligent way, they still may not be able actually to apply the concept in their day-to-day work because they refuse to give productivity priority over other cultural values which are inconsistent with it.

In one country, seven men were unloading ½-inch steel rods from a flatbed truck. In normal circumstances, this job should have been accomplished in about an hour, but in this case it took more than one day. There were four men on the truck bed. Three men lifted the rods one by one and threw them to the ground. A fourth man on the bed counted the rods. On the ground, two men picked up the rods and moved them about 5 feet to a stack. A third man supervised the entire operation.

Of particular interest was the fact that one man on the truck bed always picked up a rod on its wrong side. Two men were on one side of the rod, and he was on the other; therefore, when they stepped to the edge of the truck bed to throw off the rod, his head always was in the way! At that point, he had to turn loose of the rod, stoop under it, and grasp it on the other side before it could be thrown off the truck. The foreman watched this operation all day without offering any suggestion for improvement in productivity. Furthermore, the truck could have been driven adjacent to the stack and the rods thrown or skidded onto it. However, this was not done. It appears in this case that the supervisor

[11] Edward T. Hall and William F. Whyte give an excellent discussion of the difficulties of intercultural communication in "Intercultural Communication: A Guide to Men of Action," *Human Organization*, Spring, 1960, pp. 5–12.

as well as his men did not have an abiding interest in productivity; consequently, they were unable to discover means to improve their productivity as they worked.

Sometimes workers and supervisors understand productivity, but for more compelling reasons—from their point of view—*choose* not to emphasize it. An office in India had five secretary-typists who spent a great amount of time visiting and drinking tea and who came late, left early, and otherwise wasted time. When a friend from the United States asked one of them why they wasted their time, he replied that if they put in a full day's work, two persons could perform the job, leaving three persons out of a job. To him that answer was complete and rational.

Even government may support inefficient labor policies. The makers of Daisy air rifles worked with the state of Punjab, India, to build an air rifle plant 51 percent owned by the state of Punjab. Daisy officials were instructed to think in terms of an abundance of people when planning the plant. In one instance they proposed forklift trucks for hauling, but the Indians told them to use people instead.[12]

Managerial Understanding of Productivity. Even managers often do not understand the idea of productivity, and if they are not fully versed in the subject, how can they communicate it to their supervisors and workers? One study of native managers in ten Latin-American countries reported that "only a minority of the managers interviewed had a reasonably clear concept of productivity." [13] The majority thought in terms of production (a net increase in output regardless of inputs), rather than in terms of productivity (an input-output measure of efficiency). The experiences of one of the authors in South America confirm that many South American managers fail to see the full meaning of productivity.

The same Latin-American study reported that those who did understand productivity believed that government processes were the major impediment to it. Political favoritism, nepotism, red tape, and outright corruption were mentioned by many interviewees as obstacles to higher productivity in their enterprises in every country studied. The head of a Brazilian industrial association, however, felt that inflation was the main deterrent to productivity in his country. It was his opinion that Brazil's high inflation discouraged any favorable attitudes toward productivity. He commented: "Inflation is more powerful than any talk; why make an effort?" [14] In this kind of environment, profit from adapting correctly to inflation tends to get more managerial attention than profit from greater productivity.

---

[12] "Not Just Kid Stuff," *Business Week*, Jan. 25, 1964, p. 90.
[13] Albert Lauterbach, "Executive Training and Productivity: Managerial Views in Latin America," *Industrial and Labor Relations Review*, April, 1964, p. 366.
[14] *Ibid.*, pp. 367, 371.

The gap in understanding productivity is made worse by the fact that managers in many countries ignore the scientific method in solving business problems. They treat management as a personal art, solving problems subjectively and impulsively without adequate attention to whether their decision will increase or decrease productivity. When decision habits are so firmly ingrained, it is difficult to change them, regardless of the quality of communication and training programs. Further, these same managers seldom follow up their decisions with objective measures to try to determine whether productivity was in fact increased.

When the idea of productivity is finally understood by a firm's native managers, they are ready to communicate it to less sophisticated workers. They will do this by emphasizing the idea itself, rather than by resorting to sales gimmicks and indirect approaches such as better human relations. The central idea of productivity is an efficiency of outputs in relation to inputs, and the productive work group will be culturally dedicated to this type of efficiency as a social goal. Productivity teams which have visited the United States from other countries have consistently reported that the significant difference they observe in United States employees is their understanding of productivity and their dedication to it.

Indirect approaches seldom work in conveying the productivity idea. It does little good to change organization forms in the hope that workers will somehow come to understand productivity as a result. In Israel, for example, workers own and control many business firms through their labor union, Histadrut. Planners hoped that workers would take an ownership interest in making these firms productive and that the firms would then serve as models of efficiency for the nation. Derber's study, however, reports an opposite result. He comments: [15]

> Socialist idealists had expected that workers in Histadrut-owned plants would view these plants as their own and would take an active part in their development and operation. They found, to their chagrin, that workers did view the Histadrut enterprises differently from private enterprises but mainly in the negative sense of expecting better economic returns and employment conditions rather than of promoting efficiency and production.

Productivity is the central idea which people need to absorb in order to develop the spirit to rise above poverty and inefficiency. Without a devotion to productivity, new capital inputs are dissipated. Without a belief in productivity, more education merely increases the demand for wasteful personal aides, attendants, and helpers. Without productivity, the achievement drive mentioned in the next section merely increases

[15] Milton Derber, "Plant Labor Relations in Israel," *Industrial and Labor Relations Review*, October, 1963, p. 58.

competition for resources that are not growing. It merely causes the achiever to step harder on his neighbor's shoulder as he climbs to the top, and since national resources are not expanding, whatever one gains is at the expense of the other.

When the idea of productivity is understood and accepted, it is possible to make substantial increases in output while still keeping enough of the old culture to maintain security for the persons involved. In other words, the old culture is blended with the new. Oil companies in the Moslem East have effectively blended cultures and have thereby achieved a high level of productivity. Similarly, in its rise to advanced industrialization, Japanese industry has been able to retain much of its old culture and still be competitively productive. Japanese workers are hired virtually for life, and managerial promotions are mostly by seniority. However, most of the technological improvements of modern industry have been introduced into this cultural context. What the Japanese factory loses in rationality and efficiency it seems to gain back in stability and employee loyalty. Culture is used to reinforce productivity rather than to interfere with it.

MOTIVATION IN A LESS-DEVELOPED ENVIRONMENT

Managerial Adjustments Required. An expatriate manager who wishes to motivate natives in a host nation, not merely order them around, must make some changes first in himself. His success will depend on upgrading his knowledge of native needs, ways of thinking, and cultural idiosyncrasies. The strange environment actually requires him to have greater understanding of social systems than he would need in his own country to accomplish equal results. Since he knows less about the specifics of native culture, he needs to know more about culture in general as it affects management—and he needs to be alert, aware, and interested so that he can absorb local culture rapidly. His role of boundary mediator, mentioned in an earlier chapter, finds him mediating the boundaries of two cultures as they apply to business.

The manager will also find it necessary to make adjustments in his personal manners in dealing with people. In the United States it is the custom for people in a face-to-face conversation to maintain some physical distance between them, perhaps 1 or 2 feet. In some cultures, however, it is the custom for people who talk face-to-face to do so quite closely, at perhaps a distance of 6 inches. A manager from the United States may be uncomfortable in a conversation of this type. We observed one manager overseas who, by the end of a short conversation, had backed halfway across the room trying to increase the distance between himself and an employee, who, of course, kept following him in order to keep the distance of 6 to 9 inches with which he was familiar. Under these conditions, it is difficult for a manager to motivate employees because he appears to be uncomfortable in their presence.

Since people in most other cultures tend to defer to authority more than is the case in the United States and since language differences further handicap communication, it becomes especially important to keep upward communication channels open. They are not likely to work unless strongly encouraged to do so. Many of the ideas an expatriate manager communicates are difficult to understand and accept, such as that of productivity, which was just discussed. Even though he is greeted with "yes," "si," or "aye" in his downward communication, noncooperation may actually increase because workers do not know how to reach him with their objections.

In international management the most important point regarding motivation is to apply it *in terms of the environment of the people involved* rather than in terms of an advanced industrial economy. Most companies desire to hire native supervisors, and there is little use trying to motivate workers until these supervisors can be trained and motivated. What is effective motivation in one environment may not be in another.

In a South American factory, for example, accidents were high. The six native superintendents were not following management's instructions for accident prevention. They seemed agreeable, but somehow failed to sell accident prevention throughout the organization. The overseas top management of the company then tried a high-powered safety publicity program of the type used in its own home plants. This was of no avail. Finally, a wise staff man found an effective solution. Papier-mâché heads of the six superintendents were molded and colored, the idea being that each week these heads would be arranged on a "totem pole" at the front gate in the order of the weekly safety rank of each man's department. No superintendent wanted to see himself as low man on the safety totem pole, so the accident problem was quickly corrected. In this case, management used existing cultural values of the country in order to accomplish the desired result of better safety.

Less-advanced Need Structures. Most workers in less-developed nations are correspondingly less advanced in their need structures. Modern psychology reports that new human needs take priority whenever former needs are reasonably satisfied. In other words, man is motivated more by what he is seeking than by what he already has. Human needs are generally recognized to be in some order, with physiological and security needs preceding social and ego needs. In less-developed countries, most employees are still seeking basic physiological and security needs. Hence, some of the more sophisticated and elaborate motivational devices of modern industrial management may not be appropriate in these countries. The needs of workers may be more simply reached by direct motivation. In many countries, workers have lived in economic systems in which there was little direct connection between the efficiency of their work and the amount of their rewards. Therefore, they require management to show them simple, direct evidence that if they work more effectively, they will receive more. In other words, work must be interpreted in terms of their immediate needs, rather than waiting for indirect results through a complex economic or social system. Accordingly, action which would be inappropriate in an advanced country may be workable in a less-developed country, as illustrated by the following events.

In South America, an international petroleum company employed about twenty natives in an oil-well perforation team managed by a nonnative executive. In spite of management efforts, each perforation job averaged nine days. Since a similar job with similar equipment was done in the United States in 1½ days, management reasoned that—even considering the more primitive operating conditions in South America—the job could surely be done in six days or less. Since the job did require genuine teamwork and since the men worked in isolated locations less subject to direct supervision, management decided on a drastic step to break the cultural pattern. It offered nine days' pay for each job, regardless of the actual number of days worked. This dramatic economic incentive proved sufficient to alter long-standing cultural habits.

The employees' attitudes gradually changed. Within four years, they had reduced perforation time to 1½ days, the same as in other efficient countries. Team members readily offered suggestions to improve teamwork and adapt technology to the special conditions of that area. On two occasions, the team encouraged transfer of men who would not change their habits and were thus holding back the team.

Research supports the view that workers in less-advanced countries also have a less-advanced need structure and, consequently, require different supervisory approaches. A study of factory workers in India reports that security and wages to satisfy basic physiological needs are most important to Indian workers, although higher needs are important in the United States. The study concludes concerning the Indian worker: "Once his basic physical needs are satisfied his psychological-social needs will no doubt become more important, but today they are still of strictly secondary importance." [16]

A French study of African workers reports that the further away they get from their traditional group, the more insecure they become. It is therefore important for management to build security feelings into new factory situations to replace those which workers lose when they

[16] Paras Nath Singh and Robert J. Wherry, Sr., "Ranking of Job Factors by Factory Workers in India," *Personnel Psychology*, Spring, 1963, pp. 32–33.

leave their traditional group. Paternalism is a desirable practice to help provide these security feelings, although in the United States private paternalism is outdated.[17]

A study of Peruvian white-collar and blue-collar workers also reports contrasts with the United States. Studies in the United States show a negative correlation between closeness of supervision and satisfaction with supervision; in other words, close supervision is disliked. In contrast, both groups of Peruvian workers reported that they preferred close supervision. The same contrast in viewpoint applies to supervisory pressures to get out the work. United States workers dislike work pressure, but both groups of Peruvian workers favor this type of supervision.[18]

To restate the basic point we are making, managerial practices from an advanced country cannot be transferred directly. They need to be adapted to the particular cultural practices, level of development, and employee need structure which a host country has. In effect, neither the advanced nation's nor the host nation's traditional practices are used. Instead, a third—and situationally better—set of practices is developed which integrates the most workable ideas from both sets of traditional practices.

The Achievement Motive. Research by David C. McClelland discloses that emphasis on the *achievement motive* in a nation has an important influence on the drives of its people.[19] The achievement motive is present in everyone, but some people are consistently more oriented toward achievement than others. The achievement motive is a basic general attitude toward life, rather than a narrowly defined psychological need. It apparently can be stimulated by a nation's culture, for there are great differences in it among nations. McClelland found that the achievement motive is stronger in economically advanced countries and "growth" countries. As further evidence of cultural support of achievement, even children's readers in the achievement-motivated countries give more emphasis to this drive, compared with those in nations low in achievement motivation.

People with strong achievement motives make accomplishment an end in itself, leaving in a secondary role the profit from accomplishment. They take moderate risks, rather than high or low ones, because they feel responsible for their decisions. In contrast, a person with less achievement drive is willing to gamble a high risk because to him nothing is lost if

[17] Marc-Edmond Morgaut, *L'Afrique et l'Industrie*, Paris: Librairie Artheme Fayard, 1959, reviewed in *Personnel Psychology*, Winter, 1964, pp. 449–452.

[18] William Foote Whyte and Lawrence K. Williams, "Supervisory Leadership: An International Comparison," *Proceedings of the Thirteenth International Management Congress*, New York: Council for International Progress in Management (United States), Inc., 1963, p. 485.

[19] David C. McClelland, *The Achieving Society*, Princeton, N.J.: D. Van Nostrand Company, Inc., 1961.

the risk fails. Those with high achievement motives are realistic. They plan carefully and persist toward goals.

The achievement motive may be contrasted with competence, affiliation, and power motives.[20] These appear to be significant distinctions everywhere in the world. The achievement motive is more likely to develop the entrepreneur, innovator, and responsible leader. The achievers choose the best men to help them regardless of personal dislikes, while persons with affiliation motives choose their friends. The achiever works harder when he has feedback about progress, whereas the affiliator works best when he is complimented for his attitude and cooperation.

Perhaps the main point to be drawn from studies of motives is that there will be a different mix of them in different cultures. If an international manager wishes to motivate natives, he needs to learn the motive most emphasized in the native culture and try to use it constructively. Then he needs to try to interpret how motives vary among his people. For example, in South America the affiliation motive might be expected. Submanagers could be expected to hire, purchase supplies from, and otherwise bestow favors on their brothers, in-laws, cousins, and personal friends. However, a sample of 100 persons in the plant might be distributed by cultural motivation as follows: achievement, eleven; competence, thirteen; power, twenty-seven; and affiliation, forty-nine. If achievers can be identified and developed, they are likely to be responsible, innovating managers. The ultimate goal is to have as much native leadership managing operations as quickly as possible—and even moving to management positions in other countries, which would create a truly international work force for a business.

SUMMARY

An international business which enters a less-developed national culture needs to integrate its advanced business system with the native culture. Both the advanced and the native culture must adapt toward a middle ground which applies the most workable characteristics of each culture. This kind of adaptation requires well-prepared expatriate managers who understand social systems. Experience indicates that cultural preparation of managers for foreign responsibilities is usually inadequate.

Managers use a full range of managerial techniques to introduce change. For major changes, group discussion techniques are effective, especially with native managerial cadres. A difficult idea to communicate is productivity as an input-output relationship. Native workers and managers tend to put other cultural values ahead of it; yet it is a central idea in business growth and social development.

[20] Saul W. Gellerman, *Motivation and Productivity*, New York: American Management Association, 1963.

The most important point concerning motivation is to apply it in terms of the environment of the people involved. This approach requires changes in the viewpoint and conduct of an expatriate manager, as well as of native employees. Unless native managers can be motivated, it is unlikely that native workers can be motivated to adapt to new programs. Workers in less-developed countries also have less-developed need structures; consequently, managerial practices which are not effective in an advanced country may be desirable in a less-developed one. The achievement motive, compared with competence, affiliation, and power motives, appears to have a positive effect on economic development.

QUESTIONS

1. Choose another country, study its culture from books or personal contacts, and prepare a written presentation telling a United States automobile manufacturer how his company's managerial practice should be amended for the new branch it is starting in that country.

2. Comment on important points to consider when integrating two national cultures in an international branch plant.

3. Discuss the difficulties involved in communicating the idea of productivity in less-developed nations. Prepare your own three-year plan for conveying this idea to native supervisors in the branch mentioned in question 1.

4. Discuss how workers in less-advanced countries also have less-advanced need structures.

5. Comment on the achievement motive and its significance to business and social progress in the world.

6. Discuss what you consider management's responsibilities to be in introducing a more advanced work culture into less-developed countries.

CHAPTER 17   LOOKING TOWARD

THE FUTURE

Ours is not a finished society.

EMILIO G. COLLADO[1]

New conditions bring new issues. Certainly a central issue of modern times is the relation of organizations to their external environment. In this book our focus is upon business and its external relations. The central issue—as with all organizations—is how to meet the needs of the organization (business, in this instance) along with the needs of its individual participants and of society in general.

In short, the issue is how to keep organizations viable along with man and his whole society. If we emphasize organization viability alone, society may become an organized monstrosity with human puppets dangling from its organizational strings. If we emphasize individual viability alone, we deny man the cornucopia of benefits that derive from organized activity. And if we emphasize only society as a whole, we deny man the individuality and freedom with which nature ordained him, and we reduce both organizations and men to servitude under the "plan." The only satisfactory answer is a balance which harmonizes all interests. The modern social balance is called pluralism. It is dynamic, not static, evolving into new forms that probably eventually will give it a new name also.

In this chapter we shall take a broad look at how the issues we have discussed are moving toward a more responsible business society in the future. We shall discuss how new relationships are evolving between business and society and how the business mission is being more clearly defined for society. Society is coming to understand the importance of

[1] Emilio G. Collado, "The Central Problem of Our Times," *The Lamp*, Winter, 1963, p. 5.

business in achieving productivity and growth around the world, and the concept of a socially profitable business is emerging.

BUSINESS AND SOCIETY

The modern business is a social system in itself, but it is also part of a larger social system represented by society in general. Clearly there is a reciprocal relationship between business and this larger society. Society does affect business through religion, law, custom, and a host of other influences. But business is not a mute servant; it speaks with a voice of leadership in the affairs of society. It is a change agent influencing society in many ways. It is an important voice in a pluralism of many voices.

The society which created business could, of course, destroy its independence. Business is continually on trial before the high court of public opinion, but, in a free society at least, it is permitted to testify in its own defense by showing how its actions contribute to the general welfare. Except for the dark days of the Great Depression of the 1930s, business testimony has been effective. The public has little doubt about business's net contribution. The issue is not whether business should be stripped of power, but rather how its power and drive can be channeled into greater contributions. As explained by Taylor:[2]

> A pluralist society is obliged to proceed always on a principle of counterpoise: it discovers its equilibrium, not by eliminating oppositions, but by using them, by making them party to a larger design which exhibits the public dimension of every private act. . . .
>
> We do not solve the problem of governing the modern corporation by extinguishing its independence. We solve the problem by defining the limits within which its independence is admissible and beyond which its independence is an encroachment on the public interest.

We believe that the next few decades will be an era of pluralistic society. The idea of pluralism will tend to be used more and more to explain institutional conduct and analyze its consequences. There are two potential dangers in the rise of pluralism. First, there is the possibility that institutional *power* will be overemphasized, in contrast to present emphasis on institutional *contributions* to society. Generally speaking, institutions today justify their existence by showing how they contribute to public needs. This is a positive, worthwhile measure of institutional performance. However, power derives from good performance, and there is always the danger that organizational interests will be diverted to power for its own sake. This kind of diversion makes organizations greedy for power and leads to power blocs and private wars among institutions for

[2] John F. A. Taylor, "Is the Corporation above the Law?" *Harvard Business Review*, March–April, 1965, p. 130.

power supremacy. Power becomes the measure of success rather than the instrument by which service is rendered, and energies are diverted from more constructive public responsibilities.

As institutions become larger, there is the danger that they will lose sight of their service functions and rely on power to keep viable, unless constitutional provisions are established to limit power. Both the individual and total society need to be protected. The Labor-Management Relations Act, for example, has one set of provisions to protect the individual union member and another set to protect the public interest from union power.

A second danger in pluralism is the possibility that so many different groups will arise that their objectives will overlap and they will dissipate their energies trying to maintain coordination and keeping off each other's toes. Just as too many cooks spoil the broth, too many pluralistic organizations could reduce progress to a quagmire of confusion and red tape. Each new institution further complicates the business environment. Since each institution is related to all others, the addition of one results in a geometric increase in complexity, rather than an arithmetic increase.

The fact that some pluralism is wise does not prove that more pluralism is wiser. At some point groups can be so splintered that each lacks the power to hold responsible leadership. Political parties in some European countries, for example, are so fractionated that none is strong enough to provide much-needed leadership. Divided responsibility and compromise become ends in themselves, while genuine political needs go unheeded for lack of leadership. In the business environment, government first moved in strongly. Then the unions came, followed by trade associations, professional and scientific societies, nonprofit organizations such as the Committee for Economic Development, and others. Recently we have added the institutional investor and religious-action groups. We must be cautious not to become so enamored with pluralism that we let complexity outstrip our capacity to coordinate society.

The point of diminishing returns in pluralism is the point where the increment from one more institutional finger in the pie is offset by the loss arising from additional complexity. Comparing pluralism to democracy, we recognize that an optimally free society is not one in which every citizen votes on every public issue regardless of its importance. Similarly, an optimally pluralistic society is not one in which every conceivable interest is represented by a separate institution competing for power.

THE SOCIALLY PROFITABLE BUSINESS

In Chapter 1 we referred to the socially profitable business. In this kind of business various types of membership investments are received from many claimants. Career management, acting particularly as trustee along with its other managerial roles, takes these investments and tries to develop payoffs to claimants greater than their investments. The payoffs cover all types of claimant expectations, including social and psychological claims. The socially profitable business, therefore, gives society much more than economic payoffs.

Too often specialists have tended to look at business payoffs from a narrow point of view only. Economists have tended to make a fetish of models of price competition, emphasizing only economic decision criteria and payoffs. As one economist observes, they ". . . are defending a glaringly inadequate position. . . . Traditional theories of price competition are impossible models for business behavior." [3]

Other intellectuals here and abroad see only the material side of business and condemn the United States for being a "business civilization." An economist observes: [4]

> Peering down from their self-made Olympian heights, they view with contempt and derision an uncultured people who seem bent on squandering their vulgar energies on the modern equivalents of Rome's bread and circuses. The American, poor soul—they tell each other with an air of knowing superiority—is a lost creature who throws his life away on a materialism which, in addition to being pathetically ephemeral, elevates the ordinary and elaborates the ugly at the expense of true excellence and grandeur.

In reality, the payoffs of business are much more than material goods and have always been so. They provide opportunity, fulfillment, worthwhile associations, and many other benefits. Businessmen are beginning to give more attention to these benefits for claimants. They are also redefining the material goals of business. Together these material and nonmaterial goals give a new look to the mission of business.

The *new business mission* is largely a new interpretation of business's long-standing mission, rather than a change of mission. It does, however, put first things first and thereby sharpens perception of what business actually does. There is also one new ingredient—a high rate of technological change. It has upped the payoff potential and made employee development much more important.

The business mission today tends to be defined in terms of *creating an environment for productivity and progress toward social ends.* Perhaps the central focus at the moment is freedom from poverty as quickly as possible. Affluence becomes the means by which the social degradation

[3] John W. Lowe, "Needed: A New Model for Competition," *Advanced Management Journal,* April, 1965, pp. 66–67.
[4] Harvey C. Bunke, "Priests without Cassocks," *Harvard Business Review,* May–June, 1965, p. 103.

which surrounds poverty can be abolished. Even poor nations can provide art, culture, education, and health for a chosen few, but they have learned that to provide these benefits for a substantial part of their people they must overcome poverty. Business is prepared to help by organizing and managing resources in the most productive way possible.

In more productive nations which have already overcome basic poverty, emphasis on the business mission has shifted to innovation and adaptation of technology for public use. The focus is upon growth rather than simply overcoming poverty, but the same need for productivity exists, and the same institution—business—is there to provide it. Business comes with self-interest and with faults, but it is no different from other institutions in having these deficiencies.

In essence the business mission is to help society move toward its long-sought goals, which may be summarized as follows: a free society wherein motivation is self-generating because each person lives under equal justice and has the opportunity to fulfill himself through use of his differentiating characteristics as well as his common ones, for his own good as well as the common good.

POWER AND RESPONSIBILITY

Society's expectations of business are increasing. The idea of productivity is being defined much more broadly to include a full range of non-material payoffs to various claimants. Not only does society expect business to take material goods and produce something better, but it also wants business to take employees and make them better. Society expects that a business that enters a community will make it better. Whatever business deals with, the expectation is leadership toward improvement rather than simply meeting minimum standards of conduct. This high expectation places heavy responsibility on business to consider the consequences of its actions on the whole community. Thus business acts with social responsibility: it is influenced by public-interest considerations beyond its direct economic and technical interest. As stated by the Chairman of the Board, Standard Oil Company (New Jersey): "No businessman today can afford to stand aloof from the major issues of our time." [5]

The power-responsibility equation suggests that because business is powerful in society, it also has equivalent social responsibility in the areas where it has power. But there is perhaps even a stronger reason for emphasizing social responsibility. The Iron Law of Responsibility promises that a group which has power and fails to use it responsibly will eventually find its power slipping away to other groups which are ready to use it

[5] M. J. Rathbone, *The Businessman and the Problems of Progress*, New York: Standard Oil Company (New Jersey), 1963, p. 2.

responsibly. This means that business can hardly refuse expectations of responsible action unless it is prepared to give up power. Berle comments:[6]

> The choice of corporate managements is not whether so great a power shall cease to exist; they can merely determine whether they will serve as the nuclei of its organization or pass it over to someone else, probably the modern state. The present current of thinking and insistence that private rather than governmental decisions are soundest for the community are clearly forcing the largest corporations toward a greater rather than a lesser acceptance of the responsibility that goes with power.

The world of business is no longer just a technological and economic world—and probably it never was. Now, for sure, it is a social world also. One of the authors has said elsewhere:[7]

> Management's first social responsibility is to create an environment in which *social values* are served along with technology, because values determine how technology and science will be used. . . .
> A second social responsibility derives from the first. Since social values are determined by man, management's responsibility is to cultivate each man's individual talents to optimum capacity, because only to the extent that man improves can he make better progress toward the values he already has or choose improved values. . . .
> There is a third social responsibility derived from the first two. Since most values will be determined outside the firm, management needs to help the whole society provide optimum development and freedom of decision for all its members. A social value becomes real or virtuous only to the extent that it is freely chosen among alternatives.

The social values most important to employees were defined in Chapter 9 as improvement, independence, and justice. The value which general society expects of business is expressed in the business mission to create an environment for productivity and progress toward social ends.

EVALUATING THE SOCIALLY PROFITABLE BUSINESS

Economic profit is basic to business success. Business deals with economic inputs, and if these resources are dissipated, the organization lacks the capacity to continue its services. Economic outputs need to exceed inputs, or else there is no reason for economic investors to allocate resources to the business. These economic facts of life are as true for publicly owned business as they are for private business. If the public invests its resources in a state enterprise, it expects a favorable return therefrom

---

[6] Adolf A. Berle, Jr., *The 20th Century Capitalist Revolution*, New York: Harcourt, Brace & World, Inc., 1954, pp. 172–173.

[7] Keith Davis, "The Public Role of Management," in Edwin B. Flippo (ed.), *Evolving Concepts in Management*, University Park, Pa.: Pennsylvania State University: The Academy of Management, 1965, pp. 6–8.

just as a private investor does. Therefore, when we speak of social criteria to evaluate business performance, we think of social criteria as an addition to profit criteria. They are not a substitute for profit criteria of performance. We need businesses which are both economically productive and socially productive.

The business which measures up to both sets of criteria is the one which will be immensely stronger and better accepted by society. Looking at the situation this way, we see that the idea of social performance and social responsibility of business is in a sense an extension of the profit idea to social outputs, rather than a denial of the profit idea. The only denial which exists in this line of reasoning is the denial that man seeks only economic returns from his economic institutions. Without question, he also seeks social returns from business, and he expects a profitable return of outputs above inputs.

As the future unfolds, what kinds of measurement criteria are likely to develop for evaluating social performance? Criteria are already beginning to emerge. In the future, businesses are likely to be judged, in addition to profit performance, on their rate of growth in productivity, rate of innovation, and impact on their community. National officials are especially interested in business's influence on general economic growth, its effect on balance of payments, its stability of employment, its overcapacity or undercapacity, and its flexibility to absorb the effects of new Federal programs. Religious groups are evaluating on the basis of social justice and morality of conduct. Unions and others are evaluating in terms of retirement security, employee development, and handling of technological change.

There appear to be about as many social-evaluation criteria as there are people with an interest in business. As with any newly developing social idea, most of the criteria are nebulous and poorly defined and consist mainly of the holder's personal ethics and interests. At this stage of development, there are far too many criteria and far too few actual evaluations. As time passes, criteria may be sifted and combined into a few key ones that can be better defined and measured. Until criteria can be defined and measured, they are of little general use for public evaluation. But even poorly defined criteria can be used by businessmen as a personal ethic in guiding their decisions; hence, in the short run, emphasis will be directed toward educating businessmen about the external environment of business and encouraging them to consider social consequences in making decisions.

In the long run, public measures of social performance may be developed. Society already has this kind of evaluation in state unemployment compensation laws, which give an employer lower rates if employment stability is greater. The same kind of arrangement exists in state workmen's compensation laws.

Even such a nebulous area as the effect of a business on the general well-being of people—society's human assets—may be carefully measured and evaluated in the future. The reason is that society stands to lose if human assets are used wastefully in the production of economic assets. Blum has described an experimental social audit of a business,[8] and Likert concludes that social science tools are now available to make this type of audit.[9]

An important issue in evaluating social responsibility is whether the evaluation must be made at the point of decision or whether effects of the decision are also to be considered. It is quite possible that socially desirable effects will occur even when social responsibilities are not considered at the time the decision is made. Even antisocial decisions may, because of external, unforeseen events, have socially desirable outcomes. McGuire makes the following comment:[10]

> Obviously, the social content of a corporate decision cannot be evaluated ex post by an examination of the social benefits stemming from its outcome, for in a business world dominated by uncertainty this outcome is often unintended. Any decision process, therefore, must be appraised for its social content prior to or at the decision point. A corporate decision is socially responsible when that alternative the decision-maker believes will result in the highest social benefit is elected.

McGuire goes on to explain that there are degrees of social responsibility and that a business may for other reasons choose an alternative that advances social welfare less than the maximum possible. But, nevertheless, the decision must be evaluated in terms of whether social responsibility was considered at the time it was made. Socially responsible action can hardly be evaluated in terms of the effects of some subsequent event which interferes with the desired outcome. This reasoning is sound if society is interested only in the *intentions of businessmen* with regard to social responsibility. But society historically has also been interested in the *performance of business*. To the extent that performance is involved, effects of a decision must be considered. Allowance can be made for unforeseen events, but the final test is the social effect of a decision.

It appears likely that both intention and performance criteria will be applied in the future. It is important to know that businessmen are considering social outcomes when they make a decision, but it is also important to know that their intentions are producing worthwhile results. Consistently poor results might indicate poor judgment, inadequate edu-

---

[8] Fred H. Blum, "Social Audit of the Enterprise," *Harvard Business Review*, March–April, 1958, pp. 77–86.

[9] Rensis Likert, "Measuring Organizational Performance," *Harvard Business Review*, March–April, 1958, p. 49.

[10] Joseph W. McGuire, "The Social Responsibility of the Corporation," in Flippo, *op. cit.*, p. 21.

cation in social values, lack of sufficient power to bring about intended outcomes, or something else; but in any case society needs to evaluate *results* as well as *intentions* in order to take the necessary corrective action.

Along these lines, one point should be made regarding method. It is incumbent upon businessmen to stress the positive contribution of business performance. In many parts of the world it seems that businessmen are still trying to prove that business is not bad for society. Success with this campaign may relieve public hostility, but it will not bring positive public support for business because its psychological orientation is defensive. Business will be communicating its true situation when it takes the positive approach of showing the public the *good* it produces (rather than how *bad* it is not). This approach encourages the public to recognize both economic and social benefits of business.

Modern society is changing fast, and business is required to move with it. Work, for example, is becoming less important to some workers, compared with their other pursuits. A number of social analysts believe that modern society is heading toward a new bohemianism of plenty, in which leisure rather than work will be the center of life. The wants of man will be so bounteously met by an automated society that little work will be required of him. On the other hand, man by his nature seems to be oriented to curiosity and problem solving. He derives satisfaction from finding and overcoming challenges, so he may choose to continue creative, productive work, even though need for it declines in urgency. And surely his work will be more in service occupations and less in manufacturing; more in intellectual pursuits and less in physical labor.

Regardless of whether work is at the center or the periphery of life, the work environment is likely to be more democratized. Workers will be as committed to their intellectual specialty and its norms as they are to their company and its norms, and they will be committed in other ways to other groups. This is multiallegiant man, mentioned in the first chapter. With less employer commitment and an intellectual skill usable in many ways, workers may become more mobile, shifting from job to job with as much ease as departmental shifts are made today. Scientific attitudes will further encourage democratization, compelling decisions to be made more on the basis of data contributed and evaluated by groups of specialists, since no man can know enough about a problem to be an autocrat with it.

Some social analysts believe that the advancement of science makes democratization inevitable. In many types of organizations, public and private, science may give to bureaucracy the *coup de grâce* that moralists and human relationists earlier tried to deliver. Bureaucracy—well suited to the stable environment and routine tasks of the early twentieth century —will, according to some analysts, crumble before the dynamic onslaught of science because it is less efficient than democracy for many tasks in this new environment.[11]

With so many changes coming, business leadership in the next generation will be an increasingly difficult task, requiring intensely prepared career managers. But the challenges are exciting. The opportunities are great. The new emphasis on social responsibility opens a whole new planet for development in the business universe. No one claims that in the physical universe the job of reaching the planet Mars is easy, but it is exciting. The same excitement applies to the new planet of social responsibility which business is developing. The payoff may be far greater than that derived from reaching and developing Mars. Consider, for example, the influence of one businessman on the Renaissance:[12]

> One would like to have a record of the thinking of the great Italian banker, Cosimo de' Medici, in the mid-fifteenth century. His bank and his business had come to dominate Florence. He ran the little country, though he assumed no political title. He subsidized art and artists, and supported queer penniless refugees from Byzantium who insisted on copying and translating Greek classics. Did he realize he was laying one of the foundation piers for the Italian Renaissance, one of the greatest efflorescences of human spirit in the Christian era? He was a reflective man, and he may have speculated on the subject. There are some marked similarities between his situation and that of American business firms five hundred years later.

There are indeed some similarities between the fifteenth and the twentieth centuries. Business today is coming to an era of social responsibilities. It is pushed by world events, so that it really has no choice concerning whether to step into this era or not. The social results can be just as exciting and as beneficial as those of the Italian Renaissance—or even more so. This is business's great opportunity.

QUESTIONS

1. What, in your opinion, is the essence of the social opportunity facing businessmen around the world?

2. With regard to business, do you see any dangers in the further development of pluralistic society?

3. Is the idea of a socially profitable business a useful concept? How can it be used?

4. Can economic- and social-profit criteria both be used in business evaluation, or does the use of one freeze out the other? Explain. What problems do you foresee in applying social-evaluation criteria to business?

5. Prepare in a few pages your personal philosophy of business in relation to its environment.

[11] Philip E. Slater and Warren G. Bennis, "Democracy Is Inevitable," *Harvard Business Review*, March–April, 1964, pp. 51–59.

[12] Berle, *op. cit.*, pp. 176–177.

CASES

CASE 1 BENEFICIAL

BUILDERS

Beneficial Builders is a major subdivision home builder in southern California. During the last fifteen years it has developed seven large subdivisions in the Los Angeles area. Its policy is to buy large tracts of land on the edges of suburbs and build good-quality, low-cost homes for working families. In order to keep costs low, Beneficial Builders uses only a few house plans in each subdivision, enabling it to precut lumber and subassemble walls, door frames, windows, cabinets, and other house parts in its shops. There are several variations of the front, or "elevation," of the houses, so that the streets are not identical in appearance.

A shopping center and 800 homes had been planned for the Hills East subdivision, located in high foothills 50 miles east of Los Angeles. Over seven hundred homes had been built and sold when the heavy fall rains started. After the ground had been thoroughly soaked, an unprecedented 12-inch rainfall occurred on Monday night in the foothills just above the subdivision. A stream which drained these foothills ran through the center of Hills East. In planning this subdivision, Beneficial Builders recognized that heavy thunderstorms did occur in the area, so it widened and straightened the stream bed according to a plan approved by county engineers.

The rain sent torrents of water down the steep stream bed at an estimated 30 miles an hour. It appeared that the stream bed was adequate until the fast, high water uprooted a giant eucalyptus tree on the edge of the stream and carried it ⅓ mile to a highway bridge. The tree lodged against the bridge and held fast, soon collecting other debris until it blocked an estimated 60 percent of the streamflow. The lake created behind the bridge soon flooded a few homes, and even worse, it caused a major streamflow over a low spot in the highway 100 yards from the bridge. This overflow could not return to the stream bed, so it continued

337

down a street for several blocks, horizontal to the stream but one block away.

Soon there was a torrent of raging water 3 to 5 feet deep in this overflow route. Homeowners were awakened suddenly about 5:30 A.M by the sound of water running through their houses and cars crashing against carports and house walls. Water rose above 3 feet in over twenty-five houses, and occupants had to flee to roofs or a second story if they had one. Walls and doors were torn away, but no house was swept from its foundation. Two persons were swept away by the current and drowned.

In a few hours the flood subsided, leaving a jumble of automobiles, uprooted trees, furniture, and house parts. Forty houses and thirty-five automobiles had damages estimated at $300,000. National Guard, civil defense, armed services, and city police helped restore order and provided trucks to haul away debris. Light showers continued, but the stream was back in its bed, and no further flooding was predicted. All utilities including water were disrupted, and none of the damaged homes could be occupied.

Glen Abel, president of Beneficial Builders, heard of the flood early in the morning and drove directly to his subdivision. He talked with public officials on the scene and with dazed and shocked residents. Although some were understandably bitter, there was no evidence that they thought the flood had been caused by poor design of the subdivision. Their homes had received the same heavy rains that hit the foothills, so they knew the rainfall was torrential. A flood victim described his experience to Mr. Abel as follows: "When I woke up, the water was leaking through the walls at the joints. We all started picking things off the floor so they wouldn't get wet, and then there was a crash as the water broke a plate-glass window and an outside door.

"The furniture started to float on top of the water, and big pieces like our dresser fell over. I knew then that we had to get out, but I didn't know how or where to go.

"I started to the boys' room, but before I got there the bedroom wall gave way and they came floating right by me out into the yard, both in their beds. I started after them, sort of swimming. Finally I reached one of the boys, still on his bed, and I handed him up to my neighbor on the roof of his house. I just handed him up; the water was so high, I didn't stand on a ladder or anything. Somebody else reached my other boy and put him on a roof.

"My house is still standing and the roof is good, but most of the walls are gone. I really don't know how it all happened, because you couldn't see anything in the dark."

Abel checked with city street engineers at the bridge, and they reported that the stream bed had proved large enough to hold the flood and that there was no overflow except that caused by the blocked bridge.

On the basis of these discussions and all other evidence he had, Abel concluded that the subdivision drainage design was sound and that his firm had no liability for the damages.[1]

Although no company liability was evident, Abel was nevertheless distressed by suffering caused by the flood. He knew that there was no insurance protection against floods; hence many home buyers faced the loss of all their savings or might be forced into personal bankruptcy. He knew that these wage-earning residents, most with young families, were not financially prepared to cope with losses this large.

From a business point of view, Abel recognized that even though the Hills East subdivision was nearly sold out, any remaining sales would be handicapped by publicity about the flood. He reasoned that many persons would not be able to repair their homes, which would leave eyesores of wrecked buildings until mortgage settlements were made. He expected that various types of lawsuits and legal entanglements would develop among homeowners, automobile insurers, real estate mortgagors, chattel mortgagors (furniture and appliances), repairmen, finance companies, and others.

While on the scene Abel checked with city engineers and determined that they would work with civil defense and National Guard truckers to clear all debris and return furniture to homes. The city would rebuild streets. Abel also worked with officers of the Hills East Community Improvement Association to arrange for flood victims to live temporarily with neighbors. The improvement association was a voluntary community group encouraged by Beneficial Builders when the first home buyers moved to Hills East.

Later that afternoon Abel returned to his downtown office several miles from Hills East in order to discuss with his associates what might be done for the flood victims. They considered asking the state governor for state flood aid, but delayed for two reasons. First, they felt that government aid should be requested only when all private and public self-help, such as the American Red Cross, was insufficient. Second, government aid would probably require much red tape and delay, and action was needed now.

They were discussing what direct action Beneficial Builders might take, when Arch Smith, the union business agent for Beneficial workers, arrived and asked whether the union might help. He said that he had talked informally with several union leaders and could guarantee 200 volunteer carpenters and other selected skilled workers all day Saturday and Sunday to repair all structural damage to houses, if someone would supply materials, equipment, and supervision.

---

[1] Weeks later a special engineering report requested by the city council and made by city engineers concluded that the flood was an "act of God" and that no negligence was evident.

After extended discussion, Beneficial executives and Smith decided they would take direct action to repair all flood damage with donated labor and materials, provided Apex Lumber Company would donate lumber and building materials. Apex was considered the key to this plan, for lumber was the main building material needed. If Apex agreed, Abel and Smith believed that all lesser services would "fall in line." Apex was one of the largest building suppliers in the West, and it had been the principal supplier of Beneficial Builders since Beneficial Builders was organized.

If Apex accepted, the following plan would be used. All services would be donated. All homes would be restored to approximately their original condition, except for furniture and household supplies. A newspaper release would announce that the restoration was a joint effort of businesses, unions, and community agencies. Appeals for help would be made privately through existing groups; there would be no public appeal playing upon emotions and possibly leading to disorganized action. Unions would provide sufficient skilled labor for ten hours daily on Saturday and Sunday (an estimated two hundred men) and the following weekend if necessary. Beneficial Builders would provide supervision, shop services, and construction equipment (worth an estimated $20,000 wholesale). Apex would provide all building materials (worth an estimated $30,000 wholesale). Community agencies would be asked to supply unskilled labor (about one hundred men). Other groups employed by Beneficial Builders to construct its subdivisions would be asked to donate services, such as plumbing and electrical work, appliance repair, landscaping, and painting. All services except painting would be donated for the forthcoming weekend so that homes would be livable on Monday. Painting would be donated the following two weekends. The Red Cross or some other service agency would be asked to provide food and coffee for all volunteer labor.

Abel and Smith were convinced that 95 percent of the repairs could be made in one weekend because of the fortuitous circumstance that Beneficial's shops had completed cutting and assembling all components for the last fifty houses in the Hills East subdivision on the Friday before the flood. These components provided a ready-made inventory matching most of the houses destroyed. In the few instances where necessary items were not assembled, Abel promised to work his shops overtime to assure that all needed precut materials and subassemblies would be delivered to the carport of each home by 6:00 P.M. Friday. This procedure probably would delay by ten days the completion of the remaining fifty houses because new lumber would have to be cut and assembled. Some persons who had bought one of these fifty houses might be inconvenienced or have added expenses if they had already promised to vacate their present residence and move to Hills East on a certain date, believing that their home would be available at that time.

By the time Abel and Smith completed their plans, it was 7:30 P.M. They telephoned Abe Silver, southern California manager of Apex Lumber, at his home near Los Angeles. When he learned the purpose of their call, he agreed to an appointment in his home at 9:00 P.M. that evening.

At 9:03 P.M. Abel and Smith rang the doorbell of Silver's palatial home.

DISCUSSION QUESTIONS

1. What do you think of Abel and Smith's original plan?

2. If you were Abel, what presentation would you make to Silver? If you were Smith, what would you do? Role-play the 9:00 P.M. meeting of Abel, Smith, and Silver.

3. If you were Silver, with authority to make an appropriate decision, what would you do when you learned the facts of this case in the meeting with Abel and Smith?

4. Comment on the business-environment aspects of this case.

5. What are the different investment groups in this situation, and what are the investments and payoff expectations of each?

CASE 2 BETTER STEEL

CORPORATION

The Better Steel Corporation is a large, international steel company incorporated under the laws of New Jersey. On April 10, 1965, Joe Jones received a notice of the annual meeting and a proxy statement from the company. Jones owned 1,000 shares of common stock in the corporation, valued at $45,000. This investment represented some 20 percent of his investment portfolio. Income from this portfolio had been his primary support since he had sold his store and retired five years before. He bought the Better Steel stock at that time. Since then, the stock had declined 40 percent in value, even though stock market averages had risen. Some of the reasons for the decline, according to Jones, were:

1. Technological changes in steel markets
2. Foreign competition
3. The pricing conflict between big steel and President Kennedy in 1962, which shook public confidence and was followed by a sharp stock market dive
4. Reduced company earnings since his purchase, even though sales had increased, especially in 1964
5. A dividend reduction of 33 percent three years before, due to reduced earnings

While reading the proxy statement, Jones came upon a stockholder proposal which particularly interested him. It read as follows:

STOCKHOLDER PROPOSAL NO. 3
RELATING TO CONTRIBUTIONS

Martha Masters, Grand Central Station, New York, N.Y., 10017, the holder of record of twelve shares of common stock of the Corporation, states her intention to propose the following resolution at the meeting:

342

"RESOLVED: That the corporation's certificate of incorporation be amended by adding thereto the following provisions: No corporate funds of this corporation shall be given to any charitable, educational or other similar organization, except for purposes in direct furtherance of the business interests of this corporation, and subject to the further provision that the aggregate amount of such contributions shall be reported to the shareholders not later than the date of the annual meeting."

and asks that the reasons for the resolution be stated as follows:

"REASONS: With the amount of money being contributed by the corporation increasing over the years, it is becoming more important that all know the amount. Your dividend has been cut, and yet your company gave away 7½ million dollars of your money to charity during 1963, money which belongs to you.

"If you agree, please mark your proxy *for* this resolution; otherwise it is automatically cast against."

A *Vote Against this Resolution Is Recommended by the Directors for the Following Reasons:*

The amount of contributions is reported. The 1964 annual report of the corporation states: "Better Steel made contributions for educational and charitable purposes during 1964 of 7 million dollars. This sum included 6 million dollars paid in December, 1964, to Better Steel Corporation Foundation, Inc., a nonprofit corporation which was formed in 1953 to provide aid for charitable, educational, and scientific organizations and activities." It is the opinion of the board that such contributions advance the interests of the corporation as a private corporation and as a part of the communities in which it operates. A report of the foundation is available upon request to the office of the foundation.

Adoption of the proposal would not be in the interest of the Corporation. It might be difficult to establish affirmatively that contributions which are used for general support of universities, scientific research, and the like are in "direct furtherance" of the business interests of a corporation. Yet this corporation and all business corporations generally must depend upon the availability of highly trained people for the future well-being of their companies and hence of our economy as a whole. Support of education is one way of assuring this availability.

Also, the proposal would seriously limit the corporation in fulfilling its responsibilities to, and maintaining its position as a corporate citizen in, the commmunities in which it is located and conducts business.

Corporate support is well recognized as essential. There has long been legislative authority in New Jersey and many other states for contributions to community funds, hospitals, and educational and other instrumentalities conducive to public welfare. The New Jersey statute was revised in 1950 to give added emphasis to the public policy that New Jersey corporations are specifically empowered to contribute such moneys as in the judgment of their governing boards are conducive to the betterment of social and economic conditions. The New Jersey courts have said that such corporate aid to charitable and educational projects "amounts to a solemn duty."

Corporate support is vital to charitable, educational, and other voluntary institutions if they are to avoid being instrumentalities controlled by government and entirely supported by taxation. The benefits to a corporation from such support are many and varied and frequently much greater than those from expenditures which can be more easily demonstrated to be in "direct furtherance" of the business interests of the corporation.

The directors believe that the restrictions proposed would be contrary to the corporate and stockholder interests of the corporation, and they recommend a vote *against* this proposal.

Since this year's annual meeting was scheduled to take place in his metropolitan area in May, Jones decided he would not mail his proxy statement but would vote his shares in person. In thinking about Stockholder Proposal No. 3, Jones remembered that during the past year he had received several reprints of management speeches from the company. He remembered that one of them was on the subject of corporate giving. In his files he located three reprints. One speech was by the director of the corporate foundation mentioned in the proxy statement. Speaking before a business group, the director had supported business giving. Reading the speech for the first time, Jones was especially impressed with the following comments:

> It is time for all to realize that the existence of an economic unit in a local community, or its entrance into one, automatically sets up its proportionate share of the responsibility for achieving the community's aspirations. Any business concern doing a sufficient volume to make it a primary economic unit in the neighborhood should, as a matter of purpose, make provision in its organization structure for proper attention to community affairs and leadership. . . .
>
> The first suggestion is that you adopt a basic idea with which you undertake a larger share of leadership. The basic idea is this: When dealing with all matters affecting community needs and aspirations, business should temper any concept of "taking out of immediate profit" with the concept of "putting in for ultimate benefit to all." This must follow, since the common good, typically, represents an area that is "off limits" so far as "taking out" or immediate reward is concerned.

In the second reprint Jones noted that the foundation director established seven major areas for corporate giving:

1. Private social welfare causes such as community chests and united funds.
2. Private health and medical care such as community hospitals.
3. Cultural needs such as symphony orchestras.
4. Civic needs such as urban renewal and public sanitation.

5. Citizenship-leadership training, such as public and private education.
6. Education in physical and social sciences.
7. International development in areas where business skills can help the development of a country. "Enlightened capitalism must evidence to the world, not only to the people who already enjoy its fruits, that it has demonstrable nonmaterial values to offer peoples who hunger for the freedom and individual dignity that raises man above the condition of peonage."

The director reported that the corporate foundation supported projects in all seven areas of assistance.

Jones then turned to the third reprint which reported a speech by the company president at a community awards dinner. The president mentioned the burden of corporate taxes and community responsibilities, commenting: "We need to understand that we cannot so burden any one element in our community as to make it impossible for that element to operate successfully and thus supply the lifeblood of the city."

In May, Jones attended the stockholders' meeting. He heard the corporation president in a prepared speech state that there was no near-term probability of a dividend increase because of capital needs and continued low earnings. Later in his speech the president reported that for eight months the corporation's production facilities had been operating near capacity. He said major capital improvements were needed to expand capacity.

The time for stockholder voting was approaching, and Jones wondered how he should vote his stock on Stockholder Proposal No. 3.

DISCUSSION QUESTIONS

1. If you were Jones, how would you vote on Stockholder Proposal No. 3? Explain.

2. Discuss pro and con the corporation's stated position on Stockholder Proposal No. 3.

3. Do you see any conflict of viewpoints between the president's statements and the foundation director's statements? Explain.

4a. As a stockholder, would you favor this corporation's giving in each of the seven areas mentioned by the corporation foundation director? Support your view separately for each area.

b. As an educated citizen, would you favor the idea of corporate giving in the seven areas mentioned? Consider each area separately. What is the general guide, if any, which you are using in making your decisions?

CASE 3 THE DENVER AND RIO GRANDE WESTERN RAILROAD COMPANY, SILVERTON BRANCH [1]

On December 21, 1959, the Denver and Rio Grande Western Railroad Company,[2] a common carrier by railroad subject to Part I of the Interstate Commerce Act, filed an application under Section 1(18) of the act for a certificate of public convenience and necessity permitting the abandonment of that portion of its narrow-gauge line known as the Silverton Branch. Protests against the abandonment were filed by several city chambers of commerce, the county commissioners of two counties, the Colorado Public Utilities Commission, the Colorado State Mineral Resources Board, various railway labor organizations, the San Juan Wool Growers' and Cattlemen's Associations, and a number of ranchers and businessmen from the area.

The Silverton Branch of applicant's system is a narrow-gauge line that extends between Durango and Silverton, two towns in the rugged mountainous area of southwest Colorado. The Silverton Branch was constructed by applicant in 1881 and 1882 for the purpose of transporting ore and concentrates from many rich mines in the Silverton area to the smelter in Durango and also for the purpose of transporting passengers and freight between the two towns and intermediate points. Prior to completion of the Silverton Branch, freight could be transported only by pack animal or freight wagons.

Over the years, mining operations in the Silverton district have gradually declined, and the demand for freight service to carry ore and concentrate to the smelter at Durango, and supplies and other freight to

---

[1] Adapted from the report and order recommended by the hearing examiner in interstate commerce, Finance Docket No. 20943. The true company name is used in this case.

[2] Hereinafter referred to as "applicant."

346

Silverton, has slowly decreased. In 1924, the railroad stopped operating separate freight and passenger trains and instituted a daily (except Sunday) mixed-traffic service.[3] The amount of service was gradually reduced over the years, although the railroad continued to offer year-round service. From March, 1949, to September, 1953, the year-round service consisted of one mixed train per week. However, beginning in 1951, triweekly round-trip mixed-train service was started in the summer. This service was designed primarily to accommodate tourists and sightseeing passengers who wished to ride on an antique, picturesque, narrow-gauge train, pulled by an old-time steam locomotive through the beautiful Colorado mountains. In 1953, the railroad stopped providing any year-round scheduled service, confining its scheduled trips to the tourist season of June 1 to September 15.

The line is subject to maintenance problems characteristic of narrow-gauge lines located in the mountains. It is difficult to maintain and operate, particularly during the winter and spring months. Heavy snows block the tracks, snow and rock slides often occur, and flooding (particularly from fast and heavy thawing in the spring) causes washouts of tracks.

Applicant estimated that the cost of rehabilitating the line so that it would be suitable for year-round operation would total $447,400. Although the track between Durango and Hermosa (a distance of 11 miles) is low and subject to flooding, no damage from floods has been experienced in recent years. A number of culverts along the line need replacing, and some portions of the roadbed require ditching. Much of the existing lightweight rail needs replacing, and because of age, bridges need to be reinforced and strengthened.

Although no regular year-round service has been provided over the line in recent years, maintenance work has been on an accelerated basis for the past several years. This has resulted in a general upgrading of the bridge structures and in the restoration of the track to a level entirely satisfactory for the restricted use that has been made of it.

Applicant admits that without any increase in its regular maintenance program, the line could be adequately maintained to afford service during the summer and that the extensive rehabilitation work outlined would be necessary only if year-round service were rendered.

Each summer since 1951, the combination sightseeing and freight service has been provided from early June to the end of September. At the commencement of each summer season, triweekly service is provided. During the peak of the tourist season, it is increased to daily service and is then reduced to the triweekly basis toward the end of the season. The train, normally consisting of a coal-burning locomotive, ten passenger cars, and two freight cars, departs from Durango at 9:15 A.M. and arrives

[3] A mixed train is one which carries both freight and passengers.

at Silverton at 12:40 P.M. After a two-hour lunch period, the train makes the return run to Durango, arriving there at 6:00 P.M. Although the train normally accommodates a total of 385 passengers, including some standees, occasionally additional standees are permitted, thus increasing the passenger maximum to 485. Such freight as may be available for movement is also handled on the trains.

Since applicant's line is narrow-gauge from Silverton to Alamosa, any freight moving between points on the branch and standard-guage-line points must be transloaded into the larger cars at Alamosa. While freight has continued to move over the branch in this manner, the volume thereof has been greatly reduced in recent years.

Prior to 1952 [4] (when all passenger service over the narrow-gauge lines, other than that provided on the Silverton Branch, was discontinued), applicant rendered passenger service over the entire narrow-gauge line to Alamosa, where passengers transferred to and from trains operating on applicant's standard-gauge line. Through such service, some interstate passengers were handled, and some were moved to and from points on the Silverton Branch. Since the discontinuance of passenger service between Durango and Alamosa, only intrastate passenger service has been provided over the Silverton Branch. Applicant no longer holds itself out to provide an interstate service over the line, and no arrangements exist for the through movement of interstate passengers wishing to travel over the branch line. Tickets for transportation over the line are offered for sale at Durango only.

Although no regular service is provided after the close of the summer season, applicant does claim to hold itself out to transport freight over the line whenever a shipper has ten or more carloads to be transported at one time. Under an arrangement with its wholly owned subsidiary, Rio Grande Motor Way, Inc., less-than-carload freight moving on applicant's line to or from points on the branch line is transported by the motor carrier. Applicant asserts that this provides an adequate substitute for rail service during periods when no regular rail service is provided over the line.

Applicant has published no schedules since 1953 covering any of the services rendered over the line, and it has obtained no authority from any regulatory body authorizing any temporary suspension of service over it. Also, no adjustments have been made in its intrastate and interstate tariffs, placing any limitation on the traffic that would be transported or establishing a minimum on the volume of shipments that would be handled.

Over the years, mining operations in the area gradually declined, and in 1938 the smelter at Durango closed. After this closure the decline

---

[4] After 1952 the Silverton Branch became the last regularly scheduled narrow-gauge line in the United States.

in freight traffic moving over the line became more pronounced. Finally, applicant concluded that the slight demand for service that existed did not justify the expenditures involved in attempting to keep the line in operation on a year-round basis, and in 1953 it abandoned any attempt to provide any regular service over the line, except during the summer months, and established the arbitrary minimum carload requirement previously mentioned. Applicant made no attempt, however, to create any embargo on traffic but merely notified shippers in the area and posted notices in the stations at Durango and Silverton of the minimum rule it had established.

The number of round-trip passengers transported over the line has increased substantially from year to year during each of the past four years, increasing from approximately twenty-five thousand in 1957 to more than thirty-five thousand in 1960. During the same period, passenger revenues increased from almost $86,000 to over $163,000. In most instances the train was filled to capacity each trip, and at times the demand exceeded the space available. During the summer of 1960 there were at least twenty-five hundred persons, representing three times that number of prospective passengers (families), who were unable to obtain tickets to ride the trains because of the heavy demand.

The amount of freight transported over the line in recent years has not been substantial. In 1957 there were 277 tons of freight handled, and the revenue therefrom amounted to $1,997. In 1958 there were 371 tons of freight handled, and the revenue was $2,410. In 1959 the revenue from 444 tons of freight amounted to $5,499.

For the first nine months of 1960, the total branch-line revenue amounted to $168,216, the branch-line expenses were $76,605, and the net branch-line operating revenue was $91,611. The net revenue to the system for freight handled over the branch line amounted to $2,704, and the net return to the system from branch-line operations amounted to $94,315.

From time to time, applicant has, by license or agreement, permitted individuals to use the tracks. People having property located at points on or near the tracks have been allowed to operate small motorized vehicles over the tracks for limited purposes. Applicant considers that the agreements are a matter of private contract between it and the individuals concerned and that they are without significance insofar as the issues involved in the instant proceeding are concerned.

With respect to passenger service, applicant asserts that the line provides no service whatever to that segment of the public residing in the area and that the motor-bus service provided to and from points along its line is more than adequate to meet the needs of the public traveling to and from the area. It alleges that the only use to be made of the line in the transportation of passengers is as a mere tourist attraction, appealing to those seeking the novel and unique experience of riding on a narrow-gauge railroad but having no relation to what is considered public convenience and necessity. It admits that the potential for the continuation of this type of patronage is good; that, by leaving off the freight cars presently handled, one or two more coaches could be utilized, thus adding considerably to the revenue earned by the line; and that it reasonably may be expected that the summertime tourist service would continue to be profitable if continued. Applicant considers the service rendered the tourist trade to be a special service for the pleasure of the passengers, rather than a necessity, which it, as a common carrier, has no obligation to provide. It alleges that inasmuch as the public no longer needs the service, public convenience and necessity do not require continuance of the passenger-train operation.

If, however, it is concluded that the passenger service should be continued, applicant then requests that consideration be given to the fact it has entered into an agreement with a newly formed corporation, the Durango-Silverton Railroad Company,[5] whereby said company would purchase the branch line, if abandonment were authorized, and would undertake to render intrastate passenger service to the tourist trade over the line. Applicant recognizes that the charter of the new corporation does not authorize the performance of any freight operations or authorize the corporation to operate in interstate commerce; applicant also recognizes that the abandonment of the line is not authorized. Applicant admits that the sole purpose of the instant application is to free it from the obligation presently imposed upon it as a common carrier to serve the line, and it asserts that it is willing to lose all the net revenue now accruing to the system from the branch line in order to be relieved of all its responsibilities toward the line.

Protestants assert that applicant had no right to limit its service in the manner described without first obtaining appropriate authority from the Interstate Commerce Commission and the Colorado Public Utilities Commission, and they contend that applicant's act in so limiting its service was, in legal effect, an actual abandonment of the line without authority. They argue that applicant, having committed an illegal act, cannot now rely on it in any way to establish justification for the abandonment but, instead, must rely on the situation as it now exists, which, they assert, shows the line to be profitable and necessary in the movement of both freight and passenger traffic. They contend that no burden is imposed upon interstate commerce by the line and that the best interests of applicant will be served by requiring operations to be continued.

In brief, applicant concedes that operation of the line as it is

[5] A group of local businessmen who organized a corporation for the purpose of purchasing the Silverton Branch (if abandonment was authorized) and operating it as a tourist attraction.

presently conducted, and if rehabilitation is not required for year-round service, is not a burden on interstate commerce.

Highway 550 is approximately parallel to the railroad between Durango and Silverton. It is a paved, all-weather highway and is one of the principal north-south highways in western Colorado.

Rio Grande Motor Way provides daily (except Saturday and Sunday) common-carrier service by motor vehicle, transporting general commodities, with certain exceptions, in interstate and intrastate commerce between Durango and Silverton as a part of its through truck service over Highway 550 and other highways between Durango, Silverton, Ridgeway, Montrose, and Grand Junction, Colorado, and other points. Continental Trailways Bus System operates one bus schedule daily in each direction between Durango and Silverton over Highway 550 as part of its scheduled interstate service.

Occasionally truck and bus operations are interrupted because of weather conditions on the highway between Durango and Silverton. These interruptions, however, occur rarely and usually do not continue for more than one day at a time. Although most of the populated areas between Durango and Silverton are provided transportation service over Highway 550, between those towns there are portions of the canyon area that are not served by any motor carrier.

As mining operations in the Silverton area declined and as other means of transportation became available, the need for freight service over the branch line declined. By 1953 all mining operations in the Silverton area had terminated, and those mines which had formerly transported their ore from another mining district to Silverton for movement over the branch to Durango had begun transporting their concentrates by truck to a smelter at Leadville or to applicant's standard-gauge railhead at Montrose. Except for one 40-ton car of zinc ore transported in 1957, no ore or concentrates moved over the branch from 1953 to 1959. In 1960, there was renewed interest in mining operations at certain points along the branch, especially in the Silverton area, and one mining company became actively engaged in performing the preliminary work incident to placing one or more mines into production. This company does not intend, however, to utilize the branch line for the transportation of its ore and concentrates, but will transport its shipments by truck to applicant's railhead at Montrose.

There are other companies and individuals who own mining claims along the branch and who desire to institute production operations. The record does not indicate, however, when production at any of these claims may be expected to commence.

Although numerous shipments of livestock used to be transported over the branch line, such movements have now practically ceased. In former years applicant provided convenient service for shippers of livestock and furnished adequate loading and unloading facilities for such movements. When the service was no longer convenient and when the needs of the shippers and the loading and unloading facilities on the branch either were eliminated or, because of lack of repairs, became unusable, most of the livestock shippers found it necessary to use other means of moving their livestock to and from the feeding ranges in the area served by the branch.

In 1957, the only shipments of livestock were three carloads of cattle that moved between points on the branch and other points on applicant's system. In 1958, the livestock shipments consisted of fifteen carloads of sheep that moved to or from points on the branch. In 1959, the only livestock transported over the line consisted of two carloads of cattle and calves. No livestock was handled over the line in the period during 1960 when operations were performed.

Applicant takes the position that the transportation needs of the area are adequately served by the truck and bus service presently available therein and that, in view of the insubstantial use being made of the branch line, there no longer is any need for its continued operation.

A total of twenty-five witnesses appeared in opposition to applicant's proposal. With respect to the passenger service provided over the line, the executive director of the Colorado State Advertising and Publicity Department described the numerous activities of the state in publicizing the branch line throughout the United States and the favorable results flowing therefrom. He stressed the economic benefits accruing to the communities involved and to the state from the large number of tourists who came to Durango each year to ride the train and enjoy the scenic beauty of the area. The branch line has now become one of the most important tourist attractions in Colorado. Not only does the state of Colorado consider that the interests of the tourists are served by the operation of the train, but it also considers the continued operation of the service to be of the extreme importance to the welfare of all residents of southwestern Colorado.

Applicant's passenger traffic manager, who was one of the officers of the Colorado Visitors' Bureau, testified, pursuant to subpoena, that it is the policy of the bureau to encourage tourists to visit various attractions in Colorado, including the narrow-gauge line here considered, and that the bureau's efforts had been very successful. He expressed the view that, to the extent that tourists come to Durango to ride on the train, the needs of the public were thereby served.

The Chambers of Commerce of Durango and Silverton and officials and businessmen in Silverton consider the passenger service provided over the branch to be essential to the economic well-being of these towns and of the surrounding communities. Several business establishments in Silverton are dependent almost entirely upon the trade from the tourists riding the trains, and all businesses in the town also derive substantial benefits therefrom.

Protestants contend that by virtue of the very substantial demand that exists for passenger service over the line, it must be concluded that its continuance is required by public convenience and necessity.

With respect to the freight service provided over the line, protestants refer to the fact that there are certain areas on the line which are not accessible by motor vehicle and which can be served only by the branch line. They also point to certain mines and mining properties along the line which are not now producing ore but which the owners are endeavoring to place in production. They assert that the value of these properties would be reduced by the elimination of the only transportation services available.

At present there is approximately 47 million board feet of commercial timber in the Elk Park area of the national forest available for cutting, and the branch line affords the only means available for transporting a large portion of that timber out of the area. The United States Forest Service, however, has not authorized cutting that timber or indicated that such authorization may be given.

Protestants refer to the fact that Rio Grande Motor Way is not authorized to transport all types of freight between Durango and Silverton and that it is not physically possible for it to serve certain points in the canyon area that are served by the branch line. They therefore assert that this establishes that the needs of the communities involved and of the public can be adequately served only by the continuance of the freight service provided by applicant.

Several sheep raisers testified to a need for freight service in the movement of sheep to and from the summer range areas in the national forest near Silverton. Because of a lack of convenient service and adequate loading and unloading facilities on the line, most of the sheep raisers in the area have not utilized applicant's service for the movement of their sheep for a number of years. Instead, they have utilized truck service or have "trailed" their sheep to and from the summer ranges. Trailing involves walking the sheep along the highway through the national forest to the range areas. Each spring the sheep are moved into the national forest near Silverton, and they are then moved out in the early fall. Approximately six days are consumed in trailing the sheep between Durango and Silverton.

Sheep do not readily adapt to travel by motor truck, and for that reason the sheep raisers prefer not to utilize that means of moving their sheep. Furthermore, the truck service that is provided in the area not only is expensive but, many times, is not available when required. As a result, most of the sheep are trailed to and from the summer ranges.

Apparently applicant's freight service from Durango to other points on its lines is utilized by some of the sheep raisers in moving their sheep to market. If adequate and convenient service were provided over the branch and if applicant would provide proper loading and unloading facilities at points along the line, rail service would again be utilized by the sheep raisers opposing abandonment of the line.

The United States forest ranger for the area involved, who appeared under subpoena, testified that consideration is now being given to the imposition of a ban on the trailing of sheep through the national forest to the summer ranges but that no decision had been reached on the matter. If such a ban were imposed, the sheep would be moved either by truck or over applicant's line.

With respect to use of applicant's service for the transportation of livestock, it should be noted that applicant has the obligation of providing service and facilities adequate to meet the needs of the public. If it is found herein that the public convenience and necessity require the continuance of freight service over the line, applicant, of course, would be required to provide service and facilities adequate to meet the needs of the aforementioned shippers of livestock, and any failure on its part to provide such service might, of course, justify appropriate action to obtain the service required.

Certain operators of coal mines in the Durango area opposed the abandonment of the line on the grounds that the service was required for the movement of coal to Silverton. Although some coal is transported over the line each year, the witnesses conceded that truck service is available for the transportation of coal from the mines direct to customers in the Silverton area. One motor carrier at Silverton who was engaged in the delivery of coal from the rail siding in Silverton to consumers in the area testified, however, that he would abandon his motor-truck service if abandonment of the line was authorized.

DISCUSSION QUESTIONS

1. What are the social issues involved in this case?
2. What obligations does the railroad have to the communities it serves?
3. Do the communities involved have any responsibilities to the railroad? If so, what? If not, why not?
4. Was the discontinuance of freight service during the winter months justified?
5. Does the fact that the Denver and Rio Grande operates a truck service have any bearing?
6. If you were the Interstate Commerce Commission hearing examiner, how would you decide this issue? Substantiate your decision.

CASE 4 RODO CATTLE COMPANY [1]

The Rodo Cattle Company is located in the metropolitan suburbs of Pleasantville, a city of over six hundred thousand people in a Western state. The primary business of the Rodo Company is operation of cattle feedlots for fattening cattle for slaughter. Although cattle feedlots have been used for centuries, commercial development of feedlots as a large business operation is fairly new. The Rodo Company is a specialized business of this type. Its cattle pens cover 80 acres and will feed at one time over twenty-five thousand cattle worth several million dollars.

Rodo Company's feedlots are organized into separate pens of about 1 acre each, and modern, laborsaving methods are used throughout its facility. The pens are ringed with concrete feed bunks and water troughs. Feed is mixed from truckload batches in the company's feed mill at the feedlot. Mixed feed flows by gravity to other trucks, which distribute it to the feed bunks. The entire acreage is covered by an overhead water sprinkler system that reduces the amount of manure dust in the dry afternoons; this helps prevent cattle tuberculosis and other lung diseases. The sprinkler system also reduces the drift of dust from the feedlots to neighboring residential properties; however, the lots cannot be kept wet enough to prevent all dust, so there are many complaints from neighbors, as will be discussed later. If too much water is used in dust treatment, muddy conditions develop which increase both neighborhood odor and cattle diseases.

The company regularly sprays its pens to control flies. Its monthly expenditure for insecticide exceeds $300, and both the county health officer and neighbors agree that flies are effectively controlled. Manure in the pens is mechanically handled. After it has accumulated in a pen for several months, it is scraped up by a bulldozer and mechanically loaded into trucks which take it to the edge of the property, where it is stacked in large, flat piles 30 feet high. Portions of this manure are occasionally sold to a processor who pulverizes and bags it for sale to home

[1] All names are disguised.

355

gardeners and farmers. The supply of manure is much greater than the demand for it, so Rodo Company has an inventory of thousands of tons, which is increasing by hundreds of tons annually. The general manager and principal owner of the company, Mr. Jesse Rodo, is not sure what to do with this growing inventory because he is running out of storage space.

The Rodo Company does primarily custom feeding. This means that it accepts on consignment cattle owned by others, and it feeds the cattle until a proper slaughtering condition is reached. The company also feeds a few hundred or thousand cattle on its own account when market conditions are favorable.

The Rodo Company was established sixteen years ago on 120 acres purchased especially for feedlot operation. In the beginning there were pens for only 500 cattle, but its facilities expanded rapidly as the idea of custom feeding became popular with local farmers and business investors. At the time the feedlot was established there were three other feedlots nearby, so the property was already recognized as a stockyard area. The land was rocky and uneven, was located near a river bottom, and was unfit for residential housing. The property was 6 miles from downtown Pleasantville, and the nearest residential developments were 1½ miles away on either side. Pleasantville was toward the west, and a suburban town was toward the southeast.

The other three feedlots in Rodo Company's area have also expanded, until this area now has pens for nearly one hundred thousand cattle. Meanwhile, the Pleasantville metropolitan area has also grown, pushing residential suburbs closer to the stockyard area. One new residential area is within 500 feet of the edge of Rodo's property, and homeowners are complaining loudly about feedlot dust and odors. In fact, the whole stockyard area is surrounded on three sides by residential and commercial developments less than ½ mile away. The municipal stadium is only a mile away, and several fine motels are on the highway about the same distance. The city auditorium, the site of operas and other gala events, is slightly over 2 miles away. On winter evenings when the air settles, an intense odor from the stockyard area sometimes reaches the auditorium at about the time programs begin. This one fact has caused strong protests from several influential Pleasantville people.

The odors and dust produced by a feedlot operation are much different from those of the common farm barnyard. Because of heavy use of the ground (several hundred cattle on 1 acre), the type of odor is much more putrid, and it exists in a stronger concentration than it does on the farm. The foul odor causes nausea and illness in sensitive people. And if the pens are not properly sprayed with water when the cattle are milling about in late afternoon before bedding down for the night, clouds of unpleasant dust, similar to those which arise behind an automobile moving along a dusty road at sundown, cover the neighborhood.

This combination of factors has placed a large segment of the community in conflict with feedlot operators. Residents of the suburb southeast of the Rodo feedlot have organized a Fresh-air Committee, whose purpose is to encourage community action to control air pollution. Committee members include many influential citizens of the suburb. The group holds public meetings, and officers regularly attend city council meetings to offer proposals for feedlot regulation and city prosecution under nuisance laws, since three of the four feedlots now are within the city limits of the suburb. The group is also developing proposed city ordinances for control of feedlot pollution. The group has employed a photographer and a scientist to gather evidence of feedlot pollution, and members are outspoken against the odor and dust derived from feedlots. The committee has proposed that since the cattle feeders cannot or will not do anything about the offensive nature of the feedlots, they should move to a rural area zoned especially for long-run cattle feeding. A local journalist reported the proposal as follows:

> That hero of Western lore, the cattleman, could be headed for a reservation just like his predecessor, the Indian, if a group of unhappy citizens has its way.
>
> The reservation proposal is the brainchild of the Fresh-air Committee and is aimed specifically at cattle-feeding operations in urban areas.
>
> They propose that statewide zoning be initiated by the Legislature to provide a permanent area where cattle and dairy operators can work free from encroachment by residential areas. This zone would be buffered with a 5-mile ring of orchards to protect people against the cows, and vice versa.
>
> The Fresh-air Committee is only one of many groups troubled by the scent of "Corral No. 5" and the dust rising every evening from the community's cattle-feeding operations.
>
> The list of complainants is long. It includes hotel and motel operators, airport authorities, city officials, doctors, health officials, homeowners, and tourists. The airport manager commented: "During the height of the tourist season, the airport receives the full 'benefits' of the stockyards. People get off the plane, and they want to get right back on."

In addition, a few months ago residents of some of the worst fallout areas filed lawsuits against all four cattle companies, alleging that they were maintaining a public nuisance. Some eighty citizens filed suits asking for damages totaling $859,040. The suits allege that stockyard dust settles in homes even when they are closed, requiring more frequent cleaning than in other areas of the community. They complain that use of patios and yards is denied on many evenings, that extra money must be spent for air conditioning and filters to keep odors and dust out of homes, and that home prices have depreciated more than normal. They allege that odor and dust have become worse since they moved into their homes because more cattle are being fed and larger piles of manure are accumulating. Some also allege nausea and bronchial difficulties caused by the nuisances. One of the complainants, speaking to a reporter, warned persons interested in buying a home in the area not to close the sale in the daytime. "All the people around here bought their houses during the daytime, when the dust and odor do not settle so badly," the complainant said. "The real estate people either evade the subject or ignore it when they're selling a house."

The lawyer who represented most of the complainants in their lawsuits made the following comment to a reporter: "We don't mind the stockyards, but we do mind the dust and odor. The basic legal question as I see it is the right of habitation or the right of agriculture. I believe that human habitation is superior to that of livestock."

Meanwhile, the Citizens' Council for Beautification of Pleasantville was taking an interest in the feedlot problem. The council is a civic committee appointed by the mayor to coordinate work of all voluntary groups seeking to make the metropolitan area a more beautiful, cultured, and pleasant place to live. The council was particularly concerned because feedlots caused a large blighted area on the edge of town, several distinguished visitors had inquired about the odor when alighting at the airport, several cultural events at the city auditorium and other locations had been made unpleasant by stockyard odor, and a number of residents had complained. In fact, some businesses on the highway were so affected by the feedlots that their managers were writing letters to anyone who would heed them. Some dispatched letters to their United States senators and representatives. They also complained to the county health officer, but at one of the council meetings he told the group that his office had investigated the feedlots and was convinced that neither their dust nor their odor constituted a health hazard to citizens.

Jesse Rodo became embroiled in the feedlot controversy in two ways. First, as owner and manager of Rodo Cattle Company, he was the object of lawsuits (which included both the corporation and its manager in each complaint), and he was under pressure to move his feedlot or take corrective action, which would be expensive. Second, he was at this time serving a three-year term as president of the Cattle Feeders' Association, which was the trade association of the feedlot operators. The association was working hard to offset unfavorable publicity which feedlots were receiving.

Several years ago, when complaints first started to develop, the Cattle Feeders' Association took the position that the feedlot operators were there first; hence, anyone who built a home or business in the area did so at his own peril. As one operator stated: "An age-old concept in common law is 'Let the buyer beware.' It is the buyer's legal duty to be aware of environmental conditions which might affect his home or business prior to investing in it. The feedlots should not be blamed because people insist on moving closer to them."

This argument reduced complaints and probably would have worked for the long run, except that the feedlots continued to expand their facilities and pile their refuse. The result was that people who originally built in an odor-free and dust-free neighborhood soon found that these nuisances were reaching their neighborhood also. Then, when the Fresh-air Committee entered the controversy, its officials reported legal opinion that prior occupancy of the area did not give feedlots an easement to inflict obnoxious dust and odor on adjoining property. In other words, adjoining property owners had just as much right to use their property freely as the feedlot owners had to use theirs.

At about this time Rodo became president of the association, and he persuaded members to hire a public relations firm to improve the feedlot's public image. The firm recommended emphasis on the economic benefits of feedlots to the state. This approach gained support of operators outside the Pleasantville area because some of them were beginning to receive complaints from their neighbors also; however, nearly half the state's feedlots were in the Pleasantville area. The public relations firm prepared news releases for mailing to all papers in the state at least once a month extolling the economic virtues of feedlots. Releases reported that during the last year nearly 150 million dollars' worth of cattle were sold out of feedlots in the state. In terms of dollar value this was the second largest agricultural product in the state. Fresh-air Committee officials countered this argument by reporting that tourism brought 400 million dollars to the state and that urban feedlots were driving away tourists.

Another publicity release explained that the feedlot industry provided employment for over one thousand persons and had invested over 40 million dollars in land and equipment. Rodo and the public relations firm also persuaded leading feedlot operators to prepare speeches and seek speaking invitations to luncheon clubs and other meetings.

The number of complaints did not diminish, so association officials persuaded a number of the worst offenders to experiment with spraying a masking agent (offsetting perfume) in their lots daily. In most cases the cattle odor and masking odor seemed to combine to produce a third odor as obnoxious as the original one. In fact, the new odor aroused additional complainants not aroused by the original odor.

As a result of the failures mentioned, the Fresh-air Committee continued to gain strength and worked with the city council of the suburb where Rodo Company's pens were located to develop a stringent ordinance regulating feedlots. The ordinance required operators to remove all organic refuse at least once a week and to haul it outside the city limits entirely. The feedlot operators felt that compliance with this ordinance would be expensive and unduly restrictive; therefore, they proposed a program of self-regulation to the city council. They offered to use masking agents and sprinkler systems and to remove refuse twice a year. The council "took the proposal under advisement" and continued with its plans for an ordinance.

The council's action caused feedlot operators throughout the state to become concerned that each city might set up its own special ordinance for feedlots. Differences in ordinances might cause cost variations which would upset competitive conditions. Feeding costs now were about equal throughout the state, but a local ordinance might increase costs in one city, driving a feedlot's customers to another lot and eventually driving the feedlot from the city. One influential operator proposed that the association go to the State Legislature, which was then in session, and request a law requiring nuisance regulation by the State Livestock Sanitary Board. Since the board consisted mostly of cattlemen, this approach would put them in the position of regulating themselves; therefore, regulations could be kept reasonable. Another operator said he would move his feedlot from the state if the state law was passed.

Rodo decided to call a statewide meeting of the entire association membership to decide what the next move should be. He knew that a strong plea would be made for the law requiring regulation by the Livestock Sanitary Board. He also knew that association members were looking to him for leadership, but he was not sure what to propose next. He was further confused by the situation with his own company. He owned land elsewhere in the state and was about ready to move his feedlot from the Pleasantville area; however, whenever he hinted to other operators that a move might occur, they strongly objected. They said that all feedlot operators must "stick together and not retreat at this time." They felt that if one feedlot left, it would be an "admission of guilt" and would make it necessary for the other lots to move in a short time.

DISCUSSION QUESTIONS

1. In Rodo's role as president of the Cattle Feeders' Association, prepare his speech to the association recommending a particular course of action. Give reasons for the action chosen.

2. In the role of a local manufacturing executive not personally bothered by feedlot nuisances, give your analysis of the situation and proposed course of action.

3. In Rodo's role as general manager and principal owner of Rodo Cattle Company, appraise the question of whether you should move your feedlot in the near future. What issues are key ones in making your decision?

4. What was the extent of the social responsibility of the suburban feedlots in this case? Does this responsibility differ from the legal obligation?

5. Appraise the usefulness of the courses of action which the Cattle Feeders' Association took to reduce complaints about feedlot operations.

CASE 5 SOLO RUBBER COMPANY [1]

The Solo Rubber Company is the second largest tire and rubber manufacturer in the United States. Although its headquarters remain in Akron, Ohio, where it was founded, it is an international company whose operations extend around the world. It owns rubber plantations and factories in several nations, and its products are sold in all major countries of the free world. It is widely diversified into rubber, chemicals, merchandising centers, and allied products. Sales and assets exceeded 1 billion dollars each in 1964.

On April 15, 1965, Mr. Dick Smith, president, discussed with his executive committee a decision which had come to be called the "Romanian deal" within the company. For several months it had generated vigorous discussion within the executive committee. The Romanian deal concerned efforts of Romania, a Communist satellite, to purchase in the United States for installation in Romania a full-scale synthetic rubber plant. The plant which the Romanians desired to purchase used confidential production processes not yet publicly known.

President Smith reported to the executive committee that two days ago in Romania a Solo Rubber negotiating team had signed a preliminary contract with Romanian officials for a 45-million-dollar plant. Solo was to do a "turn-key" job, meaning that it would design and build the entire plant, delivering it to the Romanians in operating condition. The contract also called for Solo to train Romanian operators and keep the plant in operating condition for one year after it began producing.

President Smith reported that the contract should provide a profit of several million dollars to Solo Rubber Company, for the Romanians were eager to have the plant and had been willing to pay a generous price. He then commented:

"This preliminary contract specifies that it is subject to final approval by higher Romanian government officials and by Solo management in

[1] The Solo Company and its officers are fictitious, but the problems with which the company deals are real.

361

our Akron headquarters. We are now going to have to decide once and for all time whether we want to go through with this deal. As our earlier discussions have pointed out, the Romanian deal does have both favorable and unfavorable aspects. It is much more than a strictly commercial transaction because it involves grave questions of business social responsibility, public policy, and international relations.

"Newspaper releases correctly point out that this is the first time private American industry has contracted directly with a Communist nation since World War II. We must be sure before we proceed with this historic contract. I am therefore appointing a subcommittee of this group to review the whole situation and present their recommendation to this group two weeks from today. For ready reference the subcommittee should include a summary of all reasons for and against this contract, giving particular attention to our public responsibilities. The subcommittee will consist of John Dye [director of marketing], chairman; Roger Slade [director of research and development]; and Samuel Ratliff [director of public relations]. The subcommittee's report and our decision two weeks from today will then be presented to our next board meeting for ratification."

President Smith then moved on to other matters before the executive committee. He did not invite further discussion of the Romanian deal because it had already been thoroughly discussed at several earlier meetings. The events which led to the preliminary contract signed in Romania were rather complex. It seemed to President Smith that because this was a new situation, not previously faced by American industry, Solo Company had drifted gradually into the Romanian deal without any understanding of what might develop.

The Romanian deal began in the spring of 1964, when a Romanian delegation visited the United States and toured some industrial facilities. They were particularly interested in rubber and chemical plants. At that time they visited the Goodyear Tire and Rubber Company's polyisoprene rubber plant in Beaumont, Texas. They were not permitted in the plant, but were driven around it. In the summer of 1964 Romanian officials held trade negotiations with United States government officials in Washington. An interagency committee, which included representatives from the State Department and the Defense Department, studied the question of trade with Romania to determine whether it would conflict with the security of the United States. At the conclusion of the meeting, Ambassador Averell Harriman and Gheorgho Gaston-Marin, vice-chairman of the Council of Ministers of Romania, issued a joint statement. It said that the United States had agreed to issue export licenses to Romania for a number of industrial facilities, including those in the petrochemical field.

The reported reason behind the government's approval of these export licenses was that the creation of greater economic ties between the

United States and Romania would encourage the Romanians to be more independent of the Soviet Union.

Shortly after the export licenses were approved, Romanian trade officials contacted the Goodyear Tire and Rubber Company, whose plant they had visited in Beaumont, Texas. They wanted to purchase an exact duplicate of its polyisoprene facilities at Beaumont, complete with the processes, machinery, and technicians to run it.

Early in October, Goodyear withdrew from further negotiations. Board Chairman Russell DeYoung wrote Secretary Rusk of the State Department that Goodyear was withdrawing because the company felt it was not in the "best interests of the United States" to sell this type of plant to a Communist nation.

A company house organ, the *Goodyear Triangle*, later explained the company's decision as follows:

> Goodyear feels that the dangers far outweigh the possible benefits in the proposed deal. For that reason Goodyear has no intention of being a party to it.
>
> Why is Goodyear so opposed to the transaction?
>
> Because we foresee the knowledge that [what] Romania seeks to purchase from the United States [may be used by Romania or another Communist nation] in the potential role of an international agitator, we don't believe that the United States should allow any Communist nation to acquire the know-how to produce a synthetic rubber which competes head-on with natural rubber.
>
> And that's what Natsyn—Goodyear's polyisoprene—does. As you know, Natsyn is a duplication of natural rubber, offering natural's many desirable qualities that have eluded duplication in all other manmade rubbers.
>
> *While synthetic and natural rubber are now competitively priced, Goodyear believes the Communists could—if they wished—disrupt natural rubber markets in Malaysia, Liberia, and other so-called underdeveloped countries. The Communists are not governed by marketing conditions in setting their prices and in the past have, in fact, used cut-rate prices as an economic club* [italics in original].
>
> The State Department, in commenting on the situation, has said that the Romanians have assured the United States that they won't divulge the polyisoprene secrets they purchase from us to other Communist nations. With due respect for the State Department's belief in the Romanians' promise, Goodyear would prefer not to entrust its production secrets to the Communists.
>
> What's to keep the Romanians from passing techniques developed in the Goodyear Research Laboratory on Goodyear Boulevard to Communist production geniuses in Moscow or Peiping? The why's and wherefore's of Natsyn might make an interesting "I'll trade you . . ." tool for the Romanians.

With regard to Goodyear's concern about Communist manipulation of rubber markets, F. D. Hockersmith, director of the Office of Export Control in Washington, acknowledged in the *Akron Beacon Journal,* on October 23, 1964, that this was "something that could be done." But he observed that since other rubbers compete with natural rubber, the Communists could not be stopped by Goodyear's refusal to sell them a polyisoprene plant if they really wanted to upset the world market. He said that government policy in dealing with Communist countries is ". . . to permit trade in non-strategic items where there is no threat to the national security and welfare." In this particular case, the Federal government had approved the sale of the plant to Romania.

At the time the Goodyear decision was made, details were withheld because of possible effects on the forthcoming November national presidential election in the United States. Philip Meyer, Washington correspondent for the *Akron Beacon Journal,* commented in the issue of October 24, 1964:

> Goodyear officials have a reason for soft-pedaling their objections to selling a synthetic rubber process to Romania.
>
> They are afraid the question might get embroiled in the political campaign. It is a fear shared by officials in the State Dept., and other Government agencies.
>
> Both Goodyear and the State Dept. have declined to make public the contents of a letter from Board Chairman Russell DeYoung to Secretary Rusk early this month, but its general theme has leaked out.
>
> Basically, the company's position—which it confirms—is that a technical process developed only after great expenditure of time and money should not be sold to Communists.

Meyer went on to explain that State Department policy favored trade with Communist satellites to encourage independence from Russian influence but that conservatives opposed industrial trade with Communists; therefore, the conservative presidential candidate might be able to use the Goodyear letter to say, "Here is an example of private industry making a financial sacrifice in order to take the firm position on Communism which the State Dept. refuses to take."

Following their rejection by Goodyear, Romanian officials contacted the Solo Rubber Company. Since Solo lacked know-how with polyisoprene rubber, the Romanians asked it to build them a copolymer styrenebutadiene rubber plant. Although this rubber lacked the exact characteristics of natural rubber, it blended well with natural rubber, and Solo Company's advanced know-how involved some secret processes. Romanian officials noted that they had arranged for commercial credit to finance the purchase, with the credit being guaranteed by the United States Export-Import Bank, so they were ready to make the purchase immediately for cash.

Since the sale was approved by the State Department and credit was guaranteed by the Federal government, Solo officials felt they could hardly refuse preliminary negotiations with officials of the Romanian government. They felt that a preliminary refusal would be an affront to the Romanians, since the Romanians were initiating contact with the approval of the United States government. Solo officials knew, however, that their final decision would be difficult because of the volatile issues involved.

The first time the executive committee discussed the Romanian deal, several strong views were expressed. The vice-president for international operations reported that anti-Communist feeling was very strong in some of the company's foreign markets. Part of this opposition was organized, and company products could be boycotted if the company finally made a sale to Romania. Another committee member mentioned the reasons Goodyear gave for stopping negotiations and said that these reasons also applied to Solo Rubber Company. But another member pointed out that the rubber produced by the Solo plant was not an exact substitute for natural rubber, so the decision Solo Company faced was not quite the same as the one Goodyear faced.

Another member stated that Solo Company was not engaged in international relations; consequently, whatever the United States government approved, Solo Company should feel free to do. The director of industrial relations insisted, however, that the limits of law or government policy are not necessarily the *best* public conduct for a corporation. These limits set the extremes to which a company can go, he said, but usually the best action is somewhat short of the extreme permitted.

The treasurer pointed out that Communists are unalterably opposed to private industry and that this view was confirmed by the fact that the Romanians were government officials seeking to set up a *government* plant. For the stockholders' sake, he said, Solo Rubber should not help a group which sought to abolish their way of life. But another member explained that the Romanian people should be free to make their own choice of industrial organization without interference from Solo Rubber. Another member, however, argued that the Romanians' choice of communism in the beginning was not a free choice; therefore, any support at this time would simply give a stamp of approval to the original tyranny.

One committee member, a strong humanist in philosophy, said that Solo Company must help the Romanians because they are human beings who need rubber as much as any other human beings do. He announced that no human being can refuse to help another human being for any reason. A Ph.D. scientist, another strong humanist, took an opposite view. He philosophized that he loved the Romanian people as he loved his own brother but that the pending decision concerned support of the Romanian government, not help for the people. To strengthen the government would strengthen oppression of human beings and would in the long run be antihumanistic. As long as communism supported dictatorship and emphasized the state above the person, a humanist could not support the government, regardless of how much concern he had for its people.

Then the committee returned to what one member called "good business" and discussed how the Romanian deal would affect other sales. Three members pointed to the favorable publicity received by Goodyear and argued that Solo's sales and earnings would improve if the Romanian deal were rejected. The treasurer observed that, assuming a normal 5 percent net profit on sales, 100 million dollars in new sales would be required to replace the net profit of 5 million dollars expected from the Romanian deal. He doubted that sales could increase that much. He predicted that any tendency for increased sales as a result of favorable publicity would be offset by rejection of company products by those who objected to the company's decision.

During the next several months, discussion of the Romanian deal took a total of six hours in the weekly meetings of the executive committee. Two staff reports on the subject were heard and discussed. After each report, committee views seemed about evenly divided, so Romanian negotiations were continued, since there was no clear reason to stop them. Finally, the preliminary agreement was signed in Bucharest, and Solo Rubber Company faced its decision "once and for all time," as the president had mentioned at the committee meeting of April 15, 1965.

John Dye, director of marketing and chairman of the final subcommittee to study the Romanian deal, walked from the committee room wondering how he should go about preparing his subcommittee report in the two weeks of time that remained.

DISCUSSION QUESTIONS

1. In the role of John Dye, prepare a detailed plan for your subcommittee's action during the next two weeks. Then prepare the subcommittee report as you think it should be prepared.

2. Comment on President Smith's decision to let the executive committee decide on the Romanian deal and the board of directors ratify it, rather than making the decision himself as head of the enterprise.

3. Discuss from all angles the Goodyear decision made earlier and appraise its correctness.

4. Discuss and appraise Goodyear's desire to soft-pedal its decision until after the national presidential election. Discuss and appraise the similar desire of Federal government officials.

5. Is it really necessary or desirable for the Solo executive committee to concern itself with the social, political, and international aspects of the Romanian deal? Should they not confine themselves to whatever is "good business," that is, with what is reasonably profitable and within the law?

CASE 6 WAGNER CHEMICAL COMPANY

The Wagner Chemical Company was founded by Charles E. Wagner in Newark, New Jersey, in 1933, when the chemical industry was beginning to gain industrial prominence. Mr. Wagner, president and general manager, graduated from college summa cum laude in chemistry. He later received his Ph.D. in chemistry from one of the country's outstanding universities.

He began his career with du Pont as a research chemist working on applied research, where his achievements were recognized as outstanding. However, his desire was to perform pure rather than applied research. Subsequently, he left du Pont, and with the aid of money borrowed from his father, started what is now the Wagner Chemical Company. Because of his spirit of adventure, creativity, and fresh approach to complicated industrial chemical problems, his company soon became successful. Creativity became the watchword of Wagner Chemical and still remains today as one of the company's major objectives.

Some outstanding discoveries in the fields of synthetics, drugs, vitamins, pesticides, insecticides, and fertilizers were patented and contributed heavily to the early success of the enterprise. In the period just prior to World War II and during the war, top-secret work was done for the United States government. The most important contribution to the war effort was the work done in the area of gaseous diffusion used to separate uranium-235 from uranium-238.

Present Situation. The company is presently engaged in research and manufacture of a highly diversified line of products for home and industry. It ranks among the top fifteen chemical and drug companies, with an annual gross income in excess of 150 million dollars. Mr. Wagner has always surrounded himself with competent and respected businessmen and hired the finest chemical minds available. His director of research is John Gordon, a respected chemist, who is well known throughout the world for his knowledge, ability, and creativity.

Competition in the chemical industry is extremely severe, and the

367

heart of any leading company is in its research department. Finding and developing new products is essential, and to accomplish this, Wagner Chemical is constantly engaged in both pure and applied research.

Heavy emphasis on research in the chemical industries causes rapid change and product obsolescence. In order to survive and prosper in this highly competitive industry, firms find it necessary to allocate a much higher percentage of gross sales to research than most other manufacturing industries.

Wagner's Philosophies. Mr. Wagner and Mr. Gordon share the philosophy that no expense restrictions should be put on the scientists who are engaged in pure research. The budget for this activity is generous, and some scientists are performing revolutionary experiments without regard for any ultimate financial return.

Relatively low earnings of the company reflect the large sums spent on research. However, since leading stockholders lack unity and organization, no restrictions have been placed on research expenditures. The board of directors, in conjunction with Wagner, also contribute a reasonable percentage of the earnings to hospitals, community service centers, universities, the Red Cross, and other charities.

In justifying large research expenditures at the last annual meeting, Mr. Wagner expressed the belief that: "In my judgment, contributions and research are in the stockholders' best interest because they help retain public goodwill." He further pointed out that these expenditures are encouraged by tax laws, sustained by the courts and legislatures, and endorsed by the public.

The Research Department. The research department has been a major department since the corporation was founded. Mr. Wagner has always inspired his scientists and chemists to be creative and has been financially generous in order to obtain the best personnel available.

He hired Mr. Gordon shortly before World War II and found him to be an ideal man to head the research department. During his association with Wagner Chemical, Gordon has discovered and improved a vast number of new products and has written numerous papers for the Manufacturing Chemists Association. Under his direction, the company has greatly diversified its product line and has steadily improved its image in the industry. Among the new and diversified products which Wagner Chemical has been actively working on are pesticides and insecticides.

Pesticides and insecticides and their use have recently attracted wide public attention. Growing concern over the harm which these products do to human beings, fish, and wildlife has been accentuated by the book *Silent Spring*, by Rachel Carson. In addition, the Department of Agriculture, the Food and Drug Administration, the United

States Wildlife Bureau, and the Surgeon General have been reviewing the effects of these poisons. Several conclusions have been drawn from their studies. It is generally agreed that poisons do accumulate on the food people eat and that men, plants, and animals may be damaged by this accumulation; however, the long-range effects of pesticides are not known. On the positive side, it is further agreed that the yield of crops is higher, that the quality of the harvested product is better, and that insect control is necessary for human health.

Mr. Wagner's Problem. Mr. Wagner is a rational businessman. He is aware of the dangers of pesticides, and he is also aware that agricultural producers need them and that cities need weed and insect control.

The Department of Agriculture and the Food and Drug Administration have set standards concerning the maximum amount of poison allowable on food, and producers of pesticides must conform to these standards. These government agencies have been satisfied with the results obtained with the use of insecticides, but admit that they are not certain what long-range effects they may have. The Surgeon General has also voiced concern over the unknown harmful side effects of the use of these poisons.

The U.S. Wildlife Bureau has been studying the birth rate, the death rate, fertility, and changes in species of birds and other wildlife; they have found changes, but they cannot be certain of their causes or of how extensive the changes really are. There is also growing concern over water pollution due to pesticides and the harm it causes to fish and animals.

Mr. Wagner has had several meetings with his competitors, heads of government agencies, and personnel in his research department. He has authorized additional funds for research to be used to eliminate or reduce the harmful effects his products have.

There are other dimensions to the problem. Certain insects become immune to insecticides, and this increases the need for stronger poisons or new products. The cost of research is already high in the industry, and stockholders want higher dividends and less research expenditure.

Mr. Gordon has made speeches and written papers saying that the problem has been blown out of proportion by the book *Silent Spring* and that insecticides and pesticides produced by Wagner Chemical conform to government and company standards. He adds that to discontinue their use would endanger the health of the nation and cause a food shortage. He further contends that the real cause of harm to wildlife is *misuse* of the products and use of them too close to water and game reserves.

Mr. Wagner has evaluated his problem and finds that over one-third of his company's income is derived from insecticide and pesticide sales. He is convinced that his products conform to government standards, but he does not want to be responsible for the death of wildlife, pollution of streams, or possible damage to human beings.

He must also face pressures from stockholders to reduce research expenditure, from competition to keep costs down in order to get his share of the market, and from the public to make his products safe for general use. He cannot ignore these pressures.

Any research into the long-range effects upon plant and animal life is an extensive, formidable undertaking, and there is little chance of obtaining conclusive answers. He knows that competition would take over if he discontinued producing insecticides and pesticides. He feels that he is filling a need by producing them. Mr. Wagner wonders what he should do.

DISCUSSION QUESTIONS

1. Should Mr. Wagner increase expenditures for research? What kinds of research? How could he justify his choice of action?

2. Is Wagner Chemical Company responsible for damage to fish and wildlife by its chemicals? If not, who is?

3. To what extent should Mr. Wagner feel responsible for effects on human beings of his company's pesticides and insecticides?

4. Evaluate the arguments Mr. Wagner has been using in his speeches.

APPENDIXES

APPENDIX A FINAL REPORT OF

THE BOARD OF ADVICE,

WESTINGHOUSE ELECTRIC

CORPORATION [1]

Mark W. Cresap, Jr., Esq., *President*,
Westinghouse Electric Corporation,
Pittsburgh, Pennsylvania.

Dear Sir:

In the spring of 1961, the undersigned were requested by Westinghouse Electric Corporation to serve as members of an advisory group, or Board of Advice, to the management in reviewing and appraising the procedures adopted by the Corporation to assure future compliance with the antitrust laws and with high standards of business conduct.

On October 16, 1961, we made an interim report which contained a statement of our understanding with the management as to the scope of the responsibilities of the Board of Advice and of the management, respectively. It recapitulated our meetings to the date of that report with representatives of management and listed the presentations made, data supplied and, generally, the matters discussed and questions considered. For convenience, a copy of our interim report is attached hereto as Exhibit A. Since our interim report we have had further meetings with representatives of management, as described below. We fully agree with the suggestion of the management that the time has come when it is appropriate to summarize our views as to the existing procedures and further plans of the management and to submit this final report, as follows:

1. In the light of the activities described in the indictments and com-

---

[1] "A Report from the Board of Advice to Westinghouse Electric Corporation," Pittsburgh, Pa.: Westinghouse Electric Corporation, 1962, pp. 5–12. Used with permission. The "Exhibit A" mentioned has been omitted.

plaints in the criminal and companion civil actions instituted by the Department of Justice during 1960 in the Federal Court in Philadelphia against members of the electrical equipment manufacturing industry, including Westinghouse, the immediate and basic problem with which the management had to cope, and with respect to which our advice and counsel had originally been sought, was the establishment of a more comprehensive educational and enforcement program which would prevent the occurrence of any such activities in the future. Management recognized that, although those activities were contrary to established Westinghouse policy, a vigorous enforcement program coupled with an intensified educational program—and the wholehearted support of the entire organization—were necessary too attain the desired results.

2. The Corporation's problem is complex. In general, the Corporation manufactures and sells apparatus and appliances for the generation, transmission, utilization and control of electricity. It is the second largest producer of such equipment in the United States. The Corporation is organized into a number of basic product groups. It has about 109,000 employees. Approximately 1,650 of its employees have pricing and marketing responsibility and are located at numerous plants and sales offices throughout the United States. The Corporation's product mix runs from heavy electrical equipment and defense and atomic projects to various electrical devices used in the home—in all some 8,000 basic products, with about 300,000 variations. Many of these products and product groups are sold in distinct economic markets, in competition with like products offered by rivals widely different, in many of those markets, in number, economic strength, and market policy. Moreover, the Company's product mix—as wide and varied as it is—is constantly changing as a result of research and innovation. Accordingly, although Westinghouse is the second largest producer of electrical equipment in the United States, its relative position as to particular products and product lines in particular markets varies considerably. It is subject to varying degrees of competition within the various markets and its competitors in any given product or product line may provide substantially more or less of the supply in the market than it does.

At the same time the distribution channels and the sales outlets through which the Corporation sells its products are as varied as the products. Westinghouse sells directly to municipal, state and federal governments, to public utilities, to manufacturers, to distributors, to dealers and directly to consumers.

In short, the Corporation is continually confronted with virtually every economic and antitrust and trade regulation problem which a business enterprise can encounter. Moreover, because the Corporation sells throughout the United States and abroad and functions through a host of employees, communication and control are an indispensable feature of its efforts to implement corporate policy. Constant alertness is needed to identify problems as they may arise.

3. During the grand jury investigations that led to the Philadelphia cases, and before any indictments were handed down, the management of the Corporation undertook to impress upon those officers and employees of the Corporation with pricing and marketing authority a personal sense of respon-

sibility for compliance with the letter and the spirit of the antitrust and trade regulation laws. At a meeting of the Management Council in Absecon, New Jersey, on February 2, 1960, the President reiterated the policy of the Corporation to comply with the antitrust laws. A new Management Guide was read to that meeting which stated in part: "It is the policy of Westinghouse to comply fully with all laws governing its operations and to conduct its affairs in keeping with the highest moral, legal and ethical standards." At that meeting the President made it clear that any *per se* violation of the antitrust laws would be considered an act of disloyalty to the Corporation.

4. The reiteration of that policy has been carried down the chain of command through policy directives, letters, memoranda and a continuing series of personal conferences on all levels. Further, the Company has sought to strengthen the management's sense of personal responsibility by broadening the general understanding of the antitrust and trade regulation laws through a more comprehensive educational program at all levels addressed to explaining those laws and their applicability to many of the Company's day-to-day marketing problems.

An Antitrust Section was established in the Law Department to serve management in carrying out their responsibilities. The Antitrust Section has conducted a continuing educational program which during the last 14 months directly reached 10,000 management persons and which is designed to review the antitrust compliance program at least once a year with every person in Westinghouse who has pricing or marketing responsibility. The President has added his authority to this program by personal addresses to a large number of groups of supervisory personnel. At the same time, the Antitrust Section regularly reviews the activities of those persons to ensure that they understand and are applying the lessons they have learned to particular transactions. Its duties include independent investigations in areas where it deems such action advisable to prevent tendencies that could lead to violations.

A policy has been established regarding the participation of Westinghouse employees in industry activities and trade association meetings, limiting such participation to strictly business sessions under proper auspices.

A system of certificates from those who determine prices and those who supervise such functions, and a like system requiring reports on all contacts with corresponding personnel in competitors' organizations, have been established.

Finally, a definite enforcement program has been promulgated providing for punishment for violations, including dismissal in serious cases.

5. Since our interim report we have had an opportunity, as a result of an analysis made of the compliance certificates filed during the past year by employees having pricing and marketing responsibility, to appraise this part of the Corporation's enforcement program on the basis of a presentation made to us by management. The certificates indicated an understanding on the part of employees of the problems they face and of the conduct expected of them. After discussion of the certificate procedure, some suggestions were made for improving the form, review and handling of the certificates and dealing with the information obtained from them. The Board of Advice also heard a review of the educational meetings conducted by the Chief of the Antitrust

Section of the Law Department with many groups throughout the organization.

6. We are satisfied that a thorough job has been done in bringing home to the Westinghouse organization the types of activities that constitute *per se* violations of the antitrust laws and the management's determination to prevent all such activities and, where they are found, to punish the offenders. We are also satisfied that great efforts have been made to make this compliance program a part of a larger program intended to promote higher standards of business conduct generally and to win the affirmative support of the organization to it. With the memory of the Philadelphia cases still fresh, we believe that currently no one in the Westinghouse organization can have any excuse for participating in any activity constituting a *per se* violation of the antitrust laws. As we stated in our interim report, however, the management recognizes that "the success of the Corporation's policy and program will depend on constant support by the officers of the Corporation, by precept and example, on constant reiteration and constant checking and inspection, and in the gradual elimination of some habits of thinking common to many businesses."

7. During our earliest consultations with management, it became clear that the Company's program for explaining the antitrust and trade regulation laws to all appropriate levels and parts of management, and its administrative arrangements to ensure management compliance with Company policy, did not constitute the main area of our possible usefulness to the Company. The Company did not need our advice to appreciate the importance of such programs. They were in fact established and put into effect, under the direction of competent and qualified persons, before our appointment. At the request of the President, discussions at our later meetings centered around the development of suitable material for presentation to Westinghouse management groups to supplement the program of education and compliance which the Corporation had already established. These consultations have led to the development of our principal recommendation to the Company—that it plan, organize and carry out a program of education in the economics of competition, intended to develop within the organization an improved awareness of opportunities for profitable competitive action consistent with the antitrust laws, and an attitude of initiative in responding to them.

It is our view that the Corporation's problem in relation to the antitrust laws should not be regarded as solely, or even primarily, the negative task of issuing and policing strict instructions against overt collusion with competitors, price fixing, market division and the like. Measures of that sort are necessary, but the success of such "negative" programs, and, more broadly the Corporation's business success in the future, will depend to a considerable degree on the adoption by the Corporation of policies of vigorous (and even aggressive) flexible, competitive initiative, appropriate to the nature of the electrical industry and to the structure of the many product markets in which the Corporation sells, and will sell in the future. We recognize the difficulties of articulating and applying such policies to particular situations, in the light of the complexities of the antitrust laws, especially in markets where the number of sellers is small. And we have emphasized the particular importance to the Company, in many of the markets where it sells, of distinguishing between those forms of price discrimination which may, and those which do not, adversely affect competition in a relevant market. The Board appreciates the challenge of explaining such policies, as they are developed, to experienced businessmen who may have become accustomed over the years to other attitudes. Despite those difficulties, however, the Board believes that such an approach could contribute greatly to morale by giving management a greater sense of purpose and achievement, and, in the end, could place the problem of avoiding antitrust violations within a positive rather than a negative framework. Such an approach is consistent with vigorous and profitable growth and should permit the Corporation to utilize profit opportunities available to it in many markets in a more thorough and comprehensive manner than would be possible under a purely negative program of avoiding violations of the law.

In line with the management's suggestions, the Board has at our recent meetings discussed some basic economic writings designed to give insight into private competitive enterprise in the seventh decade of the twentieth century and the criteria by which such competition must be tested. We have also reviewed with management a series of practical problems and questions which the operating executives face in the marketing of Westinghouse products, questions which illustrate the application of the economic principles to the facts of life in selling products in various markets.

We recommend, therefore, that the management retain competent staff to plan, organize and carry out such a sustained program of continuing economic and legal education for its managerial and sales personnel.

In conclusion, we desire to express, jointly and severally, our appreciation for the opportunity to have participated in this pioneering effort to explore and define an important series of problems of modern economic policy, and to help bridge the gap between common business and theoretical ways of viewing such problems. Throughout, our discussions have been characterized by candor and open-mindedness on the part of the management. We have been impressed by management's determination to perfect the Corporation's policies and procedures to insure high standards of conduct in all its operations.

Respectfully submitted,

Erwin N. Griswold
(Dean, Harvard Law School)
A. D. H. Kaplan
(Brookings Institution)
S. Chesterfield Oppenheim
(Professor, Michigan Law School)
Eugene V. Rostow
(Dean, Yale Law School)

APPENDIX B   LETTER OF THE SECRETARY

OF COMMERCE, MARCH 17, 1965,

TO 600 CORPORATE LEADERS

ASKING THEIR AID IN

REDUCING THE BALANCE

OF PAYMENTS DEFICIT

The President has asked me to handle the voluntary cooperation program with American industry which is a key part of our overall effort to improve our Nation's balance of payments situation. Since the success of this program depends entirely on full cooperation and help from the heads of the U.S. corporations doing a significant amount of business internationally, I am writing to you to enlist your personal support.

As you can see from the enclosed press release, the Advisory Committee for this industry program, chaired by Mr. Albert L. Nickerson, Chairman of the Board of Socony Mobil Oil Company, is composed of outstanding leaders from the business community who have been active in direct overseas investments and international trade. That Advisory Committee met with me on February 26, and strongly urged that our program be set up on as informal and personal a basis as possible, with a minimum of formal reporting requirements and other "red tape." All members of the Advisory Committee have given me their judgment that the leaders of American industry will respond quickly and favorably to that kind of approach and that, as a result of such leaders taking personal responsibility for this effort, our voluntary program will produce significant reductions in the balance of payments deficit. The Advisory Committee is particularly in favor of a flexible approach that enables each company head to work out his own program, based on the operating facts of his own business, rather than limit the means of meeting each company's objective by having the government prescribe some formula of general application.

That advice makes sense to me, and the form of the program that we had been planning has been modified along the lines suggested.

378

Consequently, I ask for your help specifically as follows:

1. Please set up for your company a balance of payments "ledger" for the year 1964 which shows the selected debits and credits. I enclose a summary work sheet to indicate the needed figures, and some instructions to help your technical people in preparing it for you.

2. After looking at your 1964 results—and we realize in most cases a significant favorable balance will be shown—please consider how that 1964 result can be improved for the years 1965 and 1966. We have been thinking in terms of an average improvement in balance of payments terms, in 1965 of 15–20 percent over the 1964 results. We realize, however, that any such target will be inappropriate for many corporations—either on the low or high side—but the important thing is to make an extraordinary effort. Therefore, we have concluded that only you are in a position to set up a reasonable but meaningful objective for your own company, in light of your operating facts and problems. The nine suggestions listed on the enclosed press release do not exhaust the list of possibilities that you and your associates can put together in devising an approach meeting the national purpose, yet tailored to your particular circumstances. In short, I am asking you to establish, *and then let me know,* your best *personal* estimate of how much of an improvement in terms of net dollars you think your company can make overall in 1965, compared with 1964 by taking all feasible steps to help the Nation deal with this serious problem.

3. It would also be helpful for us to have a few of your summary figures for the year 1964 showing credit and debit items separately. The work sheet referred to in paragraph 1 would be appropriate for your 1964 report and should be returned to us. It may also be helpful in calculating your 1965 target. We understand that for many firms or industries, such as petroleum operations or contract construction, there may be a need to include in their "ledger" other information on foreign transactions in order to show a realistic balance of payments performance. In such situations, we would welcome any supplementary figures you wish to supply, and will take them into consideration in reviewing your results.

4. Because of the unique opportunity to shift short-term assets and make an early improvement in the balance of payments, I would also like to have your figures at the end of 1963 and 1964 for short-term assets held abroad either directly or through U.S. banking or other financial institutions. In addition, we would like to have figures on such assets held in developed countries by your subsidiaries and branches.

5. I would like to receive your first set of figures by April 15, if this is possible, and I hope it is.

6. Thereafter, I am asking you to send me quarterly reports through the years 1965 and 1966 showing the data in paragraphs 2, 3 and 4 above and revisions, if any, in your overall goal for the year. You should also give your personal evaluation of points or problems you consider to be of particular significance.

7. While prior notification regarding substantial new investments or expansions abroad, including information indicating how they would be financed, would be helpful, we have decided against a formalized program

asking for such information. It is our hope that the overall estimates and reports that I am requesting will prove to be adequate, and that the results will be clear enough to obviate the need for prior notification of new investments. We, of course, expect that care will be taken to minimize the balance of payments effects of large investments and either we, or the appropriate Federal Reserve officials when their program is involved, would be glad to discuss such situations should you so desire.

8. We shall be very glad to talk on the telephone or meet with you to discuss this or any other aspect of this voluntary program of interest or concern to you as it moves along.

Your company's report and estimates will be treated by us as strictly "Confidential" and shown only to those few government officials who are working with us directly in this program. We do plan to put together a periodic summary of the reports in aggregate terms for consideration with the Advisory Committee and for reports to the President, the Cabinet, and the public.

There are a few special problems which I would like to call to your particular attention.

First, we regard the national objective of increasing the contribution by private enterprise to growth in less developed countries of such importance that we do not wish this program to inhibit the flow of these investments.

Second, while relatively rapid progress in repatriating short-term financial funds invested abroad, wherever appropriate, would be helpful, we request that this be done with caution in the case of balances in countries subject to balance of payments problems. We are naturally concerned not to cause difficulties on the exchanges and it would be desirable for companies with large balances to consider consulting with the appropriate Federal Reserve Bank on this problem.

Third, we do not anticipate cutbacks in Canadian direct investments, but firms should take particular care to assure that short-term funds put at the disposal of your subsidiaries in Canada serve only to meet operating needs in Canada. Opportunities should be explored for obtaining at least a portion of working capital requirements from the Canadian market. In this process, we hope that short-term investments in Canada by parents or subsidiaries clearly in excess of working requirements will not be increased. No doubt opportunities will arise to reduce these balances, particularly those denominated in U.S. dollars, but this should be done only in a gradual and orderly way.

I am sure you are aware of the vital importance of improving the U.S. balance of payments position. Such improvement is essential to international monetary stability, to this Nation's economy, and to continued business progress. The capability of this nation to manage its international fiscal affairs is being carefully watched around the world.

President Johnson is confident, as am I, that you will cooperate with us in this extremely important program of serious concern to you and to our country. We urgently need your help.

Sincerely yours,

John T. Connor

Enclosures

SUGGESTED READINGS

1. The American Business System: Its Origins and Development (Chapters 1 to 4)

ANDREWS, CHARLES M.: *The Colonial Period of American History*, New Haven, Conn.: Yale University Press, 1938, vol. IV.

ARISTOTLE: *Politics*, found in Philip C. Newman, Arthur D. Gayer, and Milton H. Spencer, *Source Readings in Economic Thought*, New York: W. W. Norton & Company, Inc., 1954.

BALDWIN, SUMMERFIELD: *Business in the Middle Ages*, New York: Holt, Rinehart and Winston, Inc., 1937.

BEARD, CHARLES A., AND MARY R. BEARD: *The Beards' New Basic History of the United States* (1944), Garden City, N.Y.: Doubleday & Company, Inc., 1960.

BEARD, MIRIAM: *A History of Business from Babylon to the Monopolists*, Ann Arbor, Mich.: The University of Michigan Press, 1962.

————: *A History of Business*, Ann Arbor, Mich.: The University of Michigan Press, 1963, vol. II.

BOWEN, HOWARD R.: *Social Responsibilities of the Businessman*, New York: Harper & Row, Publishers, Incorporated, 1953.

BROEHL, WAYNE G., JR.: *The Molly Maguires*, Cambridge, Mass.: Harvard University Press, 1964.

BURSK, EDWARD C. (ED.): *Business and Religion*, New York: Harper & Row, Publishers, Incorporated, 1959.

CHEIT, EARL F. (ED.): *The Business Establishment*, New York: John Wiley & Sons, Inc., 1964.

COCHRAN, THOMAS C., AND WILLIAM MILLER: *The Age of Enterprise*, New York: The Macmillan Company, 1942.

The Code of Hammurabi (2000 B.C.). See Edward C. Bursk, Donald T. Clark, and Ralph W. Hidy, *The World of Business*, New York: Simon and Schuster, Inc., 1962.

DAGGETT, STUART: *Chapters on the History of the Southern Pacific*, New York: The Ronald Press Company, 1922.

DIESING, PAUL: *Reason in Society: Five Types of Decisions and Their Social Conditions*, Urbana, Ill.: The University of Illinois Press, 1962.

DOBB, MAURICE: *Studies in the Development of Capitalism*, New York: International Publishers Company, Inc., 1947.

EELLS, RICHARD: *The Government of Corporations*, New York: The Free Press of Glencoe, 1962.

———— AND CLARENCE C. WALTON: *Conceptual Foundations of Business*, Homewood, Ill.: Richard D. Irwin, Inc., 1961.

GREENWOOD, WILLIAM T. (ED.): *Issues in Business and Society*, Boston: Houghton Mifflin Company, 1964.

HACKER, LOUIS M.: *The Triumph of American Capitalism*, New York: Simon and Schuster, Inc., 1940.

HAMILTON, ALEXANDER: *Report on Manufactures* (1791), extracts reproduced in William MacDonald (ed.), *Selected Documents Illustrative of the History of the United States, 1776–1861*, New York: The Macmillan Company, 1898.

HEATON, HERBERT: *Economic History of Europe*, New York: Harper & Row, Publishers, Incorporated, 1948.

HECKSCHER, ELI: *Mercantilism* (1931), trans. by Mendel Shapiro, New York: The Macmillan Company, 1935, vols. 1 and 2.

HEILBRONER, ROBERT L.: *The Quest for Wealth*, New York: Simon and Schuster, Inc., 1956.

————: *The Making of Economic Society*, Englewood Cliffs, N.J.: Prentice-Hall, Inc., 1962.

HOFSTADTER, RICHARD: *Social Darwinism in American Thought*, rev. ed., Boston: Beacon Press, 1955.

KUHN, ALFRED: *Study of Society*, Homewood, Ill.: Richard D. Irwin, Inc., 1963.

LIPPINCOTT, ISAAC: *Economic Development of the United States*, New York: Appleton-Century-Crofts, Inc., 1925.

McCLELLAND, DAVID C.: *The Achieving Society*, Princeton, N.J.: D. Van Nostrand Company, Inc., 1961.

McGUIRE, JOSEPH W.: *Business and Society*, New York: McGraw-Hill Book Company, 1964.

MACHIAVELLI, NICCOLÒ: *The Prince* (1513), Oxford: Clarendon Press, 1909.

MYERS, GUSTAVUS: *History of the Great American Fortunes*, New York: Modern Library, Inc., 1936.

PIRENNE, H.: *Economic and Social History of Medieval Europe*, trans. by I. E. Clegg, New York: Harcourt, Brace & World, Inc., 1956.

PLÁTO: *The Laws of Plato*, trans. by E. A. Taylor, London: J. M. Dent and Sons, Ltd., Publishers, 1934.

————: *The Republic*, trans. by B. Jowett, Oxford: Clarendon Press, 1881.

ROLL, ERIC: *A History of Economic Thought*, 3d ed., Englewood Cliffs, N.J.: Prentice-Hall, Inc., 1956.

SCHLESINGER, ARTHUR M.: *The Colonial Merchants and the American Revolution*, New York: Barnes & Noble, Inc., 1939.

SCHMOLLER, GUSTAV: *The Mercantile System and Its Historical Significance* (1895), Gloucester, Mass.: Peter Smith, Publisher, 1931.

SELEKMAN, BENJAMIN M.: *A Moral Philosophy for Management*, New York: McGraw-Hill Book Company, 1959.

SMITH, ADAM: *An Inquiry into the Nature and Causes of the Wealth of Nations* (1776), New York: Modern Library, Inc., 1937.

TAWNEY, R. H.: *Religion and the Rise of Capitalism* (1947), New York: Mentor Books, New American Library of World Literature, Inc., 1962.

THOMPSON, JAMES WESTFALL: *Economic and Social History of the Middle Ages: 300–1300*, New York: Century Company, 1928.

UNWIN, GEORGE: *Industrial Organization in the Sixteenth and Seventeenth Centuries* (1904), London: Cass and Company, 1957.

WEBER, MAX: *The Protestant Ethic and the Spirit of Capitalism* (1905), trans. by Talcott Parsons, New York: Charles Scribner's Sons, 1958.

2. Current Issues in Business (Chapters 5 to 9)

ARGYRIS, CHRIS: *Personality and Organization: The Conflict between System and the Individual*, New York: Harper & Row, Publishers, Incorporated, 1957.

————: *Integrating the Individual and the Organization*, New York: John Wiley & Sons, Inc., 1964.

BARTELS, ROBERT (ED.): *Ethics in Business*, Columbus, Ohio: Ohio State University, Bureau of Business Research Monograph 111, 1963.

BEAUMONT, RICHARD A., AND ROY B. HELFGOTT: *Management, Automation and People*, New York: Industrial Relations Counselors, Inc., 1964.

BRADLEY, JOSEPH F.: *The Role of Trade Associations and Professional Business Societies in America*, University Park, Pa.: The Pennsylvania State University Press, 1965.

BRIGHT, JAMES R.: *Research, Development, and Technological Innovation*, Homewood, Ill.: Richard D. Irwin, Inc., 1964.

BUCKINGHAM, WALTER: *Automation: Its Impact on Business and People*, New York: Harper & Row, Publishers, Incorporated, 1961.

CLEVELAND, HARLAN, AND HAROLD D. LASSWELL: *Ethics and Bigness*, New York: Harper & Row, Publishers, Incorporated, 1962.

DALE, ERNEST: *The Great Organizers*, New York: McGraw-Hill Book Company, 1960.

DAVIS, KEITH: *Human Relations at Work*, 2d ed., New York: McGraw-Hill Book Company, 1962.

DUNLOP, JOHN T. (ED.): *Automation and Technological Change*, Englewood Cliffs, N.J.: Prentice-Hall, Inc., 1962.

GOLEMBIEWSKI, ROBERT T.: *Men, Management, and Morality*, New York: McGraw-Hill Book Company, 1965.

GREENEWALT, CRAWFORD H.: *The Uncommon Man: The Individual in the Organization*, New York: McGraw-Hill Book Company, 1959.

GROSS, MARTIN L.: *The Brain Watchers*, New York: Random House, Inc., 1962.

HABER, SAMUEL: *Efficiency and Uplift*, Chicago: The University of Chicago Press, 1964.

HAZLITT, HENRY: *The Foundations of Morality*, Princeton, N.J.: D. Van Nostrand Company, Inc., 1964.

HOFFMAN, BANESH: *The Tyranny of Testing*, New York: Crowell-Collier Publishing Co., 1962.

KAPPEL, FREDERICK R.: *Vitality in a Business Enterprise*, New York: McGraw-Hill Book Company, 1960.

LIPSTREU, OTIS, AND KENNETH A. REED: *Transition to Automation*, Boulder, Colo.: University of Colorado Press, Studies in Business, no. 1, 1964.

MILLER, ARTHUR S. (ED.): *The Ethics of Business Enterprise*, Philadelphia: The American Academy of Political and Social Science, *The Annals*, vol. 343, September, 1962.

MONSEN, R. JOSEPH, JR., AND MARK W. CANNON: *The Makers of Public Policy: American Power Groups and Their Ideologies*, New York: McGraw-Hill Book Company, 1965.

MOORE, WILBERT E.: *The Conduct of the Corporation*, New York: Random House, Inc., 1962.

PACKARD, VANCE: *The Naked Society*, New York: David McKay Company, Inc., 1964.

SAYLES, LEONARD R.: *Individualism and Big Business*, New Book Company, 1963.

SOMERS, GERALD G., EDWARD L. CUSHMAN, AND NAT WEINBERG (EDS.): *Adjusting to Technological Change*, New York: Harper & Row, Publishers, Incorporated, 1963.

STEIGERWALT, ALBERT K.: *The National Association of Manufacturers, 1895–1914: A Study in Business Leadership*, Ann Arbor, Mich.: University of Michigan, Bureau of Business Research, 1964.

SUTTON, FRANCIS X., et al.: *The American Business Creed*, New York: Schocken Books, Inc., 1962.

TOWLE, JOSEPH W. (ED.): *Ethics and Standards in American Business*, Boston: Houghton Mifflin Company, 1964.

TURNER, ARTHUR N., AND PAUL R. LAWRENCE: *Industrial Jobs and the Worker*, Boston: Harvard Business School, Division of Research, 1965.

WALKER, CHARLES R. (ED.): *Modern Technology and Civilization*, New York: McGraw-Hill Book Company, 1962.

WARNER, W. LLOYD: *The Corporation in the Emergent American Society*, New York: Harper & Row, Publishers, Incorporated, 1962.

WORTHY, JAMES C.: *Big Business and Free Men*, New York: Harper & Row, Publishers, Incorporated, 1959.

3. Business and Its Publics (Chapters 10 to 14)

BARKIN, SOLOMON, AND ALBERT A. BLUM (EDS.) *The Crisis in the American Tradeunion Movement*, Philadelphia: The American Academy of Political and Social Science, *The Annals*, vol. 350, November, 1963.

BERLE, ADOLPH A., JR.: *Power without Property*, New York: Harcourt, Brace & World, Inc., 1959.

——— AND GARDINER C. MEANS: *The Modern Corporation and Private Property*, New York: The Macmillan Company, 1932.

BROOKS, JOHN: *The Fate of the Edsel and Other Business Adventures*, New York: Harper & Row, Publishers, Incorporated, 1963.

BUNTING, JOHN R.: *The Hidden Face of Free Enterprise: The Strange Economics of the American Businessman*, New York: McGraw-Hill Book Company, 1964.

BURNS, ARTHUR R.: *The Decline of Competition: A Study of the Evolution of American Industry*, New York: McGraw-Hill Book Company, 1936.

COMMONS, JOHN R., AND ASSOCIATES: *History of Labour in the United States*, 2 vols., New York: The Macmillan Company, 1918.

DRUCKER, PETER F.: *The Practice of Management*, New York: Harper & Row, Publishers, Incorporated, 1954.

DUNLOP, JOHN T.: *Industrial Relations Systems*, New York: Holt, Rinehart and Winston, Inc., 1958.

EELLS, RICHARD, AND CLARENCE C. WALTON: *Conceptual Foundations of Business*, Homewood, Ill.: Richard D. Irwin, Inc., 1961.

EMERSON, F. D., AND F. C. LATCHAM: *Shareholder Democracy*, Cleveland, Ohio: Press of Western Reserve University, 1954.

GALLIGAN, DAVID: *Politics and the Businessman*, New York: Pitman Publishing Corporation, 1964.

GILBERT, LEWIS D.: *Dividends and Democracy*, Larchmont, N.Y.: American Research Council, 1956.

GOLDBERG, ARTHUR J.: *AFL-CIO: Labor United*, New York: McGraw-Hill Book Company, 1956.

HARRINGTON, MICHAEL, AND PAUL JACOBS: *Labor in a Free Society*, Berkeley, Calif.: University of California Press, 1959.

KAPLAN, A. D. H.: *Big Enterprise in a Competitive System*, rev. ed., Washington, D.C.: The Brookings Institution, 1964.

KEYNES, JOHN MAYNARD: *The General Theory of Employment, Interest, and Money*, New York: Harcourt, Brace & World, Inc., 1936.

LIVINGSTON, J. A.: *The American Stockholder*, Philadelphia: J. B. Lippincott Company, 1958.

McGUIRE, JOSEPH W.: *Business and Society*, New York: McGraw-Hill Book Company, 1963.

MASON, EDWARD S.: *The Corporation in Modern Society*, Cambridge, Mass.: Harvard University Press, 1959.

MUND, VERNON A.: *Government and Business*, 4th ed., New York: Harper & Row, Publishers, Incorporated, 1965.

SULTAN, PAUL: *Labor Economics*, New York: Holt, Rinehart and Winston, Inc., 1957.

TAFT, PHILIP: *Organized Labor in American History*, New York: Harper & Row, Publishers, Incorporated, 1964.

WEISSMAN, JACOB: *Law in a Business Society*, Englewood Cliffs, N.J.: Prentice-Hall, Inc., 1964.

4. Business in an International World (Chapters 15 to 17)

AITKEN, HUGH G. J. (ED.): *Explorations in Enterprise*, Cambridge, Mass.: Harvard University Press, 1965.

ARENSBERG, CONRAD M., AND ARTHUR H. NIEHOFF: *Introducing Social Change: A Manual for Americans Overseas*, Chicago: Aldine Publishing Co., 1964.

BRANNEN, TED, AND FRANCIS HODGSON: *Overseas Management*, New York: McGraw-Hill Book Company, 1965.

FARMER, RICHARD N., AND BARRY M. RICHMAN: *Comparative Management and Economic Progress*, Homewood, Ill.: Richard D. Irwin, Inc., 1965.

FAYERWEATHER, JOHN: *Facts and Fallacies of International Business*, New York: Holt, Rinehart and Winston, Inc., 1962.

GRANICK, DAVID: *The Red Executive*, Garden City, N.Y.: Doubleday & Company, Inc., 1960.

———: *The European Executive*, Garden City, N.Y.: Doubleday & Company, Inc., 1962.

HAGEN, EVERETT E.: *On the Theory of Social Change*, Homewood, Ill.: Dorsey Press, 1962.

HARBISON, FREDERICK, AND CHARLES A. MYERS: *Management in the Industrial World: An International Analysis*, New York: McGraw-Hill Book Company, 1959.

——— AND ———: *Education, Manpower, and Economic Growth*, New York: McGraw-Hill Book Company, 1964.

KERR, CLARK, JOHN T. DUNLOP, FREDERICK H. HARBISON, AND CHARLES A. MYERS: *Industrialism and Industrial Man: The Problems of Labor and Management in Industrial Growth*, Cambridge, Mass.: Harvard University Press, 1960.

McCREARY, EDWARD A.: *The Americanization of Europe*, Garden City, N.Y.: Doubleday & Company, Inc., 1964.

MEAD, MARGARET: *Cultural Patterns and Technical Change*, New York: Mentor Books, New American Library of World Literature, Inc., 1961.

RICHMAN, BARRY M.: *Soviet Management, with Significant American Comparisons*, Englewood Cliffs, N.J.: Prentice-Hall, Inc., 1965.

ROBINSON, RICHARD D.: *International Business Policy*, New York: Holt, Rinehart and Winston, Inc., 1964.

SLOTKIN, JAMES S.: *From Fields to Factory*, New York: The Free Press of Glencoe, 1960.

INDEXES

NAME INDEX

Adams, Velma A., 232n.
Andersen, Hans Christian, 164
Andrews, Charles M., 43
Andrews, Frank M., 154n.
Anthony, Robert N., 97, 208n.
Appley, Lawrence A., 178n.
Aquinas, St. Thomas, 32, 234
Arensberg, Conrad M., 307
Argyris, Chris, 17n., 125, 127, 315
Aristotle, 26, 234
Aronson, Robert L., 158n.
Austin, Robert W. 119n.

Bach, George L., 225n.
Bakke, E. W., 130n.
Barber, Arthur, 265n.
Barkin, Solomon, 247n., 248
Baumhart, Raymond C., 106n.
Beard, Miriam, 21n., 40
Bellows, Roger, 94n.
Bennis, Warren G., 128n., 315, 334n.
Berle, Adolph A., Jr., 210n., 218n., 330, 334n.
Bienvenu, Bernard J., 94n., 99n.
Bining, Arthur C., 72
Blake, Robert R., 315
Blomfield, Richard B., 309n.
Blough, Roger M., 87, 185, 191, 275n.
Blum, Albert A., 247n., 248n.
Blum, Fred H., 332n.

Bonjean, Charles M., 267n.
Bowen, Howard R., 169n.
Boyd, Harper W., 228
Bright, James R., 152n.
Broehl, Wayne, 78n.
Brooks, John, 219n.
Brown, J. A. C., 128n.
Bullock, Charles J., 25n.
Bunke, Harvey C., 328n.
Bunting, John R., 186
Burck, Gilbert, 155n.
Burke, Edmund, 46
Burns, Arthur R., 198
Bursk, Edward C., 16n., 263n.
Byrnes, Francis C., 311n.

Calkins, Robert D., 3n.
Calvin, John, 33, 34
Campbell, Robert E., 267n.
Cannon, Mark W., 120n.
Carlson, Howard C., 134n.
Cheit, Earl F., 12n., 74n., 80n., 166, 170n., 262n.
Chittenden, Hiram M., 44
Clague, Ewan, 157n.
Clendenin, John C., 211n.
Cleveland, Frederick W., Jr., 16n., 104n.
Cleveland, Harlan, 129n.
Cochran, Thomas C., 81n.
Cojeen, Robert H., 291n.
Colbert, Jean Baptiste, 37

SUBJECT INDEX